BETWEEN THE SWASTIKA AND THE SICKLE

Between the Swastika and the Sickle

The Life, Disappearance, and Execution of Ernst Lohmeyer

James R. Edwards

WILLIAM B. EERDMANS PUBLISHING COMPANY
GRAND RAPIDS, MICHIGAN

Wm. B. Eerdmans Publishing Co.
4035 Park East Court SE, Grand Rapids, Michigan 49546
www.eerdmans.com

25 24 23 22 21 20 19   1 2 3 4 5 6 7

ISBN 978-0-8028-7618-8

Library of Congress Cataloging-in-Publication Data

A catalog record for this book is available from the Library of Congress.

To Melie Seyberth Lohmeyer,
beloved wife of Ernst Lohmeyer,
who championed his life
and preserved his memory

Contents

CONTENTS

Prologue

In 1996 I published an article on the mysterious disappearance and death of Ernst Lohmeyer that appeared just weeks before the fiftieth anniversary of Lohmeyer's execution, which was commemorated at the University of Greifswald on September 19, 1996. I assumed that the publication of this article would be my only contribution, major or minor, to Lohmeyer scholarship. With the fall of the Berlin Wall in 1989 and the subsequent demise of communism, sources related to the life and death of Ernst Lohmeyer that I had pursued in a clandestine manner in East Germany were finally open to all, and it seemed proper to me for Germans themselves to air the story of this remarkable scholar and witness of faith and character. For the next twenty years I transitioned from sometime East German sleuth back to other roles related more directly to my discipline as a professor of New Testament. Lohmeyer himself remained a fixed feature of my mental world, of course, but I had no plans of developing that feature beyond the scope of the 1996 article I had written.

When I retired from full-time teaching in 2015, two things caused me to change my mind and plunge into a full biography of Ernst Lohmeyer. One was that by 2015 Gudrun and Klaus Otto, Lohmeyer's daughter and son-in-law, had died, as had Professor Günter Haufe, Lohmeyer's successor as chair of New Testament at the University of Greifswald. Gudrun, Klaus, and Günter had been my three best "informants" on Lohmeyer's life and fate. Indeed, they were genuine mentors. Their deaths left my unlikely American voice one of the few remaining to tell the Lohmeyer story within the context of those who had preserved his memory during the attempted blackout of his name in communist East Germany.

A second awareness, closely related to the above, was perhaps even more compelling in changing my mind. As I mention more than once in the book, the Soviets did not simply kill Ernst Lohmeyer, they sought to expunge all memory of him, "as though he never existed." Gudrun had reminded me that death is inevitable, but deprivation of honor is not. The first must be accepted, but the second need not—or perhaps better, *should* not—be accepted. It became increasingly clear to me that not to tell Lohmeyer's story was to abet, albeit it unwillingly, the expunging of his memory. At various points in Lohmeyer's biography I relate my personal endowments that linked me to similar endowments of Lohmeyer. The determination of the Soviets to expunge his memory seemed to *mandate* marshaling those endowments to tell a story that deserved to be told but that otherwise might not be told. This latter realization became a virtual call, a necessary counteroffensive to reverse a mendacious victory of those committed to expunging Lohmeyer's memory. Gudrun noted how her father made a rule not to refuse when asked for help that he could render. My situation conformed too closely to Lohmeyer's "paradigm" not to apply it to myself.

The theological faculty at the University of Greifswald, thankfully, continues to keep the candle of Lohmeyer's memory burning. A current member of the faculty there has written his doctoral dissertation on Lohmeyer, and a small but steady stream of academic work and conferences—one of which I note at the beginning of chapter 17—continues to explore Lohmeyer's significance as a theologian. A particularly pleasing example of this revival is the naming of the new residence of the theological faculty at Greifswald the Ernst Lohmeyer House. The plaque prepared for Lohmeyer's exoneration on the fiftieth anniversary of his execution on September 19, 1996, now adorns the entryway of the Lohmeyer House, which lies directly across the green from the main hall of the university.

Virtually all resources I used in writing this book, whether written or oral, were German. This was inevitable, for Ernst Lohmeyer was German through and through, and he lived and wrote in an era when far fewer German works were translated into English than is true today. Apart from rare instances of English translations of Lohmeyer's works, all English translations of German in this book are, by necessity, my own. For those who are interested, I have provided all German originals—whether individual words or entire paragraphs—in the endnotes of each chapter. Readers with even minimal German proficiency will profit from reading Lohmeyer's lucid, strong, and penetrating German. Within the biography I occasionally place in quotation marks conversations for which I do not provide the original German in endnotes. Most of these conversations are the result of my recall. I make no claim for verbatim accuracy in such conversations, but I wish to assure readers of the veracity of the sense of the conversations, if not of their exact words. In many instances my recall has been aided by written diaries that I kept in my various peregrinations in Germany. I did not keep written diaries while on Berlin Fellowship (an organization I shall introduce in the story) in East Germany for fear of their being confiscated at border crossings, thereby compromising our German friends in the East. I did, however, commit my itineraries, experiences, and key conversations there to personal diaries after returning to West Germany. The several conversations in chapters 15–16 transpired after the fall of the Wall, and the time lag between event and transcription was reduced to no more than a day, and often to a few hours.

One of the most personally gratifying aspects for me in the Lohmeyer pursuit has been the interplay between the living and the dead, the church militant and the church victorious. That interplay has included voices on both sides of the Atlantic. As noted throughout this book, many Germans have contributed to the Lohmeyer legacy. The foremost among them have been mentioned in the book, especially Gudrun and Klaus Otto and Günter Haufe. I am also indebted to Andreas Köhn's biography of Ernst Lohmeyer as a New Testament scholar, and his publication of Lohmeyer's sermons as president of the University of Breslau. But there are others standing in the wings to whom I am also indebted. Ted Schapp, a West Berlin pastor, and Bärbel Eccardt, a West Berlin catechist responsible for "East work" with Berlin Fellowship, both now deceased, nurtured and advanced my understanding of the church in East Germany for more than two decades. Their counterparts in the East, Gerhard Lerchner (†2018), a pastor in East Germany, and Gerlinde Haker, a catechist at the Lutheran cathedral in the city of Schwerin, both of whom I met through Berlin Fellowship, possessed the rare virtue of demonstrating staunch resistance to oppression yet without vilifying oppressors. Both witnessed to the gospel of reconciliation in a dehumanizing world of East German socialism.

Names associated more directly with the writing of this book are Barbara Peters, who offered prompt and professional assistance to my various requests during her three-decade tenure in the archive of the University of Greifswald. Similar assistance from Dr. Ingeborg Schnelling-Reinicke at the Secret Prussian Archive in Dahlem, though of shorter duration, has been equally helpful in securing access to materials crucial to this book. I wish to thank Professor Dr. Christfried Böttrich, who now occupies the chair of New Testament at the University of Greifswald once occupied by Lohmeyer, for his invitation to lecture at a Lohmeyer Symposium in October 2016, and for his expressed advocacy of this book. I am further grateful to both Ingeborg and Christfried for their willingness to read the entire English draft of this book and offer many helpful suggestions for its improvement. Finally, I wish to express my gratitude to Dr. Julia Otto and Stefan Rettner, grandchildren of Ernst and Melie Lohmeyer, for their continuation of the charitable legacy of their parents Gudrun and Klaus in support of my research into their grandfather, and especially for making all the photographs in this book available for publication.

Americans have been equally important in my Lohmeyer pursuit. Early encouragement for a biography of Lohmeyer came from my friend Gus Lee. Jerry Sittser, Adam Neder, Gerri Beal, Myra and Gary Watts, William Yakely, and my wife, Jane, our daughter Corrie Berg, and our son Mark Edwards have been magnanimous in reading earlier drafts of the work and offering both encouragement and helpful suggestions for changes. Perhaps only an author can appreciate how their advocacy and critiques have refined and improved the manuscript of this book throughout its various stages of gestation and made the work more deserving of its subject.

I wish to express my particular thanks to Eerdmans Publishing Company for its interest in a Lohmeyer biography. Theological publishers are generally reluctant to publish biographies of theologians, and several refuse even to consider submissions in this genre. Trevor Thompson, acquisitions editor at Eerdmans, believed this biography needed to be considered apart from such reservations, that Lohmeyer's story was not simply one of historical merit but contemporary significance as well. I am grateful for Trevor's work along with that of his colleagues, Tom Raabe, Jennifer Hoffman, Chris Fann, and Tom DeVries. They have played important roles in moving the biography through the publication process and improving it along the way.

The person to whom and for whom I am most indebted and grateful in the writing of this book is my wife, Jane. She has been familiar with the name of Ernst Lohmeyer since I read a baffling reference to him in the foreword to his Mark commentary in 1974. She has accompanied me in Germany more times than I can count in my endeavor to unravel threads in the Lohmeyer skein. Her willingness to accompany me on Lohmeyer journeys, both physical and mental, over many decades has been unfailingly helpful and has contributed constructively to the outcome of this book.

In the last chapter I speak of the connection that developed between Lohmeyer and myself in the research and writing of this book by means of an analogy of wiring a house, at some point during which the electrical current is switched on. When I accepted a grant from the German Academic Exchange Program in 1993 to investigate the mysterious disappearance and death of Lohmeyer, I took my family with me to Germany, along with Shane Berg, one of my students at the University of Jamestown who is now my son-in-law, and Jane Holslag, a former colleague at First Presbyterian Church in Colorado Springs who was then working for Berlin Fellowship. We all spent Christmas 1993 at Professor Eduard Schweizer's chalet in Braunwald, a Swiss village high in the Alps that is accessible only by cable car. During the day we skied, but each evening after dinner we stoked the fire in the hearth at *Pilgerhuesli*—"Pilgrim's Hut"—and gathered around the dining table to hear of progress in my Lohmeyer research. Thereupon the family transformed itself into a company of quasi detectives in an unsolved crime unit, seeking to piece together the Lohmeyer puzzle.

Three years later, in 1996, I sat next to Julia Otto, Lohmeyer's granddaughter, at a dinner reception at the Hotel am Dom in Greifswald following her grandfather's posthumous inauguration ceremony in the University Great Hall. Julia was interested in knowing how I, an American too young to have known her grandfather personally, became interested in him. In my response I reported that my family was also interested in the Lohmeyer mystery, and I shared the above story of the investigative evening discussions at *Pilgerhuesli*. Julia took particular delight in this anecdote. Only later in my research did I begin to understand why. Following Lohmeyer's arrest, his wife, Melie, and two surviving children, Hartmut and Gudrun, spent the remainder of their lives salvaging remnants of their shattered family. So indelible was the experience that Gudrun, wishing to dispel its influence from the family, told Julia and Stefan very little about their grandfather. She did this not out of disinterest or disrespect. Few daughters, in fact, could have been more valiant for their father's memory. Gudrun moderated her father's legacy in the family so that Julia and Stefan could develop their lives free from the shadow of his death and defamation. And therein lay, I think, Julia's delight in my account of *Pilgerhuesli*: her grandfather's story was, at last, no longer a cause of sorrow and loss but—for my family, at least—a cause of togetherness and justice and hope.

A second episode occurred in the fall of 2016 at the Secret Prussian Archive. I was working through Lohmeyer's voluminous correspondence of 1942–1943 in order to determine his itinerary and stations during his military service on the eastern front in Russia. I opened a letter, too casually I fear, and a small flower that Lohmeyer had pressed and sent to Melie from the Russian steppe fell to the floor. I reached down to retrieve it, but his lovely memento, which Melie had equally lovingly preserved for three-quarters of a century, disintegrated at my touch. The loss of this meek flower filled my heart with sorrow and my eyes with tears. I realized in that moment how closely my life had become bound to Ernst and Melie Lohmeyer, and how the distance of time and space separating us was momentarily closed. Their loss had become mine, and perhaps my tears would have been theirs. A pressed flower from the Russian steppe, lost. May this story give voice to what its fragile beauty represented.

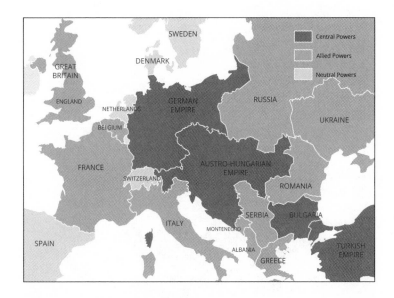

Europe at the beginning of World War I

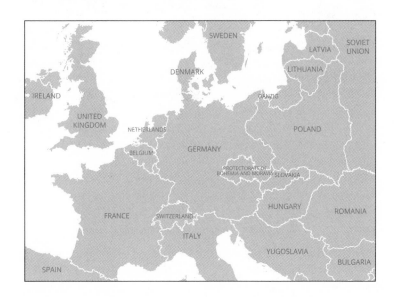

Europe during World War II (1942)

Post–World War II Germany

CHAPTER 1

A Posthumous Inauguration

No one knows where Ernst Lohmeyer's final resting place is. But we all know who he was and what he always will be for us: a preeminent theologian, a great man of integrity and innocence, a martyr for the freedom of the university, in the words of Israel, "a righteous man among the nations."

Günter Haufe[1]

An Awkward Entrance

I shuffled sideways in front of people seated in the second row. Toward the middle of the row a card with "Herr Edwards" written on it reserved an empty seat. I took the seat quickly and focused intently on the evening program in front of me, hoping to atone for my disruption. But for the moment, at least, it was a sham performance. I had just completed a six-thousand-mile journey to attend an important inauguration service—and surely the most unusual one I would ever attend—and I was late. I had flown from North Dakota, where I was professor of religion at the University of Jamestown, to Chicago, and from Chicago a night flight brought me to Munich, Germany, where I took an in-country flight to Hamburg. In Hamburg I boarded a train—not a high-speed Inter-City Express but a slower regional train that would afford me time to prepare for my unique pilgrimage. Five and a half hours later I arrived at my destination in Greifswald, a quaint, midsized university city bordered by the Baltic Sea on the north and Poland on the east.

For the previous four years I had been researching the man to be inaugurated. I had written a scholarly article on him that had been translated into German and published in a premier German journal only a month before the inauguration. That article netted my formal invitation to attend the inauguration at the University of Greifswald and sit with dignitaries for the ceremony, including family, university officials, and political representatives of Germany's northeastern state, Mecklenburg-Pomerania. The first two rows were reserved for the dignitaries. The invitation clearly announced the time and place—University Hall, September 19, 1996, 7 p.m.

I received permission from the dean of the University of Jamestown to miss a week of classes in order to attend the event. This was no minor request, for at Jamestown teaching loads were heavy and teaching assistants scarce. Four of my senior religion majors graciously volunteered to teach my classes for the week. Then, after all my preparations, I fouled up the time. Some of life's blunders have such senseless causes. I got into my head that the event began at 7:30 p.m., and failing to reread the invitation, I walked briskly to the university, expecting to be there in plenty of time. I dashed up the stairs to the stately University Hall on the second floor, arriving at 7:10. I heard music playing behind closed doors. The musicians must be practicing, I thought. I cautiously opened the door . . . and discovered a full house and the ceremony in progress. There was no way to join the proceedings at that point either gracefully or unobtrusively.

The processional—Bach's *Contrapunctus IV* from *The Art of Fugue*, performed by a pianist playing a polished black August Foerster grand piano, two violinists, a cellist, and a violist—was just concluding as I took my seat. Professor Jürgen Kohler opened the ceremony with a formal greeting. Regine Marquardt, minister of culture of Mecklenburg-Pomerania, offered words of appropriate solemnity on behalf of the German government. A second Bach fugue, *Contrapunctus I*, was now performed as an interlude. I shifted my attention to the ambience of the baroque hall, which was a visual mirror of Bach's music. The rich vermilion-colored walls were set in sharp relief by two rows of high-gloss ivory-colored columns that divided the hall into a central nave and two narrower side aisles.

The Ionic volutes that crowned the columns supported a surround balcony, also high-gloss ivory. Gilded finials and urns and ornamentation adorned the top of the balcony balustrade. The high ceiling was dominated by a large decorative center medallion with translucent chandeliers at each end. The polished chestnut flooring below mirrored the aesthetic dance of color and light.

The assuring energy of *Contrapunctus I* drew my attention to the front of the hall. There was the podium for the speeches of dignitaries. There was the rector's chair, the scuffs and mars of its patina like runes of a language known only to the university itself. Over the back of the chair was draped the rector's medallion. But the chair was empty. Beside it was a photograph of a man—his handsome face somewhat chiseled and gaunt, with knowing eyes looking slightly to his right. Above the photograph a black marble plaque was inscribed in gold lettering:

In Memory of
ERNST LOHMEYER
Born 7.8.1890
Professor of New Testament
Greifswald 1935–1946
President of the University from 5.15.1945
Arrested by the NKVD on 2.15.1946
Unjustly executed on 9.19.1946
Exonerated on 8.15.1996[2]

As I read the second to last line I mentally substituted 1996 for 1946. Exactly fifty years earlier to the day, Ernst Lohmeyer had been executed by the infamous NKVD, precursor to the equally infamous KGB, of the Soviet Union. This was a posthumous inauguration.

The Fugue as a Metaphor of Life

Fugues are the most formal and academic of European musical forms. Fugues begin with a tonic tone, a signature melody or "voice" of comfort and reassurance. This melody is then taken up by as many as three or four subsequent "voices" in new variations. The subsequent voices differ from the signature melody in two respects, however. They are dominant voices, stronger than the initial tonic melody. And they challenge and pursue the initial melody, creating tension in the fugue. The success of the fugue depends on the resolution of the tension between the initial tonic voice and the subsequent dominant voices.

The soliloquy of the Bach fugue seemed to have been composed for Lohmeyer himself. His life was as complex and metronomically precise as a fugue. The opening melody of his life had been tonic—promising, reassuring, comforting. He had achieved early and decisive success in the intellectual and academic worlds by earning two doctoral degrees, one in theology and one in philosophy. His interests encompassed Greco-Roman antiquity; ancient Greek, Latin, and Semitic languages; interpretation of the New Testament; as well as philosophy, music, and poetry. While still in his thirties, his genius bore fruit in an impressive number of articles and books published in renowned venues by equally renowned publishers. He received calls to prestigious professorial posts at the universities of Heidelberg and Breslau, receiving an honorary doctorate from the former and being named president of the latter. His productivity and notoriety seemed to have been graced by the Muses.

But in the early 1930s, new voices, more dominant and disruptive, intruded into the fugue of Lohmeyer's life. Like many of his generation in Germany, he found himself commandeered by forces beyond his control. He opposed authoritarian Nazi ideology, especially its fanatical anti-Semitism. He affiliated with the Confessing Church, a branch of the German Protestant Church that resisted the annexation of the church by the state. Through it all he held steadfastly to the original melody of his life, to be a biblical theologian. He wrote voluminously—not simply works of the mind but also on virtually every occasion works closer to his soul, in sermons, correspondence with intellectual luminaries of the day, and letters to his wife during nine and one-half years of service in World Wars I and II. His character and brilliance resulted in his being named president of not one but two German universities. His presidential responsibilities would be challenged to the core by the dissonant voices that assaulted him. At both universities, the first cloaked in Nazi brown and the second in communist red, he would be required to render unto Caesar what belonged to Caesar without rendering to either what belonged to God. In the dangerous circus of German public life in the 1930s and 1940s, this was tantamount to a high-wire act without a safety net. He succeeded in the first contest, as he also did in the second—but success in the second came at the cost of his life.

The ceremony I was attending was a replica of the one at which Ernst Lohmeyer was scheduled to have been inaugurated on February 15, 1946. At 2 a.m. on that day, the NKVD stormed into his house and took him away. The inaugural ceremony was duly held at 11 a.m. the same morning, but Lohmeyer was not present, the president's chair was empty, and all references to him were hastily deleted from speeches. In the ensuing decades in East Germany—and Greifswald was securely ensconced in the Russian sector—there was a blackout on his name and fate. All clues and information about his fate were locked in unknown archives. No questions could be asked, no information divulged. Only after the fall of the Berlin Wall in 1989, and with it the collapse of communism in the East Bloc countries and then in Russia itself, could the fate of Ernst Lohmeyer be resolved. The chief symbol of its long-awaited resolution was the ceremony I was attending—in honor of his inauguration, even if posthumously, of which he had been unjustly deprived fifty years earlier.

The inaugural ceremony, the beauty of the baroque hall, and the serenity of *Contrapunctus I* pulled my mind and spirit upward. The fierce compassion of Lohmeyer's face held me, like an icon holds a venerator. The words of rehabilitation—"unjustly executed ... exonerated"—were freeing, vindicating, and joyful in spite of the sadness. The commemoration service was like the cleansing waters of absolution, a consummation of nearly two decades of efforts on my own part, and even more on the part of his family and the University of Greifswald, to wrest scraps of information about his mysterious disappearance and death from the night and fog of the communist East German and Russian bureaucracies.

The Bach fugue also reflected, although more vaguely, my own pursuit of Lohmeyer's fate. The voice of my pursuit of a doctorate in theology had been interrupted by the voice of Lohmeyer's unresolved fate, and the voices grew in number and intensity as the years passed. They drew me, an unlikely American, into the life story of this very Prussian man whose mettle and faith were tested to their limits first in Nazi Germany and subsequently in communist East Germany. When Soviet military operatives labeled him "enemy of the state" and murdered him in 1946, it was their intention not simply to take his life but to expunge all memory of him, *als ob er nie existierte*—"as though he never existed." They nearly succeeded.

But they did not. This book tells the story of Ernst Lohmeyer, and how my pursuit to uncover his fate changed my own life in the process.

CHAPTER 2

An Inappropriate Question

> ... until a higher power carried him off to a still-unresolved fate.
>
> Gerhard Sass[1]

A Chance Discovery in a Library

I had never heard of Ernst Lohmeyer until I was in my late twenties. I came across his name in the same way I came across many names at the time, as another scholar whom I needed to consult in doctoral research. In the mid-1970s I was writing my doctoral dissertation on the Gospel of Mark in the McAlister Library at Fuller Theological Seminary in Pasadena, California. A premier commentary on Mark at the time was Ernst Lohmeyer's *Evangelium des Markus* (*Gospel of Mark*), published in the acclaimed Meyer Commentary Series in Germany. Lohmeyer first published the commentary in 1936 when he was professor of New Testament at the University of Greifswald in Germany. The edition I was using, however, was published in 1967 and was accompanied by an *Ergänzungsheft* ("Supplementary Booklet"). Not uncommon in German scholarly literature, an *Ergänzungsheft* is a supplementary pamphlet containing further evidence, corrections, changes, additions and deletions, and so forth in light of later findings, offered by author and publisher to update and extend the life of an earlier publication. There was nothing particularly unusual about the fifty-page *Ergänzungsheft* bundled with the 1967 edition of Lohmeyer's commentary, except that it was not written by Lohmeyer. It carried the name Gerhard Sass, was dated 1950, and began thus: "Although it is a joyful occasion to welcome the second edition of Prof. Lohmeyer's *Commentary on Mark*, it is at the same time regrettable for both academy and church that the author himself can no longer undertake its publication. His hand-written changes on which the new edition is based reveal how continuously he labored to improve and expand his book, until a higher power carried him off to a still-unresolved fate."[2]

Many of you may be interested, as I am, in knowing something about the life of an author you are reading. I find this particularly true when I like an author. The melancholy of Sass's preface haunted me. The fate of the author I was reading was an unsolved mystery. I showed the passage to Professor Ralph Martin, my "doctor father," and asked, "What is up with that?" Martin knew more about such things than anyone I knew, but he somewhat dejectedly replied in his clipped British manner, "It remains a mystery." The mystery aggravated me. What was the "higher power" Sass referred to—a regime, a government, perhaps an armed force? What did the power do to him? Why, after all these years, was the mystery still unsolved? Such intrigue is not the norm in the predictably safe and insular world of academia. Equally telling was what Sass did not say, perhaps could not bring himself to say. Lohmeyer's fate was final and irreversible. His disappearance was not reported as though he might be found, the mystery resolved, and everything set right. He was gone . . . forever, and no one knew why.

The note about Lohmeyer's mysterious disappearance stayed with me by the sheer power of its intrigue. But I did not pursue it. I was married at the time, my wife and I had two young children, and my work as youth minister at First Presbyterian Church in Colorado Springs was a full-time-plus call. But young couples and young families rarely live within rational limits, whether by necessity or choice. My wife, Jane, and I were no exception. We bought an older home and renovated it in our spare time and with our sparse resources. In addition, I conspired to commence a PhD program at Fuller Seminary, which entailed flying to Pasadena three times a year to research assiduously in the library for two weeks, while Jane was left in Colorado Springs to care for children, house, dog, yard, and routine unforeseeables on her own. At the end of the two weeks in Pasadena, I would fly back home to the Springs, where I wrote chapters of my dissertation from my research. My "to do" list in the 1970s was longer than it had ever been or would ever be. It was during a Fuller short term that I encountered Gerhard Sass's vexing reference. It anchored Lohmeyer's name in my memory bank, but I had no leisure to pursue it.

Resolution along a City Wall

In 1978 I received my PhD in New Testament and accepted a position as professor of religion at the University of Jamestown in North Dakota. The following summer I returned to East Germany with an organization called Berlin Fellowship, where I rekindled relationships I had initiated on a visit in 1971. Berlin Fellowship grew out of Hollywood Presbyterian Church's ministry with refugees in Berlin following World War II. The erection of the Berlin Wall in August 1961 sealed off half of Berlin from the West, and what came to be known as the Iron Curtain separated the easternmost states of Germany from West Germany. Through annual visits of American church members to pastors, churches, and Christians in the eastern zone of Germany, Berlin Fellowship became a quiet but powerful witness to the oneness of the church in a politically divided and militarily precarious world.

The essence of Berlin Fellowship was contained in its name: "Berlin," the divided city and flashpoint in the Cold War between East and West, and "Fellowship," the forming of friendships and mutually encouraging relationships. These goals were achieved by teams of four American Christians visiting a given congregation in East Germany for several days, during which they enjoyed outings, picnics, games, conversations, Bible studies, and worship and prayer together. At its most basic level, Berlin Fellowship was about people. It was not about politics or economics, nor about ideologies or military strategies. Berlin Fellowship avoided anything illegal or provocative that might jeopardize the lives of East Germans. It did not engage in subversive political activities, and it did not smuggle contraband into East Germany. Participants traveled into East Germany on legal tourist visas. Although this was not widely known, such travel was actually encouraged by East Germany as a means of garnering hard Western currencies.

In June 1979 I was translating for a Berlin Fellowship team in Greifswald, Germany. We were in our final meeting, enjoying *Kaffee und Kuchen*—coffee and cake—in *dicke Maria*—"Fat St. Mary"— as the rather squat-looking church was affectionately called. The church basement was filled to capacity with people interested in hearing and talking with American visitors. Such a visit was a rarity in remote Greifswald. Those who attended did so at some risk to themselves, for the Stasi—secret police—disapproved of public gatherings that were not controlled by the state. There were certainly Stasi agents and informants among those present, although who they were was anyone's guess. Nevertheless, conversation was flowing freely, and the meeting, now in its second hour, seemed to have plenty of life left. During a pause in the discussion, I suddenly recalled that Greifswald was where Ernst Lohmeyer had "mysteriously disappeared." Until that moment I had not made this connection. His fate and the city of Greifswald obviously seemed like two live wires that I should try to connect. "Is not Greifswald where Ernst Lohmeyer taught?" I quickly interjected. "Does anyone know what happened to him?"

The warmth and conviviality immediately drained from the gathering. I had no idea why. The pastor of Fat St. Mary, Dr. Reinhart Glöckner, did. He rose, brought the meeting to a hasty and awkward conclusion, and said to me, "Jim, let's take a walk." In a society where listening devices were placed in radios and TVs, in light sockets and under reception counters, where social settings such as this invariably had listening ears, a walk usually guaranteed privacy. We walked along Brüggstrasse to the point where it exited through the old city walls. There we took a right and walked along a gravel path. On our right was the old red-brick city wall, on our left a spacious and inviting bank of trees. I felt anxious as we walked. The crunching gravel of our footsteps became slightly irritating to me as I waited for Glöckner to speak. He broke the silence. "Jim, we cannot mention the name of Ernst Lohmeyer in this city!" "Why not?"

I asked. I had been raised in a society where an overly free inquiry might offend social etiquette, but it would not kill a healthy meeting. "Why not?" seemed justifiably obvious. To Glöckner, who had spent his life piloting churches between the Scylla of Nazism and the Charybdis of communism, it seemed almost unforgivably naïve. "Lohmeyer disappeared at the hands of the communists," he said in veiled exasperation. "He was certainly killed by them, although we do not know any details. People who are arrested and liquidated by the state are considered enemies of the state, and whoever inquires about their fate is considered an accomplice. Accomplices are enemies of the state! Your question jeopardized everyone in the room this afternoon!"

I was left smarting. Glöckner's explanation made sense, although I confess that its force would have been lost on me apart from his rebuke. But more important than the rebuke was the monstrous injustice of the cover-up itself. For thirty-three years the murder of an innocent man had been cloaked in silence. I was indignant. "Surely his death can be resolved," I said noncompliantly. "Lohmeyer was a great theologian. He was even the president of the university here. How can he be consigned to oblivion in the city where it all took place?"

I had always conceived of the Cold War as a power struggle. Glöckner and I were in the vortex of the Cold War in this moment. But we were not dealing with power. We were dealing with something more fundamental—with truth. Glöckner was as concerned with Lohmeyer's fate as I was. Probably more so. But he could not freely leave East Germany, as I could as an American. He was an East German pastor, and he was not free to consider the fate of Ernst Lohmeyer in isolation from the existential realities of his parish, a parish, like all churches in East Germany, that had to find a way to live within the confines of an all-encompassing state that sought to suppress and ultimately eradicate its existence. The church, it is true, enjoyed a range of freedom in East Germany that other institutions did not, but its optimum range of freedom never exceeded reluctant tolerance by the East German government.

Behind the wall on our right was a row of tired buildings. One of the more prominent buildings was a four-story Orwellian structure constructed of red brick with small windows high in its walls. This building had been a prison. I did not know it at the time, but in this prison Lohmeyer spent the last months of his life, and in its courtyard he may have met his death.

The sound of crunching gravel grated again on my nerves. I made a silent resolution. It was hazily formulated and I could not have expressed it clearly, but it was resolute. If the opportunity ever presented itself, I would try to get to the bottom of Lohmeyer's fate.

An Alignment of Constellations

One of the characteristics of totalitarianism is that it presumes to alter the coordinates of reality. It seeks to redefine and even abolish the concept of "inalienable rights," to eradicate values such as truth, justice, and honesty that do not exist on the basis of argumentation and proof but subsist as innate virtues. Both Nazi Germany and communist East Germany attempted such chthonic overhauls of reality. The East German blackout on Lohmeyer's fate for forty-five years was an example of such. The purpose of proscribing a name like Lohmeyer's was not simply to prevent it from being mentioned in the future but ultimately to eliminate it from the past. If a name can be expunged and deleted from both common parlance and historical record, then the unknowing will never know it and the knowing will in time forget it. The past itself can be sanitized, temporally altered and manipulated, for the purposes of a fraudulent reality.

There is only one defense against this fraudulent overhaul. It is memory. Memory is the first form of resistance to tyranny. The control of information in East Germany created something of a diorama of the actual society. Within this lifeless display isolated individuals labored quietly, sometimes secretly, always intrepidly, to keep the memory of Lohmeyer *alive* and to attempt to learn his fate. These included his wife, his son, especially his daughter and her husband, a few professors at the university, and in lesser ways people like me. When communism imploded in Germany in 1989, the fates of Ernst Lohmeyer and the hundreds of thousands of Germans like him could not only be revisited but also potentially resolved.

Several stars in the constellation of my life aligned to enable me to pursue Lohmeyer. The most important bond between us was the pilgrimage we shared as New Testament scholars. Two individuals making the same pilgrimage know a great deal about each other even before they know each other's name. Lohmeyer, of course, did not know of me, but our shared bond with the New Testament opened a doorway of insight for me into him. Other elements, if less integral, were also vital tangent points. One was German. After graduating from Princeton Seminary in 1970, I had the good fortune to study the New Testament in German-speaking Switzerland at the University of Zürich. There Professor Eduard Schweizer introduced me to the vibrancy of the German language, German theology, and to the prodigious nature of the German university. Lohmeyer was supremely German, even Prussian, and apart from a facility in German, his remarkable life could not be penetrated or publicized to the larger world. The German language permitted me access to an element of German society that was almost wholly sequestered from the West. When I studied in Switzerland, I first visited East Germany, from which, in some respects, I have never returned. In visits to East Germany over the intervening decades, I entered into the lives of Christians there. Lohmeyer spent most of his life in what became East Germany, where he also died. The church that I encountered in East Germany was a daughter of the church Lohmeyer himself led and served. In East Germany I met people who knew Lohmeyer. And those who did not know him knew the East German experience that was essential to understanding him. What I learned about Lohmeyer from friendships and conversations with East Germans was an essential supplement to what I learned about him in libraries and archives.

And a final point, not of circumstance or interest, connects me to Lohmeyer perhaps more deeply than any of the above. It was his courage to act on principles he knew to be true, and to which he dedicated his life. Some people are valiant for the truth; Lohmeyer was fierce for the truth. His ability to act decisively and assuredly, with almost supreme composure in the face of withering opposition, touches me at a deep level, not because it is a virtue I possess but because it is one I admire, and because I believe that courageous character is an unstoppable force in the resistance of tyranny. I have pursued his life because the model of one's life is as important as the words of one's mouth in communicating virtue.

In the basement of Fat St. Mary in 1979—or in the reprimand of Glöckner in its aftermath—these various stars, which shone in the night sky of my scholarship, strangely but irrevocably aligned in my conscience. As I recount these coincidences, it seems that I may not have been alone in my resolve along the city walls of Greifswald to search for Lohmeyer. Perhaps he was also calling to me, and I, for the reasons noted above, was able to hear and obey his call.

CHAPTER 3

Young Man Ernst

Be strong, my son, in the grace that is in Christ Jesus.

2 Timothy 2:1

Growing Up in Germany at the Turn of the Century

If you ask an American kid who his or her heroes are, you will probably hear names from the fields of entertainment and sports. Had you asked a young person of Lohmeyer's day—at least from his social stratum—you would have heard names from science, the arts, and literature. Lohmeyer was introduced to the cultured worlds of antiquity, classical languages, music, and the humanistic tradition early in life. That was typical in the curriculum of the *Gymnasium*— the preuniversity academic educational track—of late nineteenth-century Germany. But it was surely not so typical that students bonded so organically with this curriculum as young Ernst did.

Lohmeyer grew up in a different intellectual galaxy from the one I experienced as a boy. The educational world in Colorado Springs where I grew up was quite respectable by the standards of the day. I attended Cheyenne Mountain School, and it had many bright students. There was a genuine intellectual component, to be sure, but the educational system reflected American culture at large, and the social, practical, activist, and athletic influences, especially in combination, tended to dominate. Had Lohmeyer been a pupil at my school, he would have had to apologize for his academic interests and performance. I simply did not think of the things he did when I was his age. And if I had thought of them, they would have seemed unattainable and oddly irrelevant.

I think of my experience in the American school system of the 1950s and 1960s in quantitative terms: How many goals had we scored, who got invited to whose Christmas open house, what kind of car—or motorcycle—were you driving, did you have the latest gear in any sport or endeavor, and especially at Cheyenne School, how many ski tickets were stapled to the zipper of your ski jacket? Lohmeyer's experience, by comparison, was more qualitative. His life was simpler, to be sure, for a German boy in the 1890s did not have the array of opportunities an American boy did in the 1950s. He had not fished and hiked and skied and traveled and had the adventures I enjoyed in the Colorado mountains, and he could not have imagined the plethora of American gadgets that were available to me and my friends. His life was closely anchored to his home, but the depths of his reflection and expression were as remarkable as the breadth of my experiences. By the time he was twelve, he could write essays in proud upright script that were practically publishable. He almost seems to me not to have been a youth at all, at least not for very long. I tend to think of him in the obviously false stereotype of Byzantine paintings or medieval art where children are depicted as small adults even in their early years.

The differences between Lohmeyer's education and mine largely reflected the two different educational models that were practiced in America and Germany, each of which was accepted rather self-evidently. The goal of American education was—and by and large still is—to master a breadth of proficiencies. In Lohmeyer's day, however, German education—and this still typifies German education today—aspired to depth rather than breadth, to the demonstration of particular strengths in fewer areas, "specialization," as we say today. If the goal of the American model is being "well rounded," that of the German model is sharpness. The premium in Germany is on "*Spitzen*wissenschaft," learning brought to a point. Young Ernst had honed his learning to a very sharp point indeed.

We tend to imagine former eras as "simpler." "Simpler," however, is too often a description not of the former era but of our limitations in understanding it. Lohmeyer's childhood was defined and ordered, focused, deep and reflective, and above all, rooted. The values of a family of a German professional in 1890 were generally characterized by virtues that were intellectual and Prussian—duty and regimentation, for example. Lohmeyer's family was characterized by both, and equally importantly by the church. His maternal grandfather, Karl Niemann, was superintendent of the Lutheran Consistory in Münster,[1] which was essentially a vice-bishop, second in authority to the bishop. His paternal grandfather, Heinrich Lohmeyer, was the director of a village school in Westphalia who achieved modest fame in the 1861 publication of *Protestant Chorals for Church and Home*.[2] Lohmeyer's father, also named Heinrich, was himself a Lutheran pastor who married Maria Niemann. It was Maria's joy and laughter in life that attracted Heinrich to her, including her laughter on occasion *at* him. On their wedding day in June 1884, Heinrich waxed lyrical in celebration of their love. "My irresistible longing for you calls from the distance. Don't you also sense the sweet melody of our hearts, like the call of the Nightingale, that disrupts our stillness and aloneness until we are together?" He closed with reference to the gospel read at their wedding. "Marriage," he reassured, "is the supreme school for heaven."[3]

The marriage of Heinrich and Maria became a finishing school in learning, manners, music, faith, and virtue for the nine children they brought into this world, of whom Ernst Johannes Lohmeyer was the fourth. The tradition of a Lutheran pastor's home, then in its second generation, became a defining influence in Lohmeyer's life. When he was a month old, his father baptized him in the tall-spired Gothic church he pastored in Dorsten, a small city in Germany's northwestern industrial corridor. At age fifteen Lohmeyer would be confirmed by his father as well. In the German tradition, confirmands were invited to choose a life verse from the Bible at the time of their confirmation. Ernst chose 2 Timothy 2:1, "Be strong, my son, in the grace that is in Christ Jesus." A more providential verse could not have been chosen for the life that lay before him.

Ernst would continue the tradition of the Lutheran pastor's home to a third generation. In his first sermon, preached at his ordination to the Lutheran ministry in 1912, he gave an illustration—the only one in the sermon—of the significance of his family in his life. "Let me illustrate," he said, in speaking of his awareness of God in his life. "At the time we were children, our whole life, our happiness and joy, lay in the hands of our father and our mother. We received everything from them. We ourselves were nothing, and everything that we were existed only in their love. That love was our life and joy."[4]

In 1895 Heinrich was transferred from the church in Dorsten to a village church of Vlotho, eighty-five miles to the northeast in more rural Westphalia. There young Ernst attended the local school from ages five to nine. When he turned six, his father began to supplement his regular schoolwork with a regimen of personal tutoring. Included in the instruction were traditional subjects of reading, writing, and math, which Heinrich augmented with Latin, Greek, and music. Many boys, surely, would have chafed at such paternal initiatives. Not Ernst. He responded like a flower to sunshine and water. The combination of his father's instruction and his own will and native intelligence formed a deep and permanent alloy. "With eager interest I learned the ancient languages, above all Greek," he wrote as a boy. He was "overjoyed" when his progress in ancient languages earned him a coveted seat in the Friedrichs-Gymnasium in Herford, fifteen miles west of Vlotho, which he attended from ages nine to eighteen.

In later life Ernst Lohmeyer would often be described as an *Einzelgänger*. The word itself simply means one who "goes it alone." With reference to Lohmeyer, *Einzelgänger* did not mean "loner" but rather self-assured and independent of thought, a person capable of making decisions on his own and, when necessary, acting on them. If the term also suggests that Lohmeyer's character and intellectual achievement were autonomous and perhaps even idiosyncratic, that too would miss the mark. And it would be an injustice to Heinrich, whose influence in his son's education, faith, and character not only began early and bonded organically but also continued, although in different ways, until his death in 1918. Once Ernst left home, Heinrich wrote him a proper letter with news, advice, and his own thoughts every other month throughout his university years, and during the war years, when Ernst was deployed on both the eastern and western fronts, father wrote son twice as often.

Lohmeyer's verbal and quantitative skills were influenced by the same sense of aesthetics that influenced his life as a whole. His scholarship would be characterized by attentiveness to form and proportion, symmetry and symbolism, alliteration and pattern, rhythm and meter. Lohmeyer wrote early, he wrote prolifically, and he wrote well. If Lohmeyer did not exactly write poetry, he seldom failed to write poetically. His gift in mathematics was not satisfied by the mechanics of numbers, but rather by their significance in form and architecture. When applied to the New Testament, his combination of critical tools, Greek and ancient history in particular, and sense of aesthetics resulted in groundbreaking insights. Lohmeyer would convince the scholarly guild that New Testament authors not infrequently incorporated preexisting Christian creeds and hymns into their writings. This was especially true of the epistle writers, Paul in particular, the classic example of which is the sublime hymn to Christ in Philippians 2:5-11, which Lohmeyer believed to be an early eucharistic confession. Lohmeyer's literary sense resulted in further insights, that references to Galilee and Jerusalem in the Gospels, for example, were not simply place-names but representations of two different communities and traditions in earliest Christianity. His study of the Lord's Prayer would argue that not only its words but its very *structure* were essential to its meaning. And with regard to the conundrum of the final book of the Bible, the Revelation of John, he argued that the key to its understanding lay in the number seven.

Lohmeyer's home played an important role in the creative interplay of the intellectual and aesthetic in his life. Sunday afternoons saw the Lohmeyer home transformed into a chamber orchestra. "As in so many pastors' homes," Lohmeyer's daughter Gudrun later wrote, "the Lohmeyer home in Vlotho was dominated by music. Grandmother Marie played the piano skillfully, her husband improvised on the parlor organ in the study, and each child played an instrument. Sunday concerts belonged to every weekend schedule."[5] Lohmeyer's musical abilities expressed themselves most completely through the piano, on which he was capable of extemporizing pieces of more than one part. Among Gudrun's happiest memories of her father was playing four-handed piano pieces with him, well enough, in fact, to *improvise* "without scruple." To which she felt compelled to add, "if not always to the complete pleasure of our listeners."[6] Included in those memories was an instance from the early 1930s when Lohmeyer, then president of Breslau University, donned a Mozart costume and directed the university orchestra.

Lohmeyer's 1907 black notebooks from the Herford gymnasium reveal not only a gifted but also a preeminent student, of the quality that a teacher would see only rarely in his or her career. His fine cursive hand, produced with a needlepointed fountain pen, is fluent, flawless, and calligraphic both in script and format. As was the custom at the time, the pages of student notebooks were written front and back, with a two- to three-inch outer margin left blank on each page for teacher comments. Lohmeyer's notebooks must have been the envy of fellow students and the delight of teachers. Corrections of language or challenges to content and conclusions were remarkably rare. What was not rare was the frequent "Yes" or "!" noted in the margins.

By the time Lohmeyer entered university, he had mastered Latin. That was no mean accomplishment. Nevertheless, Latin played a prominent role in Western education at the time, and it was not unique in the early twentieth century for students entering German universities to be proficient in it. Lohmeyer's greater mastery and deeper bond with Greek were more unique. He respected the practical and political Roman spirit, but he was captivated by the aesthetic Greek spirit. If we speak of him mastering Latin, we must express his relationship to Greek as something altogether different. It would be truer to say that Greek mastered him. Greek language, art, and values awakened him to Greek's potential in fostering human flourishing. In his application to receive the *Abitur*—his diploma from the gymnasium—seventeen-year-old Ernst soared on a thermal current of exuberance to the Greek worldview.

Greek civilization has always enchanted me. It represents the extravagantly rich blossoming of the human spirit, the reason being that all Greek culture rests on an artistic foundation. The free and creative expression of human fantasy is for the Greeks the beginning of their ceaselessly rich life. For us, every inch of Greek soil is holy, every rock alive and individual, the voice of nature awakened to consciousness itself. And the people who brought forth this marvel stand before us, from the half-legendary times of the Trojan War down to Roman Empire: heroes, rulers, warriors, thinkers, poets, sculptors. Here the person was born who was capable of being a Christian.[7]

Lohmeyer's ode to the "rich blossoming of the human spirit" in Greek civilization, where nature itself seemed to be awakened to consciousness and humanity came of age as a worthy heir of Christianity, seemed to those who heard it as youthful hyperbole. Not so this seventeen-year-old. Lohmeyer was extolling more than the soul of the Greeks over the practicality of the Romans. The truth he had discovered about the Greeks was also a truth about himself. All our dreams, I believe, begin in youth. Lohmeyer's early dream awakened him to who he was and where he must go in life. In 1990 his daughter Gudrun, in addressing the Herford gymnasium on the 100th anniversary of her father's birth, quoted her father's Greek rhapsody as a germ of insight into his intellectual life. "His mastery of the vehicle of language—including Greek—in his years in the Gymnasium was so complete that he was already free to look for intellectual connections and to identify emotionally with them."[8]

Greek and German

I recount with special interest Lohmeyer's mastery of Greek and German not simply because he acquired both so early and completely but because his acquisition of both differed so dramatically from mine. German and Greek are two essentials for the study of the New Testament. Had it not been for my love of the New Testament, I most certainly would never have learned either language. And without Greek and German, I never would have encountered Ernst Lohmeyer.

In contrast to Lohmeyer, my legacy with both languages began late and unpromisingly. My two professional goals in college were to attend seminary and become an ordained pastor. Both required proficiency in Greek. I took an introductory Greek course my senior year at Whitworth University, and although I achieved the highest average in the class, I did not bond with the language and I did not like it. When I entered Princeton Seminary in the fall, I faced a predicament: I knew too much Greek to enter the introductory course but too little to pass the qualifying examination for New Testament exegesis. I decided to improve my Greek proficiency on my own in preparation for the qualifying examination. While doing so, I began eating meals in the refectory with pastors who were returning to the seminary for continuing education events. I asked them if they used Greek in their ministries, and if so, how? Of the fifty or so pastors with whom I ate, only two or three reported using Greek in any significant way. This exacerbated my Greek crisis. To invest the enormous time and energy required to learn Greek, and then lose it, struck me as folly. Only two feasible options seemed left to me: either not learn Greek at all, or find a way to make it a permanent part of my theological toolbox.

A fellow student knew of my dilemma and directed me to a doctoral student, Margaret Shatkin. Maggie, as she was known, had already completed a doctorate in classics and was now pursuing a second doctorate in the church fathers at Princeton Seminary. My spirits were at half-mast as I shared with Maggie my seemingly unsolvable dilemma. I am not sure what I expected her to say or do—perhaps only to express a scholarly requiem of sympathy. To my surprise, she responded quickly, lightheartedly, and matter-of-factly. "If you want, in a year or so you can be reading Greek about as well as you can read Shakespeare," she said. "How might that be possible?" I asked incredulously. "Throw away your English Bible," she said. "Start reading the Greek New Testament twenty minutes a day—*every day*—until you are able to read a chapter a day. If you read a chapter a day, you'll read through the Greek New Testament in a year, and if you keep doing that, you'll have Greek for life!"

In less than five minutes Maggie had broken my logjam! I repeated her advice as I walked back to my room in Alexander Hall, where I began stumbling through a verse of the Greek New Testament. A task that seemed forbidding in prospect turned out, remarkably, to be much less daunting in execution. I read through a New Testament lexicon and wrote on flash cards the definition of every word I did not know. There are nearly seven thousand different Greek words in the New Testament; my flash cards numbered about four thousand. I memorized these words—not in one year, as Maggie projected, but in two. In 1972 I succeeded in reading the Greek New Testament cover to cover. In the years since, I have read twenty-five verses daily—*every day*—in the Greek. I have now read the Greek New Testament forty-six times cover to cover. It's the most important thing I do every morning—except for breakfast. My bond with Greek is cemented. Lohmeyer's ode to Greek strums the chords of my soul.

My experience with German was somewhat different. I wanted to continue studying the New Testament after seminary, and to do so I needed to learn German. In contrast to my experience with Greek, I *wanted* to learn German. I wrote to three professors with whom I wished to study—one in England, one in Germany, and one in Switzerland. The first to respond was Professor Eduard Schweizer of the University of Zürich in Switzerland. In a postcard dated May 5, 1970, he explained the process of study at Zürich and concluded optimistically, "Let us hope that you will find some way for coming to Zürich." I am not entirely sure Schweizer meant that as a personal invitation, but I took it as such. The clock was now ticking. The successful passing of a German proficiency examination at the University of Zürich was required before I could matriculate in the fall. I went to the Princeton University Bookstore and purchased a used copy of a German grammar. I worked through the volume as if my life depended on it—which it did. On the flight to Europe in June of 1970, I studied German vocabulary cards all night long.

The study of German theology is not a little daunting. A cursory visit to a university library in Germany or Switzerland makes one quickly aware that theological and philosophical disciplines are established and honored industries in the German-speaking world—with a two-centuries' head start over the same in America. It was thus with considerable trepidation that I entered a small library in October of 1970 to take the language proficiency examination. The examination, I was informed, was short and simple: a professor would take you into a library, pull a German book from the shelf, open it at random, and tell you to read three pages aloud, after which you had to explain in German what it said. Period.

Under no pretenses did I consider my six months' study of German adequate preparation to pass this test. The only comfort I recall as the exam began was that the middle-aged professor was a man of benign manners. Anxious about the exam, I was unable to hold up my end of the conversational courtesies. My verbal contribution amounted to a few grunts and nods, similar to the way I respond to questions when the dentist is cleaning my teeth. The professor walked to one of the bookcases and pulled Albert Schweitzer's *Zwischen Wasser und Urwald* from the shelf. This was utterly remarkable. As a teenager I had been inspired by Schweitzer's life and had read the English translation of this signature book, entitled *On the Edge of the Primeval Forest*. The most famous passage in the book is one of the most inimitable reflections Schweitzer ever wrote, the recounting of his boat trip up the Ogowe River in French Equatorial Africa to found a hospital at Lambarene. Beholding the teeming life at the meeting point of river and forest, Schweitzer came to a revolutionary and life-transforming insight—*all life wills to live*. The will-to-life, moreover, should be respected by other life-forms, especially the most powerful one, the human life-form. Schweitzer was one of the first thinkers in history to include *nature* within the orbit of human ethical responsibilities. His life-affirming philosophy of "reverence for life" became an important clue to the meaning of life.

It was this passage that the professor opened before me.

Since all German words are pronounced exactly as they are spelled, I had no trouble reading the passage understandably, if not accent-free. I already knew the gist of the story in English, so all I needed to do was translate it into basic German, which I also was able to do. After two or three minutes the professor relaxed his attention and said casually, "*Ganz gut*." He scribbled something on a form, handed it to me, and told me to give it to the registrar. *Ganz gut*, for those who know German, is not the highest praise— that would be *sehr gut*, "excellent." *Ganz gut* means "fine," "okay," "good enough." No one could have received greater delight from such prosaic affirmation than I did in that moment.

As I left the room, I surveyed the library momentarily. There were perhaps three thousand volumes on its shelves. Wholly unknown to the professor—our introductory small talk scarcely included Albert Schweitzer—he had selected what was surely the only book on the shelves that I had ever read.

CHAPTER 4

University Years

The God who said, "Let light shine out of darkness," has shone in our hearts the radiance of the knowledge of the glory of God in the face of Jesus Christ.

2 Corinthians 4:6

Study

With scarcely a break in his stride, Lohmeyer commenced his university studies three weeks after graduating from the Herford gymnasium in 1908. Gudrun's description of her father's readiness for "intellectual connections"—to begin putting the pieces of life's puzzle together—when he entered university did not mean that her father's future as a theologian was already determined. Lohmeyer was eighteen years old, and he wanted to savor the symphony of knowledge open to him, where theology, philosophy, history, music and art, and also mathematics and the natural sciences were but different instruments in a grand orchestra. Or, to change the metaphor, he wanted to explore the composite of all the university had to offer—like one looks through a night telescope not to enjoy a single star but to revel in the vast array of space itself. Lohmeyer's interest in the whole over the parts was another example of the influence of the Greeks. The Greek ideal—as exemplified in Socrates, the intellectual gadfly, or in Aristotle's golden mean between the poles of harmful excesses—was always a global ideal of the whole person. Many things would change as Lohmeyer matured in life, but his passion for an integrated rather than compartmentalized life would not change.

Heinrich thought his son was destined to study music. "I am pleased that you have found a place where you can especially pursue your aptitude for music," he wrote to Ernst during his first year at university. In addition to the affirmation, he included, as usual, a paternal admonition: "Perhaps you can also polish your bowing technique on the violin."[1]

In spring 1908 Lohmeyer wrote to inquire about studying at the University of Tübingen with Dr. Theodor Haering, professor of philosophy. Haering wrote him two brief postcards in return, and shortly after his eighteenth birthday in July, Lohmeyer commenced his first semester at Tübingen. Tübingen is a picturesque university city nestled in a crook of the Neckar River. The university's history extends as far into the Middle Ages as the Neckar extends into the heart of Germany. Reflected in the river was the yellow-turreted house of Friedrich Hölderlin, a poet who enjoyed Lohmeyer's lifelong admiration. High above the Neckar a line of stately mansions, which had been repurposed into German fraternity houses, crowned the cityscape like a crenellated castle wall. The university's libraries and lecture halls and seminar rooms, its institutes and clinics and study centers, were like ribs connected to the backbone of the city on Wilhelmsstrasse. Lohmeyer thrived in Tübingen's stimulating and contagious academic atmosphere from summer semester 1908 (July to September) through winter semester 1908–1909 (October to February).

Heinrich's prediction about his son's study of music was premature. Already in his first semester Lohmeyer set a different course. The course may have surprised father and family, but it was true north on Lohmeyer's personal compass, and would remain so ever after. He commenced the study of Oriental languages—Assyrian, Babylonian, and Aramaic. The decision of an eighteen-year-old to embark on the study of Aramaic—a Semitic language written from right to left—and Assyrian and Babylonian—both written in cuneiform (stylus imprints in clay)—reveals that he was anything but academically undecided. The family's surprise in their middle son's course reveals more about the deep waters of his inner life than it does about their misjudgment of him. He continued to paddle freely in the broad river of knowledge flowing through Tübingen, but already he plied the river from the current of theology and philosophy.

Berlin

Unlike American higher education, which requires a certain number of course credits for graduation, German universities require successful completion of a series of comprehensive examinations in a chosen field of study. German students often attend lectures at two or more universities in preparation for these terminal examinations. In winter 1909 Lohmeyer wrote to inquire about the possibility of studying with Dr. Heinrich Zimmern at the University of Leipzig. Zimmern was the successor of Friedrich Delitzsch and one of Germany's leading Orientalists and Semiticists. Lohmeyer's inquiry of Zimmern reveals that the Semitic literary world remained a lively counterpart to the classical world of Greek and Latin in his academic pursuits. Lohmeyer spent summer semester 1909 at the University of Leipzig.[2] Both Tübingen and Leipzig were mere prologue, however, to his ultimate academic goal. In winter semester 1909 he transferred to Humboldt University in Berlin, from which he graduated in summer semester 1911.

Located on Unter den Linden, the grandest boulevard in Germany and one of the grandest in Europe, Humboldt was housed in the neoclassical palace that once belonged to Prince Henry of Prussia. A heraldic equestrian statue of Frederick the Great parades down Unter den Linden before the main university building. The star of Humboldt University rode high in the sky of imperial Germany. In Lohmeyer's four years at Humboldt, six of its faculty were awarded Nobel Prizes. And more Nobel laureates were waiting in the wings, including Albert Einstein and Max Planck, both physics professors at the university. Nobel Prizes are not awarded to theologians, but if they were, Humboldt professor Adolf von Harnack, perhaps the dominant theological figure in Europe at the time and one of the preeminent patristic scholars of all time, almost certainly would have been a laureate. In the forty years before World War II, thirty-two Humboldt University faculty members were awarded Nobel Prizes. Following World War II and the division of Berlin among the four victor powers, Russia, America, England, and France, Humboldt University lay within the Russian sector. The contrast between the university's postwar status in communist East Berlin and its prewar status could not be more dramatic. Between 1949, when the German Democratic Republic was founded, and 1989, when the Berlin Wall fell, Humboldt University had only one Nobel laureate. Lohmeyer would not live to witness the demise of Humboldt University in the communist era, but his experience on the eastern front in World War II tutored him well in the temper of Russian communism. As president of the University of Greifswald in postwar Germany, he exchanged letters with Professor Johannes Stroux, president of Humboldt, in which they committed themselves "to preserve the heritage of the German university from the dangers threatening free inquiry" in the Soviet sector of Germany.[3]

As a student at Humboldt, Lohmeyer corresponded with a number of professors, especially Adolf Deissmann and Reinhold Seeberg in Berlin, but also others farther afield in southern Germany and Switzerland. In the florid and dramatic script of the era, their postcards advised him on matters related to academic programs and publication of his works. Deissmann and his wife invited Lohmeyer, still an undergraduate, to dinner in their home—a rarity in Germany at the time. Adolf Deissmann left the most lasting mark on Lohmeyer in Berlin. In 1910 German scholars typically approached academic study of the New Testament through the lenses of history, original languages, theology, or comparative religions. The contributions of archaeology and the social setting of the New Testament were still in their infancy or neglected altogether. Deissmann had traveled extensively in the eastern Mediterranean, however, where he was introduced to the dramatic archaeological discoveries then coming to light, and which, especially in Ottoman Turkey, were being made available to German scholars and German museums. Along with scholars like Adolf Schlatter and Gustaf Dalman in Germany and William Ramsay in England, Deissmann harvested newly discovered monumental inscriptions and papyri—unofficial secular documents largely from Egypt—for the light they might shed on the vocabulary of the New Testament. Prior to such late nineteenth-century discoveries, the Greek of the New Testament, which differed from the classical Greek of Plato and the Greek dramatists, for example, was poorly understood. Indeed, it was often misunderstood as a strange and inferior form of Greek—frequently disparaged as "Holy Spirit Greek." The cue ball of Deissmann's sociological and epigraphic studies would significantly realign the pool table of New Testament studies by situating study of the early church squarely in the Greco-Roman world of the first and second centuries.

Deissmann was more than an academic theologian, however. He was also an ecumenical churchman. The divided churches of Europe and their eager alliances with nationalist and militarist ambitions in the lead-up to World War I distressed him deeply. The height of Deissmann's career came during the Great War, during which he largely suspended his scholarship in order to "foster ecumenical solidarity," as he described it, among Protestants in Europe. His ecumenical orbit did not include Catholics—that extended orbit would not come until the postwar era—but his advocacy of Protestant ecumenism across national boundaries was a prophetic antidote to the ecclesiastical partisanship and nationalism of the era. The English translator of Deissmann's influential *Licht vom Osten*, Lionel Strachan, was a British citizen who was stranded in Berlin when World War I broke out. Strachan was interned in the Plötzensee and Ruhleben prisons in Berlin for the duration of the war, from fall 1914 until spring 1918. In the preface of his English translation, *Light from the Ancient East*, Strachan testifies that Deissmann's commitment to "Christian solidarity" included visits to prisoners like himself. "Every two months or so a long, weary journey was undertaken [by Deissmann] just for the sake of cheering an enemy alien by half-an-hour's talk under the eye of soldiers in a guard room; 21 visits were paid in all, permission having to be obtained for each, not without difficulty, from the military authorities. Rare indeed was the privilege. And the visitor never came empty handed, but brought with him mental pabulum and always some creature comforts, even when the pinch was being felt in the homes of Germany." Strachan concluded his eulogy to Deissmann by quoting from Matthew 25:36 in Greek, "I was in prison, and you came to me."[4]

Lohmeyer produced the most impressive work of his undergraduate career under Deissmann's tutelage. His study of *diatheke*, Greek for "covenant," was one of eight undergraduate essays at Humboldt in 1910—and the only one from the theology department—to be awarded Humboldt University's highest student distinction of honor.[5] Lohmeyer did not rest on the laurels of the distinction but took it as a launchpad for further and more ambitious studies. In the spring of 1911 he produced for Deissmann three more studies, two of them on the book of Revelation. The longest, a beautifully handwritten monograph of 190 pages, attempted on the basis of evidence preserved in Revelation to construct a profile of the Christian communities to which John addressed the Apocalypse. A second and shorter study of 35 pages investigated the letters to the seven churches of Revelation. A final study in the spring of 1911, also written in handsome cursive, was a 120-page paper entitled "A Hypothesis concerning Kings and Heroes in the Hellenistic Era." This thick study commenced with a long Greek quotation of Xenophon about heraldic virtues. These impressive fledgling studies already bear Lohmeyer's methodological signature as a theologian—to remain as free as possible from citations of secondary literature in order to focus primarily on original Greek and Latin sources.

Another Berlin scholar who left a mark on Lohmeyer was fellow student Karl Ludwig Schmidt. A year younger than Lohmeyer, Schmidt earned his doctorate under Deissmann the year after Lohmeyer earned his. The two remained loyal correspondents with Deissmann until his death in 1937, and Schmidt and Lohmeyer with one another until Lohmeyer's arrest in 1946. Schmidt went the second mile by writing on behalf of Lohmeyer's release after his arrest. The careers of Ernst Lohmeyer and Karl Ludwig Schmidt both reflected Deissmann's scholarship of engagement, and they intersected with each other in unforeseen ways. Lohmeyer and Schmidt were both expelled by the Nazis from prominent New Testament professorships, Schmidt from Bonn in 1933 and Lohmeyer from Breslau in 1935. Both held offices in political parties, Schmidt in the Socialist Party of Germany and Lohmeyer in a centrist forerunner of today's Christian Democratic Union. Both engaged and critiqued the challenges to the historical veracity and literary integrity of the New Testament Gospels posed by the dominant theology of Rudolf Bultmann. And most important—and certainly most unusual—Schmidt and Lohmeyer were among the few German intellectuals publicly to defend the reputation of Jews in Nazi Germany.

Melie Seyberth

In the spring of 1910, nineteen-year-old Lohmeyer met a young woman named Amalie Seyberth on an outing to Wannsee on the outskirts of Berlin. Melie, as Lohmeyer would call her, the daughter of a member of the city council in Wiesbaden in southwest Germany, was born in 1886 and was four years his senior. She was a young woman of poise and strong purpose—and character-to-the-core. She was not a person of superficial friendships but of deep and abiding relationships. She found such a relationship with Ernst Lohmeyer. She later reflected on her early impressions of him thus: "Ernst seemed to me the purest, most transparent, and most genuine person I had ever met in life. His rather childlike appearance was something of a contrast to his expressive green eyes, which he inherited from his father, and his high and pensive forehead that harbored many thoughts. Those features admitted an inner will and passion. What was not yet clear to me was his tender charm, willful balance, sensitive disposition, and gallantry. These were so pronounced and predominant that they dispelled all illusions about him."[6] As far as we know, Lohmeyer had not dated or shown much interest in girls before he met Melie. He had too much in common with Melie, however, not to be interested in her. Both loved music, not simply listening to music but making music. Ernst was an instrumentalist, primarily pianist, but Melie was an alto vocalist who enjoyed a reputation in and around Wiesbaden before their marriage. Singing was a minor vocation throughout her life. Whatever shyness she exhibited in other public venues dissipated when she sang an aria of Bach or Schumann or Mendelssohn with a chamber orchestra.

Ernst and Melie were intentional, and intense, although in different ways. Ernst's scholarship attests to his inner drive: few twentieth-century German theologians got more seminal scholarship into print in the brief span of their lives than did Ernst Lohmeyer. Melie's drive did not produce a life's oeuvre, as did Ernst's, but it *preserved* the common life they shared together in scrapbooks, guest books, itineraries, calendars, and, in Lohmeyer's final years, important diaries. She was intent and indefatigable in keeping memories alive, the past ever present, in her marriage and family.

Courtship through Correspondence

No interest was more common and constitutive of Melie and Ernst, and none would bind their marriage more indissolubly together, than letter writing. Words offered more than a medium of communication between these two different but equally passionate souls. Both found the written word as natural as breathing or walking, and almost more vital than if they were physically present. Their letters are revealing and expressive, but without ostentation or affectation. Rather than muffling their voices or inhibiting their spirits, the literary clothing of their correspondence seemed to make the pulse of their lives more intense and palpable.

Correspondence was more than a choice; it was a necessity. They *had* to write. They wrote each other even when they were not apart. Their thirty-five-year relationship is preserved in thousands of letters. I spent several months in the Secret Prussian Archive in Berlin-Dahlem combing through boxes and boxes of letters; they wrote four or five letters per week, especially during the nine and one-half years they were separated by World Wars I and II. Many were postcards and some, less than postcards, simply two or three sentences scribbled on a scrap of paper at hand. But the majority are proper letters, written in handsome cursive on several pages of unlined stationery. In 1915—the bowels of the war years—Lohmeyer sent Melie a dozen missives that were nothing short of wartime field diaries, each sixty-plus pages in length. Melie saved Ernst's letters.

Ernst saved Melie's letters. Every letter. They even saved receipts of hotel rooms, restaurants, and purchases of a hat or pair of trousers for Ernst. Melie sorted them all by year, each letter in chronological sequence, then tied them with thin brown string into thick bundles, with a cover note identifying each bundle.

Their letters, like life itself, were mostly about ordinary events of ordinary days—the kinds of things most of us find too mundane and humdrum to record. But for Melie and Ernst, no event seemed devoid of significance, and hence no event was too small to recount. I was often struck more by the letter writers themselves—these two souls who devoted themselves so tirelessly and fully to the act and art of communication—than by the actual contents of the letters. If the events were ordinary, Ernst and Melie were extraordinary—genuine, self-revealing, loving—in relating them.

Lohmeyer's relationship with Melie began, as it would end, in separation. Both separations were primarily the result of war. After Lohmeyer graduated from Humboldt, he took a yearlong position as private tutor to the two sons of Count Max von Bethusy-Huc at Klein-Gaffron, near Breslau—today Wroclaw, Poland. Lohmeyer had known Melie for about eighteen months when he sent her the following letter about "my children," as he called the two boys he tutored. He promised to write about both boys, but the younger, Clemens, so captivated him that he never reported on the older.

> Shall I describe him to you? He is a sweet little boy, almost beautiful, with long dark hair hanging down to his shoulders and with large bright brown eyes. One moment his movements are childish and clumsy and the next youthful and precise. He stands on the threshold between little child and young man and is, as is so often the case, a strange and charming mix of both. His entire nature is inwardly dear and kindred to me. He fixes his big eyes on me when I tell a story, hanging on every word. And then those childlike questions, wonderful and thoughtful, come from his mouth. I once told him a story from the Old Testament as simply as I could. "Then dear God said . . ." and so forth. Then he asked me: "Oh, please tell me if dear God speaks that way today." I: "Of course, if one is very quiet and asks him for something, then

he still answers." He: "Does he then speak like I am speaking to you? Can you hear him?" I: "No, not like that. But when you pray for something, then you will suddenly become very happy and know what you should do. Then you'll know that dear God has spoken to you." And then after a quiet pause, he: "But when I get to heaven, will he speak to me so I can understand him?" I: "Yes, you can be sure of that." He: "I want so much to go to him right now." ... And then further, "Is dear God always alone?" I: "No, he has lots of good little angels around him. He is always with them and he rejoices in them." He: "Tell me, when was dear God born?" I: "O, God was never born. He has always been, before any people were on earth." He: "But doesn't he have a father and a mother?" I: "No, he has no father or mother." He: "Is dear God then an orphan? I want to go to him right now and speak with him. That would make him so happy, wouldn't it?" Then I took the dear little fellow who had been leaning against me the whole time up in my arm and gave him a kiss. "Yes indeed," I said. "You will go and talk to dear God real soon, and that will make him very happy." At this the little guy jumped from my arms and ran around happily like a kid in a park and wanted to catch a squirrel.[7]

Dissertation

Lohmeyer did not shelve his academic pursuits during his year at Klein-Gaffron. While tutoring his two young charges, he expanded into a doctoral dissertation the 1910 word study on *diatheke* (Greek "covenant") that had been awarded highest honors by Humboldt University.[8] In July of 1912, just after his twenty-second birthday, he successfully defended the 160-page work in Berlin.[9]

The purpose of a doctoral dissertation is to show mastery of the fundamental content and methodology of a given field of study, while demonstrating its significance in a new area of that field. The narrow ridge of a doctorate is to be novel without being radical, to extend the "assured results" of a discipline but not abandon or subvert them. Lohmeyer followed the narrow ridge in his approach to "covenant" by exploring the history of the word's usage, beginning with its use in the ancient Greek world, followed by its use in the He-brew and Greek Old Testaments, in intertestamental Judaism, and concluding with its uses in the New Testament. The sequence of this historical approach, although not exactly pioneered by Lohmeyer, was exhibited to near perfection in his dissertation. This same his-torical sequence would be adopted by the nine-volume *Theological Dictionary of the New Testament*—the preeminent German study of the vocabulary of the New Testament—that appeared from 1933 to 1973.

In addition to demonstrating mastery of New Testament philol-ogy in *Diatheke*, Lohmeyer also exercised scholarly independence. A case in point was his discussion of "the Damascus Apocalypse" (today known as the Damascus Document), which had been dis-covered by Solomon Schechter in the Cairo Genizah in 1896. A *genizah*, which was usually attached to a synagogue, was literally a "book morgue," that is, a Jewish repository for old writings and ritual objects that contain the name of God and hence are forbidden by Jewish law from being destroyed. The Damascus Document be-longs to the same family of documents later discovered in the caves above the northwest shore of the Dead Sea in 1947, known today as the Dead Sea Scrolls. Schechter's discovery of the Damascus Doc-ument might be regarded as the *first* Dead Sea Scroll—discovered fifty years before the main corpus of scrolls. Lohmeyer described the Damascus Document as "of uncommon importance"[10] for the New Testament because, like Jeremiah 31, it linked the fulfillment of the *diatheke*, the covenant, with the arrival of the Messiah. The past century of scholarly research has soundly vindicated Lohmeyer's judgment regarding the Damascus Document.[11]

Lohmeyer further exercised his scholarly independence in his skepticism of the various strands of literary tradition in the first five books of the Old Testament, the Pentateuch, commonly identified as the J and E sources. Regarding the Documentary Hypothesis, he was skeptical of the "labyrinth of literary-critical hypotheses."[12] Though Lohmeyer was only twenty-two years old when he wrote *Diatheke*, his scholarship was already sufficiently mature to char-acterize the impressive body of work yet to come. In *Diatheke* and ever after, he grounded his discussions in original rather than in secondary sources. His scholarship was governed throughout by logical progression, control, succinctness, and focus. He pursued the root of the matter under discussion rather than following tendrils and offshoots that, though perhaps of interest, were of secondary importance. Above all, Lohmeyer pressed the grapes of his historical, sociological, linguistic, and epigraphic evidence for the theological wine they might yield. With regard to *Diatheke*, the crux of its biblical significance lay in Jesus's words at the Last Supper, in which he interpreted his death as a "new covenant." Jesus understood his messianic self-sacrifice as a fulfillment of Jeremiah's vision of the new covenant (Jer. 31), which was echoed in the Damascus Document, as the inauguration of a new and eternal relationship between God and humanity. The long history of the concept of *diatheke*, not surprisingly, included a tangle of tangents and byways and asides, but its essential shoots all converged in Jesus's eucharistic teaching on covenant, which was the "nucleus," the "sum of all Christianity." Lohmeyer set a quotation from the philosopher Johann Gottlieb Fichte—the first president of Humboldt University exactly a century earlier—at the head of *Diatheke*: "The source of all science and all truth and all certainty and all reality is love."[13] That covenantal love was inaugurated by Jesus at the Last Supper.

Ordination

The writing and defending of his doctoral dissertation were not Lohmeyer's sole theological pursuit in 1912. Six months after he received his doctorate, he successfully completed his church examinations for ordination in the Lutheran Church. Ordination was a two-track process, one track of academic theology, which Lohmeyer had completed at Tübingen, Leipzig, and Berlin, and a parallel track of ecclesiastical preparation overseen by the Protestant Consistory of Münster. The ecclesiastical license was a Latin tongue-tangler, *pro licentia concionandi*, which simply meant the sum of everything necessary to become licensed. That sum included both professional and practical sides of church ministry, such as preaching, liturgy, pastoral care and counseling, church administration, and so forth. Candidates were required to take an oath of submission to Holy Scripture and the Augsburg Confession. Lohmeyer submitted to both and was certified to preach the Word of God. His fellow students jovially christened him "Frater Ernestus"—Brother Ernst.

The conclusion of the ordination process, to which friends, family, and acquaintances were invited, was the sermon, which Lohmeyer preached in Berlin on 12/12/12—December 12, 1912. His sermon text was 2 Corinthians 4:1–6, concluding with "The God who said, 'Let light shine out of darkness,' has shone in our hearts the radiance of the knowledge of the glory of God in the face of Jesus Christ."[14] Lohmeyer made four points. Foremost was his conviction, repeated throughout the sermon, that the gospel is an objective truth, without which we are "like refugees wandering aimlessly, not knowing where we belong until the conviction (*Bewusstsein*) is granted to us that our life rests in God, that we are allowed to live in him and in his love until mercy encompasses us."[15] Here Lohmeyer echoed Augustine's famous conviction that "God has made us for himself, and our hearts are restless until they rest in him."[16] His second point was that the office to which he was being ordained was not limited to him alone as a clergyman but was a responsibility of grace for all Christians, whatever their professions and works. Here Lohmeyer appropriated Luther's concept of the "priesthood of all believers," but he extended it beyond the church to include work in society at large. Thirdly, the transforming light of Christ was not communicated through disembodied truths but through fellow believers "who approach us and talk with us as trusted friends, who themselves longed for what we long for and found rest in the longings."[17] The gospel, in other words, is "incarnational." In some way unknown to them, believers become for others what Christ has become for them. Then Lohmeyer concluded. These realities equip believers to do the one thing in life that humans were not only made to do but also meant to do in order to be truly human—to act responsibly, to do meaningful work. "When we live in the world by forces that come to us from above the world, then we have the privilege and deep certainty that we are equipped for work—and with unquenchable joy in doing it. Life impels us to action and the inexhaustible energy contained in action. In work, life unfolds itself in free abundance."[18]

Most ordinands intend their ordination sermon to be not simply first in time but first in importance, charting the course of their life and ministry. Lohmeyer's ordination sermon clearly fits this second category. The drive for certainty, for inalterable truth, would characterize all facets of his subsequent theological endeavors. His sense of calling or *office* would be evident in his conduct as professor, preacher, and university president. Openness to the influence of others on his life, above all Melie, but also and equally subsequent colleagues, would testify to his incarnational understanding of the gospel. And perhaps above all, the sermon declares his unflagging energy and resolve for work, to which his productivity as both scholar and leader would bear witness.

Lohmeyer closed the sermon by quoting John 8:32, "The truth will make you free." Truth grounds and focuses one, making one whole and single. Truth saves one from distractions, from partial truths, half-truths, and compromises. Truth is empowering. Lohmeyer received the truth that makes one free in the Christian gospel, and it formed him to follow a unique course in life as a scholar, leader, and witness.

CHAPTER 5

The Great War

> Freedom is present for us as long as reason is present in us.
> The job of reason is to discern righteousness, the job of the
> will is to preserve it.
>
> Ernst Lohmeyer[1]

Second Doctorate

Not long after Lohmeyer defended his theological dissertation under Deissmann—although exactly when we do not know—he began
work on a second dissertation in philosophy. Eighteen months later,
at the end of January 1914, he presented to the philosophical faculty
at the Friedrich-Alexander-University of Erlangen the dissertation
"The Doctrine of the Will in Anselm of Canterbury," written under
Professor Richard Falckenberg, an authority on the history of German philosophy and particularly on Nicholas of Cusa.[2] At the time
Lohmeyer submitted the dissertation, he had been in active military duty for four months, having volunteered for military service
in October 1913. The world was not yet at war in January 1914—that
would come six months later—so Lohmeyer's military life consisted
of training rather than combat. He took full advantage of the relaxed
discipline while completing his dissertation.

No doctoral dissertation could be leaner than his seventy-five-
page study of Anselm, which consisted of a brief introduction, three
main chapters, and an even briefer conclusion. Lohmeyer repeated
in the second dissertation the modus operandi followed in his dis-

sertation on *diatheke*—bypassing secondary literature and commentary in favor of original sources, focusing on essential rather than secondary issues, citing original languages rather than translations, evaluating all data—whether historical, linguistic, philosophical, etc.—in terms of its ultimate theological significance. These would become signature elements in all of Lohmeyer's future academic work.

The Limitations of Scholasticism

The figure of Anselm crowns the gothic medieval intellectual edifice known as Scholasticism. Scholasticism was the attempt, on the basis of logical methods and categories inherited from Aristotle, to undergird, explain, and defend the entirety of Christian dogma. In addition to Aristotle, Scripture and church fathers (and among the latter, particularly Augustine) remained the chief sources of the "Schoolmen," as the Scholastics were called. The achievement of Scholasticism lay not in its content—in new theological insights and truths—but in its novelty of method. Scholasticism thus referred to a *way* of doing theology rather than its actual content.

Lohmeyer began with a treatment of two foundational distinctions of medieval thinking—substance and accidents. Substance is the more important of the two, for it is the essence of a thing that makes it the kind of thing it is, and therefore does not change. Accidents, on the other hand, are properties of a thing that can change without changing the essence of the thing to which they belong. A horse, in terms of substance, is a large, solid-hoofed herbivorous mammal that has been domesticated as a beast of burden, but in terms of accidents, horses can range in color and size. For Anselm, the human mind belongs to the category of substance, whereas human will belongs to that of accident. The mind is placed within the human creature by God, but will is an instrument of the mind deriving from human nature and has been corrupted by its fall from grace. The power of the will over man is supreme, but it is not complete, for it is unable to permeate the human creature sufficiently to reconcile it to God. A dualism results, which characterizes all medieval theology—the conflict between mind and will, spirit and matter, heaven and earth, God and the world.

Human freedom reveals the renegade nature of the will. Prior to human disobedience of God's commandment and the fall from grace in Genesis 3, the human will freely and joyfully chose what it "ought." "Ought" refers to the God-ordained good that was both commanded by God and achievable by the unimpaired human will before the Fall. But the Fall corrupted the human will, and ever since the Fall, it chooses not what it ought but what it "wants," *self-fulfillment* rather than righteousness ordained by God. The conflict between humanity and God is now played out in the arena of human freedom. The conflict between divine transcendence and goodness on the one hand and human willfulness on the other hand, which is shackled with finitude and fear, and devoid of righteousness and peace, is unresolved. This divide cannot be overcome by the two most common medieval means to bridge it—*vita contemplativa*, monasticism, or *vita activa*, service.

Lohmeyer's dissertation was largely descriptive, analyzing the complex train of Anselm's reasoning on the relation of reason and will. Why, we may ask, was Lohmeyer, a New Testament scholar, interested in this subject, and what did he conclude from it? The answer seems to be that he wanted to demonstrate the inadequacy of human reason as a foundation for the gospel of Jesus Christ. A passing comment in the introduction hints at his motive. Anselm's philosophy, he noted, was the first step in a long journey that was only completed when the Reformation liberated human consciousness and filled it with true content. Scholasticism had built the edifice of Christian dogma on a foundation borrowed from Aristotelian logic and methodology. This foundation was alien to a uniquely Christian perspective and ultimately inadequate. The Reformers—the Luthers, Calvins, Melanchthons, and Bullingers—were the first to build a Christian dogma on the proper foundation of God's self-revelation in history. Anselm demonstrated the insufficiency of human reason as the basis of Christian dogma. He could go no further—that would require the Reformers—but he took an all-important first step toward it. The purpose of Lohmeyer's dissertation was to show the significance of that first step.

Summons to War

The German Reich required one year of military service of all eligible young men. On October 1, 1913, Lohmeyer joined Jäger-Batalion Seven in Bückeburg, not far from his home in Vlotho. Three months before his obligatory year was scheduled to end—on June 28, 1914, to be exact—Archduke Franz Ferdinand of Austria and his wife, Duchess Sophie, were assassinated in Sarajevo. The archduke was a figure of secondary importance, at best, on the world stage. But in the overwrought European political climate of 1914, the assassinations of the archduke and duchess were like a strike at a subsidiary power station that effectively triggered a failure of the global power grid. The lights went out, and the world was suddenly and inexplicably at war. Lohmeyer's intended year of military service would be protracted to nearly five years on both the eastern and western fronts of the war.

World War I was the first "modern" war. It introduced mechanization, weaponry, and tactics that had never before been seen in human warfare, including the development of trench warfare and the employment of submarines, tanks, machine guns, mortars, poison gas, and airplanes. The last of these were initially used for aerial reconnaissance, but soon thereafter they were used for aerial bombing. The German Reich was prepared to wage war with all these means. Britain disparaged many of these methods and means, opting instead for the nineteenth-century myth of the gentleman soldier. General Douglas Haig, British commander in chief, rejected the machine gun as a useful weapon on the grounds that it was a disincentive to bravery at the front. He limited the number of machine guns in each battalion. For similar reasons, he resisted the introduction of steel helmets for soldiers, which had proven to significantly reduce head injuries in combat. He dismissed the airplane as an overrated contraption and even considered the rifle suspect. What counted, maintained Haig, was the horse and saber, the future of which was "likely to be as great as ever."[3] The ineptitude of such leadership sent three-quarters of a million British young men marching to their deaths into the hail of machine gun fire from the German lines.

The exact number of war dead between 1914 and 1918 is unknown, but more than ten million soldiers died, and at least half that number of civilians. The better part of an entire generation was effectively lost in Europe. Of the ten million–plus soldiers killed, one-third came from the Central Powers, that is, from Germany, Austria-Hungary, Bulgaria, and Turkey. The Central Powers fought the war not on a single front as did the Allied Powers in the west and Russia in the east, but on *two* fronts—on the Russian front in the east and on the French front in the west. On these two fronts the Central Powers, and Germany above all, suffered greater losses than did any other combatant nation.

In his nearly five years of military service, Lohmeyer saw combat on both fronts. Surprisingly, the destruction and disillusionment of the brutal conflict are not reflected in photographs of Melie and him during the war years. Both posed for the camera in evocative settings. Lohmeyer's handsome face, his strong stature, and his smart dress display his self-esteem, as confident in a pensive pose with hand on chin as in directing his piercing gaze straight at the camera. Melie was not camera-comfortable. Her smile was reluctant, even slightly mistrustful. The glamorous poses of women in the scrapbook that Melie made during the First World War were not of herself but of her attractive voice teacher, Else Schünemann. Melie was also attractive, but not immediately so, like Else. She directed attention away from herself by holding something in her hands. In one photograph she held aloft a bouquet of flowers, like a priest raising the Holy Sacrament at the words of institution. The occasional shot of Melie alone is not a close-up.

There are surprisingly few pictures of Ernst and Melie together. Indeed, there are as many photographs of Melie and her dog as there are of her and Ernst. From the beginning of their courtship their togetherness had spaces in it. The spaces would remain as the relationship matured and lengthened in marriage. Some would be widened by yet another war, others by problems resulting from demands on their lives. If any relationship could weather such separations, even grow through them, it was theirs, for it was not the bond of physical proximity that had brought them together in the first place. It was their love for music, language, and poetry, their joy in self-revelation in correspondence. These sparked and blew the flame of their lives into union. These sparks seemed to need spaces in order to survive and fuel the fire of their union.

Melie was as reliable as a Swiss clock in saving letters, telegrams, photographs, newspaper clippings, and memorabilia of the war years. Her scrapbooks of the time have dried flowers on most pages, and they preserve a half-dozen playbills of church concerts, especially at Christmas, featuring her as alto soloist. She also composed music, a two-part musical score, for example, precisely staffed for her and Ernst. During Ernst's absences at the fronts she wrote sonnet-length poems. The European nations rushed into the Great War with pride, patriotism, and naïveté. Melie joined in the march. I have translated the beginning of one of her poems as follows:

> Over rock and over root
> Tramps the hardened German boot.
> Cloaked in finest wool about,
> Made with hands of love throughout.
> All the German troops to aid
> Thus the march still better made.[4]

The poses Lohmeyer struck in war photos were demonstrably individualist. A photo taken early in the war shows a dozen uniformed soldiers in a beer hall, their beer steins displayed prominently and their faces set in resolve. In their midst sits Lohmeyer, beer stein forgotten on his lap, head propped on his hand, looking bored, or perhaps, like Diogenes, cynical at the waste of precious time.[5] A photograph taken in January 1916 shows three officers standing erect and proud outside a wooden country house in East Prussia. In their midst is Lohmeyer—seated casually with his legs crossed.[6]

On August 1, 1914, Lohmeyer's military status was ramped up from reserve to active. He reported for duty at Bückeburg in Westphalia, and his unit was transferred quickly to the west. By the end of the month his letters to Melie were posted from Cambrai in northern France, and by the first of September from Crepy-en-Valois.

The latter location, he noted at the end of one letter, was only "30 kilometers from Paris." Soldiers were not allowed to report details of military actions and information in their letters, but Lohmeyer probably saw action in the first battle of the Marne in September of 1914. He was in the precise region at the time, and in January of 1915 he sent Melie an article from the *Cologne Newspaper* describing the battle. General Joseph Joffre, commander of the French army, succeeded in regrouping the retreating Allied forces and outflanking the advancing Germans, thus halting their advance and achieving victory at the Marne. One of the generals leading the German advance was Alexander von Kluck. Lohmeyer highlighted the point in the article where von Kluck described the bold French maneuver as "one of the most suspenseful episodes" that he had experienced in the war.

In mid-November 1914 Lohmeyer wrote Melie that he would be passing through Germany and wanted to meet her in Kiel. "Passing through Germany" meant only one thing—he was being transferred to Russia on the eastern front. Lohmeyer closed most letters with a simple note of location, "From Cambrai" or "From Lille." By December the place-names were Slavic, "Ruszki on the Bzura [River]" or "Bralla." He and Melie continued exchanging several letters per week. We forget—or perhaps never knew—how advanced German communication systems were in the first half of the twentieth century. The train from Berlin to Breslau, which today takes over four hours, took two and one-half hours then. The postal and telegraph systems were similarly advanced, expediting mail to and from multiple fronts of the war in France, Russia, and Greece. Lohmeyer and Melie made maximal use of the communication system, sometimes humorously so. In his first three months on the eastern front, in addition to letters, Lohmeyer wired five telegrams. He even sent a one-line letter to Melie announcing that she should expect two or three letters the next day. "Innermost Thoughts Big Letter Coming. Yours, Ernst."[7]

In February 1915 Lohmeyer saw Melie briefly when he was back in Germany recovering from a sprained ankle. In March he was back in East Prussia, near Königsberg (modern Kaliningrad), where he remained until June. In March he ordered a small jeweled pillbox to be sent as a gift to Melie from Siegen, Germany. In April he sent a telegram on the fifth anniversary of the beginning of their dating relationship. In May he enclosed a harrowing newspaper report of a courier riding horseback between the German and Russian battle lines. Above the article he wrote "Many greetings," a clue that he had been present at the battle. The several photographs that Lohmeyer sent to Melie of himself on horseback during the war years and the specific highlight in the article invite the conclusion that Lohmeyer himself was the intrepid rider.

In June 1915 Ernst visited Melie when he was home on leave for a week. A month after he returned to the front, he sent her a sixty-page diary chronicling each day since they had parted. The small tome was only one of 160 letters he wrote her in the next six months. In July he enclosed several two-inch-square black-and-white photographs in a letter to Melie. One was of himself on horseback, another of two women sitting on the ground before a primitive thatched-roof house on the Russian steppe. In September and October, Jäger-Battalion Seven engaged the Russians in a major battle on the Düna River to the east of Riga, Latvia. Lohmeyer sent a newspaper article of the battle to Melie. Underlined was a reference to his battalion, which, the article reported, had distinguished itself in taking eight hundred Russian prisoners, giving the Germans victory. The article celebrated the particular heroics of a "musketeer"—a hand-grenade specialist—named Weiss, who swam across a lake at night, cut the Russian wire defense perimeter on the far side, and, along with a dozen German prisoners whom he freed, succeeded in taking a citadel overlooking the Düna. The German general awarded Jäger-Battalion Seven with honors, and Musketeer Weiss with the Iron Cross. What the article failed to note was that Jäger-Battalion Seven suffered eight hundred casualties in the battle, nearly all fatalities, many from Lohmeyer's Bückeburg unit.

Marriage

In February 1916 Lohmeyer wrote Melie of severe headaches, the result of a "fall." Its effects were apparent in his erratic script. Further details of the injury were not forthcoming, but the injury may have resulted from a fall from his horse. The horse played a major role in the First World War, and there were, sadly, almost as many horses and mules killed in the war as there were humans. Lohmeyer was treated in two infirmaries in East Prussia (modern Poland) for a month after the fall. In mid-March he was sent back to Germany to convalesce in military hospitals in Cologne, Bückeburg, and Paderborn.[8]

By 1916 the war in Europe had ground to a standstill. A deadly no-man's-land laced with land mines and strewn with corpses separated the sodden and disease-ridden trenches of the combatants in eastern France, on one side the German troops and on the other the British, French, Canadian, Australian, and Italian troops. By spring Lohmeyer had recovered from his head injury. The stalemate in the war and his proximity to Melie allowed them frequent, if short, chances to be together. He and Melie decided to exchange six years of courtship and a thousand letters of correspondence for the permanence of married life. On July 16, 1916, Lohmeyer's father, Heinrich, united them in a service of holy matrimony in Vlotho. They enjoyed the remainder of July together. August separated them once again, Lohmeyer back at the front and Melie staying for longer or shorter periods of time with family, friends, and acquaintances in various parts of Germany. For the next two years their married lifestyle remained much the same as their unmarried lifestyle had been—further separations and the exchange of another thousand letters.

A major improvement for Lohmeyer in the remainder of the war years, however, was his transfer back to the western front, first in the region of Alain-de-Cote, between Metz and Nancy in eastern France, and later in the Saarbrücken region of western Germany. His closer proximity to Melie afforded not infrequent leaves, and leaves meant time together. In October of 1917 they enjoyed two sumptuous weeks together in southern Germany, attending classical concerts and a performance of *The Magic Flute* at the opera, vacationing on the idyllic Walchen See, and topping it off with several nights in a first-class hotel in Munich.[9]

Scholarship in the Trenches

Lohmeyer's personal experience of the war was ameliorated not
only by leaves from the front, especially after mid-1916 when he
was transferred back to the west, but also by the increased time for
scholarship that the final stalemated years of the war afforded him.
In both world wars scholarly activity for Lohmeyer consisted of carrying in his backpack a Greek New Testament, something to write
on, and his lifelong instrument of written expression—a green-black
fountain pen with a gold nib. Further scholarly resources were but a
dream. The early morning hours from five to seven offered the least
encumbered time, before military routines and duties commandeered his schedule. Within such time fragments his concentration
had to compete with fatigue, makeshift work spaces and writing surfaces, noise, interruptions, poor lighting, and other inconveniences
that he could not foresee and we cannot imagine. Whatever the circumstances, if he could redeem time daily for scholarship—and his
dedication for such was indefatigable—he could cope with whatever
duties, distractions, and even hardships might arise. Scholarship
was an elixir in the mud-and-blood trenches that witnessed such
carnage and produced such disillusionment and despair in his generation. No characteristic left a greater impression on his daughter
Gudrun than his powers of intellectual concentration and productivity. "Whether vacation or semester, weekday or holiday, city or
country, no day elapsed without scholarly work," wrote Gudrun in
1989. "It is hard to imagine, especially for the young today, what
it had to mean for my father to have spent almost nine years of his
life as a soldier."[10]

With pen or pencil in hand, Lohmeyer had the one requisite to
be right with the world. Scholarship laid a foundation for every other
activity in his life. When that foundation was laid and maintained,
even if only for an hour or two a day, he was grounded and endowed
with composure to face whatever might come his way. Writing was
a stream of living water. "When I write," he wrote in a 1932 diary,
"I can be joyful and sad in all the heights and depths of life."[11] This
sense of atonement, if that is the right word, was not free of cost,
of course. For people who share Lohmeyer's passion, more than a

tinge of guilt usually accompanies the decision to study and write rather than attend to other duties that, if not more important, are usually more urgent. People who live by strong priorities know this feeling well, as I am sure Lohmeyer did. I am equally inclined to believe that he discovered what all who bear this burden of grace discover, that in giving priority to primary matters he also found time for secondary matters. Indeed, the secondary matters were usually done better and with greater justice than they would have been had he given them priority. Augustine—whose works ranked high on Lohmeyer's lifelong reading list—described this phenomenon in terms of rightly ordered loves. Sin and chaos were the result of disordered love, whereas rightly ordered love produced purpose and fruitfulness in life.

Two weeks after his discharge from active duty in November 1918, Lohmeyer presented his *Habilitation* to the University of Heidelberg. For candidates to receive a call to a professorship in Germany, they had to augment their doctoral dissertation with a second scholarly monograph called a *Habilitation*. The purpose of the *Habilitation* was to demonstrate the ability to produce scholarship on one's own that equaled the quality of scholarship produced under the tutelage of a doctoral supervisor. Lohmeyer's *Habilitation*, entitled "Divine Aroma," was a study of the role of smell—specifically incense and ritual aromas—in divine revelation.[12]

He began with the role of incense in the religious and cultural milieu of the Bible. In the Greek world the narcissus and hyacinth, and above all ambrosia and incense, were "the sweet symbol of divine nearness." In Egypt, incense was considered the aroma of the gods; in Persia, the symbol of the blessed in paradise. By curious contrast, in the culture and scriptures of Israel the sense of smell played no role in divine revelation. Smell occasionally appears in later Old Testament writings, but only as a simile: God is *like* a pleasing fragrance. But God is not the fragrance, nor is fragrance a medium of petition to God or revelation of God. The sense of smell plays no greater role in the New Testament, with the rare exception of Paul's description of God, who "manifests the fragrance of his knowledge through us in every place, for we are the aroma of Christ to God among those who are being saved" (2 Cor. 2:14–15). In contrast to surrounding pagan and Gnostic cults where incense wafted heavily, the Judeo-Christian tradition was an exceptionally smoke-free environment. Indeed, maintained Lohmeyer, the popularity of incense in surrounding cults virtually eliminated the possibility of its positive use or assessment in the early church. If incense crept into medieval Catholicism—and it did—"the annihilating attack [of Protestantism] drove its use into the sphere of folk superstition," he declared.[13] He left unmentioned the significance of incense in Roman Catholicism and Orthodoxy in the modern era, perhaps because its absence from the origins of the Christian tradition eliminated its credibility, at least in his mind, in later tradition.

A *Habilitation* on the subject of divine aroma may strike some readers as an exercise in academic irrelevancy. But consider the following. The subject once again exhibits Lohmeyer's aesthetic sense. The other human faculties—speaking, seeing, hearing, and touch—play prominent roles in scriptural revelation. It would be reasonable to assume that smell would join the other human faculties as an empirical counterpart of divine revelation. After all, smells, aromas, and fragrances, though less concrete and definable than sight and sound, are more immediate and evocative. The sense of smell can rouse forgotten memories and awaken hidden longings like no other sense. Lohmeyer's esoteric study of aroma is particularly important in his case, because he demonstrates the fallacy of an unexamined assumption. The sense of smell is the only one of the five sense that plays no role in divine revelation in Israel and early Christianity. Indeed, it seems to have been proscribed in order to prevent Israel and the early church from the pagan practice of burning incense to idols.[14]

An Attempt to Process the War: *Attack*

Conditions in Germany could scarcely have been more volatile when Lohmeyer presented his *Habilitation* at Heidelberg in the fall of 1918. The wave of enthusiasm that had swept Germany into war four years earlier had by 1918 spent itself, leaving Germany exhausted and demoralized. The extreme loss of life in the war—

and to what purpose?—left Europe in a worse state in 1918 than it had been in 1914. The Great War delivered a knockout blow to a widespread optimism of a world evolving toward perfection. The moral and spiritual house of the West was left in profound disarray, the subsequent nihilism stronger than the optimism it ingloriously crushed. The undertow of pessimism affected the arts, literature, politics, morality, economics, and culture in general.

Lohmeyer had kept his personal life and professional goals on track during the war—indeed, in marriage and completion of academic work he had advanced them. But not even he escaped the fallout of the *bellum cataclysmos* that took place between 1914 and 1918. By May of 1918 it was clear that Germany had lost the long and costly war on both fronts. Lohmeyer processed this upheaval in a long essay, a personal philosophy of history, entitled *Angriff (Attack)*. *Attack* is a deep trolling of his thoughts, expressed in equally chthonic imagery and language about Germany's place in the world. His inner turmoil was signaled by the work's title, which was uncharacteristically aggressive. He sought in Alexander the Great and the glory of Rome metaphors for Germany's destiny, a destiny that the inglorious end of the war gravely imperiled. Wherein lay Germany's "spirit," "essence," "people," "state," and "standing in the free world"? How could Germany's cultural wellsprings, "so wide and high that they comprised the noblest and most sacred values, in all their depths and heights, of all people," survive the weight of blood, fire, and iron that had befallen them in the war? Lohmeyer sought a way forward, if not for the German nation or even its *Volk*, then "in the German *spirit* that would move through the world in the fulfillment of life without end."[15]

Lohmeyer was stationed in southwest Germany, near Saarbrücken, when he wrote *Attack*. He sent it by post to Melie, asking her judgment. She read and interacted with it assertively, returning it to Lohmeyer by post three days later. "No, that's not true!"[16] she wrote bluntly in a marginal comment. Another comment dissented with more moderation: "This seems overstated to me."[17] Overall, however, she thought it excellent, "Yes, Yes, my Dear One. I'm quite pleased,"[18] she wrote in conclusion. She typed the entire document and sent the typescript back for his proofreading.

Expectations of an earthly fulfillment of the kingdom of God were not uncommon in the pre–World War I era. The frequent and facile identification of national policies with divine purposes throughout the pulpits of Europe reflected such hopes, as did the "social gospel" movement in America. *Attack* was the one—and only—instance in which Lohmeyer fell in line with this dangerous and inevitably futile march, so widespread at the time, of identifying the kingdom of God with a nation's policies and destiny. It is hardly surprising that he would, if not succumb to this siren song, be tempted by it. How could one who had experienced the entirety of a war of widespread and senseless carnage be expected *not* to process his thoughts so ultimately, so eschatologically? The attempt was inevitable. In my judgment it was perhaps even necessary, for apart from the attempt, Lohmeyer could not have recognized its futility. Fortunately, he did not publish *Attack*. Lohmeyer recognized the error of seeking in a nation's destiny, and even more in its political agenda, the fulfillment of the eschatological purposes of God. There would be many in the Nazi years to come, the Gerhard Kittels and Ludwig Müllers, who would fervently embrace such Faustian fantasies. Had Lohmeyer not seen his own errors in *Attack*, he may not have been as trenchant in recognizing and critiquing the same errors in others.

German Capitulation

Widespread confidence of a German victory in 1914 made its eventual defeat the more devastating. The final downfall of Germany was not the result of defeat on the battlefield but of collapse in morale. Once Bulgaria, Turkey, and Austria fell to Allied forces, the German navy mutinied and political demonstrations erupted in the streets. The convulsive outcome was more catastrophic than the loss of the war, for it swept away the foundations of the German Reich itself. Germany's conservative political and military leadership, including the kaiser who embodied it, had propelled the country to war, but they could not survive the social revolution that arose in the wake of the collapse of the Central Powers. On November 9,

1918, Kaiser Wilhelm II abdicated the throne and fled to Holland, bringing the German Reich that had been christened by Otto von Bismarck fewer than fifty years earlier, in 1871, to an inglorious and perilous end.

The vacuum left by Germany's discredited conservative monarchist leaders was quickly filled by liberal leftist parties, especially the Social Democrats. The leftist parties were not exactly bedfellows with Russian communists—at least not all of them—but their agenda was far to the left of anything advocated by the kaiser and the old regime. Social and political tensions stretched Germany's political fabric to the tearing point.

This was actually the best of Germany's bad news. Far worse were the punitive conditions meted out to the "Huns" by the Allies in the Treaty of Versailles. Versailles required Germany to yield Alsace-Lorraine to France, and to give up other territories contiguous to Belgium, Denmark, and Poland. The loss of these agricultural and industrial regions, and their natural resources, imperiled Germany's economy. Included in the territorial losses were the Saar and Rhineland, Germany's industrial drivetrain, which Versailles conceded to the Allies for fifteen years of occupation. The war reparations imposed by Versailles sent Germany's monetary system into a tailspin. Had the conditions imposed by Versailles been fulfilled, Germany would not have made its final war payment until 1984! Hitler would make sure that never happened. But the worst of the bad news was the war-guilt clause of Versailles, which heaped blame for the war squarely—and solely—on Germany's shoulders. In the words of Versailles: "The Allied and Associated Governments affirm and Germany accepts the responsibility of Germany and her allies for causing all the loss and damage to which the Allied and Associated Governments and their nationals have been subjected as a consequence of the war imposed upon them by the aggression of Germany and her allies."[19] World War I ended in Germany's defeat; Versailles ensured that it also ended in Germany's disgrace.

The failed war, the collapse of imperial rule, the imperiled economy—all these precipitated a political free-for-all in postwar Germany. The one effect of Versailles that might have helped Germany was the requirement to build a postwar democratic superstructure on the foundations of the failed monarchy. Not surprisingly, the negative effects of Versailles's other conditions on Germany conspired to doom this potentially positive overture. The forces against democracy succeeding in postwar Germany were formidable. The Weimar Republic would see thirty-five political parties vying for power in Germany's first, fledgling, and ultimately failed democratic experiment. The bombshell that the Allies had been unsuccessful in dropping on Germany during the war—for only a fraction of combat in World War I took place on German soil—was ironically delivered to Germany after the war by the Treaty of Versailles.

The League of Nations, surely the most positive offspring of the Treaty of Versailles, echoed the slogan of American president Woodrow Wilson "to make the world safe for democracy." The optimism, perhaps even euphoria, shared by the Allies in the formation of the league was shared by few Germans. The Central Powers had lost nearly 3.5 million soldiers in the war, the vast majority of them Germans. It was a rare household that had not lost a husband, father, son, or grandson in four costly years of combat. And what had been gained? The kaiser had abdicated. The exorbitant loss of German soldiers—as cited by the political opponents fighting it out in postwar Berlin—had been for a failed cause. Versailles's verdict that Germany alone was to blame for the war draped her war dead with a rag of shame. The roots of bitterness grew quickly—and deeply and widely—in Germany. Few Germans considered the conditions of Versailles to be just; none, I think, considered them honorable. What the future held for Germany no one of course could predict. Hitler's Promethean rise to power and the disaster and destruction that he brought upon Europe could not have been foreseen, not even imagined. Even less so the ensuing Russian occupation of the entire eastern sections of Germany. But one thing was deeply felt. The Great War had not settled matters. It had, in fact, set the stage for something ominous to come. Many Germans would be fated to play roles on that stage, but few would have to play the role assigned to Ernst Lohmeyer.

CHAPTER 6

Transplant in Breslau

All our dignity consists in thought. Let us endeavor, then, to
think well; that is the principle of morality.

Blaise Pascal[1]

Assistant Professor in Heidelberg

How does one reenter civilian society after nearly five years of war?
It probably depends on who one is, what one has experienced, what
one has done—and left undone. World War I did not in any fundamental way alter the coordinates that oriented Lohmeyer's life. It
brought changes in life, to be sure, but the changes, at least so far as
they were noticeable, were positive. His deprivation of scholarship
left him like a climber returned from a strenuous expedition with
a ravenous and insatiable appetite. The appetite, in Lohmeyer's
case, was for scholarly productivity. This appetite, however, only
reinforced something Lohmeyer and everyone else already knew.
The focus and energy with which he returned from the war made the
next fifteen years the most productive of his academic life. The war
also taught him something he may not have known. "The hardships
of the war and long years as a soldier," wrote Gudrun, "left [my fa-
ther] a stronger man. They cultivated his practical abilities, which
he possessed by nature, and also his sense for what is possible, both
of which would later prove useful to him as a university administrator."[2] If Lohmeyer always knew he was a scholar, he now knew he
also had the capacity to be a leader.

By 1918 he claimed an enviable *curriculum vitae*, fully half of which had been completed *during* the war. That was an epic achievement. He had completed a doctorate in theology on "covenant," another in philosophy on Anselm's doctrine of the will, and a third opus, a *Habilitation*, on the role of aroma in the Judeo-Christian tradition. In July of 1918 he received a handwritten letter from the theological faculty at the University of Heidelberg offering him the position of *Privatdozent* of New Testament. *Privatdozent* was an "assistant professor," the first rung on the ladder to full professorship. An earned doctorate, plus *Habilitation*, were necessary prerequisites to receive a *call* as professor at a German university, but they did not give one the right to teach. That right—the final turn in the labyrinth of German academe—was bestowed by the *venia legendi*. Latin for "permission to teach," *venia legendi* was conferred not by the university but by the state, which held ultimate jurisdiction over German universities. *Venia legendi* was the state's approval of the candidate's preparedness to teach and authorization of him or her to do so.

Inaugural Lecture

On Lohmeyer's final war leave in mid-October 1918, less than a month before the armistice ended World War I, he delivered his inaugural lecture at the University of Heidelberg as a prerequisite to receiving *venia legendi*. The lecture, entitled "Christuskult und Kaiserkult" ("Christ Cult and Caesar Cult"), was published the next year.[3] As the title suggests, the lecture investigated the Roman emperor cult and its possible influence on the worship of Christ in Christianity. Lohmeyer traced the roots of the emperor cult to the Greek East, all the way back to Plato's ideal of the philosopher king, but more directly to the influence of Alexander the Great in the late fourth century BCE. The East proliferated with cults of semi-divine heroes believed to have descended in various ways from the gods—rulers of all sorts, philosophers, poets, and wonder-workers. Lohmeyer considered these "divine man" cults rather like trumpet blasts that prepared for the grand entry of the Roman emperor cult, commencing with Caesar Augustus's proclamations of himself as savior and son of god shortly before the birth of Jesus Christ. In Lohmeyer's view, the divine pretensions of Augustus birthed a fledgling emperor cult that influenced the way early Christians thought of and referred to Jesus, especially as "Savior," "Son of God," and "Lord." Lohmeyer extended the influence of the emperor cult beyond the New Testament era, however. He regarded it as a blueprint for the doctrines of papal supremacy and the cult of saints in Roman Catholicism. Its crowning influence, in his judgment, was the transformation of the emperor cult into the Christ cult during the reign of Constantine in the early fourth century.

The wealth of archaeological discoveries and advance in our knowledge of the emperor cult since Lohmeyer wrote this treatise have not supported all his conclusions. The imperial garment of the emperor cult that extended from Augustus to Constantine was not as seamless as it appears in Lohmeyer's lecture. True, the imperial cult functioned in the second century as a test of allegiance to the Roman state—and with the threat of death for those who refused the test. But the cult was not defined as clearly nor promulgated as widely in the first century as Lohmeyer assumed. The story of Jesus's birth in Luke 2 may presuppose the pronouncements of Augustus Caesar as "son of god," and references to "the whore of Babylon" and "the beast" in chapters 16–18 of the Revelation clearly cast the Roman Empire in unsavory imagery, but these sporadic allusions and references do not assume a systematic "emperor cult" in the first century. Nor is there evidence that imperial sacrifice—the pouring out of a libation to Caesar—was required of all Roman subjects at the time, and certainly not at the cost of the lives of those who refused it.

Lohmeyer's lecture also rehearsed the commonly held view in early twentieth-century German scholarship that New Testament titles for Jesus were fashioned from Hellenistic prototypes. Lohmeyer maintained that Christians applied not only Roman imperial terminology to Jesus, "Son of God" and "Lord" being the most important, but also Roman *understandings* of the terminology. The New Testament seems to question both assumptions. Several load-bearing titles for Jesus in the New Testament—"Messiah," "Word," and "servant" are examples—were Jewish and do not appear in the emperor cult. Some titles that do appear in the cult, "Son of God" and "Lord," for instance, carry over meanings from the Old Testament rather than from the emperor cult. But most important, religious devotion to the emperor cult was understood very differently from devotion to Jesus in the New Testament and early church. The emperor cult was but one expression of multifaceted Roman religion, which was more defined and demonstrated by public observance and etiquette than by personal faith and conviction. The pledge of allegiance in America or display of the flag on patriotic occasions would be modern counterparts to the level of devotion that typified Roman religion. Such public ceremonies and observances are inadequate parallels to religious devotion in early Christianity, however. The gospel laid total claim to a believer's life, and that claim was signified by a changed heart and life. No such personal transformation was expected of Roman religion or the later emperor cult, and certainly no one sacrificed one's life for the emperor cult. That thousands of Christians in the post–New Testament era willingly sacrificed their lives rather than worship the Roman emperor reveals the categorical difference between worship of Caesar and worship of Christ.

Lohmeyer's inaugural lecture on the emperor cult, like his doctoral dissertation on "covenant," again reflected Adolf Deissmann's interest in tracing the development of early Christianity within the Greco-Roman world. If conclusions of *Christuskult und Kaiserkult* need to be revisited in light of today's understandings, the importance of Lohmeyer's study is not wholly nullified. One point of enduring significance is its setting of the study of New Testament Christology squarely within the sociology of the Roman Empire— specifically within the context of the (in)famous emperor cult, in this instance. The trail that Lohmeyer blazed in the inaugural address has since been furthered and refined, but it has not been reversed.

Lohmeyer commenced his assistant professorship at Heidelberg on December 1, 1918. The university was still readjusting its academic calendar to peacetime when he arrived. His first lectures were scheduled in a "War Emergency Semester" running from late January to mid-April of 1919. By summer semester Heidelberg was fully readjusted to the traditional German academic schedule. From the outset of his career, Lohmeyer lectured on the vital organs of the Christian corpus: Romans, Corinthians, and the passion narratives of the Gospels. Already in the War Emergency Semester he lectured on the New Testament book on which he would write his most important commentary—the Gospel of Mark.[4] It was that commentary that introduced me to his name.

Breslau: Jewel on the Oder

On October 10, 1920, Lohmeyer wrote to Rudolf Bultmann, who was leaving Breslau to accept the chair of New Testament at Marburg: "I received an invitation from the Prussian Minister of Culture today to become your successor at Breslau. It is an honor for me and a joy at the same time to assume the academic chair that you have occupied."[5] Shortly after arriving in Breslau on December 5, Lohmeyer again wrote to Bultmann, reporting that he found Breslau "quite strange and quite 'eastern.'" Despite its foreignness, however, two faculty colleagues, Hans von Soden and Karl Bornhausen, had been "very friendly" to him.[6] With this correspondence Lohmeyer signaled the transition from a brief two years at Heidelberg to what would become fifteen fulfilling years at Breslau.

The city of Breslau (today Wroclaw, Poland) is bordered on its northern side by a sweeping bend of the Oder River. Over the centuries the Oder had been diverted into channels and canals, resulting in a virtual encirclement of the city by water and the formation of a dozen islands. The insinuating tendrils of water make Breslau a Venice of the north. A hundred bridges link the urban archipelago into a picturesque city of towers, church steeples, charming streets, and especially on the city square, neo-Renaissance facades. The stately university main building, symmetrically situated between two bridges spanning the Oder, overlooks the broad northern bend of the river.

The university was founded in the seventeenth century by Jesuits, and its architecture, appropriately, is sumptuously baroque. Frescoed hallways, academic rooms more reminiscent of churches than lecture halls, walnut staircases richly carved, observation towers offering panoramas of city and river—all these make the University of Breslau uniquely magnificent. A decade after his arrival, Lohmeyer would become its president. Perhaps the most famous photograph of Lohmeyer is his presidential photograph in a velvet tam and broad-collared cassock covered in ornate brocade and trimmed in metallic-corded piping. This gilded image would be prodigally extravagant in practically any other setting, but in the baroque and Prussian magnificence of the University of Breslau, it was in perfect character.

Breslau itself was on the outer edge of places where Lohmeyer envisioned teaching. He further sought Bultmann's advice on procuring housing—no fewer than five rooms, he stated.[7] He procured the house, and a vacation home as well—in Glasegrund, in the highlands of Silesia to the south of Breslau. Melie made her first entry in the Glasegrund guestbook on May 9, 1920, enjoying the sunshine on the porch while little Beate Dorothee, born in February, was asleep in an adjoining room. The entry was an idyllic vignette of what would be a season of contentment in the Lohmeyers' life.[8] But it was not free of sorrows. The first sorrow began with little Beate Dorothee herself. On February 19, 1921, the Lohmeyers published an announcement in the *Heidelberger Tageblatt*—the *Heidelberg Daily News*: "On February 17 at 1 p.m. our only child, our little Beate Dorothee died at the tender age of one year after bravely enduring five weeks of agony."[9] The cause of death was not given. The most likely culprit was the influenza pandemic that claimed so many millions of lives in the late teens and early twenties. So ubiquitous was the pandemic that people like the Lohmeyers no longer bothered to name it.

Three more children would be born to Ernst and Melie, two sons—Ernst-Helge in 1922 and Hermann-Hartmut in 1923—and one daughter, Gudrun-Richarda in 1926. The children would grow into their early teenage years in Breslau. Lohmeyer would flourish in the university's intellectual community, and Melie would do the same in Breslau's music culture. Otto von Grünewald, a leading musical personality in Breslau, wrote her a long letter of warm praise, imploring her to sing in Breslau concerts as she had in Heidelberg and elsewhere during the war. The Lohmeyer home became a stimulating hub of friends. Lohmeyer's academic colleagues became Melie's friends as well, and Melie befriended many of their wives.

The Social Setting of Early Christianity

In the latter half of the twentieth century, sociological methods and approaches made a major entrance on the stage of biblical and theological scholarship, and they show no sign of abatement still today. Investigations into social conditions prevailing in the eastern Mediterranean and in early Christian communities rank as a blue-ribbon contribution to the advancement of our present understanding of the New Testament and early church. Lohmeyer's 1921 *Soziale Fragen im Urchristentum* (*Social Questions in Early Christianity*), written fully fifty years before virtually any biblical scholar addressed the subject, remains one of his more distinctive contributions to biblical and theological scholarship.[10] Adolf von Harnack, Germany's theological titan at the turn of the twentieth century, declared somewhat pontifically that the literature of early Christianity knew nothing of social principles, that all influences on early Christianity were only religious and moral. Harnack may have believed that social principles played no role in the conception of early Christianity, but others in his day, Marxist theorists for one, were dogmatic in their belief that social forces played the major role in historical change. It was inevitable that such principles would be employed in the study of early Christianity. Some social theorists would indeed attempt to demonstrate the proletarian character of early Christianity.[11] Lohmeyer was not a Marxist social theorist, but, as he noted in the introduction to *Social Questions*, he believed that early Christians and modern Europeans, for all their distance in time and space, shared an acute commonality. Both were caught in a collision of tectonic social forces, and both were unalterably changed by them. If the precise outcomes of social changes were debatable, the existence of social forces producing them was undeniable.

Social Questions is characterized by elements now typical of Lohmeyer's scholarship—directness, precision, and descriptiveness, with not infrequent flares of imaginative and lyrical style. Lohmeyer followed Jacob Burkhardt in dividing the social world of the ancient Near East into three major divisions, state, society, and religion/church. Lohmeyer further subdivided the divisions into urban life, agriculture, commerce, free citizenry, slavery, family, religious and philosophical sects, and so forth. The result is a schematic analysis of the social topography of the Greek, Roman, Jewish, and early Christian worlds. The book is thus a presentation of various social categories operative in the ancient world more than, as the title may suggest, an engagement with actual social issues and questions faced by the early Christian movement. An early commentator on *Social Questions* observed that Lohmeyer depicted ancient societal *forms* more philosophically, even metaphysically, than sociologically.[12] Once again, he applied philosophical analysis to theological subjects.

Two premises ruled Lohmeyer's study: first, that Christianity penetrated the ancient Roman world more rapidly and fully than any other faith, philosophy, or movement, and second, that Christianity remained less affected by the vicissitudes of that world than did any other faith, philosophy, or movement. The long-term result was that Christianity exerted a transformative effect on the Roman world without the essential nature of Christianity being transformed by the Roman world. Christianity, in other words, existed in the Roman world and engaged it, and in time profoundly influenced it, but did not forsake its distinctive character in doing so.

Lohmeyer pictured Jesus in *Social Questions* as "torchbearer of the Almighty," a ray of light from the mild and supernal deity. This seems very reminiscent of Ernst Renan's romanticized and docetic figure of Jesus, who hovers slightly above the world rather than entering it fully. Lohmeyer also portrayed early Christianity as a primarily lower-class movement, consisting of gentile outsiders, the rural poor, Galilean foreigners, slaves, and women. It is tempting to read this emphasis in light of sociological forces at work in Germany in the 1920s, that is, the privilege that the German *Volk* would enjoy over the "foreigner" and "alien" in the approaching Nazi years. To what extent Lohmeyer could have foreseen this already in 1921, however, is not clear, and even if he could have, was he inclined to leverage historical conclusions for their "prophetic" relevance in the church of his day? Neither of these questions can be affirmed with any degree of certainty, and it is best to take Lohmeyer's conclusions at their face value.

Although "the down and out" constituted a significant quota in early Christianity, perhaps even the majority, they were not its sum total. In the New Testament the claims of the gospel are also presented to the upper social echelons and powerful—the nobility, wealthy, and military leaders—who were not absent from early Christian communities. Members of the Herodian dynasty were counted in early Christianity's inner circle (Luke 8:3; Acts 13:1), and Luke-Acts, especially, emphasizes the proclamation of the gospel to powers and principalities and their reception of it. The prolific culture of early Christian letter writing itself presupposes semi-literate audiences. Attention to such constituencies would have illustrated and supported Lohmeyer's ruling premise that Christianity permeated the ancient world more *fully* than any other religious or social sect.

Lohmeyer's compact study of early Christian sociology was written at a time when the wealth of ancient material culture that we take for granted today, which contributes so fundamentally to our understanding of first-century Christianity, had not come to light. His perspective on the past was afforded through a low-power telescope in comparison to modern higher-power social and historical telescopes. What significance then, if any, does *Social Questions* still have today? I believe it remains important in at least two respects. *Social Questions* is one of the earliest studies to treat the social history of early Christianity as a viable academic genre within New Testament scholarship. The flood of monographs, series, articles, presentations, and publications on this subject today is all indebted—whether scholars know it or not—to Ernst Lohmeyer's *Social Questions in Early Christianity*. Today's four-lane scholarly freeway on the social history of early Christianity follows the route that Lohmeyer pioneered into virgin territory in *Social Questions*. And secondly, *Social Questions* is an early instance—but not the last—of Lohmeyer hoisting the sails of his scholarship to the winds of his own character and erudition rather than to the prevailing winds of scholarship of his day. An important motto in his life came from a quotation of Blaise Pascal: "All our dignity consists in thought. Let us endeavor, then, to think well; that is the principle of morality."[13] *Social Questions* is an instance of attempting to think well—to stand as an individual in the face of the superior authority of a Harnack who insisted there was no such thing as a social perspective on early Christianity, and to stand equally independently in the face of growing Marxist theories that history consisted wholly and solely of social forces.

Intellectual Community

In chapter 2 I related the story of my qualification examination in German at the University of Zürich. A second story from Zürich may help set the stage for the remainder of this chapter. Every couple of weeks Eduard Schweizer, with whom I studied New Testament in Zürich, would enter the lecture hall, pull a calendar from the vest pocket of his sports coat, and announce: "I have Thursday evening free this week. All who are interested are invited to come to my house for beer and wine, and we'll talk theology." I showed up promptly on Thursday. A Japanese student also came, but he was not confident in his German and rarely spoke. My exultation at Schweizer's invitation was matched by my surprise that none of the Swiss and German students accepted his invitations. "Why?" I asked them, to which they somewhat shamefacedly admitted to being intimidated by such close proximity—in his home, no less—to a renowned professor. They also admitted, equally shamefacedly, their envy of those who overcame such intimidations!

I had experienced various clubs in America—church youth groups, ski and mountaineering clubs, Boy Scouts, sports teams, school band, Latin club, and so forth. But I had never experienced, nor do I remember hearing of, an intellectual club, a circle of people dedicated to discussing the methodology and content of a given subject. Schweizer did not invent the idea. It was unusual for German professors to do the same—hence the intimidation of the Zürich students—but it was not unknown. Schweizer had been a student of Karl Barth, who had invited students into the community of unstructured intellectual inquiry in a convivial atmosphere. Schweizer invited his students into similar intellectual community in his own home.

Schweizer's "Open Evenings," as he called them, were the pinnacle of my academic experience. Schweizer had studied with influential theologians in German-speaking Europe—with Rudolf Bultmann, Emil Brunner, Gottlob Schrenk, Rudolf Otto, and, yes, with Barth himself. When I studied with Schweizer, he had joined their ranks in academic stature. In his living room I pursued questions that I had brought with me from Princeton, and I learned new questions as well. Approaches to the New Testament that were murky in my understanding—form and redaction criticism, for one, Bultmann's program of "demythologizing," for another—could be pursued unstintingly with one who had been taught by their originators. We talked about the relationship of theological scholarship to preaching, about the importance of the laity in the mission of the church, about the blunt force of Nazism to the intellectual world of Europe, including to theology—and why some professors collaborated with it. We talked about Marxist influences in theology that were reflected in the 1970s in liberation theology and "theology of hope." But above all, we talked about theology itself, that God's action precedes all human reaction; about Jesus, on whom Schweizer wrote *four* books, in the last of which he inimitably described Jesus as "the parable of God." Schweizer summarized his theological pilgrimage in these words: "God is a reality compared with which all that we call 'reality' is but an image and feeble copy. Compared with his love all that we call love is but an emanation of God's own love. Therefore, only God's own engagement of us, as it has happened in Jesus Christ, is able to bridge the gap between God and man."

Our conversations ventured freely over the theological landscape, but their homing instinct always returned us to the New Testament and its responsible and faithful exegesis. Schweizer was indomitably committed to theology, and especially the New Testament. His mastery of languages and breadth of secondary scholarship was impressive. What remains most enduring in my memory, however, was his personal humility and willingness to learn from other scholars, even in disagreement, and to acknowledge how much he owed them.[14]

"Open Evenings" were an incomparable gift in my formative years as a scholar. They left me feeling profoundly *alive*. Intellectual community hosted by Eduard Schweizer introduced me to a call that determined my life.

Something similar happened to Lohmeyer in Breslau.

Poet

Breslau witnessed the emergence of Lohmeyer's poetic style of expression and philosophical orientation in theology. Neither trait began expressly in Breslau, for both had appeared earlier *in nuce*. Even innate gifts require stimulus and nourishment, however. Lohmeyer received both in Breslau, and they came from creative circles of colleagues and friends.

A number of *Kreisen*—"circles"—developed among German intellectuals in the 1920s and 1930s, nearly all of which were dedicated in one form or another to the renewal of cultural and spiritual life, broadly speaking, in post–World War I Germany. It is important to remember how late Germany arrived as a *nation* on the European scene. Not until 1871 did Otto von Bismarck constitute Germany as a nation-state. In 1920, Germany as a *nation* was still in its infancy, barely fifty years old. The catastrophe of the Great War raised serious questions whether it would reach maturity. The various intellectual circles that arose in the interim between the Treaty of Versailles and Hitler's accession to power—a mere dozen years—believed that Germany's survival required the recovery, perhaps even discovery, of moral and spiritual groundwaters capable of cleansing and redeeming the losses of the war, the capitulation of the monarchy, and the encroaching political and economic darkness of the postwar era. This humanistic objective, and others like it, defined the various intellectual circles in Germany.

Many circles were formally constituted and named. The most famous of them—at least from our perspective today—was the Kreisau Circle in Berlin, formed by Helmut James von Moltke and Peter

Graf Yorck von Wartenburg. Kreisau encompassed leading social, political, economic, and military thinkers, nearly all of Judeo-Christian persuasion, who endeavored to topple the Third Reich and replace it with a legitimate moral and democratic government. One of Lohmeyer's close colleagues at Breslau, Eugen Rosenstock-Huessy, would later join the Kreisau Circle. Rosenstock-Huessy later immigrated to America, where, among many contributions to our national life, he designed and directed the Civilian Conservation Corps under President Franklin Roosevelt. Several members of the Kreisau Circle participated in the July 20, 1944, plot to assassinate Hitler—and they paid for its failure with their lives.

There were other circles as well. Paul Tillich's Kairos Circle approached the renewal of Germany from distinctively theological and social perspectives, although without developing a political program. The Eckart Circle, another intellectual fellowship, dedicated itself to the revival of Protestant spiritual life in Germany. Many of its members would be sympathizers and even members of the Confessing Church in the 1930s. One of them, Jochen Klepper, a Christian of Jewish ancestry who became a leading journalist in Germany, was a student of Lohmeyer's at Breslau. Klepper became an important—perhaps the most important—Christian poet and hymn writer of twentieth-century Germany. Klepper would also pay for his resistance to Nazism with his life. Kreisau and Eckart Circles, in particular, counted women, some of them wives of male members, as full-fledged participants.

Perhaps the most widely known circle of Lohmeyer's day was the George Circle, named for the quixotic German savant Stefan George (pronounced *gay-OR-guh*). The George Circle aspired to a reawakening of Germany based on spiritual and mythical values of classical antiquity, especially as these were transmitted through poetry and the lyrical power of language. Many of Lohmeyer's native gifts and inclinations aligned with those of Stefan George and his circle. These included George's sensitivity to aesthetics, especially in language but also in music and poetry, his attention to the significance of structure and numbers in texts, and his love for antiquity and writers inspired by it, such as Friedrich Hölderlin and Hugo von Hoffmannsthal. George and Lohmeyer both believed that scholarship should be more than analysis, no matter how pure and perfect the analysis. It should be equally about felicity of expression in which analysis was conveyed. Lohmeyer and George did not simply use language. They *believed* in language, not merely as a medium of expression but as a content essential for the conveyance and meaning of truth.

Stefan George was an enigmatic figure in twentieth-century Germany. A self-taught savant, he mastered a dozen languages completely enough to translate their epics and masterpieces into German. He was so fascinated by language that, like J. R. R. Tolkien in the English-speaking world, he invented secret languages. He recorded his personal notes in secret languages so complex and impenetrable that they have never been decoded. His experiments with the German language resemble those of e. e. cummings with English. He invented fonts resembling his handwriting in which to publish his books, and he devised unique formats and punctuation for such fonts. He personally assumed the robust and mythical characters of his writings, somewhat like G. K. Chesterton did of his characters. He dressed in priestly robes when he read his works in public. Most unusual of all for an author, he sought to *limit* the sales of his books and the audiences to which he lectured. His elitism, perhaps not surprisingly, attracted overflow crowds to his readings and stimulated his book sales.

George was idolized by the Weimar Republic. His transcendent mythic and moral vision, his literary artistry and individual persona, inspired adherents in the post–World War I era with a vision they believed—or hoped—was capable of withstanding the nihilism engulfing Germany. And it inspired some of them to acts of great courage. One was Hans Scholl, a student at the University of Munich who had never met George. Along with his sister Sophie, a philosophy professor named Kurt Huber, and a dozen Munich students, Scholl produced and circulated throughout Germany in 1942–1943 a half-dozen issues of *The White Rose*, a literary leaflet of moral wisdom and Christian social responsibility decrying Nazi barbarism. The resistance of *The White Rose* was crushed by the Gestapo, and both Scholls, Huber, and most of the students were executed. The day Hans Scholl was beheaded, these words were found written on the table of his prison cell: "Cross, you will remain the light of the world for a long time. Hellas, our love is eternal" (Stefan George).[15]

Eighteen months later the influence of George appeared in connection with a similar act of heroism. Among George's most loyal apostles were the three von Stauffenberg brothers, two of whom, Claus and Berthold, would lead the July 20, 1944, plot against Hitler. The night before the plot they took a vow to recover the "hidden" but true Germany to which George had directed them. The following night, the plot having failed, Claus died before a Nazi firing squad in the courtyard of the German Admiralty in the "Bendlerblock" in Berlin. Three weeks later his brother Berthold was executed in Berlin's notorious Plötzensee Prison.[16]

There were unmistakable cultic, even occultic, facets to Stefan George. But in one cardinal respect George was atypical of a cult leader: he steadfastly refused public acclaim and power. In 1927 the city of Frankfurt honored him as the first recipient of its most prestigious honor, the Goethe Prize. He refused it. In 1933 Joseph Goebbels offered him the presidency of the Third Reich's Academy of Literature. He refused that, too. Nazi propagandists knew how to harness the power of symbolism in promoting their cause, and they longed to hitch Stefan George to their cart. He was not so easily tamed. When Hitler came to power in 1933, he left Germany for Switzerland, where he died in November of the same year.

Stefan George was a living Sphinx, a creature in which disparate animal parts combine to form a new and powerful mythical reality. His intellectual magnetism was a conglomerate of Pythagoras's numerology, Luther's robust development of the German language, Goethe's Eternal Man, Friedrich Hölderlin's romanticized antiquity, and Nietzsche's *Übermensch*—"superman." These pagan and poetic elements were forged into a mythic *gestalt* that plumbed Germany's deep longing to recover that which had been lost—or had not yet been found.

So far as we know, Lohmeyer never met George personally. No personal relationship developed between the two, at any rate, for among the volumes of correspondence of Lohmeyer preserved in the Secret Prussian Archive, not a single letter exists between George and him. Lohmeyer's contact with George seems to have been mediated through Melie, who during the war years became acquainted with George's chief apostle in Heidelberg, Friedrich Gundolf. George's influence on Lohmeyer was thus indirect, although perhaps not insignificant, for both were kindred spirits in their commitment to the essential role of language and symbol and aesthetics in the service of truth.

Philosopher

The professors with whom Lohmeyer fraternized in Breslau were not a formally constituted or named circle, nor did they affect the ostentation of the George Circle. Nevertheless, they functioned as a working group of philosophers and theologians, and the magnetic north to which the group's compass pointed was Ernst Lohmeyer. The cast of characters met regularly and read one another's works. Their names, most of which can be found in the guestbook of the Lohmeyer summer house in Glasegrund, were Richard Koebner (†1958), Otto Strauss (†1938), Eugen Rosenstock-Huessy (†1973), Ernst Joseph Cohn (†1976), and Richard Hönigswald (†1947). All were Jewish—although some, like Hönigswald, had converted to Christianity. Most were philosophers, Kantians in particular, neo-Kantians more particularly, and this orientation stamped Lohmeyer's theological work distinctly.

As its name suggests, neo-Kantianism was a revival of the philosophy of Immanuel Kant, who died at the turn of the nineteenth century. Kant founded his philosophy on the concept of human autonomy that presupposed four ideals: the existence of God, freedom, ethics, and immortality. These ideals, and Kantian idealism as a whole, were besieged from various fronts in the nineteenth century. The chief assault, which spared virtually no aspect of Western culture, came from materialism. Materialism affected economics by fueling the Industrial Revolution; it affected science in the wide array of scientific discoveries; and it affected philosophy and politics by providing Karl Marx with a theory to account for all human history on the basis of material causality, particularly economic causality. Theology itself was affected, for in the late nineteenth century the pendulum was swinging away from theology as discourse about God to theology as discourse about human morality. Indeed, the nineteenth-century fascination with archaeology was a particularly fruitful combination of both scientific and materialistic influences.

A corollary of materialism was determinism, which likewise played a major role in nineteenth-century Western intellectual history. All realities, according to determinism, can be attributed to prior empirical causes in the natural order. Reality, in other words, exists within a closed system of known—or knowable—factors. The philosophical system that results from the commitment to explain reality on the basis of materialist-determinist factors is naturalism. Naturalism excludes the possibility of causal factors outside the natural order, such as God, freedom, or ethics based on nonquantifiable values. Philosophical naturalism thus claimed to refute the foundations and conclusions of Immanuel Kant.

Naturalistic methods that had yielded such positive results in the natural sciences—biology, chemistry, physics—were inevitably extended to human nature itself. Sociology, psychology, history, philosophy, and religion were likewise investigated according to criteria that could be quantified, measured, empirically described, and statistically calculated. In religion, the result was Deism, which, with the single exception of the doctrine of creation, made God virtually identical with the natural order. In ethics the result was utilitarianism, which sought to calculate the good in terms of numerical quantity.

Neo-Kantianism

The fields of human endeavor most imperiled by this intellectual revolution were philosophy and religion. For both, freedom of human thought and behavior was essential, and for religion, God and immortality as well. Enter neo-Kantianism, which sought to defend Kant's quadrivium of God, freedom, ethics, and immortality from the onslaught of materialism and determinism. The defense came at the point of epistemology, that is, the theory of knowledge that undergirded the materialist-determinist program. Neo-Kantians maintained that empiricism—knowledge achieved through the five senses of sight, sound, touch, taste, and smell—was not the sole or even most important way by which we know things. Other means of knowledge also led to truth, and to deeper truth. These included human intuition, truths communicated by art forms, truths grounded in reliable authority, and above all, truths mediated by faith in God.

A leading figure in the neo-Kantian defense team was Lohmeyer's colleague and confidant at Breslau, Richard Hönigswald, who was fifteen years his senior. Hönigswald was an Austro-Hungarian by birth, but he had studied in the West—medicine in Vienna, and later philosophy in Halle (Germany) and Graz (Austria). The range of his thought and academic proficiencies was exceptional, as indicated by his title: professor of philosophy, psychology, and pedagogy. His theories of knowledge, mind, thought, and method are standard subtopics in modern philosophy today, but in his day they were unusual and advanced.

It is not difficult to understand why Lohmeyer found an intellectual ally in Hönigswald, who defended philosophy, and by analogy theology, from being reduced exclusively to materialist realities. If the nineteenth-century materialist-determinist philosophical revolution were successful, it would reduce New Testament exegesis to mere linguistics and word studies. The biblical narrative would simply become the ethnic history of the Jewish people. The gospel would become a human invention without reference to a reality beyond itself. The success of such a revolution would spell the end of theology per se, that is, of God, faith, prayer, and the spiritual foundations of virtues such as love and hope and of ethics as a whole. If the concept of God were dismissed from the field of permissible realities, then there could be no God to know and love, no revelation of God in Jesus Christ, no word of God in Scripture, and no people of God in the church.

Neo-Kantianism itself was not a single unified philosophy, however. Indeed, by the 1920s it had become a henhouse of competing philosophies. Feathers flew in the henhouse, forming no fewer than seven neo-Kantian schools, each associated with a particular German university, each publishing its own journal. Hönigswald's philosophy aligned more closely with Immanuel Kant than did those of most other neo-Kantians, for Hönigswald—and in this he was followed by Lohmeyer—believed that human thought (which Kant referred to as *phenomena*) was actually based on natural realities (which he called *noumena*), that is, that the various modes of human conceptualization are authentic reflections of objective realities.[17] This insight provided Lohmeyer, who was a theologian top to bottom, inside and out, with a bulwark safeguarding the possibility of theology. His writings are replete with references that celebrate that possibility: "eternity," "objectivity," "factuality," "transcendent values," "supernatural principles," "unconditional," "unending," "eschatological," "timeless." On and on. I have never read a German theologian who uses the word *sachlich*—"factual," "objective"—with reference to such metaphysical realities more often than Ernst Lohmeyer.

Personal Reflections

The figure of Richard Hönigswald and the philosophy of neo-Kantianism were exceptional influences in Lohmeyer's life. In concluding this chapter I wish to say a word about both influences.[18] First, Hönigswald. Aristotle described friendship as "one soul dwelling in two bodies."[19] No two academics more completely fulfilled that model than Ernst Lohmeyer and Richard Hönigswald. Hönigswald's second wife died in 1921, the same year Lohmeyer moved to Breslau. Following the loss of his wife, and perhaps because of it, Hönigswald formed a fast and lasting friendship with Lohmeyer. Although the two were on the same university faculty and saw each other almost daily, they continued to correspond regularly in writing. The hundreds of letters that exist between Hönigswald and Lohmeyer are second in number only to the letters between Ernst and Melie. An entire book of Hönigswald's letters to Lohmeyer was published in 1999.[20] Hönigswald included Melie in his friendship with her husband, addressing letters almost always to both of them. The fact that Ernst and Melie named their daughter after him—Gudrun-*Richarda*—suggests that Melie, too, valued his friendship.

The intoxication of the Breslau intellectual community, and Hönigswald in particular, was not entirely positive in the Lohmeyer family, however. Hönigswald was a senior scholar whose intellectual formation, and above all, whose academic trajectory, was more firmly set than was Lohmeyer's. In a final letter from prison, Lohmeyer wrote Melie a long and full disclosure of his life, his hopes, and his failures. One of the failures Lohmeyer regretted had to do with Hönigswald. Lohmeyer confessed that he had dedicated himself to his academic work at the expense of his marriage and family, "misled perhaps by the allurement and imposing example of Hönigswald."[21] It is important to hear what Lohmeyer said in this confession and what he did not say. He did not attribute deleterious intentions to Hönigswald, nor did he blame him for misusing his influence in his life. In light of Lohmeyer's respect for Hönigswald and bond of friendship with him, it is unimaginable that he would suggest either of the above. The problem, rather, by Lohmeyer's own confession, was his own. He had *allowed* Hönigswald, who was a widower and whose sole family responsibility at the time was the care of a young son, to exercise undue influence in his life, and his allowance impeded his own responsibilities—both to his family and to the course his academic career might otherwise have taken. Lohmeyer's perspective on Hönigswald in 1946 thus exhibited a critical component that it lacked twenty years earlier in Breslau.

Second, neo-Kantianism. Heavy reliance on any one system runs the danger of warping and misconstruing the object investigated. Lohmeyer did not escape this danger. The New Testament can often appear in his writing as a metaphysical sourcebook, its authors appearing in his commentaries as Greek thinkers pondering questions. He can describe Christianity in words and categories more appropriate to Platonic idealism than to Jewish-Christian authors in Palestine. The New Testament can appear as an enshrinement of the supreme religious-ethical principle; Paul as a contender for the metaphysical certainty of the faith; Jesus as the proper embodiment of final principles; God as the unchangeable eternal reality; ethics as "the idea of the good." Lohmeyer's contemporaries often criticized him—sometimes sharply—for interpreting the New Testament in such categories. Hans Windisch critiqued his Philippians commentary as novel, creative, and theologically stimulating, but "the question remains how correctly he captures the intention of Paul himself."[22] Bultmann's concerns were more frequent and harder hitting. Again with reference to the Philippians commentary, he noted that theologians had often been accused of using philosophy as the handmaiden of theology, but Lohmeyer had made theology the handmaiden of philosophy![23] Seventy years hence the critique remains. "Lohmeyer's mixture of meticulous criticism and creative vision [leaves] the observer dazzled," notes William Baird. Nevertheless, "he has imposed a nineteenth-century philosophy on the ancient sources."[24]

The apogee of Lohmeyer's planet is at its furthest and most distant point from my own planetary orbit in his neo-Kantian orientation. I suspect it is for most modern readers as well. I have even met professional academic philosophers for whom neo-Kantianism is a foreign concept. It is easy to lose touch with Lohmeyer at this point. But before dismissing the matter—and perhaps Lohmeyer as well—consider the *issue* posed by neo-Kantianism rather than the philosophy itself. The issue, to reword slightly William Baird's above critique of Lohmeyer, is to impose an alien ideology on the gospel. This is a lesson worth heeding. Every age is tempted to impose its ideologies on the gospel in order to tame it for the preferences and purposes of the age. If we are in no danger of overwriting Scripture and faith with neo-Kantianism, we are not free from other dangers posed by the prevalence and power, both subtle and outright, of a score of modern isms—including materialism, consumerism, hedonism, militarism, racism, and, especially today, egoism. We too can and often do impose these values not only on the ancient sources of the faith but also on the faith itself.

CHAPTER 7

Full Bloom in Breslau

> Always make truth your first concern. Good feelings and ev-
> erything else will follow.
>
> Wilhelm Karl Raabe[1]

Gudrun, circa 1990

In December 1993 I received a grant from the German Academic Exchange Service (DAAD)[2] to investigate the circumstances surrounding Lohmeyer's mysterious disappearance and death. In preparation
for my trip to Germany, I made contact with Ernst Lohmeyer's daughter, Gudrun (Lohmeyer) Otto, who lived in Wannsee, on the outskirts
of Berlin. When I arrived in Berlin, I took the S-Bahn to Wannsee,
then a taxi to the address on Bergstrasse where Gudrun lived with her
husband, Klaus. She was sixty-seven years old, of medium height or
slightly taller, slender, with rather short hair. I immediately saw in her
face features reminiscent of photographs of her father—her chin and
mouth, nose, and her kind and knowing eyes. She received me with
warmth and openness, and a comfortable rapport quickly developed
between us. I was a newcomer in a matter that had dominated her
family for more than a half century, but Gudrun never acted in a patronizing manner or left me feeling tolerated or resented. I felt more
like a child whose big sister takes him to a secret fort or hideout in the
forest that she had built in hopes of securing his help to make it better.

In my pursuit of Lohmeyer, teamwork with Gudrun was as
effective as it was gratifying. She shared information freely, and

her critical acumen thoughtfully and carefully. As I learned more about Lohmeyer, I also came to see that her judgments, whether in personal conversations or in subsequent letters, invariably aligned closely with my own. Our teamwork included my wife, Jane, and Klaus, Gudrun's husband, whose scent on the chase was no less acute than Gudrun's. Jane and I were back in Berlin in 1996, and Gudrun and Klaus invited us to stay with them. It was June, and the Ottos took us on a walking tour of Potsdam, which had been in former East Germany. The weather was warm and sunny, and the meadow through which we were walking beside a lake was green and lush. Klaus and I were walking in front, talking. A woman who had been sunbathing to our right got up and walked across the path in front of us. She was entirely naked. After she passed, Klaus remarked coolly, "People are celebrating the end of communism in East Germany in the most expressive ways."

Gudrun, circa 1930

The Lohmeyers increased from a twosome to a family of six in Breslau. We have noted one-year-old Beate Dorothee's sad and unexpected death in 1921. The year after her death the Lohmeyers' first son, Ernst-Helge, was born, in January 1922. A second son, Hermann-Hartmut, followed eighteen months later, in May 1923. Three years later the fourth and final child was born, Gudrun-Richarda, in spring 1926. Twenty years later, in 1946, Lohmeyer wrote to Melie recalling a "hard conversation"[3] they had had when Melie told him she was pregnant with Gudrun. He had not wanted another child, and he confessed to pulling back from Melie and immersing himself in his work. Distance grew between Ernst and Melie over this matter, but—perhaps not surprisingly—it did not grow between Ernst and Gudrun. Children have a way of altering the most entrenched of adult attitudes. This is especially true of the youngest child, who inherits a unique place in a family. Young Gudrun inherited a special place in her father's heart. On April 9, 1926—the day she was born—Lohmeyer proudly wrote to the university administrator at Breslau, "Please allow me to communicate that early this morning our daughter was born who will bear the name Gudrun-Richarda." The second sentence of Lohmeyer's announcement explains why he informed the administrator, whose name might not be expected at the top of the family's notification list. "I respectfully ask you to confirm that you will increase my financial allocation for this child."[4]

Many of Gudrun's early recollections were recalled from the perspective of her father's lap.

> I was the youngest child, the only girl, and I received the kind of special attention the littlest member of the family usually gets. My father never reprimanded me and never ever punished me. He helped me with everything when I asked. When I recall the times we spent together I don't remember a trace of impatience in my father. I spent countless hours sitting on his lap, which he never refused, whether it was at the end of midday rounds or when students met in our house. We played together all the normal children's games alone or with my brothers. He didn't play with us simply out of duty, but because he enjoyed it, especially in our Silesian country house where we played Skat. And then came four-handed piano together. We started slowly, but later got so good that we fearlessly tried anything together. He helped me in schoolwork with his objective and mature manner, but with a certain enjoyment even when the clock was ticking or he had to interrupt his own work.[5]

Later in life Gudrun summed up her relationship with her father thus: "I am so fortunate. I could not have had a better father, and I could not have wished for a different father than the one I had."[6] Lohmeyer's affection for Gudrun and her brothers was deep and special, as only a father's love can be. Nor was it absent in his relationships with others, even if expressed in different ways. Her father had a natural gift of befriending people, said Gudrun, "whether it was my brothers and me, the farmers around our Silesian summer home, or the soldiers he commanded in the wars."[7]

A Place at the Publishing Table

The 1920s were an exhilarating season in Lohmeyer's intellectual and professional life. He received invitations to speak at conferences. His articles were published in leading theological journals. His very first scholarly article on the transfiguration in the Gospel of Mark,[8] published in 1922, so impressed the prestigious Göttingen publishing house Vandenhoeck & Ruprecht (V&R) that its publisher, Gustav Ruprecht, invited Lohmeyer to update the commentaries on Paul's prison epistles, Ephesians, Philippians, Colossians, and Philemon, for the acclaimed Meyer Commentary Series. Vandenhoeck & Ruprecht had published a full complement of Meyer New Testament commentaries in the nineteenth century. Subsequent advances in New Testament scholarship necessitated a second generation of commentaries in the series. Ruprecht invited Lohmeyer not only to write the foregoing volumes but also to advise the publishing house on the format and choice of contributors for forthcoming volumes. It was a scholar's dream come true. I have had to stand on street corners with a tin cup in my hand, so to speak, begging for attention from publishers. Lohmeyer was instantly and early offered a place at the table—the chair at its head, in fact—of Germany's most prestigious theological publishing house.

A long and lively correspondence developed between V&R and Lohmeyer. In the next fifteen years Lohmeyer would publish seven books with the house, advise it on the format and "weight" of its theological orientation, and influence the roster of contributing scholars to the Meyer series. The correspondence was frequent, frank, and of obvious consequence for both parties. The rapidity, length, and rhetorical flourishes in Lohmeyer's letters indicate the seriousness with which he took the opportunity, which became a virtual mission for him. Both Gustav Ruprecht and his son Günther would play unusually important roles in Lohmeyer's professional life. And the role would extend to his family as well. Melie would find no more steadfast, wise, and compassionate counselor following Ernst's disappearance in 1946 than Günther Ruprecht. He became a genuine and excellent pastoral counselor to her. Even three-and-half-year-old Gudrun entered the relationship. In a long and important letter to V&R in 1929, Lohmeyer circled some messy ink marks in the margin and added a postscript begging forgiveness for the artwork that his "little girl" had appended while he left the letter unattended on his desk.[9]

Lohmeyer vigorously seized the reins to upgrade Meyer's prominence in German scholarship and theology. The bane of the Meyer series, he wrote to Gustav, was that the old volumes were so clogged with ancient history and language citations that they were uninspiring, unreadable, and unaffordable. Karl Barth's *Römerbrief—Commentary on Romans—*had just been published and was being read in Europe as no theological volume had been read before. There was a lesson here for V&R, said Lohmeyer. Let the new Meyer series strike a healthy balance between historical and philological material and theological substance. Historical and philological considerations should be limited to material essential to the understanding of the biblical text and context, and theological significance should, like Barth's *Römerbrief,* be given primary consideration. Unlike *Römerbrief,* however—and here Lohmeyer betrayed his reservation about Barth's approach—theological consideration should remain connected to the text and not soar in free flight above it.

The correspondence between Lohmeyer and V&R continued unabated for a decade. A more satisfying and productive professional correspondence would be hard to imagine. Lohmeyer's commentary on Philippians appeared from V&R in 1927, his commentary on Colossians in 1928, and the three volumes of Philippians, Colossians, and Philemon bound together in 1929.[10]

Philippians 2:5–11

One of Lohmeyer's more significant theological contributions is now so axiomatic in New Testament scholarship that even some scholars have forgotten—or never knew—that Ernst Lohmeyer first brought it to light. The particular discovery was a new and revolutionary understanding of the Christ hymn in Philippians 2:5–11, but the *significance* of the discovery would extend to many passages throughout the New Testament.

In Philippians 2:1-4 the apostle Paul exhorts believers to a life of humility and mindfulness of others. In verses 5-11 the apostle proceeds to give believers the supreme model for such a life in Jesus Christ. Christ Jesus, says Paul, existed originally in the form of God, indeed was equal to God, but he did not hold on to his form and equality at all costs. Rather, he "emptied" himself and became a human being, indeed a human *slave*, and gave himself up to a shameful death upon a cross. Because of his self-surrender, God exalted him above every name in heaven and on earth, so that every person should confess Jesus Christ as Lord.

A century ago scholars regarded this declaration, and others like it in the New Testament, as late additions to the New Testament. The dominant evolutionary and naturalistic paradigm at the time argued that a "high Christology," that is, a belief in Jesus as the divine Son of God, was not part of the earliest Christian gospel. Exalted and deified understandings of Jesus were regarded as later—and in some considerations *alien*—developments that were indebted not to the Old Testament and Jewish cradle of Christianity but rather to Greek myths about heroes like Hercules or Aesclepius, who, after their deaths, were "apotheosized" into gods and goddesses.

In 1927 Lohmeyer published a grassroots study of Philippians 2:5-11 in a monograph entitled *Kyrios Jesus* (*Lord Jesus*).[11] *Kyrios Jesus* shattered virtually every consensus about this important text that had prevailed until then. Lohmeyer began not with the theology or ostensible date of the text but with its form. His aesthetic eye saw a pattern that other eyes had not seen: a poetic composition of eighteen declarations that was divided into two halves. The first half in verses 6-8 recounts the descent of the eternal Son of God to earth. It consists of three strophes, each of three lines. The second half in verses 9-11 recounts the exaltation of the earthly Christ to heaven, and it too consists of three three-line strophes. Lohmeyer noted that in the Greek text (this is less clear in German and English translations), the first verb in each strophe is followed by verbs bearing similar senses in lines 2 and 3. The result, in his words, was "a hymn to Christ in the absolute sense."[12]

Though existing in the form of God
>he did not clutch tightly
>his equality with God,

but he emptied himself,
>taking the form of slave,
>he was born in human likeness;

and being found in human likeness
>he humbled himself
>and became obedient to death (—death on a cross).

Therefore God also highly exalted him
>and gave him the name
>that is above every name,

so that at the name of Jesus
>every knee should bend
>in heaven and on earth and under the earth

and every tongue confess
>that Jesus Christ is Lord
>to the glory of God the Father.

Once Lohmeyer had determined the original form of the Christ hymn, he proceeded to overturn all previous understandings of it in academic theology. He began with a presupposition that he and Stefan George considered elementary to literary criticism, that form is essential to content and meaning. This is especially true in poetry and hymnody. Lohmeyer declared that the form of the hymn did not derive from the hand of Paul, for its relationship to its context in Philippians is unclear and its load-bearing vocabulary and poetic rhythm are non-Pauline.

Nor was the hymn Greek and Hellenistic. Several Greek forms, slightly barbarous in themselves, are explainable as translations of an original Semitic text. Moreover, the dominant themes of humiliation and "descent" are not typical of Greek mythology but are reminiscent of the Suffering Servant of Isaiah. Further, the central motif of the hymn is *faith*, which is a Judeo-Christian characteristic. If the hymn were Greek, its central motif would have been knowledge. Lohmeyer even detected early Trinitarian elements in the hymn, the Father and Son, of course, but also the work of the Spirit in the concluding confession of Jesus Christ as Lord.

Nor was Philippians 2:5–11 a late, postapostolic creation. No epistle in the New Testament was more authentically Pauline than Philippians. The Pauline Epistles represent the *earliest* stratum of the New Testament writings, composed in the fifties of the first century. If in Philippians 2:5–11 Paul quotes a preexistent hymn to Christ, then the hymn necessarily *pre*dated Paul. Far from being a late addition, the Christ hymn was one of the first confessions of Christian faith, already in use in the forties, perhaps even the late thirties, of the first century. Lohmeyer conjectured that the hymn arose in celebrations of the Eucharist among early Jewish Christians in Jerusalem. This last conjecture, although interesting, lacks either confirming or refuting evidence.

Finally, and above all, the oft-repeated and widely held assumption that "high Christology" was late Christology had been toppled. Philippians 2:5–11 represents perhaps the highest Christology in the New Testament, and it existed already prior to the earliest stage of the writing of the New Testament! "High Christology" is not a late and alien appendage to the gospel tradition but present in its earliest literary record.[13]

Martyrdom

Lohmeyer's theological output at the University of Breslau was prodigious. By the time he became president in 1930, he had published a dozen scholarly books, half again that number of scholarly articles, and nearly fifty reviews of prominent books. At the crest of such success and the growing acclaim that it brought him, Lohmeyer turned to a most unexpected subject. The subject was martyrdom, and he treated it not once but three different times. His interest in martyrdom was certainly not prompted by any existential storm clouds in his life in the late 1920s. Skies were clear in his personal life, with fine weather forecasted. Nor was martyrdom prompted by storm clouds in Germany's social and political prospects. True, ten years later Jews and Christians would be giving their lives for their faith and convictions. But when Lohmeyer first wrote on martyrdom in 1926, the Weimar Republic was at last beginning to look like a viable government. If Germany was not exactly enjoying a "roaring twenties," it was in fact enjoying an optimistic upswing. What would happen in Germany ten years later could not have been imagined.

Lohmeyer developed his thoughts on martyrdom in three separate venues. He published a major commentary on the book of Revelation in 1926 in which he cast its author, John, as a "seer" and the Revelation itself as a "witness." A "seer" and "witness" of what? Of martyrdom! In his words, "The Book of Revelation is a book of a martyr that is written for martyrs, and through them for all believers!"[14] The following year, at a theological conference in Paris, he developed his thoughts more fully in a lecture entitled "Die Idee des Martyriums im Judentum und Urchristentum" ("The Idea of Martyrdom in Judaism and Early Christianity"), which was published in *Zeitschrift für systematische Theologie* in 1927. Lohmeyer asserted that the Christian understanding of martyrdom grew out of the soil of Jewish history. Like their Jewish counterparts, in the act of martyrdom Christians were both witnesses to the gospel in the church and advocates of the gospel in the world.[15] The fullest development of martyrdom, however, came in his 1928 commentary on Philippians in the Meyer series. From beginning to end, Philippians was interpreted by Lohmeyer as an epistle of martyrdom. The apostle Paul anticipated his martyrdom in the epistle, and the martyrdom of the Philippian church as well. The structure and content of Philippians, maintained Lohmeyer, were determined by martyrdom: comfort in martyrdom, dangers attending martyrdom, and admonitions in the face of martyrdom.[16] Lohmeyer regarded Philippians 3:10 as a capsule of the entire epistle, as well as the claim of the gospel on church and believer: "That I may know Jesus Christ and the power of his resurrection, and may share his sufferings, becoming like him in his death."

What attracted Lohmeyer to this unusual topic, on which virtually no theologians were writing at the time? We need look no further than his neo-Kantian persuasion. Kantian idealism was forever in search of essences, the heart of a matter, the irreducible element in any given thing that constituted its "objective," "certain," "absolute," and "timeless" core. When Lohmeyer examined the New Testament and Christian faith through the microscope of neo-Kantianism, he found himself looking at martyrdom. Martyrdom was the irreducible kernel of Christianity because it was the essential link between the gospel and the world. In martyrdom the Christian individual and the church collectively testify to the essence of the gospel with a purity and totality that they nowhere else render for the gospel. And also in martyrdom the world witnesses and experiences the truth and power of the gospel in a way and to a degree that it nowhere else witnesses and experiences the gospel. Martyrdom is the most uncompromised witness the believer or the church can offer to God, and as such martyrdom is the most uncompromised witness the world can receive of the gospel.

It is tempting to read Lohmeyer's early and atypical interest in martyrdom in light of his own fate twenty years later. Did he have a personal premonition of what awaited him? Or did he perhaps see in martyrdom a prophetic witness to the church? The answer to these questions is almost certainly negative. To interpret Lohmeyer's discussion of martyrdom as a closet reference to himself would be to misjudge both his character and his purpose as a theologian. At no place in his various discussions of martyrdom did Lohmeyer treat the subject existentially, as a possibility of his own physical fate. To the contrary, the topic was always and only treated in terms of its theological significance as the essential nature of Christian witness. That was typical Lohmeyer. Truth always came first, and once first, whatever followed was determined by the power of truth. Truth set one free, and once free, no other reality could compromise its freedom. Lohmeyer must certainly have recalled his work on martyrdom when he faced his end, of course. From the little we know about his end from eyewitnesses, he faced it with the faith and fortitude of a martyr.

President Lohmeyer's Inaugural Lecture at Breslau

German university presidents are chosen by a plenary vote of the faculty rather than by a board of trustees, as is customary in American universities. German university presidents are thus chosen by the same body and according to the same criteria by which American universities choose *faculty* presidents. The primary criteria in both cases are intellectual respectability and trustworthiness of character. In the German system, however, the president is responsible not simply for faculty affairs but also for the collective affairs of the university as a whole. In 1930 the faculty of Breslau University voted Ernst Lohmeyer Rektor Magnifizenz—university president—for the 1930/31 academic year.

Lohmeyer's election was perhaps somewhat unexpected for one who, by and large, was disinclined to politics. He had drifted into political waters in his unpublished *Attack* at the end of World War I, which, though chauvinistic by today's standards, was rather mainstream at the time. Apart from that abortive venture, however, Lohmeyer did not pursue political positions or strategies. As the influence of Nazism—and later, communism—grew in Germany, however, a complex tension resulted in his life. An inherently nonpolitical personality was forced to address inescapable political realities. Lohmeyer did not engage in political resistance movements or in the various plots on Hitler's life. Once the Third Reich was in power, he did not channel his implacable opposition to Nazism into political means and strategies. He sought alternative means and an alternative voice—even if it was a voice crying in the wilderness. He allied himself with the Pastors' Emergency League from its inception, and then with its successor organization, the Confessing Church. Lohmeyer would oppose Nazism where it strongly and adversely influenced his life—in the church, in the university, and with his Jewish colleagues. At these points Lohmeyer employed his most powerful forms of defense—his undaunted courage, his razor-sharp intellect, his theologically grounded faith. It was, in fact, precisely these abilities, strategies, and commitments that resulted in his election as president of Breslau University in 1930.

Lohmeyer was forty years old when he was elected president of Breslau University. The university had 6,000 students, of whom 150 were students of theology. He anticipated that the presidency would be a one-year—or two-year at the most—responsibility, after which he could catch a second wave of scholarship and publication that would carry him through the 1930s as a first wave had carried him through the 1920s. But "way leads on to way," as Robert Frost said of life's journey.[17] Until his death fifteen years later, this man, so motivated by the world of antiquity and the biblical, theological, and philosophical currents related to it, would not be free to pursue those motivations without interference and often opposition from the two most infamous totalitarianisms of the twentieth century— the first brown, the second red.

In 1930, Hitler's accession to power was still three years hence, but the Nazi tide was already on the rise. The National Socialistic German Student Association,[18] an organization founded in 1926 to promote Nazi principles and loyalty to the führer among university students, already claimed the allegiance of a majority of university students at Breslau by the time Lohmeyer took office as president. The Nazi Zeitgeist of "will to power" was rapidly becoming the dominant ideology not only of German culture but also of German universities and churches. This Zeitgeist was championed by influential intellectuals. Emmanuel Hirsch, church historian, theologian, and specialist in Luther and Kierkegaard, became a leading ideologue and virtual scriptwriter for the German Christian Movement. The German *Volk*, thundered Hirsch, was the sole antidote to the poison of internationalism and pacifism that had brought Germany to its knees after World War I. Voices like Hirsch's were commandeering the public agenda by 1930. A conservative Protestant journalist wrote that "the German *Volk* was no mere human idea, but the idea of God"—to which, he added, the church was bound to obey! At the 1927 *Kirchentag* in Königsberg—the national church conference—the influential Luther scholar Paul Althaus unveiled the guidelines of a new political theology that he christened "German Faith." "The world today is political through and through," declared Althaus. "Our questions about 'salvation' find their fulfillment in the political dimension. Today, people are not concerned about peace with God, but about overcoming political problems."[19] Althaus was specific about the chief problem the church needed to address: corruption of "the German *Volk*."[20]

These were the waters Lohmeyer had to navigate as he delivered his inaugural address at Breslau. The surface of the waters was still reasonably calm at the time, but riptides and countercurrents were writhing underneath. The title of Lohmeyer's address was safely academic, "Faith and History in Ancient Near Eastern Religions." Its literary felicities—wordplays, alliteration, step repetitions, dramatic contrasts—promised to make a ponderous address pleasing, validating the choice of Lohmeyer as the new president. The title and academic subject and literary flares were but the wrappings, however, of a surprise package.

One of the surprises was Lohmeyer's ability as an orator. Most academics are good scholars; some are good writers and even good lecturers as well. But not all are good public speakers. Lohmeyer was all of these. Some years earlier Gustav Ruprecht had invited Lohmeyer to participate in the development of a midlevel commentary series on the New Testament. The series that was subsequently developed, Das Neue Testament Deutsch, was highly successful, communicating serious scholarship to an uncommonly wide audience. Lohmeyer declined Ruprecht's invitation on the grounds that the theological needs of the hour required rigorous scholarship, "cutting-edge" scholarship, as we say today. I personally regret Lohmeyer's decision in this matter. In oral communication he was in his prime. It was the educated but nonscholarly audience that Ruprecht invited him to address in the proposed series. In this medium and for this audience, Lohmeyer achieved inimitable clarity, use of imagery, and power of conviction. This was especially evident in his sermons—and in his inaugural address at Breslau.

A second surprise was Lohmeyer's ability to leverage the past for its prophetic significance in the present. He did this in his inaugural lecture. His opening thesis was that history is the root of our existence, "where knowledge becomes deed and deed is grounded in knowledge . . . for the unchangeable form and content of life manifests itself in the changeable form of history."[21] History is unique as a field of inquiry, he maintained, because history can be approached with equal justification from the perspectives of both scholarship and faith. Scholarship charts the erring search of humanity for inerrant truth. He made this point in Latin for any smug detractors who might be present—*per varios errores sero pervenitur ad veritatem.* But faith, he went on, "affirms eternal meaning and eternal reality in unerring truth and unequivocal certainty."[22] Lohmeyer then launched into an impressive survey of ancient civilizations to demonstrate that in them all history was rooted in "inalterable and eternal laws."[23] The relationship between faith and history is thus one of stability rather than fear, order rather than chaos, individual enlightenment rather than foreordained *Volk.* "History is not fixed fate, but freely-offered goal, to which we are invited to strive. . . . It is not the triumph of power but the victory of virtue of God's wise and eternal laws."[24]

Only when Lohmeyer was two-thirds through his address did he address the one civilization and people that more than all the others— more than Babylon, Greece, Rome, Egypt, India, Persia, Germania, China, and Mexico—had tutored the world in the meaning of faith and history. That people was "the Israelite-Jewish people," to whom God said, "Those who were not my people, I will call my people; and those who were not loved, I will call my Beloved" (Rom. 9:25). Lohmeyer's German is crucial here, for the word for "people" is *Volk,* which was a virtually sacred word in National Socialist propaganda. This small and seemingly insignificant people bore witness to a synthesis of faith and history that occurred nowhere else in the world. From this marginal *Volk,* the world was introduced to the saving faith of the *individual,* faith reduced to *one,* the Messiah of Israel, the Messiah for the world.

One of the foundational ideas in all history comes to expression in Judaism, in which the Messiah and his community become the crown of the historical process. This Messiah is a particular "I," who lives in history and works for history; and the form of this particular life and work is nothing other than the form of the community, which he both creates and rules.[25]

The key to the relationship between faith and history is also the key to the relationship between the individual and the larger community of peoples, nations, and states. "The One whom God elects is he whom God determines to be the single place of his truth and reality. Through this One 'who became flesh,' God brings all humanity and history to completion."[26]

Lohmeyer concluded with a crescendo comparable to Beethoven's Fifth Piano Concerto:

> Here is the certainty of the One who is eternally present and the longing for the One who is yet to come. Fulfillment and promise are present in One and the same Person. In the eschatological fulfillment of that which until now has been unfulfilled, history now becomes free to complete its original course. History continues in eternal change of events and in eternal unchangeability of its purpose, inexhaustible and diverse in its becoming and passing, transparent and uniform in its meaning, always directed and always redeemed. History is a whole in movement, and in each separate event its unending stream is present. History is always what it is, and is always what it is becoming. . . . The relationship between faith and history is consummated when the Gospel of John says of Jesus, "And the word became flesh and dwelt among us, and we saw his glory."[27]

Lohmeyer's inaugural address was a tour de force of intellectual history. In its own way it resembled C. S. Lewis's *Abolition of Man* in grounding a moral universe in the deepest roots of human history. But it was more than a survey of the *past*. Without once mentioning "National Socialism," its tenets, slogans, or caricatures, Lohmeyer subjected the Nazi myth of hate and fear to the crushing weight of historical reality and truth. The individual cannot be dissolved into the *Volk*. The state cannot be deified. *Macht*—raw power—cannot be glorified as the chief virtue of the state. The historical and religious witness to the eternal moral order cannot be replaced by arbitrary values of a false ideology. Finally and above all, the testimony of God to the gospel of Jesus Christ was revealed ineluctably and solely through "the Israelite-Jewish religion," for "salvation is from the Jews" (John 4:22). The object of Nazism's poisonous venom and brutal violence was the very cradle of Christianity.

Ernst Lohmeyer's inaugural address at Breslau was a devastating intellectual and theological denunciation of Nazism even before it officially came to power.

CHAPTER 8

Swastika!

Hitler fought not one war but two wars between 1935 and 1945. One war was against the nations—against Russia in the east and the remaining Allies in the west. The other war was the attempted annihilation of eleven million European Jews. When the first war was lost, Hitler poured all remaining energies into winning the second.

Sebastian Haffner[1]

Heat Wave

The year following Lohmeyer's presidency of Breslau got off to a bad start. It should have been a good start, for Lohmeyer, liberated from responsibilities as president, was once again free to pursue his scholarship. A disagreement with a fellow scholar, however, shifted from an issue of genuine significance for twentieth-century biblical scholarship to personal rancor, and the ensuing rancor smothered the issue at stake.

In late 1931 Hans Lietzmann, editor of the premier *Zeitschrift für die neutestamentliche Wissenschaft* (*ZNW*), rejected an article on John the Baptist that Lohmeyer submitted for publication. There is nothing abnormal nor necessarily blamable about such a rejection. I could wallpaper my study with rejection letters from publishers. Every scholar I know receives them. Lietzmann was a first-class church historian, successor to Adolf von Harnack in the prestigious chair of church history at Humboldt University. He was a theological polymath who had successfully edited *ZNW* for a decade. His editorial judgment, if not infallible, was worthy of consideration. Lohmeyer knew all this, for he had already published a half-dozen articles in *ZNW* under Lietzmann's editorial eye.

Lietzmann intended his rejection of Lohmeyer's article to be a speed bump, but Lohmeyer took it as a brick wall. Perhaps not surprisingly, there was a back story to the clash. Lietzmann was alarmed by Lohmeyer's 1929 book *The Fundamentals of Pauline Theology*.[2] More than a hundred pages of *Pauline Theology* had appeared in three separate articles in *ZNW* in the late 1920s, and Lietzmann was disturbed by what he saw. He lamented the developing trend in German biblical scholarship of complex language and theological jargon intended for guild academics, "esoteric speciality speech," as he called it. Lietzmann was distressed to see Lohmeyer writing for this elite inner circle. *ZNW* was read internationally, and he wanted its articles to be written in German understandable to a wide readership. Lietzmann confessed difficulty in understanding Lohmeyer's article and announced bluntly, "I do not publish articles that I cannot understand."[3]

And there was more. He was vexed by Lohmeyer's "false" methodology. By this he meant that Lohmeyer had not followed "the final principles of historical methodology."[4] Theological scholarship needed to follow the same methodology followed by other sciences, grounding arguments and conclusions in empirical and historical evidence rather than in philosophical and theological presuppositions such as Lohmeyer had employed in his article.

Lohmeyer rarely lost his composure, but he did with Lietzmann's criticism. He immediately wrote to Hönigswald, including a copy of the rejection letter. "The copy of Lietzmann's letter makes me indignant," wrote Hönigswald back to Lohmeyer. "Above all I also would absolutely *not* remain silent."[5] A rejection letter leaves one smarting, and it is not surprising that Lohmeyer turned to his confidant in this matter. It is lamentable, however, that Hönigswald weighed in bullishly on his behalf. Hönigswald did not belong in the squabble, and his partisanship almost certainly induced Lohmeyer to overreact. Which he did. On Christmas Day (!) of 1931 Lohmeyer responded, not to Lietzmann personally, but in an open letter to

Theologische Blätter (*Theological Papers*). This turned a personal issue—at least in Lietzmann's mind—into a public free-for-all. People took sides. Lietzmann became a bully, Lohmeyer a poor loser, and a positive debate was aborted.

Lohmeyer admitted his change in style but defended it on the grounds that *Fundamentals of Pauline Theology* was not "merely historical" but was devoted to the principles and presuppositions of theology itself. "How should one speak about such principles in a scholarly way other than by submitting to the scholarly tradition in which they have been discussed. That tradition extends from Plato to Leibniz and Kant. I am echoing their speech and I seek to do likewise with their thoughts."[6] This defense seems to sidestep rather than address Lietzmann's critique of Lohmeyer's turgid language. Behind the critique was, once again, Lohmeyer's imposition of philosophical idealism on the biblical tradition. Lietzmann's critique at this point was worth heeding.

It was Lietzmann's methodological critique, however, that Lohmeyer took especially personally, and to which he responded aggressively. "May I ask who promoted you watchdog over the theological enterprise? Are you presuming to be a headmaster in a school of German theology, grading pupils on what is 'legitimate' and what is not?"[7] Lohmeyer reminded Lietzmann that intellectual breakthroughs and advancements often come from the new perspectives of outsiders and outliers—perspectives that the academic guild may consider disreputable. With regard to the rejected article specifically, Lohmeyer decried the rejection of theological criteria in favor of an exclusively "historical" perspective.

Lohmeyer justified his article by noting that the Baptist himself is insignificant as a mere historical character. Rather, it is his work and his figure that bear witness to an act that God earlier in the history of Israel promised and now, in the promised word and its historical fulfillment, brings about a greater act that calls for a response of faith.[8]

We can only wish that a healthy debate had taken place. Would that Lohmeyer had heard Lietzmann's critique of his literary style. Even more, that Lietzmann had heard Lohmeyer's critique that a methodology determined solely by naturalism was insufficient to account for the *theological* substance of the New Testament. The methodological monopoly for which Lietzmann was appealing would dominate New Testament scholarship for the next fifty years. Lohmeyer's open letter sought to break the historical-critical cartel that only one methodological foundation was valid on which to erect the superstructure of New Testament studies. Had the theological guild heard Lohmeyer, the more open field of play that developed in New Testament studies around 1980 might have developed earlier. That field of play did not eliminate the higher critical method—that is, the critical study of the literary methods and sources used by the authors of the books of the Bible. Nor did it intend to. It intended to supplement it with other methodologies and approaches, also of relevance, for greater understanding of the New Testament. Unfortunately, Lohmeyer's appeal for a more open field of play was not heard, and he was further relegated to the status of *Einzelgänger*—the isolated individual.

Hate Wave

Even before Hitler came to power in January 1933, Ernst Lohmeyer clashed with National Socialism at its most virulent point, its anti-Semitism.

A political spectacle took place in 1932 that left no doubt about two new realities of German life: the rise of National Socialism and the impotence of the Weimar Republic. The stage of the spectacle, significantly, was the German brain trust, the university system, which even before Hitler's accession to power accommodated itself to National Socialist policies and in many cases actively embraced them. As a signal of its intent, the Nazi Party publicly denounced five professors in the fall of 1932 whom it intended to eliminate from the university system. One of the five, Ernst Cohn, was at Breslau. But before telling his story, it is worth recounting briefly the stories of the other four.

The Nazi intent to muzzle and eliminate Jewish influence in Germany made the fates of three of the four virtually inevitable. Theodor Lessing, a philosopher of culture, was a Zionist. Hans Nawiasky, a professor of law, had offended Nazi political correctness by expressing sympathy for some aspects of the Treaty of Versailles. And Emil Julius Gumbel, a mathematician, had argued from statistical studies that political terror was counterproductive. The use of "political stage" to describe the conspiracy against the scholars is misleading, for a stage only simulates reality. The outcome of the conspiracy in the lives of the five scholars on the Nazi hit list was anything but simulated. On the orders of Hermann Göring, Lessing was murdered by the Gestapo and his body thrown into the forest as he returned from the Prague Zion Congress in August of 1933. Nawiasky and Gumbel survived with their lives, fortunately, but with little more. They were stripped of their university positions and of their German citizenship, and forced into exile.

Names four and five on the list of opprobrium were more surprising, for they were not politically dangerous Jews. Indeed, one of them was not a Jew. The inclusion of these atypical names signaled that Nazism would offer no islands of political immunity, whether in German universities or in culture at large. The transgressions of the five were also varied, which was a further harbinger of the degree to which the Nazi terror would metastasize: all academic disciplines were under scrutiny and vulnerable to retribution.

Victim number four was a Christian, Günther Dehn. Dehn had grown up in a poor working family of no religious commitments. At university he had undergone a conversion experience. In his own words: "I was not converted by an evangelist, not brought to faith by a sermon, and not redeemed from an unusually sinful life. I was not in search of the forgiveness of my sins but in search of the meaning of life. I found that meaning at the end of my first semester at the university in a meeting with the figure of Jesus Christ."[9] Dehn became a pastor in Moabit, a blue-collar neighborhood in Berlin whose economic and social conditions resembled those in the neighborhood in which he had been raised. Like Dietrich Bonhoeffer, Dehn would undertake clandestine theological education for the Confessing Church, and also like Bonhoeffer, he would be imprisoned by the Gestapo for doing so. The "Dehn affair," no less than the "Cohn affair," illustrates the particular adeptness with which the Nazi Party sanctioned individuals. Death for the Fatherland had assumed a virtual sacrosanct status in Nazi rhetoric by 1930. Dehn argued against the sacrifice of human life for a semi-deified state. Military deaths were not martyrdoms, he maintained, because soldiers themselves intended to kill, whereas Christian martyrs had no intention of killing others. Dehn conceded that governments were justified in honoring war dead in public monuments, but he argued that it was not appropriate for governments to erect monuments and plaques for the war dead in churches. The Nazi Party seized Dehn's careful reasoning and distorted it, asserting that his refusal to grant Germany's fallen soldiers martyr status in churches was tantamount to calling them "murderers." For this Dehn's name was added to the contemptuous list, and his call to a professorship at Heidelberg revoked.[10]

The Ides of November: The Cohn Affair

The fifth victim of the professor purge was perhaps the most curious, a twenty-eight-year-old law scholar at Breslau named Ernst Joseph Cohn. Cohn's demerits, whatever they were, fell considerably short of those of the other four persons on the list. The primary reason for proscribing his name seems simply to have been his Jewishness. In this respect the name of Cohn was the most alarming on the list, for it signified that in the new Nazi order Jewishness alone was a punishable offense. Elie Wiesel would later sum it up thus: "Not all who suffered under Nazism were Jews, but all Jews suffered under Nazism."[11]

In the fall of 1932, Ernst Cohn, an assistant professor at the University of Frankfurt, received a call to the law faculty at the University of Breslau. He received the call to Breslau, in part, by joining the Social Party of Germany (SPD), which had established thirteen law professorships at various German universities. Breslau may have seemed a safe call for Cohn, for its faculty had a higher percentage of Jews than did other German universities. His appointment, however, became a catalyst for perhaps the most public anti-Jewish spectacle in Germany prior to Hitler's accession to power. In August the rightist newspaper *Allgemeine Deutsche Waffenring* (*The General*

German Battle Circle) opposed Cohn's appointment on the grounds of political nonconformity, that it "did not accord to the disposition of the Breslau student body."[12] The Breslau organization of "free students," pro-Nazi in orientation and purpose, joined the chorus, condemning Cohn for "belong[ing] to the race that bears the guilt for betraying our German people on November 9, 1918."[13] The university dean, Ludwig Waldecker, sought official support from Berlin for Cohn's appointment. Berlin was silent. Hoping the unrest would subside, he postponed Cohn's opening lecture for two weeks—until November 9, 1932.

November 9, it will be remembered, was for Germany the ignominious anniversary of the signing of the Treaty of Versailles in 1918. Waldecker could not have chosen a more inflammatory date to introduce to the faculty a Jewish professor already under siege in the press. In Waldecker's defense, it is doubtful that he intended to set up Cohn for a fall, for the following year he himself was released from the University of Breslau because of his inability to prove that he was not Jewish, and in 1935 was forced into early retirement. No matter, the choice of November 9 was the kiss of Judas. Before Cohn began his lecture student protests erupted. Helmut Heiber, a student present, wrote in his notes: "Lecture hall V filled to overflowing, crowds, whistles, 'songs about the Fatherland,' 'Away with Jews!,' 'Away with Cohn!'"[14] University president Carl Brockelmann and Vice President for Business Affairs Albrecht Fischer personally escorted Cohn into the lecture hall. Rather than securing Cohn's position, the advocacy of the two highest university officials fueled student protests. From the lecture room and hallways students shouted, "Jews, get out!," "We want German professors!," "Synagogue!," "An end with Jews!," "Away with the Jews!"[15] A melee broke out with punching and kicking. President Brockelmann called in the police. Heiber's notes continued, "President, police, clearing out, flight to the classrooms and then under police protection through the University, out of the University, and into the old city."[16] Ernst Cohn's inaugural lecture had sparked a riot at the University of Breslau. The university was closed for two weeks.

It reopened on November 22. Cohn's lectures were transferred to the third floor of the university main building. Eugen Rosenstock-

Huessy, a member of "the Lohmeyer circle" in Breslau, tried to secure the stairs to the third floor with barbed wire. Heavily armed police patrolled the university on foot and horseback. Student IDs were required for entry to university buildings. President Brockelmann, who was away from the university on the twenty-second, designated Lohmeyer as deputy president in his absence. When Cohn resumed his lectures, insurgency broke out again.[17] Here is Cohn's personal testimony of the mayhem.

> Shortly before the coming to power of Nazism Nazi-inspired students' riots broke out at the University which were chiefly directed against me. During that trying time I found in Professor Lohmeyer the strongest and most determined supporter. I am still convinced that if he had been the Rector instead of being the Deputy-Rector, he would have succeeded in quelling through his strong personality and with his unfaltering democratic faith . . . the riots at their very start. On one occasion when Professor Lohmeyer believed me to be personally threatened he tried to shield me against students who wanted to attack me with his own person.[18]

Lohmeyer called for police support, and once again the university was closed. His student assistant Hannah Sommer recalled the incident in a 1946 letter on his behalf. "Professor Lohmeyer stood in strong opposition to the influence of National Socialist politics on the life and work of the University. . . . He faced the heaviest attacks in his defense of Cohn. Unintimidated, he defended his position several times against the severe hostility of student masses. His person—and also his house and summer house in Glasegrund—became a refuge for Jewish students and colleagues at the time."[19]

Sommer's testimony of the "severe hostility" to which Lohmeyer was subjected, yet without being intimidated, evokes memories of my experiences in connection with antiwar and civil rights protests in America in the late 1960s. In a particular protest punches were thrown, one of which hit one of my seminary professors in the face. Such incidents were not uncommon in heated demonstrations. Nevertheless, it is easy to underestimate how traumatic the effects of such an experience can be. The professor who was hit suffered something of an emotional collapse that took him out of the classroom for a full semester, and the event's residual effects lasted even longer. Lohmeyer, as Ernst Cohn and Hannah Sommer testify, knew from personal experience what it was like to be on the receiving end of malice and violence.

In December the university reopened yet again, but the momentum against Cohn was not to be halted. Professor Karl Bornhausen, a pro-Nazi theology professor, opened an ethics lecture by thanking students for their participation in the "battle against Cohn." It is important to note that Bornhausen's lecture was not interrupted! He concluded the lecture by leading six-hundred-plus students in an anti-Semitic march through the streets of Breslau.

Shortly before Christmas 1932, Cohn weakened his already tenuous position at the university with an unguarded reply to a newspaper reporter's question. When asked whether he believed Leon Trotsky should be granted political asylum in Germany, Cohn failed to give a sufficiently negative answer. Naïve political statements were costly in Germany at the time; Cohn's was particularly so, for it suggested that he was a communist sympathizer. The press pounced on the comment, sure evidence, Nazi propaganda maintained, that Jews supported Germany's archenemy in Russia.

A bottle of foul-smelling liquid was hurled through the front window of President Brockelmann's house in an apparent attempt at firebombing. Brockelmann withdrew his support for Cohn, as did several professors, further eroding Cohn's support within the university. Cohn's lectures were resumed at the end of January 1933 on the eve of Hitler's accession to power. Protests again ensued, more violent than before: two students were critically injured and several were arrested. Only five professors still remained in Cohn's corner, including Lohmeyer, Rosenstock-Huessy, and three members of the theology and philosophy faculties. Hitler's accession to power in January 1933 made him a fixed and formidable feature of German life, and the intoxication with National Socialism was not to be stemmed. Jewish businesses were subjected to enforced boycotts, and the April Law for the Restoration of Civil Service made it legal to retire Jewish professors. Ernst Joseph Cohn was officially dismissed. Shortly thereafter he emigrated to England.

The "Cohn scandal," as it was known, was six months of Nazi political theater. The long and arduous process of removing Cohn led not to a respite but to revived momentum in purging the university. Carl Brockelmann resigned as president and was replaced by Gustav Adolf Walz, an implacable Nazi Party member since 1931. Dean Waldecker also retired and was replaced by National Socialist Anton Jirku.[20] This left Lohmeyer, the remaining member of the university administration, to blame for the "Cohn scandal." Walz and Jirku made sure that blame was not forgotten.

The Fate of Richard Hönigswald

The relentless assault on Ernst Cohn served notice to Jewish faculty members of what awaited them at the University of Breslau. Membership in "the Lohmeyer circle" was largely Jewish in number, and its members were defenseless against the anti-Semitic bile surging through the university. Each member of the fellowship faced his fate alone. Richard Koebner emigrated to Israel, where he would teach for many years at the Hebrew University. Eugen Rosenstock-Huessy left for America. He took a post at Harvard University but did not find Harvard receptive to his conviction that God was a living presence in history. He transferred to Dartmouth, and later into social programs in the Roosevelt administration.

Richard Hönigswald's fate deserves brief consideration not only because he was Lohmeyer's most important confidant but also because his story illustrates what happened to Jews who sought to remain in Germany. Before the dam broke against Jewish professors in Breslau, Hönigswald sought to reestablish his career in a less volatile context by accepting a call in 1929 to become professor of philosophy at the University of Munich. The same year, he married Hilde Bohn, hoping to begin a new life in Munich. In April 1933, however, the Law for the Restoration of Civil Service was enacted, empowering a racially despotic state to eliminate Jews and political opponents from German civil service. Hönigswald had been received into the Christian church by baptism twenty years earlier, but his Jewish ancestry still made him a Jew in German law, and thus well within reach of the law of restoration. Many German academics and philosophers appealed on his behalf in his effort to secure his professorship at Munich. In the end, however, their appeals were unsuccessful, largely because Germany's most famous philosopher at the time, Martin Heidegger, wrote a denunciation of Hönigswald. In 1933, Heidegger, a member of the Nazi Party, became a "führer president" of the University of Freiburg. Hönigswald, wrote Heidegger, was "dangerously smart,"[21] but he "championed a futile neo-Kantian dialectic"[22] that threatened to deceive and lead young German students astray. "The call of such a man to the faculty of the University of Munich can only be deemed a scandal," he insisted. Heidegger had been raised and educated as a Roman Catholic, and he conceded that "the Catholic system of education might look with favor on professors who are so-called politically inoffensive liberals."[23] But the wave of Nazism sweeping through Germany carried Heidegger swiftly away from any such sympathies, and he added defiantly that he would not look with favor on such professors! Along with Alfred Loewy, Edmund Husserl—to whom Heidegger had been a professorial assistant!—and several other professors of Jewish descent, Richard Hönigswald, in the words of Lohmeyer's daughter Gudrun, "was driven out of the university under the direct influence of the philosopher Martin Heidegger."[24]

Richard and Hilde Hönigswald lived in virtual isolation for the next five years, mostly in Munich but for long stretches of time also in Italy. In 1938 Hönigswald's doctorate of philosophy was officially revoked, thus eliminating all future prospects to be a professor in Germany. Hönigswald received a call to become professor of philosophy at the University of Scranton in America in 1938. But *Reichskristallnacht*—"Night of Broken Glass"—intervened on November 9 of that year, and in the pogrom that followed Hönigswald was rounded up and put in the concentration camp of Dachau for the remainder of the fall. Despite a decade of persecution, in comparison to the vast majority of Jews in Nazi Germany, Hönigswald belonged to a very fortunate few. International protests on his behalf succeeded in securing his release from Dachau. He sought temporary refuge in Switzerland, after which he emigrated to America in 1939. He died in New Haven, Connecticut, in 1947.

In 1995, I met with Hönigswald's son, Henry. The son of Richard and his first wife, Gertrud, Henry was born in 1915. He had been educated at the places where his father had taught—Breslau, Munich, Zürich, Padua, Florence. When the family emigrated to America, Henry was in his midtwenties and already an accomplished linguistics scholar. He taught at the University of Pennsylvania as professor of linguistics from 1948 until 1985, during which time he was elected to the National Academy of Sciences and served as president of the Linguistic Society of America.

Henry Hönigswald invited me to lunch with him at the Faculty Club of the University of Pennsylvania. He was eighty years old at the time and retired, inviting and convivial in conversation. His eyes sparkled as he recounted the friendship between his father and Lohmeyer. He reported his father's amazement at Lohmeyer's intellectual breadth and critical faculties. As a young man, the foremost personal memories of Henry were that the Hönigswald-Lohmeyer relationship included their families as well, their wives, and also an occasional letter of Hönigswald to Gudrun, "Puppi," as she was called, and of Ernst to Henry. Henry marveled how naturally and harmoniously Hönigswald and Lohmeyer combined the intellectual and personal in their long relationship. "It is rare," he said, "for such a strong bond to exist between two especially strong characters."[25]

Hitler Takes Power

Germans are not entirely agreed on how to refer to Hitler's accession to power on January 30, 1933. Was it a *Machtübernahme*—a *reception* of power—or a *Machtergreifung*—a *seizure* of power? The latter is the more common interpretation. To be sure, it is kinder to the German conscience to say that Hitler took power than to say that they handed him power. But seizure of power is still the better of the two descriptions. In no election did the Nazi Party ever win more than one-third of the popular vote. Despite their minority status and inability in a plebiscite to achieve majority status, the party's strategy of destabilization so disabled German democracy, not least through street violence and terror, that Hitler was able to clear the board of all opposition once he had checkmated the Weimar Republic.

There were reasons—a host of reasons—why Hitler's accession to power, however it occurred and whatever it is called, was not altogether unwelcome. The financial collapse of the late 1920s had devastated Germany's economy, which had been battered and hamstrung by economic sanctions imposed by the Treaty of Versailles. The rise and expansion of "Bolshevism"—Soviet communism—were not an imaginary danger but a genuine threat to Germany's sovereignty. The unprincipled version of Weimar Republic democracy, which departed radically from customary Prussian mores, was widely viewed to undermine Germany's social and moral fabric. Above all, and always, the residual shame of Versailles's war-guilt clause poisoned Germany's national identity and pride. The one person who alone seemed capable of stemming and reversing such debilitating historical forces was Adolf Hitler. Many—very many— Germans regarded him as a salutary force in the precarious 1930s.

When Hitler assumed power on January 30, 1933, the storm that had been brewing since 1929 broke with sudden and unrelenting force over Germany. The Nazi Party did not come into existence in 1929, of course. It had been founded in the early 1920s, but improvements in the economic climate of the Weimar Republic in the latter half of the 1920s dampened the early momentum of the Nazi Party. By the spring of 1929 the appeal of the party was waning. Like so many other German political parties of the day, the Nazi Party seemed destined either to wither and die or to be absorbed into more moderate movements. Its decline was unexpectedly halted and radically reversed in the fall of the year, however. The Wall Street stock market crash in New York City on Black Tuesday, October 29, 1929, was like a malevolent defibrillator of Nazi Party fortunes. Especially Hitler's early speeches not infrequently invoked the favorable hand of "Providence" in his own affairs and in those of the party. Never would he have greater cause for gratitude to "Providence," whatever Hitler meant by the term, than for the worldwide economic crisis of 1929. The stock market crash, and the fear and panic in its aftershocks, sent Germany into an economic sinkhole. The crash sent unprecedented numbers of Germans, like a miraculous transfusion of frustrated energy, into the arteries and veins of the Hitler movement. Color and strength returned to the pallid Nazi body politic, strength upon strength, in fact. By early 1933 Adolf Hitler was supreme ruler of Germany.

Naysayers and skeptics who thought Hitler's political fantasy was mere hysteria and bombast were quickly disabused of their notions. Events that followed on the heels of his accession to power removed all doubt about Nazi determination and ability to translate political rhetoric into the cold steel of action. Within six months, perceptible changes were appearing throughout Germany. Autobahns were being stretched in long straight lines across Germany. The gears of heavy industry were turning again, manufacturing goods essential for strong economies—and strong militaries. Germany was sharply defining itself in disjunction from Europe, indeed in isolation from it. Isolation was followed by xenophobia. The economic upswing and improved mood in Germany needed to be liberated from everything that would constrain their further recovery. The most important obstacle in the way of Germany's economic and moral recovery, according to the Nazi narrative, was human rights, chiefly the rights and protection of minorities—the aged, infirm, physically and mentally disabled. And of course, the rights of Jews, at whose feet all of Germany's economic woes and national dishonor were placed. These minorities were first disdained; then their rights were revoked; and soon legal and industrial measures were introduced to eliminate their very existence.

These changes were legally binding throughout Germany, but in some areas they were enforced earlier and more rigorously than in others. The city of Breslau and its university were one such area. Some of the reasons for this were easily apparent. Breslau lay on the eastern frontier of the German Reich, in what today is Wroclow, Poland, where the number of Jews living in the city, and the number of Jewish professors at the university, was well above the average of other German cities and universities. Other reasons were subtler but perhaps more important. The Nuremberg Laws of 1935 that deprived Jews of German citizenship would play a more consequential role in the populace and politics of Breslau than they would in most other German locales. Since the late 1800s, Breslau had been close to 100 percent German, and hence—for the Nazi Party at least—it represented something of a "firstfruits" of what Hitler envisioned for Poland. In the early 1930s, Hitler's program of *Lebensraum*—room for German expansion—in the east had not been unveiled, but it would be shortly. Breslau seems to have been a symbol of the führer's plans to establish a German demographic bulwark on the eastern border of the Reich against Russia. As if to signal the portentous change to come, Hitler traveled to Breslau in the fall of 1933 to appeal for the election of a single-party Nazi slate to the Reichstag. The vote was to be held on November 12. Such a victory, he assured his hearers, would finally vindicate Germany of the shameful disgrace of the armistice of Versailles. "See to it that this day," he admonished a rally in Breslau on November 4, 1933, "shall later be recorded in the history of our people as a day of salvation—that the record shall run: On an eleventh of November the German people formally lost its honor; fifteen years later came a twelfth of November and then the German people restored its honor to itself."[26]

The accession of Hitler to power in January 1933 was like the violent intervention of fate in a Greek play, turning a prosperous scene into an irreversible tragedy. The signs of the times were apparent to Lohmeyer before January 1933, as his presidential address and the Cohn affair made clear. But what lay ahead would be an intensification and absolutizing of the Nazism he had experienced. A totalitarianism, as the term implies, implements not only authoritarian policies but also their absolute authority among the masses. Small incidents arouse suspicion, suspicion provokes denunciation, denunciation leads to reprisal. The Nazi authorities at the University of Breslau were prepared to invoke this unforgiving chain reaction when necessary.

CHAPTER 9

The Jewish Question

The Christian faith is Christian only insofar as it bears the Jewish faith in its heart; ... and the Jewish faith is Jewish only insofar as it preserves within itself a place for the Christian faith.

Ernst Lohmeyer[1]

Literature Locked in a Cupboard

In the late 1980s I received a sabbatical from the University of Jamestown in North Dakota, where I was teaching at the time, to study for a semester at the University of Tübingen in Germany. My primary objective in studying at Tübingen was to avail myself of its outstanding New Testament faculty. Among secondary objectives was a desire to investigate the role that Tübingen theologians had played during the Nazi years. German universities were largely "Brown" between 1933 and 1945, which is to say that in general they accommodated themselves early and comfortably with Nazism. This was particularly true of some of Tübingen's more celebrated theological faculty members.

When I was a student at Princeton Seminary in the late 1960s, one of my professors who had studied at Tübingen mentioned in passing that its theological faculty had a collection of "hate Jew" literature written during the Nazi era. The collection was not catalogued, and it was kept under lock and key. The theological faculty was located in a building called the Theologicum, a large courthouse-like structure that had been in use for nearly a century. I assumed that the cache of literature I was interested in was located somewhere in the Theologicum, but I could not determine where. In time I succeeded in befriending one of the attendants in the Theologicum, who confided that the alleged collection did in fact exist. I expressed my interest in seeing the materials, and he agreed to allow me to view them on condition that I do so only when the Theologicum was closed.

But where was it kept? The attendant ushered me upstairs to a large cupboard in the hallway of the second floor that I—and every other student—walked past daily. Inside this unassuming receptacle was a cache of papers, articles, speeches, pamphlets, booklets, and books—all anti-Semitic to one degree or another. Most were copies or offprints, but there were also original typescripts. The attendant showed me where the key was kept. After the Theologicum was closed, when it was dark and quiet, I would unlock and open the cupboard, sit on the floor, and read the materials at will. Once finished, I returned the materials to the cupboard, locked it, replaced the key, and exited the building.

I spent many evenings alone in the vacated and quiet Theologicum. The cupboard became a living artery into Tübingen's fateful past. Locked and disguised, the cupboard seemed to me a closed wound but not a healed wound. I read inordinate promises of peace and prosperity in Hitler speeches—a salutary reminder back in the election year of 1988 . . . or in any election year. Minutes, reports, and conferences devoted to "the Jewish question" were bureaucratic, academic, and sanitary—and lethal in implication. Some of the anti-Semitic literature came from beyond the German-speaking world; one example was an anti-Semitic book written in English by Henry Ford in 1921. And there were materials written by German theology professors. Walter Grundmann was one of them, the founder and leader of the Institute for Research and Removal of Jewish Influence in German Ecclesiastical Life. The institute sought to legitimate Christian anti-Semitism by attempting to prove the utterly impossible—that Jesus was not a Jew but an Aryan. Exposure to such literature evoked obvious and expected sensations within me—depression, fear, anger, disgust. But it also worked a less anticipated sensation. When I faced the enemy, I became less fearful and stronger in conviction. The Greek word for "repentance" in the New Testament is *metanoia*, which means "conviction that leads to change." The person who most strongly evoked this conviction in me was the man whose writings predominated in the cupboard, Professor Gerhard Kittel.

Gerhard Kittel: Scholar in Jackboots

Like Nazism itself, Kittel was a bewildering paradox. His father, Rudolf Kittel, was famously associated with the Hebrew Old Testament, which he edited, the *Biblia Hebraica* (1905). Gerhard proudly followed in his father's footsteps, learning Hebrew from a Jewish scholar, Issar Israel Kahan, whom Kittel warmly called "a true Israelite, in whom there is no guile" (John 1:47).[2] Gerhard Kittel joined the Tübingen theological faculty in 1926; while he was there, during the latter years of the Weimar Republic, he published a number of academically respected studies in Judaism. Some studies were coauthored with Jewish scholars, and all demonstrated the close ties that exist between early Christianity and Palestinian Judaism. Throughout the 1920s Lohmeyer, as we have seen, corresponded with Gustav Ruprecht about the contours of the Meyer Commentary Series. Lohmeyer repeatedly encouraged Ruprecht to enlist Gerhard Kittel to author the volume on Hebrews.[3]

With Hitler's assumption of power in Germany, however, a switch flipped in Gerhard Kittel. He joined the Nazi Party in 1933. He became a charter member of Walter Frank's National Institute for History of the New Germany, a Nazi Party organ that endeavored to endow anti-Semitism with intellectual respectability. And he produced a significant literary apology for National Socialism throughout the duration of the Third Reich. Kittel did not advocate a street Nazism, the kind that sluiced through *Der Stürmer* (*The Stormer*) or that resulted in ugly caricatures of Jews in Nazi tabloids. He became an apologist for a more sophisticated and intellectual Nazism, "genuine Nazism" as he described it.[4]

The Jewish Question

The same year Kittel joined the Nazi Party, he published *Die Juden-frage* (*The Jewish Question*), a 136-page book that set fire to the tinder-dry landscape prepared by Nazi anti-Semitism. The uniqueness of *The Jewish Question* was not in its promotion of anti-Semitism, for by the early 1930s Nazi propaganda had gained virtually unstoppable traction in Germany. The uniqueness of *The Jewish Question*, rather, consisted in its intent to justify anti-Semitism within the intellectual culture of Germany, and especially within the church. Given its significance in this latter respect, the chief arguments of *The Jewish Question* are worth reviewing.

Kittel began with the issue of societal minorities. Most German minorities, he maintained, were natives of the country from which they came, Poles from Poland, for example, or Greeks from Greece. The Jewish minority, however, was different. Jews had no one country of origin but represented an *international* Jewish network. Such international influences, argued Kittel, inclined Jews to be disloyal to Germany and destabilize it. The particular German "Jewish problem" was further exacerbated in Kittel's thinking by Germany's long contiguous border with the Slavic East. This porous border was a gateway for east European Jews to enter Germany. Thus, concluded Kittel, whereas Jews were a potential and sporadic problem in other European countries, they were a standing and dangerous influence in Germany.

By "Jews," Kittel was not thinking primarily of *religious* Jews, that is, observant Jews who maintained Sabbath, kosher, and circumcision, for example, and who lived within communities of Jewish faith. Kittel affirmed and even advocated the rights of religious Jews to continue their lifestyles because he believed that in holding true to their Old Testament faith they would, in time and in God's will, accept Jesus Christ as their savior. For Kittel, the danger in the "Jewish question" was posed, rather, by Jews who had abandoned their Jewish faith and secularized, who "assimilated" into German society. Such Jews were especially influential in Germany's professional social stratum as bureaucrats, politicians, journalists, writers, especially in the fields of business, finance, law, medicine, and education. These assimilated Jews had intermarried with the German *Volk* and corrupted its racial purity. Assimilated Jews were not simply a polluting and "decadent" element in Germany, Kittel argued. Their true danger was their desire to dominate Germany.

This apocalyptic estimation called for a conclusive solution in Kittel's mind. He entertained three possible alternatives. The first was the extermination of Jews. This he dismissed as infeasible, for Germans surely could not succeed in exterminating a populace that the Spanish Inquisition and Russian pogroms had failed to exterminate. The mention of "extermination" naturally—and rightly—causes intense alarm and revulsion in the minds of readers familiar with the history of Nazi Germany. It is doubtful, however, that use of "extermination" connoted anything as sinister as the Nazi Holocaust. Kittel can scarcely have imagined the scale on which Nazi Germany would attempt its "Final Solution to the Jewish Problem." This does not justify the outrage of his suggestion, but his analogy of the Spanish Inquisition or Russian programs suggests that he was thinking more in terms of local and sporadic acts of violence than of a systematic program of industrialized genocide.

The second option was Zionism—extraditing Jews to Palestine. This too was dismissed as impractical, for Palestine was too small to accommodate all Jews. This led to his third option, which was to redefine and reconstitute Jews in Germany. Specifically, their German citizenship should be revoked, and they should be assigned the status of "alien guests" and resettled into benign ghettos. Kittel championed this third option in *The Jewish Question*.

Whether Kittel intended "ghettos" literally or more generally is not clear, nor is it very important, for "alien guests" would effectively make Jews social pariahs and deprive them of their rights as citizens. "Alien guest" status would forbid them from intermarrying with non-Jews and further exclude them from the professions of medicine, law, and teaching, as well as from politics and journalism. Kittel sought to justify "alien guest" status as the obverse side of the Mosaic law as prescribed in Deuteronomy 24:14 and 27:19: as non-Jews were relegated to "alien" status in Jewish communities in the Old Testament, so Jews should now be relegated to the same status in Germany. It was a moral duty to disenfranchise Jews of civil rights in the German nation, argued Kittel, "a right and obligation, if [the German nation] does not wish to surrender itself."[5]

The constant in Kittel's argument throughout *The Jewish Question* is his defense of the *Volk*—the German people, its race, blood, and land. Everything else—Christianity included!—is subordinated to this inviolable end. Kittel's understanding of Jews who had converted to Christianity made this constant particularly clear. A Christian Jew, he declared, "is my Christian brother, but not my German brother."[6] Kittel may live in heaven with a converted Jew, but not on earth—at least in Germany! Citing the example of segregated churches in America at the time, Kittel declared that Christian Jews should attend Jewish-Christian congregations, but they should not be received into membership in gentile Christian churches nor should they preach in them. No aspect of *The Jewish Question* is more damning for the *Christian* integrity of Kittel's argument than this pronouncement. In making Germanness—blood, race, and soil—more decisive with respect to the treatment of fellow human beings than the saving faith of the gospel, Kittel honored Hitler as führer above Jesus as savior. The defining issue in *The Jewish Question* was thus not Scripture or the gospel, but the German *Volk* as construed by National Socialism.

"German Christianity"

Kittel's voice was but one in a chorus of similar voices that dominated an entire wing of the German Lutheran Church. The wing, known as "German Christians," comprised no less than three-quarters of German Protestants throughout the Nazi era. The views of Gerhard Kittel, unorthodox and startling as they seem today, were actually the majority voice—or better, the majority *public* voice—in Germany at the time.

"German Christians" espoused "positive Christianity." Positive Christianity attempted to incorporate those elements of Christianity that were serviceable to the Nazi program in order to defend the Germanic peoples from biological and cultural degeneration. Positive Christianity sought to purge Christianity of "obsolete" elements, such as the Old Testament and its teaching that Jews were a chosen people. Positive Christianity jettisoned the weak and suffering Jesus of the Gospels for a heroic Jesus who championed the two forces upon which Nazism depended: nationalism and militarism. In 1933, the year Hitler assumed power, German Christians incorporated their seven hundred thousand church youth into the Hitler Youth. They planted the Nazi flag next to the altar in their churches, swearing an oath of allegiance to Hitler in worship services. Positive Christianity greeted the Third Reich as the necessary completion of the Protestant Reformation, resulting in a truly German national church. The theological foundation of positive Christianity was not limited to *sola Scriptura*—"Scripture alone"—as it was in historic German Lutheranism, but was broadened to include "orders of creation," blood, soil, the German *Volk*, and nationalism. The ecclesiastical embodiment of positive Christianity was the German Christian Church, a church-state amalgam of "One People, One Reich, One Faith." This amalgam committed itself spiritually to the same struggle to which the Nazi state committed itself politically and militarily: anticommunism, antipacifism, anti-internationalism (as in the Treaty of Versailles), anti–Free Masonry, and anti-Judaism.

The Centrality of Anti-Semitism in National Socialism

Anti-Semitism was not simply one plank among others in the Nazi Party platform. It was the central plank. As Sebastian Haffner noted in the epigraph for chapter 8, Hitler fought two wars between 1933 and 1945. The better known of the two was the war against the nations fought with largely conventional military tactics, "World War II," as we know it. The lesser known of the two—at least in the West—was the war against "subhuman" *Untermenschen*, fought primarily against the Slavs on the eastern front and against Jews throughout Europe.[7] The war against the Jews was fought with greater cruelty and determination than the war against the nations. It also began before the war against the nations. The construction of the first concentration camp at Dachau already in spring 1933, the revocation of Jewish civil rights by the Nuremberg Laws of 1935, and the torching of Jewish businesses and synagogues on *Kristall-nacht* ("Night of Broken Glass") in 1938—all these began before the opening salvo of cannon and gunfire in the invasion of Poland in September 1939.

Nor did the two wars complement each other. They more often competed with each other. The industrial resources required to eliminate eleven million Jews—that was the number of Jews consigned by the Wannsee Conference in January 1942 for extermination—did not serve the military objectives of the war against the nations. As supplies, materiel, and transportation grew scarcer at war's end, transport of Jews to extermination camps in the east often took priority over transport of troops to the various fronts. When the war against the nations had effectively been lost at the Battle of Stalingrad in early 1943, the Nazi juggernaut shunted all remaining resources into the extermination of Jews. More Jews were killed in the two years after Stalingrad than in all the years before. The precise role that anti-Semitism would play in the Nazi program was not entirely clear when Gerhard Kittel wrote *The Jewish Question*, but its general character and direction were clear enough. Assaults and vilification of Jewish professors like Ernst Cohn, the Law for the Restoration of Civil Service that disqualified Jews from civil service offices, the anti-Jewish Nazi street gangs, and above all, the slanderous defamation of Jews in Nazi speeches—all these took place *before* Kittel wrote *The Jewish Question*. Given such ominous signs, the sanitized version of National Socialism that Kittel imagined was nonsense.

A Most Dangerous Nazi

Although Kittel opposed extermination of Jews, his justification for doing so—its impracticality rather than moral abhorrence—was nevertheless chilling. I have suggested that Kittel could scarcely have anticipated the "Final Solution to the Jewish Question," at least its attempt to exterminate *all* European Jews in industrial killing centers such as Auschwitz or Treblinka. When Kittel was confronted with its reality after the war, he claimed to be horrified. He saw himself as a moderate, salutary influence in the Nazi Party. He endeavored to halt its worst excesses, mitigate its most vulgar expressions, and rehabilitate its true, even God-given, mission to be a bulwark against the liberal and enlightenment influences of the Weimar Republic that, in his mind, had weakened and corrupted Germany. National Socialism—or Kittel's ideal of it—was the sole saving force that could stem the tide of Jewish infiltration and pollution of the noble German *Volk*.

Nothing I have said about Kittel, however, is terribly different from what could be said of tens of thousands of other Nazi Party members in the 1930s. What made Kittel different, indeed paradoxical, is that at the same time he was promoting Nazism in *The Jewish Question* and in Frank's National Institute to expunge Jewish influence from German history, he commenced editing the massive, new *Theological Dictionary of the New Testament* (*TDNT*). The *Theological Dictionary of the New Testament* offered a comprehensive treatment of the vocabulary of the Greek New Testament, especially its theological significance. Kittel commenced the project in 1928, envisioning collaboration of perhaps 15 scholars who would work three years and produce two volumes. The project ultimately enlisted 105 scholars, required fifty years, and resulted in ten thick volumes. Kittel did not live to see its completion, but as editor of *TDNT* he harvested the cream of Germany's New Testament scholarly guild. Unlike Kittel's *Jewish Question* and work with Frank's institute, *TDNT* is a legitimate scholarly enterprise. If *TDNT* is not entirely free of anti-Jewish biases—and it is not, especially among some contributors and articles—its anti-Judaism is nevertheless the result of the unexamined assumptions that prevailed throughout the New Testament guild of the era in which it was written rather than the vicious and shameless invective that poisoned Kittel's *Jewish Question* and the work with Frank's institute.

Herein lies the awful paradox—a Hitler ally whose theological work benefited the church. Gerhard Kittel was an exemplary family man, an intellectual capable of conscientious scholarship, whose upright behavior was attested by students and colleagues alike. He did not do the things we normally associate with evil. His personal morality was beyond reproach. He did not lie or attempt to deceive, he was not malicious, he exhibited neither anger nor inordinate pride, and (in his own mind) he was not prejudiced. In his correspondence with Martin Buber, as we shall see, he displayed the semblance of humility and sincerity. If such a thing was possible, Kittel was a "nice Nazi."

One of Nazism's most successful evils was its ability to co-opt personal virtues of its adherents for the evils of the party, yet without corrupting the virtues or burdening the adherents with undue responsibility or guilt. Albert Speer, Hitler's chief architect and after 1943 minister of the war economy, could employ his technological genius in architecture, economics, and armaments for the Nazi program without feeling overly compromised or guilty that the Nazi Party used his talents for purposes he did not ordain. Gerhard Kittel, likewise, was able to retain both his personal integrity and his sense of innocence while adamantly promoting a view of Jews that was cruel and inevitably led to greater cruelty. He did not sing the crass "Horst Wessel" Nazi fight song. He did not identify with the theological errors and vulgar tone of the German Christians. His case for Nazism was pitched to what we today would call "the moderate middle." If in *The Jewish Question* he quoted Hitler and Nazi sources far more often that he did Scripture, Kittel was nonetheless a formidable theologian, and those who wished to challenge him needed to be equally formidable.

Was, then, Kittel a "nice Nazi"? If the central core of Nazism was its unmitigated hatred of non-Ayrans and its equally unmitigated determination to subjugate and, especially in the case of Jews, exterminate them from the earth, then Nazism itself was an unmitigated evil. One could not participate in such a program "nicely." What, then, was Kittel? In my mind he was a fool, as only an intelligent person, not least an academic, can be a fool. He adopted a utilitarian rationale, arguing that his views and theories were of greater importance than the misfortune and suffering that their consequences necessarily caused others. If Jews were deprived of their professions, denied civil rights, driven from their jobs and homes and families and places of birth, if they lost all sovereignty over their lives because of views like his, then such, in his proud mind, was the inevitable if unfortunate consequence of the rightness of his views.

And he was a fool in another respect, again the kind of folly to which the gifted and intelligent are especially vulnerable. He overestimated his importance, as though his personal influence could arrest and retard the most evil consequences of Nazism. This particular flaw made Kittel, in my estimation, a particularly dangerous Nazi, for he employed his considerable energy and influence to make Nazism respectable, and once respectable, to make it credible. His comfortable combination of such repugnant polarities—editing the *Theological Dictionary of the New Testament* at the same time that he advocated for the essence, if not the excesses, of Nazism—inevitably made people who trusted his learning more tolerant and accepting of Nazism.

And finally, from a Christian perspective, in assigning priority to the Nazi worldview of race, blood, and nation over the redemption of the gospel, Kittel was an idolater. We cannot know what Kittel prayed for when he said "Thy kingdom come" in the Lord's Prayer, but what he *argued* for in *The Jewish Question* was not the kingdom of the Father but the kingdom of the führer.

In the end, Kittel's justifications for his views did not matter. The Heinrich Himmlers and Reinhard Heydrichs and Hermann Görings gladly took the baton that he and men like him handed them, and transformed a view that Kittel merely considered "impractical" to an unimaginably evil end.[8]

Martin Buber

On June 13, 1933, Kittel sent a copy of *The Jewish Question* to Martin Buber, the noted Jewish scholar who four years later would publish the book for which he is best known, *I and Thou*. Like many German Jews, Buber was thoroughly assimilated into German life and culture, having studied at Vienna, Leipzig, Berlin, and Zürich. He had founded and edited a periodical for German-speaking Jews called *Der Jude* (*The Jew*), and at the time Kittel wrote, Buber held the first chair of Jewish philosophy of religion and ethics in Germany at the University of Frankfurt am Main. Additionally, Buber was then at work on what today stands as a magisterial translation of the Hebrew Old Testament into German.

In a cover letter to Buber, Kittel expressed "how seriously I take your life's work and how deeply I believe myself bonded to you and people like you."[9] Buber, Kittel confessed, would certainly find some of his points "hostile,"[10] but he expressed the hope that Buber would agree with his main point, which was "to set forth the 'people's' (*völkisch*) movement in such a way to justify those who were entitled by it, and *at the same time* that Jews would truly find the entitlement of German Gentiles justified."[11] Kittel hoped Buber would sense the *Redlichkeit* with which he had written *The Jewish Question*. *Redlichkeit*, meaning "honesty" or "sincerity," is crucial. Kittel had persuaded himself that his *sincerity* was not only more important than truth and justice but that it compensated for whatever injustice and evil it would bring. That Kittel imagined he could gain Buber's understanding, much less approval, for views set forth in *The Jewish Question* exhibits the utter folly to which he had succumbed.

Buber wrote a remarkably gracious and measured response to Kittel that he published as an open letter in the August 1933 issue of *Theologische Blätter* (*Theological Papers*). Buber had read the whole book "particularly closely,"[12] he confessed, especially the parts to which Kittel had directed him, looking for places "where agreement existed or might exist between"[13] Kittel and himself. The composite effect of *The Jewish Question*, however, was so dire that Buber could not concur that Kittel's position "was really just to Jews."[14] Buber politely rejected the stereotypes of "*the* Jewish doctor," "*the* Jewish lawyer," "*the* Jewish businessman" that Kittel projected onto all Jews. He rejected that Jewish writers should be forbidden to write and teach in German, a language that for centuries had been their mother tongue. That he should be dismissed from his university professorship solely on the grounds of his ethnicity he found unjust. Should German minorities living elsewhere in the world, he asked, be subjected by their host countries to the same punitive status of "alien guests"? Above all, the laws regarding aliens in the Old Testament to which Kittel appealed were not intended to harm and vilify them, as Nazi laws intended for Jews. In conclusion Buber cited Old Testament laws—laws that Kittel twisted to discriminate against Jews—in favor of humane treatment of Jews. "The same laws and regulations will apply both to you and to the alien living among you" (Num. 15:16; see also Lev. 24:22). "For the Lord your God . . . shows no partiality. He defends the cause of the fatherless and the widow and loves the foreigners residing among you. You are to love those who are foreigners" (Deut. 10:17–19).[15]

Lohmeyer to Buber

When Lohmeyer read Buber's open letter to Kittel, he immediately wrote Buber from his Schlesian summer house at Glasegrund:

Glasegrund near Habelschwerdt, August 19, 1933

My Esteemed Colleague,

I have just read your open letter to Gerhard Kittel, and I am compelled to say that each word of it is spoken as if from my own heart. What compels me is not only the spiritual bond that I feel with you—although its rarity in these days makes me especially aware of it—but rather to say openly how shameful it is that theological colleagues are able to think and write as they do, and that the Protestant Church, like a ship without a captain that is driven off course by the shifting political windstorm of the present, is able to remain as silent as it does. May this letter be a token of assurance to you that not all theological professors, not even all New Testament professors, share Kittel's opinions.

Please do not imagine that I do not take the matters about which you write absolutely seriously. If only people would be honest about what is actually at stake in all this. The issue is not simply about persons, not even about the state, or *Volk*, or race, or the sense—or better, *nonsense*—of the horrible slogans that are hurled about. It is not possible either to question or answer any of these because every assured consensus has vanished, and all discourse is polarized into point and counterpoint, feelings and sentiments. The oppression that results should not be met with words but rather with help.

The issue here is one of faith—for the one Book that both binds and constrains us is also the Book that divides us. It seems to be very difficult for German Christendom to understand and embrace the two sides of this reality. What is needed is an extensive clarification of all the historical and material presuppositions on which this two-sided reality rests. I cannot address these presuppositions now, nor do I need to explain them to you. I hope that you will be in agreement with me in this, that the Christian faith is Christian only insofar as it bears the Jewish faith in its heart; I do not know if you will be able also to affirm the reverse, that the Jewish faith is Jewish only insofar as it preserves within itself a place for the Christian faith.

This is not to say that the differences between Judaism and Christianity should not be vigorously debated. Nevertheless, at root in the debate is the inner issue of the sincerity, truth, and ineffability of faith itself. I know almost nothing more paramount for a Christian theologian than this question of Judaism. And it is a bitter experience for me that in our Christian and theological publications one so easily succumbs to politically or similarly tainted slogans as happens in Kittel's concept of "duty with respect of aliens," which is a flimsy moth-eaten religious cloak for a political expedient. More bitter still is that once the defamation is politically or socially carried out, no theologian and no church speaks the word of their Master to the victim: "You are my Brother!" Demands are made, but no help is offered. If we are to come to terms with all that is happening, we must repeatedly remind ourselves that we have never drifted further from the Christian faith than we have at present. All that remains for us is the faint hope of the renewal of Christianity, as you personally hope for the renewal of Judaism. Only then, in my mind, will the ground be properly prepared for each fruitfully to resolve the questions posed by the other.

I express to you my heartfelt thanks for your open letter and offer my sincere collegial greeting. Even though you do not know me personally, I nevertheless stand united with you, as of old, now anew.[16]

Nazi Anti-Semitism in 1933

Lohmeyer's letter was one of the earliest and most definitive protests against Nazi anti-Semitism to be heard in Germany. It was also a signature witness to the inseverable relationship between Judaism and Christianity. The "Aryan paragraph," which extended the Nazi exclusion of non-Aryans from civil service to the church, had been implemented only two months earlier. Already in summer 1933, six months after Hitler's accession to power and before the Pastors' Emergency League had been formed, or the Marburg declaration on the "race question" issued, or the Confessing Church organized, Lohmeyer raised a prophetic voice in defense of Martin Buber and against an idolatrous perversion of Christianity.

What might have accounted for Lohmeyer's solidarity with Jews? It is important to remember that less than 2 percent of the German population was Jewish in 1930. It was thus quite possible for Germans to live day to day, even their whole lives, without any meaningful contact with Jews. Lohmeyer had had greater exposure to German Jews than had the average German, for Vlotho, where his father was a pastor when he was a boy, had a Jewish synagogue. Dealings and acquaintances between Jews and gentiles in Vlotho would have been inevitable. Moreover, Lohmeyer's circle of Jewish colleagues at Breslau increased and deepened his relationships with Jews.

Lohmeyer's letter to Buber was grounded in more than personal association with Jews, however, important as that was. It was grounded in a theological understanding that was rooted in Scripture. Other New Testament scholars and theologians, of course, could claim equal scriptural erudition. But the climate change of Nazism caused most of them to distance themselves from "the Jewish question," and some of them to become forthright apologists for anti-Semitism. Kittel's elevation of "Germanness" over Christian confession was a prime example of the latter. Lohmeyer, by contrast, did not confuse the leading of the führer with that of the Good Shepherd. The revelation of God in the Old and New Testaments provided the proper and saving truth on "the Jewish question," and for Lohmeyer it was decisive, the final truth.

By the time Lohmeyer wrote to Buber, he had already experienced the vulgar and violent side of Nazi anti-Semitism. The Cohn affair, mentioned in the last chapter, was an ugly omen of things to come. Once Hitler came to power on January 30, 1933, such acts ceased being criminal and quickly assumed legitimacy in Germany. The Reichstag fire of February1933, a month after Hitler's accession to power, resulted in a wave of arrests and terror throughout Germany against Jews, communists, and social democrats. On April 1, twelve weeks after Hitler came to power, Nazi boycotts of Jewish businesses commenced.

The response of the church to these early outbursts of anti-Semitism was regrettably flat-footed. No voice of protest, naturally, came from the majority Protestant church, the "German Christians," which principally supported anti-Semitism. The voice of the Catholic Church was muted as well, although for different reasons. In July 1933—a month before Buber's open letter to Kittel was published—the Vatican signed a Reich's Concord with the Third Reich. The concord was a treaty that guaranteed Catholics freedom from interference by the state, including exemption of Catholic youth from joining the Hitler Youth, in exchange for noninterference by the church and Vatican in National Socialist rule of Germany. There would of course be many individual Catholics who bravely and sacrificially resisted Nazism, but the Reich's Concord effectively neutralized opposition of the Catholic Church as an *organizational entity* against Nazism. A "concord," by definition, signifies "oneness of heart." It was never a wise idea—above all for the church—to seek oneness of heart with Hitler.

The remaining branch of the church left to resist Nazi anti-Semitism was Protestants opposed to "German Christianity." This constituency was not defined or organized when Lohmeyer wrote Buber, although within a year the Barmen Declaration was published and the Confessing Church was formed. One could hope that the Confessing Church would have expanded its protest against the Aryan paragraph to a plenary condemnation of Nazi anti-Semitism. Sadly, that was not the case. Even Confessing Church warhorses like Martin Niemöller, Karl Barth, and Otto Dibelius opted for silence on "the Jewish question." Given the circumstances at the time, this was not surprising. From a strategic perspective it may even have been advisable, for it limited the fronts on which the Confessing Church had to contend against Nazism. Nevertheless, the expedient of silence on "the Jewish question" left the Confessing Church with no protest to the most diabolical element of Nazism. And it left the church with a troubled conscience. When the Confessing Church conducted its moral housekeeping at the end of the war in October of 1945, it issued "The Stuttgart Confession of Guilt" for its failure to speak out for Jews.

"You Are My Brother"

It was within this context that Lohmeyer wrote to Buber. The most important aspect of the letter was his unambiguous declaration of opposition to anti-Semitism. Lohmeyer stood *with* Buber as a victim, and he raised his gentile German voice *for* the victim. No less important, Lohmeyer unmasked the fraudulence of Kittel's position. Lohmeyer was a man of restraint and composure, a model of Christian and Kantian ethics in virtually every respect. Kittel's attack on Buber kindled righteous indignation in him, however. Twice in the letter he named Kittel personally. He shamed him—a "theological faculty member" and "New Testament scholar"—for slogan mongering and attempting to justify Nazi barbarism theologically. Most damning of all, Lohmeyer accused Kittel of betraying Jesus Christ: "no theologian and no church speaks the word of their Master to the victim." Lohmeyer's frontal assault indicates not only his opposition to Kittel's anti-Semitism but also the *danger* he perceived it to represent.

Lohmeyer was not a Jew, but he was not invulnerable to Kittel's influence. Gerhard Kittel's scholarly influence exceeded Lohmeyer's at the time, and he may have used it against Lohmeyer. As editor of the *Theological Dictionary of the New Testament*, Kittel relied on scores of Germany's leading New Testament scholars as contributors. Lohmeyer's commentaries and scholarly articles put him in the top echelon of New Testament scholars at the time. Some fifty German New Testament scholars contributed articles on hundreds of Greek New Testament words in the four volumes of *TDNT* that Kittel edited during Lohmeyer's lifetime. Perhaps the most remarkable observation that could be made about the contributors in the first four volumes is that Ernst Lohmeyer was the most important German scholar *not* to be included among them. It is difficult to imagine that the omission of Lohmeyer was an oversight on Kittel's part.

Two further aspects of Lohmeyer's letter deserve note. The first is its *scope*. Lohmeyer's advocacy for Buber was revolutionary not simply because he stood in contrast to the church's muted response to anti-Semitism in the early Nazi years but equally because he broached the larger question of the relationship of Judaism and Christianity. He ventured a unique understanding of the relationship between the two religions in terms of progression rather than opposition. In a charitable overture, he asked if Buber could not endorse the same understanding. "I hope that you will be in agreement with me in this, that the Christian faith is Christian only insofar as it bears the Jewish faith in its heart; I do not know if you will be able also to affirm the reverse, that the Jewish faith is Jewish only insofar as it preserves within itself a place for the Christian faith."

It has been typical in Christianity to characterize the relationship between the Old and New Testaments, Judaism and Christianity, in terms of *contrast*. According to this construct, the Old Testament and Judaism teach "law"—works, obedience, judgment; the New Testament and Christianity teach "gospel"—faith, freedom, the love and grace of God. This law/gospel dichotomy is partly true, but only partly so, for the Old Testament and Judaism also witness to God's love and grace, and the New Testament and Christianity also appeal to works and obedience. The dichotomy too easily pits law and gospel against one another, encouraging the assumption of Christian privilege and superiority, and with it, supremacy and pride. The law/gospel dichotomy was wet clay in the hands of German Christians in the Nazi era.

Lohmeyer surmounted this dichotomy by setting Judaism and Christianity in complementary relation to one another. The relationship was one of continuity—of promise and fulfillment—rather than of conflict. It echoed Augustine's famous depiction of the New

Testament concealed in the Old Testament and the Old Testament revealed in the New Testament. The apostle Paul had typically been interpreted as the champion of the superiority of gospel to law, and hence of Christianity to Judaism. But in his 1929 *Fundamentals of Pauline Theology*,[17] Lohmeyer interpreted Paul's understanding as one of development rather than antithesis, as "extension" (*Verlängerung*) or "renewal" of the divine purpose from Judaism to Christianity. Israel was not a failure of the divine purpose but a formative kernel at the heart of Christianity, and Christianity is not a corruption of Judaism but its necessary and essential point of maturity. In his 1937 commentary on the Gospel of Mark, Lohmeyer would illustrate this same understanding with the messianic hope. In the flow chart of salvation history, there was an indivisible development between Isaiah's "Servant of the Lord" and Jesus as "Son of Man." Jesus Christ was the fulfillment of the prophetic promise in Isaiah. Both promise and fulfillment, type and realization, constitute the *one* revelation of God in both Old and New Testaments.[18]

And now the second noteworthy aspect of the letter—Lohmeyer's reference to Buber as "brother." We know of no other Christian leader or theologian or biblical scholar at the time who said to a Jew, "You are my brother." It would be another seven years before Dietrich Bonhoeffer would call Jews brothers. It would not be until the second half of the twentieth century that Jewish-Christian dialogue, provoked in large measure by the horrors of the Holocaust, would think in terms of a sibling relationship between Judaism and Christianity. Not until Pope John Paul II's 1987 visit to the Jewish synagogue in Rome—the first such visit in history—would the Jew as "brother" be heard in a pontifical utterance.

"Brother" signifies a genetic relationship between Judaism and Christianity. "Brother" is also the New Testament word for "neighbor" in the Old Testament, signifying a relationship established by Jesus Christ, and thus the impossibility of Lohmeyer abandoning Buber as a brother. Buber was twelve years Lohmeyer's senior, and German grammar obliged Lohmeyer to address Buber formally, "*Mein Bruder sind Sie.*" Instead, Lohmeyer addressed Buber intimately, "*Mein Bruder bist Du.*" In so doing, Lohmeyer followed Buber's lead in his theological and philosophical classic of the twentieth century, *Ich und Du*, the English title of which is *I and Thou*. Buber believed there were two types of relationships in the world: "I-It" relationships and "I-Thou" relationships. The former were relationships with *things*—quantifiable, weighable, tangible. I-It relationships were necessary, of course, but not fulfilling and not humanizing. I-Thou relationships were *personal*, providing meaning and purpose in life. An I-It relation was one of "content," in Buber's words, but an I-Thou relationship was one of "personal presence and strength."[19]

Lohmeyer wrote an I-Thou letter to Buber. In addressing Buber as "*Du*," Lohmeyer, a virtual stranger, joined him as a strengthening presence. The Nazi stigmatized Buber as "alien"; the Christian honored him as "brother." Buber never forgot Lohmeyer's solidarity. In November 1946, Lohmeyer's son Hartmut visited Buber in Israel, where he had emigrated in 1938. Buber told Hartmut, "When things got ugly in Germany after 1933, your father paid me a visit in Heppenheim, the small town where I was living in southwest Germany. When he checked in at the hotel, he announced, 'I have come here to visit Herr Professor Buber!'"[20] The curiosity in this pearl of family lore is that Gudrun, who related the story from her elder brother Hartmut, never said whether Lohmeyer actually met with Buber. We presume—and hope—he did. But Nazi regulations may have prevented it. The simple gesture of *coming* nevertheless remained for Buber "a personal presence and strength."

In National Socialism, Martin Buber was an *It*, stripped of his citizenship and vilified for his religion. Lohmeyer *came* to Buber, *announced his name and title*, and in so doing treated him as *Thou*.

The Benedictine Monks of Beuron

I began this chapter with a cupboard of forbidden literature in the Theologicum at the University of Tübingen. I likened the cupboard to an artery to the past, a secret passage, perhaps. Like all secret passages, this one took me to places I never expected, and not simply to the past. It led to unexpected places in the present, to a monastery, in fact, where the darkness of the cupboard led to a foreshadowing of light.

There were so many visiting scholars studying in Tübingen when I was there in 1987–1988 that I was forced to find a place outside Tübingen where my family and I could live. We found a place near Ravensburg. Ravensburg was far enough away from Tübingen that I occasionally spent nights in Tübingen rather than drive home. When I did so, I often stayed with the mother of the man from whom we rented our house near Ravensburg. Her name was Frau Rapp, and her deceased husband, Rev. Paul Rapp, had been a pastor in Tübingen during World War II. Frau Rapp and I often lingered after breakfast and talked. I never failed to profit from her wealth of knowledge about Tübingen. In one of our conversations I mentioned that I had been reading anti-Semitic literature in the Theologicum. She mentioned, somewhat offhandedly, that Gerhard Kittel had been a friend of her late husband, as had Martin Buber. When they visited their home, in fact, both had sat in the same chair I was sitting in.

"What eventually happened to Kittel?" I asked. Frau Rapp reported that Kittel was arrested as a Nazi collaborator by the French when they occupied Tübingen in May of 1945, imprisoned for a year and a half, and then released. His pension as a university professor was annulled, however, and he was forbidden from returning to Tübingen. Kittel was homeless and penniless. Fortunately, the Benedictine monks at Beuron took him in for the final season of his life. At Beuron, Kittel commenced work on the fifth volume of the *Theological Dictionary of the New Testament* before he died in 1948.

Sometime later my wife and I were driving along the headwaters of the Danube where Beuron is located. We stopped at the magnificent Benedictine monastery. I asked the monk attending the visitors desk if he could tell me where Kittel had lived when he was there. The monk looked at me quizzically. "Do you mean the Kittel of *TDNT* fame?"

"Yes," I said. "Gerhard Kittel."

"Kittel was never here," the monk said. "Whatever gave you that idea?"

I preferred not to tell him that an old lady told me so. I had learned not to distrust Frau Rapp's information, however, unlikely as it seemed at the moment. The attending monk was perhaps forty-five years old, and not old enough to have been at Beuron when Kittel was allegedly there. "Is there a monk still alive who lived at the monastery in 1945?" I asked. "If so, would you please call him on the phone and inquire about Kittel?" I was straining the credulity and patience of the monk, but I persisted as cordially as I knew how.

The monk's Benedictine forbearance fortunately overcame his annoyance, and he dialed a number. He dutifully repeated my request to the man who answered. A rather long silence ensued, punctuated by occasional inflections—"Really?" ... "Is that so!" ... "Hard to believe." When the monk put down the receiver, he turned politely to me and said, "Brother So-and-So remembers Kittel. He says you are the first person to ask about him. The Brother is too old to come and meet you, but it is as you said. Kittel was here for over a year. He spent his time working on the *Theological Dictionary of the New Testament*. He was finally allowed to return to Tübingen where he died."

"Why would Beuron take in a man like Kittel?" I asked.

"The Rule of Benedict teaches us to receive all guests as Christ," the monk said. "There were many people like Kittel who had nowhere to go after the war. We took them in."

The fates of Kittel, Buber, and Lohmeyer ended in ironies of providential proportions. Kittel's final years were particularly dramatic. Like King David, who called down holy wrath on sinners, only to be told by the prophet Nathan, "You are the man!" (2 Sam. 12:7), and like Haman, who himself perished on the scaffold from which he intended to hang Jews (Esther 7), Gerhard Kittel, the influential university professor, died in the status he had prescribed for Martin Buber—an alien in Germany! Martin Buber, on the other hand, did not die in the status to which Kittel consigned him. He died as an honored citizen of the new Jewish state in Israel. And Ernst Lohmeyer? His fate became the not-unusual fate of those who take a stand for truth and justice.

CHAPTER 10

Battle at Breslau

Herr Lohmeyer's anti–National Socialist behavior and his anti–National Socialist way of thinking are a commonly known fact!

Dr. Gustav Walz[1]

Preaching in Breslau

Throughout his Breslau years, Lohmeyer preached regularly in chapel services. Breslau was a Jesuit university, and Lohmeyer did not preach in its magnificent baroque chapel but at the Protestant church of St. Christopher several blocks away. In his ordination sermon back in 1912, Lohmeyer had set forth a short slate of essentials for the Christian, or at least for himself as a Christian pastor. The life required of a pastor, he concluded, was the same life, if in slightly different ways, required of all disciples of Jesus Christ. "All life presses restlessly toward action," he wrote. Withdrawal and passivity were not Christian options. "The life we bring to others can only be brought in personal ways, just as others brought life to us in personal ways. . . . A life in God and in his love, and a life among people and in service to them—both are inseparably bound together. That is the gift and task of our 'call,' which comes to us new every day."[2] The gospel needed to be communicated not only through the pastor's mouth but also through his hands and feet.

Lohmeyer practiced such a ministry at Breslau, one form of which was preaching at fall and spring convocations. He focused on a scriptural text, often a single verse, posing rhetorical questions that engaged hearers. He developed his ideas in wordplays, alliteration, homophones, and contrasts. His sermons were carefully and artistically structured yet free from affectation. His message was purposeful and passionate but not melodramatic. His preaching met hearers in their daily lives and called them to *acts* of trust and hope. German academics were strong on *logos*—rationality— but Lohmeyer was equally strong on *ethos*—trust and credibility, not only with fellow professors but also with his student hearers. His hearers were witnessing the demise and collapse of the Weimar Republic, the evisceration of the German economy first in Treaty of Versailles reparations and later in the financial crisis of 1929, and in the rising, unstoppable tide of Nazism. Especially his younger hearers must have felt very alone and vulnerable at a large and impersonal German university as they witnessed such things. When we hear Lohmeyer's sermons through such ears, we hear a cure of souls. The sermons reverberate with the conviction that God knew what was going on in Germany. They assure hearers of God's promise, "I am with you."

Lohmeyer did not preach what might be called "political sermons." By the early 1930s, certainly, direct and adverse references to Nazism were not tolerated. A preacher might not make it home safely that day, or if he did, his house might be torched that night. Nevertheless, Lohmeyer's sermons were delivered during the ominous changing of the guard in Germany from the Weimar Republic to Nazism. This context was seldom absent from Lohmeyer's mind as he prepared and delivered his sermons, and it conditioned their reception and effect. His February 1931 text was the temptation of Jesus in Matthew 4. He began by reading his hearers' thoughts. "Jesus teaches us to pray, 'Lead us not into temptation,' and among 'us' no one—including Jesus himself—is excluded. Temptations are ever present, and they remain as long as people know and choose what to do. No one is exempted. If temptations were to cease, a life of choosing and acting would itself cease."[3]

No one, of course, wants to be tempted. Did not Jesus teach disciples to pray, "Lead us not into temptation" (Matt. 6:13)? Does not the New Testament assure readers that God cannot be tempted

(James 1:13)? It is only natural that we wish to be like God in this respect. But we are not like God. We are creatures, fallible and tempted. We lament the reality in which we live. Lohmeyer encouraged his hearers to face this temptation rather than lament it. "Dear friends, don't shy away from this question: if only misery and horrors would cease, if only people could live in peace and harmony, if only the world wasn't splintered and torn apart as it is today."[4] This blissful longing, Lohmeyer warned, was actually the most dangerous of temptations. "All unlimited longings are in the deepest sense directed against God."[5] Why? Because such longings long for a reality of our own making rather than of *God's* making. Nay, worse: they long for propitious circumstances rather than for God himself. "God is not a fanciful dream, and there is nothing fantastical in him: to speak of God means to speak of the strong bond of our life with all of God's vulnerabilities."[6] Whoever is bound to Jesus knows what it means to be a bearer of God's light in a world of darkness. Here Lohmeyer made a critical connection with his hearers: their temptations and even their fears are evidence of the light of God's Spirit within them. In this respect they share a similar fate with Jesus. But they also share the same blessing. God, in his grace, sends his ministering angels to believers, as he did to his Son Jesus.[7]

Nazism had not prevailed in Germany when Lohmeyer preached this sermon in 1931. Nor was it named in this sermon or in any other. Lohmeyer's prescience and admonition, however, could not be clearer. The way of Christ lay not in escape from the struggle besieging Germany, nor in succumbing to the myth of a national redeemer. It lay in "binding" oneself to the revelation of God's light in this world in the cross of Jesus Christ.

Lohmeyer was clear about the vital nerves of the National Socialist agenda, and he was equally clear about the mandate of the gospel in relation to them. A particularly exposed nerve was paranoia. Nazism sought from the outset to direct the national gaze inward, toward the German *Volk*. The inward migration and absorption with the *Volk* inevitably led to German isolation and xenophobia. Everything outside the sacred inner circle became the enemy—"outsiders," "foreigners," and "international interests." Already in 1925, in a sermon on Matthew 18:13, Lohmeyer warned against taking refuge in a nationalism defined in terms of ethnic collectivism.

> We hear so much today about the duty of the individual to maintain community with those who share his bonds of blood or race, or whose manner of life is compatible with his own. And we are further told that this duty is incontestable. But all these roots of community fail to reach the soil in which the community of faith is grounded. In this ground, the believer does not have or hold community, rather, the believer *is* the community. This community is as real as the believer's community with God himself. That is the meaning of Jesus's double commandment: "You shall love God and your neighbor as yourself."[8]

As Germany shut its windows and doors in national isolation, individual Germans experienced personal isolation as well, especially if their hearts and minds were not in absolute accord with Nazism. Lohmeyer addressed this unspoken fear toward the end of his tenure in Breslau in April 1934. By then Germany was eighteen months into full-on Nazism. In a sermon on John 16:7, "Unless I go away, the Comforter will not come to you," Lohmeyer asked a rhetorical question: Where might believers find a place to stand amid the inescapable contrasts of joy and sorrow, death and glory, abandonment and truth? "When we look around today, where do we find a safe place either to stand or from which to move forward? Our alternatives are chaotically confused—rejoicing and crying, peril and salvation, death and life. . . . We are told, 'A new springtime is going through our land,' and yet we see grief and trouble etched deeper and deeper into the hearts and faces of the people of this land."[9] He needed say no more. The listening ear could hear the fanatical rants of Hitler and Goebbels, the inner eye could see boycotts and marauding Nazi street gangs, the throbbing heart could feel spreading malignancy in civic life, scapegoating of Jews, irrational fears. If such was the Nazi "springtime," what would winter hold?

Lohmeyer then shifted to Jesus's disciples. Their faces were etched with the same sorrows and apprehensions when Jesus told them he must go to the Father. Their hearts were troubled. "What did Jesus say to them?" asked Lohmeyer. He did not commiserate with them. He said the wholly unexpected. "It is good for you that I go!"[10] This dismayed the disciples, just as Germany in 1934 dismayed many of Lohmeyer's hearers. What good could there be in Jesus leaving the disciples . . . or in the darkness engulfing Germany? But Jesus remained steadfast: "It is good for you that I go." Lohmeyer remained steadfast: "It is good!"[11] " 'It is good'—even and indeed precisely the death of the Lord himself. This is the final security, this the only truth. The issue is no longer about you and me, about our wills and wishes, no longer about laments and despair. In all life and death, in all chances and changes, stands this one thing: 'It is good.'"[12] How can this be good, either for the disciples or for Germans? When we affirm the rightness of the path God sets before us, said Lohmeyer, only then can we submit to God's will. "In so doing we hear in the words of the Lord simply of God's reality in this one death, in which all truth and consolation are anchored. These words speak of guidance and not of demand, of promise and not of ultimatum. They speak of a once-for-all occurrence that changes all misery and all death into the one path on which we walk safely and protected."[13]

As I hear Lohmeyer's sermons, I think, How dangerous it is to preach! How dangerous to declare the divine irony of the gospel that it is good for Jesus to go to his death in Jerusalem, that it is good for the disciples to lose their lives in order to save them. How dangerous to proclaim freedom in the face of fear and resignation, truth in the face of misconceptions and false gods. How dangerous to announce that the gift of God in times of terror is not to cower or seek false refuges, but to *live* in joyful and bold action. Why is such preaching dangerous? Not because it is untrue; no human would preach thus unless it were given to him or her by God's Spirit. It is dangerous because the word of God is always personal. The word of God does not explain everything that happens in the world. It confronts the believer with the call of Jesus, "Follow thou me." And the call is to die to self. "Unless a grain of wheat falls to the ground and dies, it bears no fruit" (John 12:24). Lohmeyer was confronted with the same call he set before his hearers. When he was executed on September 19, 1946, the Bible verse for the day in the church lectionary—the lectionary he read daily—was "[Jesus] has done all things well!" (Mark 7:37). In all our living and all our dying stands Jesus's promise, "It is good."

Gathering Opposition to Nazism

"The end of the Breslau years was hard on my father. People were terminated from one day to the next, a depressing end to fifteen years of productivity." So wrote Gudrun about Lohmeyer's evening years at Breslau.[14] She evidently learned this later from her mother, for at the time, not yet ten years old, she was shielded from the gravity of the situation. Her reflections on their family life cast a telling light on Lohmeyer's personality. "It is remarkable that as children we did not notice or even sense in our father's reactions to us the tense circumstances in which he lived at the time."[15] As an adult, she accounted for this remarkable reality by the vitality of her father's intellectual world. The sordid Nazi drama through which he lived was not the only, or most important, reality of his life. Whether Lohmeyer came to his conceptual powers by nature or discipline—or more likely by both—he possessed the ability to see life, including its difficulties, according to his intellectual and theological convictions, and to act in life, including in its difficulties, relatively unencumbered by anxiety and fear. In this chapter we shall see this remarkable characteristic demonstrated most clearly, when Lohmeyer, against a withering onslaught of opposition, continued fighting for his position and convictions. Anyone who has experienced the intense opposition he experienced at Breslau knows how remarkable this is. We may be inclined to regard his commitment to Platonism and neo-Kantianism as a scholarly irrelevancy in a world of Nazi brutality. If so, our inclination is mistaken. It was precisely this world of eternal truths and unchangeable beauties that made the ugly brutality of Nazism so intolerable and constructive action against it so necessary.

We might expect the above to result in aloofness on Lohmeyer's part, but the opposite seems to have been the case. His student assistant Gerhard Sass—the same Sass who wrote the foreword to the supplementary booklet of Lohmeyer's commentary on the Gospel of Mark that first caught my attention—described Lohmeyer's presence with students in these words: "He was always open to other views and willing to listen, always balanced and therefore a balancing element in relationships. He was never abrasive, but even when challenged he remained objective and held the higher course. He did not think he had a corner on truth, but saw himself as part of the process of learning and exploration, that by its very nature is an unending process."[16] It is a rare photograph of Lohmeyer that fails to transmit in his piercing eyes his personal sincerity and bearing.

In the final two weeks of January 1934—exactly a year after Hitler's accession to power—a newspaper clipping was removed from the Theology Department bulletin board at the University of Breslau. This insignificant act, which even a year earlier might have attracted no attention, became a catalytic drop in the volatile Nazi chemistry that now prevailed at the university. It triggered a chain reaction and ended Lohmeyer's tenure at Breslau.

To understand how the chemistry at the university had changed, we need to review the opposition to Nazism that had developed in various quarters of Germany following Hitler's seizure of power. Nothing on the scale of the "Cohn affair" had transpired in Breslau in the preceding year, but the calm was simply a pent-up delay in a pressure cooker. Lohmeyer continued to oppose the most dangerous changes introduced at the university. This included his "Jewish friendliness," to use Nazi semantics, with Jewish professors at Breslau—at least with those who remained. In his lectures and sermons he did not adopt a provocative course of opposition to Nazism. Such was not in his nature to begin with, but even if it had been, by 1933 the time for it had passed. He did not avoid speaking the truth as he saw it, however, when critical issues were at stake. His sermons, as we have seen, were evidence of his attempt to speak the truth so that it might be heard and heeded.

Despite the deceptive calm, there had been open conflicts. In May of 1933 a tawdry parody of Luther's burning of the papal bull of excommunication before the city gate of Wittenberg took place in the Schlossplatz of Breslau, its main city square. The Schlossplatz burning was not of a papal bull, however, but of ten thousand books that Nazi fanatics deemed unworthy of the German *Volk*. Theology students donned SA (*Sturmabteilung*) uniforms, and as they threw the books into the flames, National Socialist professor of theological ethics Karl Bornhausen delivered a *Feuerrede*—"fire speech." Lohmeyer's research assistant, Hanna Bedürftig, was superintending the theological library when students burst in to seize the books and carry them to the Schlossplatz. Bedürftig quickly called Lohmeyer on the phone. Lohmeyer ran to the library and confronted the students. The books, he declared, were the property of the state and were untouchable!

He succeeded in saving the books, but the propaganda mill sought, not unsuccessfully, to turn the event for the Nazi cause. Georg Walter, one of Bornhausen's students, wrote a rabid pamphlet entitled *An die evangelischen Theologen!* (*To the Protestant Theologians!*) in which he pilloried pastors and theologians who resisted the German Christian Movement. They were "futile pseudoscholars"[17] incapable of leading Germans to faith, he mocked. "The obvious duty and task of theologians is to think and feel German."[18] The German church needed to "free itself from slavish dependence on the Bible," which was "unchristian and un-German,"[19] and receive the revelation of God that comes through culture. "It was not without reason," Walter concluded, "that we burned German-hating books on the Schlossplatz in May 1933."[20]

In June, Lohmeyer began his semester lectures on the Christology of the New Testament by stating publicly that National Socialism was an *Ungeist*, "an antispirit" that crippled all free intellectual inquiry.[21] Already in May of 1933, Herbert Franke, Nazi Party liaison to National Socialist faculty and students at Breslau, described the situation there as a "crisis in the Protestant theological faculty." "A tough battle needs to be waged against the ongoing opposition to National Socialism," he warned.[22] The opposition, Franke continued, was especially evident in Gottfried Fitzer, Lohmeyer's assistant, and Friedrich Gogarten, whose "middle-class, democratic, and national interests" sharply opposed National Socialism.[23] Worst of all was Lohmeyer himself, whose expressed "Jewish friendliness" during his tenure as university president was an affront to National Socialism.[24]

In late summer 1933, as we saw in the last chapter, Lohmeyer spoke out in advocacy and defense of Martin Buber, who had been attacked by Gerhard Kittel. Shortly thereafter two noteworthy protests arose against Nazi anti-Semitism. The first came from the church. On September 11, Martin Niemöller, pastor of the St. Anna Church in Berlin-Dahlem, along with other Protestant pastors, formed the Pastors' Emergency League, which rallied the church in opposition to the "Aryan paragraph." The Aryan paragraph, as noted earlier, sought to extend the jurisdiction of the Law for the Restoration of Civil Service, which eliminated persons of Jewish ancestry from civil service positions, eliminating them from positions of authority in the church as well. The Emergency League declared the Aryan paragraph a heresy and staunchly opposed all attempts to exclude Christian pastors of Jewish ancestry from ministerial posts. The league quickly swelled to seven thousand supporting German pastors by January of 1934.

The second protest came from the academy. It, too, directed uncompromising opposition to the Aryan paragraph. In the fall of 1933, two professors from the Marburg theological faculty, Rudolf Bultmann and Hans von Soden, circulated a document entitled *Neues Testament und Rassenfrage* (*The New Testament and the Race Question*) among German New Testament scholars. The "Marburg Declaration," as it was called, declared that on the basis of Galatians 3:28, both Jewish and gentile Christians were entitled to hold office in the German Protestant Church. By October the declaration had garnered signatures from twenty-one New Testament scholars, Lohmeyer among them.[25]

Lohmeyer was an early member of the Pastors' Emergency League, a chapter of which was formed in Breslau in 1933. Gottfried Fitzer, Lohmeyer's assistant, also joined the league and ushered it through the process of becoming the Confessing Church in 1934. The membership of Lohmeyer and Fitzer in the Emergency League not only set them distinctly apart from the majority German Christian faction of the theology faculty at Breslau but also made them vulnerable to its retaliation.

Fortnight of Fury

Throughout 1933 Lohmeyer was like a mountaineer traversing beneath a hanging cornice. At every step the cornice threatened to break loose, releasing an avalanche that would sweep him from the mountainside. But the cornice held, and Lohmeyer continued his traverse. Even with the November appointment of Dr. Gustav Adolf Walz, a staunch National Socialist, as president of the university, the cornice seemed to hold. Walz's appointment endangered Lohmeyer's leadership of the Theology Department, however. As chair, Lohmeyer commanded the respect of his department colleagues as a scholar, but the predominant German Christian sympathies of the department conflicted patently with his theological convictions.

Two months after Walz became president, the cornice fell. The ostensible cause of the avalanche was the bulletin-board incident mentioned earlier. In reality, the cornice broke not because of any particular misstep on Lohmeyer's part but because Walz had engineered its fall well before the news-clipping incident.

It began with a "pink slip." On January 20, 1934, Dr. Anton Jirku, professor of Old Testament and dean, wrote Lohmeyer thanking him for his direction of the Theology Department and informing him that he was relieved of his responsibility as chair. Jirku had named a German Christian, Dr. Hans Leube, as his replacement. This was no ordinary "pink slip," that is, a simple notification of firing. It meant that the university was putting the leadership of the theology faculty and its curriculum in the hands of the German Christian Movement. In short, the Theology Department of Breslau would no longer be orthodox, but heretical. January 20 was a Saturday. Should Lohmeyer have been so inclined, it would be difficult for him to mobilize the faculty over the weekend.

The following Wednesday Lohmeyer replied in writing that the majority of the faculty stood solidly behind him and that Jirku lacked the authority to relieve him. Lohmeyer wanted the matter referred to the university administrator, Dr. Adolf von Hahnke.

The next day, Thursday, January 25, Lohmeyer wrote a second letter to Jirku, repeating that Jirku did not have the authority to relieve him as chair of the Theology Department. The same day the news-clipping incident occurred. Lohmeyer was informed that two articles from the *Völkischer Beobachter* (*People's Observer*) had been posted on the bulletin board of the Theology Department. One, entitled "Small Ghosts in a Great Era," reported with approval the arrest of the Tübingen Catholic theologian Karl Adam; the other, "Scandalous Provocations of National Socialism," attacked the Pastors' Emergency League.[26]

Nazi newspapers generally appeared in one of two genres. One was exemplified by *Der Stürmer* (*The Stormer*), a rag akin to those available at checkout counters of American supermarkets. But unlike the sexual puerility of the latter, *The Stormer* purveyed political sludge. It bypassed readers' reason and sense of humanity, at whatever level they existed, and went straight for their fears, prejudices, and stereotypes. More than the word or thought, it was the *image*—the exaggerated parody, the cartoon, the grotesquerie—that delivered *The Stormer's* foul cargo. The stereotypes were all too familiar: the rich fat Jew sucking blood from upstanding Germans; the blockheaded communist with blood dripping from his bayonet; English industrialists wringing blood from Germany through reparations from the Treaty of Versailles. German blood was a Nazi quasi sacrament in *The Stormer*. The images were capable of moving its readers to the impulsive action that Nazism desired and knew how to evoke.

A second genre was represented by the *People's Observer*, from which the clipping on the bulletin board came. It was not as vulgar as *The Stormer*. Correction: it was equally vulgar, but simply less offensive stylistically. The *Observer* circulated the same malice and lies and fear, but in more conventional tabloid style. It was not as obviously jaundiced as *The Stormer*, and therefore perhaps the more dangerous of the two genres.

When Lohmeyer was informed of the *Observer* clippings, he did what any scholar who defended truth and honored his colleagues would do: he directed his student assistant Hanna Bedürftig to remove them.

One further point about this trifling incident. On Wednesday, January 24, the day before Lohmeyer removed the clipping, the *NS-Parteiblatt* (*National Socialist Party Paper*) ran an article about several clergy who had been imprisoned. The article was an undisguised warning to all members of the clergy. Let Catholic priests who speak of Nazism as "the work of the devil" and "sick Protestant ministers"[27] who confuse their theology and politics be forewarned, the paper threatened. Antagonists will come to their senses in the confinement of a prison cell! "Reactionary circles" that obstruct the "upbuilding of the National Socialist regime" need to know one thing: "Saboteurs will be neutralized, even if they ply their reprehensible craft under the cloak of being servants of God."[28]

It is possible that the threat of the *Party Paper* on January 24 and the appearance of the news clipping from the *Observer* on Lohmeyer's bulletin board on January 25 were merely coincidental. In light of the measures President Walz had already set in motion to drum out Lohmeyer, however, the timely appearance of the two pieces looks suspiciously related. It was the fatal step needed to blame the avalanche on Lohmeyer.

On Friday, January 26, Walz wrote an impassioned letter to the minister of science, art, and public education in Berlin urging the unconditional dismissal of Lohmeyer. Dean Jirku, Walz assured the minister, was acting in concert with himself when he relieved Lohmeyer as chair of the Theology Department. Lohmeyer's refusal to accept Jirku's authority in the matter was a refusal to accept the president's authority! Walz attempted to tighten the noose. "By chance," he wrote, he had learned that Lohmeyer had appealed his dismissal to the minister of education without informing himself as president. This procedural breach was "absolutely intolerable."[29] Walz conceded that the provisional regulations currently in force during the transition to Nazi control at the university could, technically, be interpreted in Lohmeyer's favor. In my research of this particular point, I have read and reread the documentation. Given the lines of authority in play during the transition period, Lohmeyer looks to me as justified in rejecting Jirku's authority to dismiss him as Jirku thought himself justified to do it.

None of this mattered to Walz, however. Lohmeyer's recourse to legal procedure and precedent was irrelevant in light of the greater issue—indeed, the *only* issue—which was Walz's authority! Walz was a "führer president." The new authoritarian Nazi era was at hand—and Lohmeyer had "deliberately and illegally" resisted it.[30] Walz's missive to the minister reached a vituperative crescendo. Lohmeyer's resistance was but a further instance of "a whole series of reasons"[31] that were too numerous to recount, too widely known to neglect, and too offensive to tolerate any longer. "Herr Lohmeyer's anti–National Socialist behavior and his anti–National Socialist way of thinking are a commonly known fact!"[32] The minister of education should effect his "immediate dismissal."

Bureaucratic Blitzkrieg

The gloves were off. The next day, January 27, Walz wrote to Lohmeyer. No salutation, no personal address. Lohmeyer's circumvention of his authority was utterly "disapproved,"[33] and his presumption to reject the decision of the dean was equally "surprising." "You will have to bear the full consequences of your actions," he warned.[34] The "full consequences," which he did not specify to Lohmeyer, had already been set in motion with the minister of education.

Totalitarian rule inevitably shifts the interests of people away from seeking the common good to self-preservation. An effective method of self-preservation is denunciation of others. A denunciation now came into play. Walz informed Lohmeyer that he was told that Lohmeyer had referred to an article in the *People's Observer* as "provocative"[35] in or around the time Lohmeyer had ordered the clippings removed from the bulletin board. To publicly question a Nazi news source was a serious infraction. Lohmeyer owed the president an explanation. Lohmeyer promptly drafted a letter, respectfully addressing the president, "Your Magnificence." He did not remember making such a statement, he reported, and in any case he did not intend a slur on the *Observer*.[36]

On the same day, January 29, the Nazi-controlled student body piled on in a gang tackle of Lohmeyer. They wrote to Walz: "The behavior of Prof. Lohmeyer is totally unacceptable and his further tenure at a university in a National Socialist state is unbearable. The student body therefore demands his immediate termination.

Simply removing him as Director of the Theology Department does not satisfy the student body."[37] Lohmeyer's ship was being torpedoed. In an effort to plug the holes, he responded to the accusations against him in a four-page letter on January 30 to Dr. Hahnke, the university administrator. He repeated his first two points, namely, that Dean Jirku did not have the authority to dismiss him, and second, that the proper protocol, in any case, was between the university administrator and the Theology Department. But there were more and bigger holes for Lohmeyer to plug. The longest and most surprising point was the third. At a faculty meeting on January 24, President Walz had circulated among the faculty a procedural plan for stripping nonconforming faculty members of their doctorates! This was tantamount to firing a faculty member, for a doctorate was a *sine qua non* in an academic appointment at a German university. The plan was evidence, if any were needed, of the absolute control that Nazism sought to exercise over German universities. It would be more than a year before the Nuremberg Laws would rescind civil rights of Jews; Walz's proposal already sought to deprive professors of intellectual freedom apart from political authorization. The plan did not name Lohmeyer specifically. It might well begin with him, of course, but it would not end with him. It needed to be general enough to include others like him. Lohmeyer replied shrewdly and stoically: the only institution that could retract a doctorate would be the institution that granted it. His two doctorates had been granted by Berlin and Erlangen and were thus ostensibly immune from question at Breslau. Walz's proposal even included the establishment of a doctoral delegitimizing commission, a member of which would necessarily be the leader of the Nazi Storm Troopers with Responsibility for University Affairs! Lohmeyer weighed in again. Such a commission should consist of the president and the deans of the four university faculties, that is, of internal academic personnel, not of outside political personnel. His proposal was carried by the faculty, and the matter was by and large neutralized.

But his defense was not complete. The "Cohn affair" continued to rankle Lohmeyer's adversaries, and in point four he was required to devote a full page to justifying his summoning of the police. Lohmeyer reminded the university administrator that the summons took place *before* Hitler's accession to power on January 30, 1933. The date was important, for prior to it the Nazi Party was not a legal political entity and the student riots were illegal. His action had of course been unpopular with Nazi students then, and was even more so now that the Party enjoyed legal status in Germany. But Lohmeyer held the fort: the political winds may have changed, but those winds could not change either the unacceptability of the students' actions or his response to them. The students had no more right to expect immunity from disrupting university life because they wore Nazi uniforms, declared Lohmeyer, than professors had a right to expect free beer and bratwurst because they wore academic gowns! At only one point did Lohmeyer offer penance in the Cohn affair: he had, it was true, failed to return the Hitler salute to the police when the affair had been quelled. He asked for forbearance of his oversight. "Ever since the introduction of the German greeting it is possible that I raised my hat, as I have been long accustomed to do, when a student raised his right hand to greet me."[38]

Fifth—and finally—Lohmeyer had to defend his support for the Pastors' Emergency League. Protestant students at Breslau had written a declaration in support of the league, and the majority German Christian professors in the Theology Department who detested the league suspected Lohmeyer's influence in the declaration. Lohmeyer remained unmoved. The declaration, he affirmed, was drafted by students, its signatures were gathered by students, and by the time he learned of it on January 11 it had already been submitted by the students. It was a responsible student initiative, intended for internal use in the department, and not a propaganda ploy.[39]

Lohmeyer ended the apology with his signature but without the customary "Heil Hitler." His dispassionate tone and absence of invective in the face of such perniciousness are remarkable. Only in the mechanics of the letter do we see his stress fractures. His typewriter did not entirely cooperate in his hurried defense to the university administrator. There are several capitalization errors, scratch-outs, and a vacant line—perhaps the result of throwing the carriage lever too forcefully. Such errors would be negligible in virtually any other writer, but for Lohmeyer they are subtle yet unmistakable reminders of the opposition he endured.

Public Humiliation

Walz was no match for Lohmeyer's intellect and character. Unfortunately, he did not need to be, for as president he possessed the power to degrade him. On Monday, January 29, he demanded that Lohmeyer read a public apology before the students on Thursday next, February 1, for referring to the *People's Observer* as "provocative." Lohmeyer sought to avert it. It made little sense, he argued, to read an apology that would require students to take positions for or against a matter about which they were uninformed. Lohmeyer ended on a come-let-us-reason-together note. Assuming that Walz agreed, or if Lohmeyer did not hear back from him, he would forgo the apology on Thursday.[40] Walz did not agree, and he was in no mood to reason. "I cannot express strongly enough," he wrote adamantly, "that you commence your next lecture with the required apology. I have informed the president of the student body of the same, and he assures me he will prevent any protests. I am absolute master of the student body. I must insist for your own sake to conclude this matter in the above-mentioned manner."[41]

At 4 p.m. on Thursday, February 1, Lohmeyer read a public apology before an overflow crowd of students of the University of Breslau. Earlier in the day he had provided President Walz with a copy of his apology. In a cover letter he repeated that he did not remember using the word "provocative." He informed Walz that he would not summon as witnesses the two theological students who could attest to his innocence in the matter, Fräulein Bedürftig and Herr Pohle, in order to spare them from being tainted by the affair.[42] Lohmeyer was personal in the apology rather than sullen and protectionist. A conversation that transpired in a circle of friends, which Lohmeyer said need not be repeated, had led to misunderstandings and rumors. "I have not taken back what I then said, nor will I take it back," he asserted.[43] The point was not what he said but rather the false conclusions that were drawn from it about his political convictions. Consider the facts, he said in conclusion: he had served four years as an officer in the trenches of the war, and as president of the university he defended it from influence from the Social Democrats, for which he was sharply reprimanded at the time.

According to Lohmeyer's later account of the apology, students "rapped their knuckles on the table in thundering applause" when he concluded the apology.

Lohmeyer fought with indomitable resolve in the last two weeks of January 1934 to salvage his professorial call at Breslau, seeking all the while to protect students more vulnerable than he. He conducted himself with unusual integrity in nasty circumstances. He did not lie or sacrifice truth for strategic gains. There are storms, however, that cannot be weathered. This was one. Following his apology on the evening of February 1, 1934, he penned a seven-line letter to Dean Jirku relinquishing his leadership of the Theology Department to the German Christian Movement and the likes of Gerhard Kittel.

A month later, on March 1, Lohmeyer produced a handwritten personal account, presumably at the request of university authorities, of the events that led to his dismissal. His thirteen-page, 3,500-word defense required him to refill his fountain pen four times in writing it. In this account, as in the letters referenced above, Lohmeyer focused on the issues at stake rather than on his personal feelings. Whatever internal battles he fought we do not know, for they surface neither in the correspondence nor in the memory of his family. To be forced to justify the use of the word "provocative," to be punished for defending the integrity of honest scholars, to be threatened with the revocation of one's doctoral degree—such things seem beyond the realm of possibility in an academic and intellectual community. But that was the ugly *Realpolitik* of Nazism. A more inglorious battle and degrading end can scarcely be imagined. But the choice of battles and battlegrounds is not given to us. Lohmeyer fought an ignoble battle nobly.

One may wonder why he fought such a battle in the first place, or fought as long as he did. Did he not know that the power arrayed against him would not allow him to prevail? After all, victory had already been granted to the Brown Shirts. In retrospect, these points seem obvious. But in 1934 Lohmeyer did not know—and neither he nor the world could have imagined—what the Nazi experiment would lead to. When Lohmeyer struggled to preserve the Theology Department from the stain of Nazism, its worst offenses, which would begin with the revocation of civil rights in 1935, still lay in the future. But more importantly, the idea of contending for issues on the basis of their winnability is the wrong perspective in Lohmeyer's case. He was not a utilitarian who measured engagement on the basis of outcome. He was an idealist—a Platonic idealist, a Kantian idealist, and above all, a Christian idealist who engaged issues on the basis of virtue and merit and on nothing else. The battle worth fighting was not the battle that could be won but the battle that virtue—truth, justice, love for the other—demanded one to fight, irrespective of outcome. The one and only virtue for Lohmeyer was always to live—and if necessary to die—as a man worthy of the freedom that was both given and required of the tradition of Christian humanism.

Ernst Lohmeyer as tutor of the two young sons of Graf von Bethusy-Huc, Silesia, ca. 1912. © Andreas Köhn

Ernst Lohmeyer, President of the University of Breslau, 1930. © University of Greifswald

Bronze bust of Ernst Lohmeyer produced when he was president of the University of Breslau, displayed today at the University of Greifswald. © University of Greifswald

Ernst Lohmeyer with his daughter Gudrun, ca. 1931 © Julia Otto and Stefan Rettner, born Otto

Ernst Lohmeyer, Melie, and Gudrun as a child, 1934. © Julia Otto and Stefan Rettner, born Otto

Melie Lohmeyer, 1937. © Julia Otto and Stefan Rettner, born Otto

Ernst Lohmeyer and Melie in Sweden, 1937. © Julia Otto and Stefan Rettner, born Otto

Melie Lohmeyer, 1940.
© Julia Otto and Stefan
Rettner, born Otto

**Ernst Lohmeyer,
1945.** © University of
Greifswald

Ernst Lohmeyer's identity card during the Soviet occupation of
Greifswald. The date of issue, September 28, 1945, was less than a
year before his execution. © Julia Otto and Stefan Rettner, born Otto

The University of Greifswald, 1996. © James R. Edwards

Lohmeyer house in Greifswald, 1996. The family occupied the third floor. © James R. Edwards

The NKVD prison in Greifswald where Lohmeyer was imprisoned, 1996. © James R. Edwards

Author standing at the main portal of the University of Breslau, 2016.
© James R. Edwards

CHAPTER 11

Ouster

When something to which we are deeply and wonderfully
bound is taken from us, much of ourselves is taken with it.
God nevertheless wills that we find ourselves again, richer
despite all the loss, increased despite the unending pain.

Rainer Maria Rilke[1]

The Politics of Diminishment

The clash between Lohmeyer and the university administration
in January 1934 had been unyielding. President Walz orchestrated
his moves throughout the assault, rallied the necessary allies, and
succeeded in stripping Lohmeyer of whatever residual influence he
had as president and of active leadership of the Theology Department. Lohmeyer was reduced to the status of mere professor. It was
a definitive victory for Walz. Inevitably so, for in January 1934 the
prevailing winds of Nazism were blowing at Walz's back.

But it was not a complete victory. Walz had appealed to the
minister of science, training, and public education that Lohmeyer's long-standing conduct warranted "an immediate recall of Herr
Lohmeyer" from the university.[2] In this he had been unsuccessful,
at least for the present. Lohmeyer was still a professor at Breslau,
and he opened a second front at Breslau; or if that metaphor is too
dramatic, he applied himself to effective moves still remaining to
him on the chessboard of university politics. Lohmeyer, as we have
seen, was an active member in the Pastors' Emergency League

that Martin Niemöller had formed in September 1933. By January 1934 the league had grown from thirteen hundred initial pastors to some seven thousand pastors and was rapidly transforming itself into what in the spring of the year would become the Confessing Church. Walz had succeeded in curtailing Lohmeyer's influence in the Theology Department at the university, but he had less control over his work in the Pastors' Emergency League and Confessing Church, through which Lohmeyer succeeded in exerting continued influence at Breslau.

In May of 1934, church leaders of the Pastors' Emergency League, including Karl Barth, Hans Asmussen, and Thomas Breit, met in Barmen, near Dusseldorf, in northwestern Germany, to frame and adopt the Barmen Declaration, which expressly forbade the state from interference in Protestant church order. Barmen called the church to the authority of Scripture and the Reformation confessions, especially the Augsburg Confession, thereby becoming the foundational document of a new church entity, the Confessing Church, which would stand as the ecclesiastical bulwark against the German Christian Movement. At its zenith in the mid-1930s, the Confessing Church would include nearly one-third of all Lutheran and Reformed pastors and congregations in Germany. Advocacy of Confessing Church ministerial candidates at Breslau became a means for Lohmeyer to counteract the dominant influence of the German Christian professors in the Theology Department. But it also sealed his fate at Breslau, offering the pro-Nazi university the final ground to dismiss him from the faculty.

The Theological Declaration of Barmen was signed by 138 church leaders who participated in the Confessional Synod of Barmen in May 1934. Lohmeyer was not a signatory of Barmen, nor did he attend the synod that produced it. The absence of his signature from the document and his own absence from the synod were not surprising. Barmen's objective was above all ecclesiastical and pastoral, to undergird the evangelical Protestant church with a theological defense capable of resisting the encroachment of the German Christian Movement, thus preventing the smaller Confessing Church from being swallowed by "German Christianity." The rallying call of Barmen, accordingly, went out to pastors and church leaders rather than to professors. With the single exception of Karl Barth, who was a professor and chief drafter of the declaration, the Confessional Synod of Barmen was attended and the declaration signed by pastors.

But professors who aligned themselves with Barmen were not left without a voice. Hans von Soden, a theology professor in Marburg, wrote and circulated *Bekenntnis und Verfassung in den evangelischen Kirchen* (*Confession and Constitution in the Protestant Churches*). *Confession and Constitution* was a theological defense against *Gleichschaltung*, a Nazi word for the party's attempt to reroute all tributaries in German life—especially unaligned and resistant tributaries—into the mainstream of Nazi ideology. Such tributaries existed in all sectors—economics, finance, industry, politics, cultural movements, arts, literature, and religion. The Roman Catholic Church had been successfully rerouted or co-opted by the Reich's Concord of 1933, but the Protestant church, which was the majority church in Germany, had not been similarly co-opted. The Protestant church was a greater potential danger to Nazism because it was larger and, with its various and disparate denominations, less easily controlled. The Nazi attempt to expand the Aryan paragraph, which excluded persons of Jewish descent from civil service positions in Germany, to the church, thereby excluding persons of Jewish descent from serving as Protestant pastors, was an attempt at *Gleichschaltung*.

Hitler redoubled the attempt at *Gleichschaltung* by personally seizing the reins to consolidate the disparate and potentially disruptive Protestant churches under a single head, a virtual Protestant pope. In September of 1933 he named fifty-year-old Protestant cleric Dr. Ludwig Müller, who had been a party member since 1931, as "Reich's Bishop." Müller was theologically incompetent, power hungry, devious, and vain—just the man for the job. More zealous in his anti-Semitism than in any theological doctrine, orthodox or not, Müller lacked any redeeming qualities as a bishop of the church. Indeed, his excess of Nazi romp and pomp in church theatrics eventually made him nearly as distasteful to Hitler as he had been all along to the Confessing Church. The introduction of the Aryan paragraph and naming of Müller as Reich's Bishop evoked an immediate and uncompromising backlash from the church. The same month that Hitler installed Müller as Reich's Bishop, Martin Niemöller rallied the church with the formation of the Pastors' Emergency League. Two months later, in November 1934, Hans von Soden drafted and circulated *Confession and Constitution*, demanding the recall of Müller as Reich's Bishop. A hundred university professors signed it, including Lohmeyer, as did some eighty theology students at the University of Breslau.[3]

Important as Barmen and *Confession and Constitution* were, they alone were not sufficient antidotes to the cancer infecting the church. Effective plans, procedures, teaching, and catechism needed to be infused into the bloodstream of the church, like theological white blood cells, to defend it from malignant Nazism. In summer 1934 Lohmeyer taught on the Gospel of John and its uncompromising Christology. Additionally, and more confrontationally, he introduced a new course at Breslau, "Christianity and Judaism," in which he developed the idea of the mutual relationship between Judaism and Christianity that he had broached a year earlier in his letter to Martin Buber. The same summer he supported his professorial assistant, Gottfried Fitzer, in establishing Confessing Church communities in Silesia.

Termination at Breslau

It is tempting to think of effective witness to tyranny in terms of dramatic confrontations. Martin Luther's intrepid defense at the Diet of Worms in 1521 comes to mind, when, as a lone monk, he declared to the combined temporal and ecclesiastic authorities arrayed against him, "Here I stand!" Bishop Thomas Cranmer's renunciation of his recantation under the reign of Bloody Mary is another. Immediately before his burning at the stake in 1556, he put his hand into the flames and said, "This hand hath offended!" Or, who can fail to be moved by the testimony of Professor Kurt Huber, the only German university professor to be executed for resistance to Nazism in twelve years of Nazi dictatorship. In courageous testimony before the fanatical Nazi judge Roland Freisler, in which he defended his support of the *White Rose* student resistance movement at the University of Munich, Huber quoted Johann Gottlieb Fichte:

> You must act as though
> On you and your deeds alone
> The fate of German history hung,
> And the responsibility—your own.[4]

Lohmeyer's concluding overture against Nazism at Breslau was not as dramatic, but in my mind it was, in a very different way, also heroic. The Confessing Church in Breslau and Silesia was comparatively weak in relation to churches of German Christian persuasion, whose numbers and strength were far superior. Nothing was more important for equipping the Confessing Church for witness and resistance to Nazism than the committee work required in the ordination process of pastors. It was to this mundane responsibility that Lohmeyer addressed himself, thereby keeping alive the voice of the orthodox faith of the churches. He was a minority voice, in some instances the only voice, but defense of pastoral candidates made a *tangible* difference in the witness of the Confessing Church in Silesia.

Günther Ruprecht offered him the services of Vandenhoeck & Ruprecht in publishing "academic theology of substance" to offset the raft of German Christian theological propaganda. Without such theology, Ruprecht warned, "no true and lasting peace" can be expected under the circumstances.[5]

In 1935, however, an event transpired that jeopardized Lohmeyer's tenuous position in opposition to Nazism in the church of Silesia. In the spring of the year, nearly a year after Barmen and *Confession and Constitution*, the Confessing Pastors of the Old Prussian Union in Silesia jointly read a denunciation of the theology and objectives of the German Christians from their pulpits. Given the time and place, the boldness of this witness cannot be doubted, although some might question its wisdom. The Nazi response was swift and severe. Two hundred Confessing pastors were arrested and put in prison, among them Lohmeyer's former doctoral student and assistant, Werner Schmauch. The imprisonments lasted between two weeks and two months, which indicated that the arrests were primarily a strategy of intimidation. They were nevertheless an ominous forewarning, and they simultaneously signaled the open intervention of the Nazi Party in church affairs. Pastor Otto Zänker, bishop of the Confessing Church in Silesia, had to delay the inaugural meeting of the Provisional Silesian Synod scheduled for March. The meeting finally took place on May 10 in St. Christopher's Church, the same church where Lohmeyer had preached regularly throughout his tenure at Breslau. Lohmeyer was the lone member of the Breslau theological faculty present at the meeting.

Confessing Church ministerial candidates were increasingly at the mercy of the majority German Christian professors who administered and graded their theological examinations. The mood of the German Christians in Breslau was decidedly unmerciful toward the Confessing Church. In conformity with the third Confessional Synod in Augsburg in June 1935, Bishop Zänker sought to exclude German Christian members from the examination process of ministerial candidates. The High Consistory of the Lutheran Church, firmly controlled by German Christians, retaliated swiftly, denying Zänker access to examinations and rooms in which to administer them. The High Consistory further declared the theological examination system of the Confessing Church illegal. Lohmeyer interpreted the High Consistory's response as a proscription of Zänker, not of himself. He therefore remained on the examination committee in Breslau throughout the remainder of 1935. In early January of 1936, however, his continued participation in the examination process evoked a blistering reprimand by the dean of the Breslau theology faculty. Lohmeyer, declared the dean, had expressly violated the prohibition of Confessing Church pastors from participating in the examination of ordinands and owed a full explanation for the irregularity of his behavior.[6]

In mid-January Lohmeyer drafted a four-page, handwritten letter of eleven hundred words to the dean that set forth his defense carefully, objectively, and perhaps most impressively, without invective. He rehearsed events as they unfolded. What the dean referred to as "illegal examinations" were, on careful reading of the law, left to the discretion of the participants concerned. Bishop

Zänker was a legally appointed chair of the process, and Lohmeyer was a legal fellow member. As a full professor and member of the Lutheran Church, Lohmeyer maintained his right to participate in ordination examinations. Perhaps the most important thing about Lohmeyer's response was its date—January 1936. By then his termination from the theological faculty at Breslau was four months past. He was writing the dean from Greifswald, where he had relocated. For Lohmeyer, however, the issue was not whether he was still a member of the faculty of Breslau or where he was living. The issue for him—always!—was *truth*, to which he would testify if he were the last man standing.

President Walz's long-engineered termination of Lohmeyer was finally achieved in October of 1935, eighteen months after the memoranda mauling of January 1934. Negotiations had been under way throughout the summer of 1935 with regard to Lohmeyer's *Strafversetzung*—heartless bureaucratic-speak for "disciplinary transfer"—to Greifswald. Joachim Jeremias was leaving Greifswald to become professor of New Testament at Göttingen, and a successor was needed for him. Lohmeyer, along with Karl Heinrich Rengstorf and Julius Schniewind, was a finalist for the position. In early August the dean of the theological faculty at Greifswald informed the minister of science, art, and public education in Berlin that he thought Schniewind the best candidate but feared that "as the keenest defender of the Confessing Church in Königsberg,"[7] as the dean described Schniewind, he might destabilize the Greifswald faculty. In contrast to Schniewind's "unusually strong influence on students,"[8] the dean proposed Lohmeyer, on the grounds that his "personal influence might not be so strongly felt."[9] How wrong that prediction would be! By mid-October 1935, supporting letters from university officials at Greifswald, including from its president, Carl Engel, had secured from the minister in Berlin the transfer of Lohmeyer to Greifswald.[10]

The full dismissal of Lohmeyer from the faculty of the University of Breslau had finally happened. The presenting reason for the dismissal had been President Walz's denunciation of Lohmeyer's "anti–National Socialist attitudes and behavior" back in January 1934. But in Lohmeyer's mind the ultimate reason was not his anti-

Nazism. It was his advocacy of the Confessing Church. In a confidential letter to Günther Ruprecht on March 18, 1936, he wrote that "the report of my 'call' [to Greifswald] was a typically deceptive maneuver. It was, in fact, a 'displacement,' as was communicated to me orally, a punitive measure on account of my ecclesiastical convictions and behavior with respect to the Confessing Church."[11]

Greifswald

Lohmeyer did not like change. Most scholars do not—change disrupts their productive routines. The move from bustling Berlin to academic Heidelberg almost twenty years earlier had not been particularly easy. Nor had the move from Heidelberg to Breslau. It took a long time to get used to Breslau—it was so far "east." Greifswald, too, presented the Lohmeyer family its particular challenges. It was considerably smaller than Berlin or Breslau, or even Heidelberg, as was its university. Weather on the Baltic Sea was not as cold as inland northern Germany, but it was grayer, wetter, and windier. Greifswald was also farther removed from the academic hubs from which Lohmeyer had come.

But Greifswald held pleasant and significant surprises. The university's theological tradition was particularly robust and long-standing. Since the late nineteenth century, students from throughout Germany had boarded trains and headed north, bypassing Heidelberg and Göttingen, Leipzig and Berlin, to study with theological heavyweights at Greifswald like Julius Wellhausen, Hermann Cremer, Wilhelm Lütgert, and Adolf Schlatter, and Levant savants like Gustaf Dalman and Victor Schultze. Nor was Greifswald's theological preeminence a thing of the past. Rudolf Hermann, Hans von Campenhausen, Walter Elliger, and Ernst Lohmeyer ensured its theological vitality in the 1930s.

Greifswald itself was a refreshing change from baroque Breslau. From the latter half of the seventeenth century until the early nineteenth century, Sweden had ruled Greifswald, and its Scandinavian influence was apparent in cleaner and simpler architectural lines and in a cityscape of predominantly red brick. The size and layout of Greifswald reminded Lohmeyer of Tübingen. Both had main streets that traversed the length of the city, Wilhelmstrasse in Tübingen and, in Greifswald, Langestrasse—"Long Street"—which united city, university, and harbor in a single artery. But Greifswald's most distinctive characteristic was the dominant characteristic of the great Flemish painters of the Baltic north—the *sky*. Huge, heavy, and scudded with gray clouds one day, expansive in its blueness and sea breezes the next, the sky was Greifswald's most striking feature.

Breslau authorities intended to "banish" Lohmeyer—what else could *Strafversetzung*, "disciplinary transfer," mean? Lohmeyer, however, *chose* to see in the move the call and providence of God. His last official sermon in Breslau on October 13, 1935, when his position in Greifswald was secured, gave voice to this choice. His text was "Sing to the Lord a new song" (Ps. 98), and his subject was God's redeeming presence in the midst of unredeemed circumstances.

> The word of God does not free us from conflicts, and it does not relieve us of life's troubles. Indeed, only where the unredeemedness of our lives is inescapable do we see God's redemption. If God were to snatch us out of trials we would then be tried in ways that would be endlessly deeper and greater than all the trials that we must endure in human circumstances. But, dear friends, even in the deepest trials the sound of his voice is perceptible, blowing over us like incense. You know this is not something that can be proven.... We can of course forsake the voice of God; many people do, as we ourselves often do. But even to those who forsake it, God still gives the gift of his voice, like the sea that roars and is never stilled, like streams of water that frolic and will not be tamed. God's voice rings through our lives. We can pull back from it or open ourselves to it, but the miracle of his voice remains, incomprehensible yet ever perceptible. And those to whom God gives the gift of his voice—and to whom does he not give it?—can respond in no other way than does the psalmist, "Sing to the Lord a new song."[12]

The word I have translated "trials" is *Anfechtung*, a frequent and important term in Lutheran language and theology. For Luther,

Anfechtungen were not signs of God's abandonment of the believer but the very opposite—signs of God's operative presence in the believer, for the devil and world test most severely those who choose to follow the Lord. Lohmeyer closely followed Luther's lead in his sermon. He would learn its meaning for him in Greifswald as he had in Breslau. He had been pressed from all sides in Breslau, "battles without and fears within," in the apostle Paul's words (2 Cor. 7:5). The trials would come in other forms in Greifswald. It was not as close to the front line of Nazism as Breslau had been, but it was not free from dangers—nowhere in Germany was.

Withdrawing from the Fray?

When I received a grant from the German Academic Exchange Program in 1993 to research the mysterious disappearance and death of Lohmeyer, I contacted former Bishop Albrecht Schönherr to talk about Lohmeyer. Schönherr had been a student leader in Dietrich Bonhoeffer's underground seminary for the Confessing Church, which was located outside Stettin, about fifty miles southeast of Greifswald. Unlike Bonhoeffer, Schönherr would survive the Hitler era to become the bishop of Berlin-Brandenburg in communist East Germany. As a pastor, Schönherr would shepherd the flock of Christ under Adolf Hitler and Erich Honecker—two of the world's most infamous tyrants. In 1935 Bonhoeffer had established a student house of the Confessing Church in Greifswald, and he appointed Schönherr as "inspector"—his personal representative—of the student house and its ministries. Only three university professors supported the Bonhoeffer initiative in Greifswald—Otto Haendler, Erdmann Schott, and Ernst Lohmeyer. Lohmeyer was the leading proponent of the three. The student house became an "affront" to the majority church and faculty members who were sympathetic to the German Christian Movement. Pro-Nazi elements in the church of Greifswald targeted the house with repeated searches by the Gestapo, and succeeded in closing it in 1938.[13]

Schönherr was in his early eighties when I met with him. He was then retired but still tall and erect, his face chiseled with character.

Given the posts he had served as pastor and bishop, I anticipated a forceful, perhaps even polemic, personality. As he recounted his life's narrative, I found a man of gentler manner than I expected, reserved and modest. I cannot say exactly what profile Schönherr cut as Bonhoeffer's assistant at Greifswald, but when I was with him on a half-dozen occasions over several years, I was struck by his irenic temperament and moderation, as if to say, "All is well." As bishop of Berlin-Brandenburg throughout the 1970s, Schönherr followed a golden mean between the poles of uncompromising and vacillating. I could see why Bonhoeffer put him in charge of the student house in Greifswald: Bonhoeffer's crystalline theological insights and unflinching convictions needed the pragmatism of a Schönherr to make them viable in Greifswald's conflicted ecclesiastical environment.

Schönherr had met with Lohmeyer several times after the latter's arrival in Greifswald in early 1936, although Schönherr did not claim to know him well. In light of the antagonism Lohmeyer had encountered in the final years at Breslau, I was interested in learning how he interfaced with the faculty at Greifswald. Schönherr said Lohmeyer was the only member of the Confessing Church on the faculty. (The situation was actually not so dire. Six members of the faculty belonged to the Confessing Church—Deissner, von Campenhausen, Hermann, Haendler, Schott, and Lohmeyer—but, as noted above, only the last three supported the student house of the Confessing Church in Greifswald. Schönherr's recollection that Lohmeyer was the *only* Confessing Church faculty member at Greifswald indicates the significant role he played.) Lohmeyer appeared to Schönherr as an *Einzelgänger*, an individualist. He noted that Lohmeyer did not preach at Greifswald. "It was my impression," he said in summary, "that he pulled back from the fray."

It may have appeared that Lohmeyer "pulled back from the fray" in Greifswald, but I do not believe it. If he had pulled back, it would have been the first time in his life that he had done so. The difference that Schönherr perceived is better explained by the altered circumstances Lohmeyer experienced in Greifswald. The fact that he had barely edged out Julius Schniewind for the New Testament post left his position there somewhat tenuous. Nor did he enter

Greifswald with the same prominence he had when he left Breslau. Above all, the political climate at the University of Greifswald was less charged and volatile than the climate at Breslau. One responds differently in a cold war than in a hot war.

But there was no change in his expressed opposition to Nazism in Greifswald. His vigorous defense to the dean of the theological faculty at Breslau—written *after* the battle there had been lost—testifies that his antipathy to Nazism had not slackened. Indeed, in his first year at Greifswald he again crossed wires with Nazi authorities. In early 1937 a Nazi gauleiter delivered a farcical speech to the theological faculty in the baroque hall of the university—the same hall in which the posthumous inauguration was celebrated in 1996. The Nazi Party had divided Germany into thirty-one (later expanded to forty-three) state-like geographical units called *Gaus*, a term that derived from the reign of Charlemagne a millennium earlier. A "gauleiter" was the official head of a *Gau*, endowed with authority analogous to a governor of an American state. The patronizing gauleiter in question, Franz Schwede-Coburg, lectured the Greifswald theological faculty on the great variety of the world's religions that were not Christian, further asserting that the Bible was transmitted in a confusing array of manuscripts that contradicted one another. He admonished the Greifswald theological faculty to "consider informing their students of these things."[14] The lecture was transmitted via loudspeaker to a room overflowing with students. On hearing such commonplaces about the world religions and falsehoods about biblical manuscripts, the students whistled and shuffled their feet in ridicule. In totalitarian regimes such responses can be dangerous. Lohmeyer was reported to have described the lecture as "slightly below what you would expect from an average high school student."[15] Lohmeyer's assessment may have been overly generous. The authorities, at any rate, did not consider it so. Lohmeyer was slapped with a violation of the Law against Insidious Persons. Five months later, in May of 1938, he was dragged to Stettin for trial, from which he extricated himself only after producing a suitcase full of testimonials on his behalf.[16]

Lohmeyer's posture in Greifswald was also misperceived by Gerhard Sass—the same Sass whose cryptic reference to Lohmeyer's disappearance in the preface of his commentary on the Gospel of Mark sparked my initial interest in the theologian. Lohmeyer desisted from preaching in Greifswald, according to Sass, because of the "unfathomable scope and weight of standing in the pulpit and presuming to speak in behalf of God. . . . How can fleeting human words express that which is ever constant, how can imperfection throw light upon that which is perfect and complete? How can mere man show the way to the source of life? These reasons explain Lohmeyer's reticence to preach in his professional years."[17] It is difficult to imagine that Sass is correct in this judgment. Is not all human preaching subject to the folly that Sass describes? Such folly, in fact, is the defining characteristic of all genuine preaching, according to the apostle Paul (1 Cor. 1:18-31). Had not Lohmeyer regularly engaged in such folly throughout his Breslau years? Why would he quail before this task in Greifswald?

His failure to preach in Greifswald is more simply—and properly, in my judgment—accounted for by practical realities. Invitations to proclaim the Word of God are rarely extended to the unknown and untrusted. Lohmeyer fit both of these categories: he was a relatively unknown newcomer to the faculty, and in light of his "disciplinary transfer" in an angst-ridden Nazi environment, his placement in a controlled lecture hall made more sense than promotion in an open pulpit. His three-year tenure in Greifswald before being called up for the war was too short to allay such apprehensions.

The changes that Schönherr and Sass noted in Lohmeyer were due more to different circumstances in Greifswald than to changes in himself. He now had respite from the interminable conflicts of his final years at Breslau that had drained his energies and interfered with his writing. The relatively stable political climate in Greifswald permitted him in October of 1937 to travel to Sweden to lecture and meet with theological colleagues. The reception he enjoyed and the relationships he made, especially with Anton Fridrichsen, Hugo Odeberg, and Anders Nygren, would be repeated three years later, with equal enthusiasm, when he was on leave from the war in Belgium. The move to Greifswald also marked a new era in the Lohmeyer family life. He and Melie had been married twenty years. The children were entering their teenage years—Ernst-Helge, fourteen years old; Hartmut, thirteen; and Gudrun, ten. Melie and the children needed him. Greifswald promised to be a providential season.

Ernst Lohmeyer's Uniqueness as a Theologian

Theology was air in Lohmeyer's lungs, blood in his veins. The distractions and hindrances of the last years at Breslau, massive as they were, had not stanched the life-giving flow of theology in his life. They had merely dammed it up, and he took with him to Greifswald a six-year reservoir of clean, deep theological water. In Greifswald, he published six books, seventeen scholarly articles, and ten book reviews. Some of these publications had been begun in Breslau and brought to Greifswald as works-in-progress, but in Greifswald they were completed and birthed. Joseph's word to his betraying brothers, "What you intended for evil, God used for good to give life to many people" (Gen. 50:20), was true of Lohmeyer in Greifswald. The silver lining in the cloud of his "disciplinary transfer" was the space, time, and less-distraught political atmosphere that it afforded to resume his theological calling.

And here is not the least remarkable thing about his concluding theological legacy—although at the time he did not know it would be the end. It would be produced during Germany's descent into the darkness of World War II, but it would not be determined by it. Once again he displayed the characteristic that so impressed his daughter, Gudrun, who more than anyone except for Melie knew the obstacles that her father faced. He chose the course governed not by crisis or emotion but by ideals and objective thought, by what was lasting and important rather than what was emotionally crippling and transitory.

It is important to understand what *type* of scholar Ernst Lohmeyer was, for not all scholars are alike. Many scholars gravitate to issues that capture the interest of their generation, hoping, if possible, to further or refine "assured scholarly consensuses." Other scholars prefer to avoid busy scholarly thoroughfares, opting for roads less taken and paths seldom trodden in hopes of making contributions that, if more modest, are nevertheless more original and groundbreaking. Still others forsake the goal of discovery or invention entirely and opt for a descriptive mode of scholarship, summing up the history of the discipline or its state-of-the-art at the current time. The forms and objectives and subjects of theological scholarship, as in all fields, are many and varied.

In a 1936 letter to Vandenhoeck & Ruprecht, Lohmeyer reminded the publishing house precisely what type of scholar he was. In defense of his refusal to produce a midlevel commentary for V&R, and in further defense against the charge that his scholarship was often tendentious and imbalanced, or alternatively, too philosophically determined, Lohmeyer wrote the following: "In the present circumstances of theology and church, and for the future of the Meyer Commentary series, nothing seems more necessary for me than to introduce fundamentally 'new ideas' into New Testament research. . . . If in the intervening years you have altered your outlook, then I am genuinely disappointed, but I am not thereby willing to alter the principles of my work."[18]

The key point here is "new ideas." Lohmeyer was a theological pioneer. He did, of course, enter the major debates of his era, but when he merged into heavy theological traffic patterns, he did so with almost sovereign critical independence, and he followed common currents to uncommon ends. He refused to be infatuated with fashionable falsehoods that prey on all intellectual disciplines. The madness to give theological justification to the German *Volk* was an example of a trend he avoided and sought to refute. More frequently, he took up issues that the scholarly guild did not address, or perhaps had not even thought of. Examples of the latter are his studies in the social context of the New Testament, the topic of martyrdom, a positive and reciprocal relationship between Judaism and Christianity, and many more. Lohmeyer had an aversion for trends and conformity, and a profound trust in rigorous historical scholarship, objective judgments, and independence of thought. Above everything else was his discontent with reducing theology to the mechanics of the discipline or to consideration of individual parts divorced from the pattern of the whole. His indomitable commitment to the theological significance of biblical texts was his solution to the fragmentation of both methods and conclusions. For the Christian interpreter, biblical languages, archaeology and epigraphy, ancient history and sociology, and all exegetical methods were insufficient and meaningless unless they served "believing theology." "By this," explained Lohmeyer, "I mean a theology which starts with faith, raises it to a knowledge informed by faith, and produces a theological system. Every word of faith and every word of revelation which faith apprehends is not content until it has found its proper place in a believing theology."[19]

The Gospel of Mark

Lohmeyer saw the seemingly inauspicious move to Greifswald as an opportunity to produce his long-planned commentary on the Gospel of Mark. He had been interested in Mark from the beginning of his academic career. The previous century of German scholarship witnessed a spectacular reassessment of the Second Gospel. For nearly two millennia Mark had been considered a later and inferior copy of the Gospel of Matthew. By carefully comparing the Greek text of Mark with the texts of Matthew and Luke, however, Friedrich Schleiermacher and his disciples came to a radically different conclusion: the Second Gospel was not an abbreviated clone of the Gospel of Matthew but the first and oldest gospel, indeed the *prototype* for both Matthew and Luke. In his first semester teaching at Heidelberg in 1919, Lohmeyer offered a course on the Gospel of Mark. In the next fifteen years, he offered ten more courses on Mark or aspects related to it, including the passion narratives, Synoptic problem, Son of Man, and early Christian Christology. A decade before he went to Greifswald, he signed a contract with Vandenhoeck & Ruprecht to write the Mark commentary for the Meyer series. By 1934, however, work on the commentary had slowed to a crawl. Disruptions from student demonstrations, church battles, and academic affairs had produced a constant state of confusion. Lohmeyer had told Ruprecht in his final years at Breslau that he "could see no pathway out of the darkness."[20]

The move to Greifswald offered him a serendipitous opportunity to revive the long-forestalled project, and in the Mark commentary we see the quintessence of Lohmeyer the theologian.

Insights and innovations abound in the commentary. One is a thesis he proposed in a monograph entitled *Galilee and Jerusalem*, written a year earlier in preparation for the commentary. Lohmeyer's thesis, specifically, was that especially in the Second Gospel, geography had theological significance. According to Lohmeyer, Mark presents Galilee as a place of blessing, where Jesus first appeared, where throngs gathered to receive his ministry and hear his teaching. "God chose despised Galilee for his eschatological work and gospel."[21] But God also ordained that the gospel should proceed from blessed Galilee to condemned Jerusalem, a city of "enemies" and "sinners." "The way of eschatological fulfillment is so determined by God that what began in chosen Galilee must lead to condemned Jerusalem. God leads Jesus from the chosen homeland of eschatological dawning in Galilee to Jerusalem, the city of enemies and sinners—which are the double homes of the gospel and Son of Man—to the place of hostility and death."[22] This "must" happen (Mark 8:31), says Lohmeyer, but Jesus commanded the disciples to return to Galilee after his rejection and death in Jerusalem, thus indicating that the place where the eschatological work began would also be the place where it was fulfilled (Mark 14:28; 16:7).

The most important "new idea" broached in the Mark commentary was the central and supreme significance of Jesus Christ. If this seems high praise for the predictable, it needs to be remembered that in the first half of the twentieth century German New Testament scholars by and large followed Rudolf Bultmann in attributing the inception of Christianity to the apostle Paul rather than to Jesus. Jesus and John the Baptist were both relegated to the era of the old covenant, not the new. In this schema, the Gospels were viewed as teaching more about the early church than about Jesus. More precisely, the schema purported that the Jesus portrayed in the four Gospels is not a genuine reflection of the historical Jesus but is rather a reflection of his significance for the *early church*. Indeed, in some instances the early church was even believed to have fabricated material about Jesus to vindicate its beliefs. The Jesus of history was relegated to a figure of lesser importance.

The above view was a Goliath in the first half of the twentieth century in German scholarship, and Lohmeyer approached it with the boldness of David with his five smooth stones. The gospel tradition did not begin with Paul, he maintained, but absolutely with Jesus. Indeed, it began with John the Baptist as forerunner. So essential was John as forerunner that Lohmeyer delayed writing his Mark commentary until he had produced a separate volume on John the Baptist, which he intended to be the first of a seven-volume opus on the history of early Christianity.[23] In support of his claim that the gospel was the proclamation of Jesus rather than a self-presentation of the church, Lohmeyer reviewed the various titles that Mark assigned to Jesus—teacher, prophet, anointed, Son of God, and Son of Man. Throughout the gospel, maintained Lohmeyer rightly, Mark interpreted these titles not with reference to the church but with reference to *Jesus*, who stood in the closest possible relation to the person and will of God himself.

With regard to Jesus's teaching, Lohmeyer believed Jesus's most distinctive speech form was parables, which were without parallel elsewhere in the biblical tradition or in other religions. In contrast to the academic theology of his day, which regarded parables as moral maxims, inimitable stories, to be sure, but not essentially different from other sagas, Lohmeyer maintained that parables were distinctive of Jesus, both his artistry in words and his intimate contact with his hearers.[24] Moreover, parables could only be understood with Jesus as their chief referent. The essence of parables was located not only in the message but above all in the Messenger—Jesus. The one who speaks in parables is, in fact, a parable *in nuce*.

Lohmeyer traced Jesus's ethnicity and theological worldview in the Second Gospel to their Jewish roots in the Old Testament. German New Testament scholarship in the first half of the twentieth century commonly interpreted the New Testament in the context of Hellenistic culture and set it in antithesis, even hostility, to Judaism. We saw earlier how the German Christian Movement, and Gerhard Kittel in particular, had capitalized on this latent antagonism to Judaism. Lohmeyer unreservedly affirmed Jesus's Jewishness and regarded it as essential to understanding his mission and message. Christianity was not a Hellenistic religion antagonistic to Judaism, asserted Lohmeyer, but a reform movement within Judaism, a fulfillment of Isaiah's "light to the nations" (Isa. 49:6).

It was common at the time to consider the Synoptic Gospels— Matthew, Mark, and Luke—the more historically accurate gospels and the Gospel of John a later theological treatise virtually devoid of historical value. The Jesus Seminar follows a similar line of thought today. Lohmeyer refused to dismiss the historical veracity of the Fourth Gospel, seeing its narrative of Jesus closer to the Synoptics than was often admitted, and in some instances more historically accurate.

His understanding of the gospel genre was unique for his day. The primary approach to Gospels research in early twentieth-century German theology derived from what was known as the history of religions school. This school believed that all religions began as myths or moral philosophies or came from extraordinary *human* founders. Any claims of the divinity of such founders accrued from later theological legend. In a nutshell, the history of religions school believed that a human Jesus had been later fashioned by the church into a divine Christ. The school further believed that the Gospel of Mark represented the earliest nontheological human historical framework of the Jesus narrative, to which Matthew, Luke, and John applied later theological padding and upholstery.

In an article on John the Baptist published five years before his commentary on Mark, Lohmeyer burst the bubble of this illusion. The Gospel of Mark was not a naïve and pedestrian historical narrative. "Every sentence and every word of it exhibits a distinctive theological perspective . . . and the same is true for Matthew, Luke, and John."[25] Theological perspectives, insisted Lohmeyer, are not the late and final veneer of the Christian tradition but the *earliest* and most formative factor of the Gospels. The sequence was not history first, then faith, but the reverse: the Gospels are the story of Jesus told from the foundational perspective of faith, and thus all four of them are equally valuable for both faith and history.

Lohmeyer's erudition and independence called into question other "received consensuses" of biblical scholarship. Already in early twentieth-century German scholarship, the "Q" hypothesis had achieved wide acceptance in the New Testament scholarly guild. The hypothesis maintained that the earliest stratum of Jesus tradition was a source ("Q" derives from German *Quelle*, "source") of Jesus's sayings that had been drawn upon by the three evangelists (Matthew, Mark, and Luke) and utilized by each evangelist for his unique editorial purposes. Q was purported to be only a *sayings* source, without Jesus's travels, miracles, exorcisms, human encounters, or passion narrative (crucifixion and resurrection). Q thus elevated Jesus's teachings over his saving *activity* in the gospel narratives. In so doing, it diminished or even eliminated the atoning significance of Jesus's death and displaced the person of Jesus with his teaching on the kingdom of God. Q delivered exactly what the Enlightenment expected—or *required*—of religion: Jesus was a moral teacher but not a divine redeemer.

Lohmeyer lamented the fracturing and fragmenting effect of the Q hypothesis, and not only of the Q hypothesis but of *all* source theories. Source theories mired scholars in the putative evolution of the gospel narratives, whereas Lohmeyer was interested in their *Sachlichkeit*, their essence and meaning, the saving significance of Jesus's life. As early as the planning stages of his commentary he wrote to Gustav Ruprecht, "My presupposition will obviously be that the question of source theories will no longer occupy front row in the discussion, as they have for a long time, but be moved three or four rows back."[26]

Lohmeyer was similarly skeptical of the prevailing method of gospel interpretation known as "form criticism." According to form criticism, the earliest Jesus traditions circulated as independent units—"forms"—without any historical context. These units were preserved because of their relevance for the life of the church at the time the Gospels were written. The theory further maintained that the metanarrative, the original narrative structure in which such units or "forms" first appeared, had long been lost. Form critics believed that the gospel writers inserted the disparate "forms," the orphaned units of tradition, into a narrative framework that they themselves fabricated. Mark was believed to be the first fabricated framework, which was essentially followed by Matthew and Luke.

Lohmeyer's artistic and Kantian sense of the whole asserted itself in his rejection of the underpinnings of form criticism. He believed that a meaningful and functional whole, whether in art, music, engineering, or literature, was never the result of a random assemblage of parts. The same was true of the Gospels. They were not "crazy quilts," snippets of dubious authenticity repurposed for later historical contexts, but substantially authentic preservations of the Jesus story *as a whole*. It was, indeed, the essence of the whole that determined the inclusion of the various parts.

The Refiner's Fire

The foregoing discussion gives a sense of the complexity of the issues involved in Gospels research and, hopefully, of Lohmeyer's significance as a theologian in relation to them. His commentary on the Gospel of Mark summarizes the fruition of two decades of research. In my judgment the results are remarkably mature, insightful, and still today largely defensible. This is all the more remarkable because he was forty-five years old when he wrote it, relatively young for a biblical scholar. Moreover, he had produced scholarship of equal significance in several other fields of theology outside Gospels research. And perhaps most significant, he produced this insightful and diverse body of work while enduring over nine years of active service in both world wars—and the attacks on his academic career in between.

Scholars depend on order and predictability and lack of distractions to be productive. It is easy to lament the lack of those factors in Lohmeyer's experience as a scholar. But perhaps we should also consider their possible significance for his scholarship. Perhaps it was not in spite of such things but because of them that Ernst Lohmeyer was the New Testament theologian that he was, that in the refiner's fire of the war years and opposition at Breslau, what otherwise might have remained dross was forged into purer and more permanent metal.

CHAPTER 12

Barbarossa

The most difficult thing about the war is that one is inextricably caught up in its gruesome chaos of horrors and guilt, certainly as guiltless, sometimes even as one who has made every effort outwardly and inwardly to make up for a fraction of the guilt—but the guilt still remains.

Ernst Lohmeyer[1]

War

The contrasts and incongruities that are exceptions in normal life became the norm for Lohmeyer in World War II. Some of the incongruities are strange but interesting curiosities. Duty at the front suddenly relieved by a week's leave to attend the opera with Melie and join the family in Vlotho. Unabated correspondence between Ernst and Melie throughout the war. Two weeks' leave for Lohmeyer to lecture in Sweden . . . or two months' leave to teach at Greifswald. Dried flowers from the Russian steppe carefully enclosed in a letter to Melie. But these curiosities are inevitably overshadowed by questions of greater magnitude. Why would the Third Reich require a forty-nine-year-old professor to fight in the war? How did Melie and Gudrun fare in relative safety in Greifswald knowing the peril their three men faced on the eastern front? And most perplexing—why was Lohmeyer, a believing Christian of uncommon moral rectitude and courage, required to participate in a military campaign on the eastern front that was conducted in flagrant violation of standards of international law?

Hard questions confront us in this chapter, and hard questions are rarely satisfied by easy answers. No chapter in Lohmeyer's life—and in the writing of this book—has left me with a greater sense of inadequacy than this one. How can I, who have never fought in a war, understand Lohmeyer's experience in World War II? How can we in the modern West who acknowledge the inviolability of moral conscience and the inalienability of fundamental human rights understand what Lohmeyer, who believed in both, experienced as he was forced to fight in a war that valued neither? How can we righteously condemn the infamies of the German Wehrmacht on the eastern front without unrighteously condemning individuals in the same Wehrmacht who opposed such infamies and sought to counteract them? How should we think about the astronomical death tolls without profaning the persons who died by reducing them to statistical analyses?

I have tried to forestall impulsive judgments on such matters. I have sought to allow the narrative to remain Lohmeyer's narrative rather than require it to conform to my preferred constructs. Above all, I have sought to preserve the difficult and torturous dilemma that a man of faith and morality like Ernst Lohmeyer faced—and there were many such men in the German Wehrmacht—who was forced to participate in a military campaign that transgressed virtually all canons of human morality.

The Bromberg Massacre

On August 27, 1939, Ernst Lohmeyer was drafted as a lieutenant into the Wehrmacht, the German army. Five days later Germany invaded Poland. The Reich did not refer to "total war" in 1939—the actual phrase would erupt from Goebbels in a rabid tirade in February 1943 following the catastrophic German defeat at Stalingrad. The drafting of a forty-nine-year-old university professor nevertheless clearly indicated the implacable resolve with which the German High Command initiated the war.

Lohmeyer's first responsibility was as platoon commander of Guard Battalion Fourteen, which was sent to Poland. His battalion arrived in Bydgoszcz on September 8, was transferred in rapid succession to Inovrozla on September 10 and to Serius on September 12, after which it returned to Bydgoszcz on September 14, where it remained for the remainder of the fall of 1939.

This itinerary of hard-to-pronounce and obscure place-names would be inconsequential had it not played a role in his arrest in early 1946. In the wake of the German invasion of Poland, Guard Battalion Fourteen massacred a large number of Polish citizens in Bydgoszcz, the German name for which was Bromberg. Since Lohmeyer belonged to Battalion Fourteen, his name became associated with the Bromberg Massacre or Bromberg Bloody Sunday.

The pretext for the massacre took place on Sunday, September 3, three days after the German Wehrmacht invaded Poland, when Nazi partisans fired on a column of Polish regulars marching through Bromberg. A skirmish ensued, in which the Polish regulars killed 170 Nazi partisans and captured 700. The success of the skirmish prompted further Polish resistance groups to attack German citizens, many of whom had moved into Poland following the Treaty of Versailles. The exact number of Germans killed in the reprisals is unknown, although it was perhaps as high as 5,000. The Nazi propaganda mill seized the reprisals as a pretext for merciless retaliation against Poles. The Reich's propaganda minister Joseph Goebbels decreed that the Poles had slain 58,000 Germans. That staggering figure was at least a tenfold exaggeration, but it nonetheless provided the pretext for vehement retaliation. In the five days from September 5 to September 10, the number of Poles massacred by Gestapo, SS troops, SD *Einsatzgruppe* IV, and Nazi police equaled or exceeded Goebbels's figure of slain Germans. The atrocity became, in turn, a pretext for Russian retaliation against Germans at war's end. When Soviet troops entered Greifswald in May 1945, punishment of Greifswald members of Guard Battalion Fourteen was at the top of their list. Within the first week of Russian occupation of Greifswald, several Greifswald members of Guard Battalion Fourteen were arrested.[2]

There is no evidence that Lohmeyer was in Bromberg before September 10, when the massacre ended. Melie and Gudrun both testified that his unit of Guard Battalion Fourteen had not left

Greifswald at the time of the atrocity. The Russian trial record of 1946 corroborated their testimony in this matter, for the Bromberg Massacre, which in itself would have been grounds for Lohmeyer's execution, was never cited in the trial record. It was not included because Russian prosecutors knew that Lohmeyer could verify his absence in Bromberg at the time the massacre was committed.[3]

Lohmeyer was of course not ignorant of atrocities committed by the German army in the invasion of Poland and Russia. Already in November 1939, while still in Poland, he wrote to Rudolf Bultmann lamenting the barbarism of the German invasion, which was not limited to Bromberg Bloody Sunday. "What is happening in the occupied territories is so impossible and unspeakable that it would have been a thousand times better never to have started this war. . . . From a moral perspective we have lost everything in these territories."[4]

Holland and Belgium

In early January 1940, Lohmeyer's battalion was transferred from Poland to the border between Germany and Holland in preparation for the invasion of Holland in May. During the transfer he enjoyed a week's leave back in Greifswald. The five-month stay of military activity on the western front in the first half of 1940 provided him with further relief from the war. He was able to visit Melie again in Greifswald, on another leave to attend the opera with her in Berlin, and on still another to visit his hometown in Vlotho with her in April.[5] From February 27 until March 7 he lectured in Sweden at the invitation of the theological faculty in Uppsala. His theme, "Kultus und Evangelium" (Cult and Gospel), would later appear in monograph form.[6] The lectures were attended by both students and faculty in growing numbers day by day. He was received by Archbishop Erling Eidem and enjoyed warm and collegial dialogue with Anton Fridrichsen, Bishop Gustav Aulen, and Hugo Odeberg. Odeberg was the foremost scholar of ancient Near Eastern languages in Europe at the time, and Lohmeyer agreed to work with Ruprecht in bringing out his work in German. At Lohmeyer's last seminar in

Uppsala, Fridrichsen presented him with a "peace pipe of friend-ship," a gesture of both levity and solemnity, assuring Lohmeyer of the faculty's enduring relationship with him despite Germany's potential military threat to Sweden.[7]

In April 1940 the German Wehrmacht invaded Denmark and Norway, and a month later, on Friday, May 10, it fell upon Holland. Lohmeyer entered Holland with the invading forces and was stationed as commandant of the city of Emmen and environs, an area that included forty-eight villages. In early June of 1940, he was briefly assigned as commandant of a prisoner of war camp in Lokeren, Belgium, east of Ghent.

Throughout 1940, leaves allowed Lohmeyer several visits with Melie, both in Greifswald and elsewhere in northern Germany. During this time he wrote her no letters, surely the longest suspen-sion of correspondence during separations in their married life. Me-lie wrote only three letters to him in the same period, reporting the lows, highs, and in-betweens of life in Greifswald. The first letter reported a low: domestic stress at home during Ernst's absence. In January she had invited two women friends to the house for coffee. Helge, the oldest son, was playing the radio so loud that they could not carry on a conversation. Melie told him to turn the music down. He refused, an argument ensued, and blows were barely averted. Melie was still shaken when she wrote, reporting that she feared "Helge was going to hit her."

Her mood had improved in an April letter, although the tardi-ness of spring's arrival touched a melancholy chord within her. She sent four poems she had composed, handsomely handwritten, each consisting of four quatrains with an *abab* rhyme scheme. One of the poems, "Spring," voiced her longing and melancholy:

> O springtime, springtime, thou art so coy.
> Come at last, strong and sure!
> Springtime, springtime, mock not my joy,
> With thee alone we can endure.

The third letter, in late November, rose several octaves. A small orchestra had performed Bach, Mozart, Brahms, and Schubert at

St. Mary's Church in Greifswald. Melie included a flyer of the concert in her letter. The name at the head of the list of musicians read: "Melie Lohmeyer, Vocalist."[8]

On June 10, 1940, Lohmeyer was transferred from Guard Battalion Fourteen to Territorial Command Unit 708 stationed in Aalst, Belgium, where he served as adjutant, responsible for oversight of a civilian population of some three hundred thousand Belgians. While there he was promoted to first lieutenant. He would remain in Aalst nearly two years—until April 1942—his longest single assignment of the war. Frequent leaves at Aalst provided Lohmeyer with auspicious opportunities to reenter civilian life and pursue his scholarship. His 1940 pocket calendar contained references to Breslau, the summer house at Glasegrund in Silesia, Berlin, and Greifswald, and meetings with colleagues, friends, and family in these and other places. Perhaps most surprising, the Theology Department requested leave for Lohmeyer to resume teaching at the University of Greifswald. The request was approved. For winter semester—January through March 1941—Lohmeyer was back in Greifswald, lecturing at the university and preparing his Sweden lectures for publication, which Vandenhoeck & Ruprecht published in 1942. In *Cult and Gospel* Lohmeyer furthered the thesis he had broached in his letter to Martin Buber, that the worship community from which both the Jesus movement and early church emerged was that of priests, temple, and sacrifices, that is, *Jewish* rather than gentile Greek. This thesis, which seems self-evident today, had to be argued in Lohmeyer's day. Liberal academic scholarship at the end of the nineteenth century and in the early twentieth century, at least in Germany, routinely traced the inception of early Christianity to Hellenistic rather than to Jewish roots. Lohmeyer's intellectual independence boldly cut against the grain of this trend, which unfortunately was often not free from anti-Semitic assumptions.

Aalst was an enviable assignment for Lohmeyer, but it was not without its sorrows. In late January 1942, he received perhaps the saddest news a father can hear. His eldest son, Ernst-Helge, who had turned twenty only two weeks earlier, was missing in action at the Battle of Leningrad. Lohmeyer wrote to Fridrichsen, the friend to whom he often and frankly confided during the war, "We are in deep distress over our son from whom we have heard nothing from the Eastern Front since January 23rd. We live from day to day expecting either good news or bad news. In such circumstances I cannot write or presume to bring out a book. I could only do it with a heavy heart."[9] He closed the letter with a paraphrase of 1 John 5:19, in Greek: "The world is in an evil state." No further word would ever be heard from or about Helge.

The routine and stability of life at Aalst, and the loss of Helge, stimulated correspondence between Ernst and Melie. He wrote her almost daily, and she him nearly as often. The long stretches of inactivity and boredom were reflected in their correspondence. He would have written two days ago, he reported in one letter, but he got a cold that almost developed into the flu. But it didn't. A moment of light humor was the high point of another letter: he had ordered a beer and schnapps from a waiter at a train station, but the waiter brought him two beers instead. When Lohmeyer asked about the schnapps, the waiter said that after 11 p.m. no hard liquor was served, so he substituted a second beer instead. In another letter Lohmeyer rued having to take a slow train with filthy windows and no lighting, robbing him of precious time to read. Given the horrendous tragedies of the war, celebrations of such commonplaces were assuringly newsworthy.[10]

Russia

The Aalst springtime was abruptly terminated in June 1942 when Lohmeyer was transferred with Territorial Command Unit 708 to the eastern front. He would remain in Russia, the most brutal theater of the European war, until April 1943. He dashed off a postcard to Melie on June 23, her birthday. In hundreds of previous letters his signature salutation had always been *"Mein Liebes Herz"* (My Dear Heart). Now it became simply, "L.H." (D.H.). "We are now really in Russia; the landscape remains poor and sandy, with large forests and woods."[11] In early summer his unit passed in short intervals through several Ukrainian cities situated immediately to the north of the Black Sea. He was awakened at 5 a.m. one day—not

knowing exactly where he was—by an army of men talking a foreign language. From his window he saw prisoners of war arriving by
train, broad- and brown-faced, some with Oriental features, from
Georgia, Azerbaijan, and further east in Turkestan. "We have advanced so far and so fast that one can no longer remember what it
was like to stay put in one place," he wrote to Melie in late June, less
than a month after he had left Aalst. Lohmeyer was given temporary
command of several Ukrainian cities: two weeks in Kremenchug,
three days in Stalino (modern Donetsk), a week in Voroshilovgrad
(modern Lugansk), another week in neighboring Azov, southwest
of Rostov, on the northeast tip of the Sea of Azov. In each place he
sought to interact with the inhabitants as people rather than as conquered subjects. The Russians were keen and eager, he told Melie,
"even friendlier than people had been in Flanders."[12]

Lohmeyer arrived in Russia exactly a year after the commence-
ment of Operation Barbarossa, the largest military invasion in history. On June 22, 1941, Germany hurled two hundred divisions, total-
ing three million soldiers, along an 1800-mile front extending from
the Arctic to the Black Sea against the Soviet Union. Barbarossa bore
the hallmarks of terror that stamped the invasion of Poland in 1939,
but the invasion of Russia was, if anything, more savage, a war of
annihilation. Compared to the so-called master race, Poles and Russians were considered "Slavic subhumans" by Nazi ideology, whose
sole future purpose was to serve German interests. At no point in
the Nazi war effort was the military destruction of the enemy more
intertwined with the extermination of the Jews than in the war to establish an "Eastern Imperium" in Russia. The German Wehrmacht
planned not simply to conquer the Soviet Union but to terrorize and
destroy it by deliberate violation of the standards of international
law. Its key objectives, to be achieved by any means, were the destruction of the Soviet state, ruthless exploitation of the economy,
and total subjection of Russia to Germany. Its darkest infamy was the
murder of fourteen million civilians in German-occupied territories
of Russia.[13] It was Lohmeyer's fate—the most unenviable of his life,
to my thinking—to be conscripted into this campaign of infamy, and
in it to follow the course Lohmeyer sought to follow—whenever possible, to lessen the evil, and however small, to ameliorate it.

As the Red Army ceded territory to advancing Wehrmacht and Panzer divisions that extended in ever-long trails of dust into the Russian interior, German occupation forces secured the conquered areas. Lohmeyer's participation in the Russian theater consisted in this second occupational phase. His copious correspondence with Melie continued unabated through the summer of 1942, consisting of no fewer than four or five missives weekly, a few of which were postcards but most of which were letters of no fewer than four pages. Lohmeyer's correspondence makes no mention of Command Unit 708 engaging the Red Army militarily. His reports to Melie describe a nonhostile and often welcoming populace, resulting in a cooperative interface between invaders and invaded. The interface, in fact, was so conflict-free that Lohmeyer, contrary to all expectations, found himself underemployed in his occupational oversight.

It usually took from one to two weeks for Lohmeyer to receive Melie's replies to his letters. Lohmeyer found the intervening silences unbearable. "It's hard to put my thoughts into words each day knowing how long it will be before I hear an answer or echo in return," he protested.[14] We have no trouble imagining Lohmeyer's—and Melie's—aggravation at the time lag. Nevertheless, the ability of the German postal system to deliver a letter, almost always by surface transportation, in a matter of days over a seventeen-hundred-mile war zone was not the least remarkable feat of Germany's war accomplishments.

German artillery had left the areas commanded by Lohmeyer in various degrees of destruction. Of Voroshilovgrad, Lohmeyer reported to Melie in early July that "the city suffered massive devastation. The only buildings still standing are low, small houses, and even these are half destroyed." Communist party leaders of the Russian communities had fled before the advancing Germans, leaving the hoi polloi behind to fend for themselves. Lohmeyer felt a strong attraction to the people. He was impressed by their friendliness and pluck, looking on them as sheep without a shepherd. There was an ethnic amalgam in the Ukraine—Ukrainians, of course, but also Russians, Tatars, Armenians, Georgians, and Jews—all of whom were united in their impoverishment and defenselessness before the onslaught of the Wehrmacht. Lohmeyer was moved by their meekness and ability to find contentment by the simple relief of their daily needs. The young boys and girls liked to mix with Lohmeyer's troops, the girls adorning their hair with flowers.[15]

Lohmeyer alleviated what needs he could. On July 26 he wrote to Melie that a group of his soldiers in search of bread had found a number of soldiers hiding in the fuel depot, having been abandoned by the Ukrainians. Lohmeyer did not identify the hiding soldiers more specifically, perhaps to avoid the charge of aiding the enemy if the letter were intercepted. Lohmeyer's soldiers did not want competitors for scarce food supplies and pressed him as commander to drive the interlopers away. Lohmeyer thought otherwise. He provided a local baker with three zentners—150 pounds—of flour to bake bread for both units. All the soldiers, he wrote Melie, laid into the bread "like flies on honey."[16]

In November of 1939, immediately after his deployment to Poland, Lohmeyer had written to his publisher, Günther Ruprecht, that he was reliving his experience of twenty-five years earlier in World War I, "torn away from all academic pursuits." As a consequence, he would not be able to submit a completed draft of his projected commentary on the Gospel of Matthew.[17] But now, by late fall 1943, a formerly dire situation had turned serendipitous. He resumed his scholarly pursuits with grateful vigor. He reported to Melie that he had many new thoughts after reading and reflecting on the passion narratives of the Gospels, specifically the betrayal of Judas and the trial of Jesus by Pontius Pilate.

Topography of Terror

I wrote this chapter while I was in Berlin in the fall of 2016. My grandson and a friend of his were both studying at European universities for the fall semester, and they visited my wife and me in Berlin for a weekend. They asked to see what I regarded as the single best exhibition of World War II. I took them to the Topography of Terror Museum, located at the intersection of what during the Third Reich had been Wilhelmstrasse and Prinz-Albrecht-Strasse. At this intersection the Reich's three most brutal and infamous terror organizations were headquartered—the SS (*Schutzstaffel*), SD

(*Sicherheitsdienst*), and SA (*Sturmabteilung*). The headquarters was almost totally destroyed during the battle for Berlin in 1945. The site lay vacant until 2010 when the Topography of Terror was erected to offer a complete exhibition of the Nazi reign of terror. Topography surveys the twelve years of Nazi hegemony, the geographical extent of Nazi aggression, and the atrocities wreaked not only on Jews but also on Poles, Russians, and citizens in the various countries occupied by the Third Reich, as well as on Gypsies, Jehovah's Witnesses, political opponents, Catholics and Protestants, homosexuals, and the aged, infirm, vulnerable, and defenseless throughout Nazi-occupied territories. Topography of Terror is an unabridged epic of the Nazi legacy—all the years, all the places, all the peoples, all the crimes—narrated in historical text and original photography, both still and motion.

Topography endeavors to present the epic not simply in callous statistics, but whenever possible it seeks to identify the face of every victim and the face of every perpetrator with a name and a date. To conceal identities is a first step in condoning infamies. Topography of Terror lives up to its name: it is terrifying. But it seeks to be something more, and it succeeds in being something more. It is also salutary. It cannot reverse what happened, of course, nor can it bring back the dead. But it can ensure that neither victims nor perpetrators of evil are forgotten. It is a place of *remembrance*, and remembering is not only a way of honoring the dead but also an important defense against the recurrence of evil.

The day we went to Topography there was a special exhibit on Operation Barbarossa. The subject of the exhibit was not the military invasion, however, but the contingent terror units that accompanied the invasion of Russia—the *Einsatzgruppen* (killing squads), SS and/or Gestapo units, and select units of German soldiers whose sole purpose was to mete out "special treatment" on defenseless victims, always and everywhere to Jews first, but also to many other noncombatants. "Special treatment" was a Nazi euphemism. It meant lining victims up at the rim of an open pit, shooting them in the back, and covering their corpses in mass graves. The exhibition identified 573 locations where, between 1941 and 1944, the above-mentioned killing squads shot to death five hundred or more Jewish men, women, and children, as well as communist functionaries, Roma, psychiatric patients, resisters, and undesirables of whatever sort. Not all the mass killings were done in secrecy. Many photographs show sizable groups of local Russians present, observing and some clearly enjoying the executions. The number of people killed in these shooting operations totaled 1.52 million. This figure is actually far below the actual number of persons murdered, for shootings of *fewer* than five hundred people were not represented on the map. One can only guess how many hundreds, more likely how many thousands, of shootings took place in which fewer than five hundred people were murdered. These staggering statistics are accompanied with photographs of sites and people, the names of which can be identified with certainty.

The special exhibition of the eastern front was not as crowded as the permanent exhibition. Solitary viewers browsed through the exhibit alone, silent, speechless at the atrocities depicted. They moved as though their hearts had stopped beating. My heart had not stopped beating. It was pounding fitfully. The southern regions of the map were where Lohmeyer had been stationed. As I perused the exhibit, I was tormented by a single thought: What if his name was listed, what if I saw his face in a photograph? German crimes and perpetrators of crimes were ubiquitous on the eastern front, and persons of even a modicum of integrity were seemingly rare. What would it mean to be a person of integrity in such a campaign of depravity? I did not see Lohmeyer's name. I knew in my mind that I would not. But even though Lohmeyer was personally absolved of guilt, corporately he was not. In his own words to his colleague Anton Fridrichsen in Sweden, "One is inextricably caught up in the gruesome chaos of shame and guilt of this war." Anyone who watches the flickering motion pictures of Jews being shot in the back as they stand facing a trench sees momentarily the gruesome chaos Lohmeyer described.

Descent into Darkness

By late August 1942—exactly three years after his induction into the Wehrmacht—Lohmeyer was transferred with Unit 708 south to the land bridge between the Black Sea and the Caspian Sea. The Caucasus Mountains extend on a roughly east-west axis between the two seas. There Lohmeyer and his troops would remain until the spring of the year when they, along with the entire German Wehrmacht, would be driven en masse westward out of Russia. Melie cut a map of the area out of a newspaper, marked the cities in red where Ernst was stationed, and kept it with his incoming letters for reference. The area for which Lohmeyer was responsible was larger than the German state of Pomerania in which Greifswald was situated. The region was known as "the Kuban," for the river of the same name that flowed northward from Mt. Elbrus in the Caucasus Mountains and then westward to the neck of the Black Sea and the Sea of Azov. There, in the region south of Krasnodar, Lohmeyer was placed in command of the lower Kuban River valley, especially the cities of Kurtshanskaya and Slavyansk. In accord with his heightened responsibilities, Lohmeyer was promoted to captain.

To the north of the Kuban lay the major Russian city of Stalingrad. There, in January and February of 1943, the most fateful and costly battle in the European theater of World War II took place, a battle that effectively assured Germany's loss of the war and exposed Germany itself to the retaliatory onslaught of the Red Army. Lohmeyer would remain in the Kuban south of Stalingrad until March of 1943. By then General Paulus's Sixth Army had been crushed at Stalingrad and German troops had to find their way, however they could, westward out of Russia. The letters that had flowed so swiftly to Melie throughout the summer now ceased abruptly and completely. The details of Lohmeyer's life in the final six months in Russia can no longer be reconstructed in detail. Only snippets of information and solitary images remain. One snippet speaks volumes. In a letter of November 1942 to his friend and fellow New Testament scholar in Sweden, Anton Fridrichsen, Lohmeyer gave momentary voice to the gravity of his experience. "My family is home and in relative safety, and things are not unbearable for me," he wrote. "But service here is infinitely harder and taking a greater toll on me. I am thin and gaunt, skin and bones, and very gray. Humanity has a capacity to create an inferno, and I have experienced it."[18]

Lohmeyer wrote the above to Fridrichsen *before* the Battle of Stalingrad. What took place at Stalingrad is without comparison, virtually beyond belief. Hitler and the High Command had committed Germany's maximum remaining forces to Stalingrad in a bid to gain access to necessities without which the war could not be sustained—Russian oil, grain, steel, and rubber. A total of 235,000 German troops converged at Stalingrad in the fall of 1942. Russian troops fortified the city but did not fully engage the Wehrmacht amassed on the western side of the city. German troops dug in for the winter, seeking refuge in chop-outs, caverns, earthen huts—anything to protect them from the snow and cold, which plummeted to 40 degrees below zero. The Germans had been unable to take the city of Stalingrad itself—although they had completely destroyed it—but the Russians had not mounted a serious counteroffensive. The Russian enemy remained elusive, seemingly absent.

But it was not absent. Furtively and systematically, the Red Army was encircling General Paulus's entire Sixth Army. In January, the Russian encirclement—1 million soldiers strong—was complete. A quarter-million freezing, starving, and exhausted German soldiers had their neck in a noose. The outcome was disastrous for Germany. The Reich lost 125,000 soldiers in the Battle of Stalingrad—100,000 of them in the last three weeks of January. One hundred ten thousand German soldiers surrendered to the Red Army following the defeat at Stalingrad and were marched by foot, in winter, six hundred miles north to Moscow for a victory parade. From Moscow they were schlepped into the Gulag Archipelago. Of the roughly 235,000 German soldiers dispatched to Stalingrad, only 5,000 returned alive to Germany. That is to say, for every forty-five German soldiers sent to Stalingrad, one—one German soldier—survived![19]

Lohmeyer was not present at Stalingrad, but he suffered the consequences of it in his ten months in the Kuban. He became gaunt and his hair turned gray. Everything essential for the maintenance of life was lacking: food—even for his soldiers—was in short supply, as were medicines, fuel, clothing, and functional housing. The local population, otherwise fearful of the German occupation, trusted Lohmeyer. They came begging, often in droves, for things that he wished to supply them but could not.

Years later, in September of 1989, one of Lohmeyer's students at Breslau, Margarete Tschirley, wrote to Gudrun describing a meeting she had had with Lohmeyer in 1943 after his return from Russia.

> I almost didn't recognize him. Before me no longer stood the young and winning professor whom I once knew, so capable of impressing his students. He had lost his teeth, his face was sallow, and he had aged terribly. Only when he spoke did his old self return, considered and thought-provoking. "You're shocked by my appearance. Loss of teeth. Scurvy. Malnourishment. No vitamins." In connection with this he told me that in one of his areas of command there had been a large apple orchard—a square kilometer. The processing plants connected to it had been destroyed. Previous German commanders had strictly forbidden the populace from picking the apples. Lohmeyer posted an announcement that allowed whoever wanted to, to pick the apples and take as many home as they could carry. "Not an apple was left on the trees, the soldiers and locals took them all." In connection with this story he said something I have never forgotten: "I have nothing to brag about in my life (in the context it was clear that he was referring to his university *Vita* and publication record) except for one thing: I escaped the sentence of death in the war. You have no idea how dispensable life was."[20]

In the early 1980s, Gudrun reflected on her father's ability to endure such desperate circumstances. "It is hard to imagine today that a man who had suffered such oppression as a leader during the Nazi era had the ability in carrying out his duties as an officer of the occupation forces to gain the trust of the Bolshevists, that a man of such high intelligence and deeply rooted human compassion took upon himself such a command."[21] Gudrun found the answer to her question in two characteristics of her father. First, "my father did not withdraw from responsibility when it was required of him. He had a unique gift to engage on behalf of others without taking into consideration the negative consequences doing so might have on him personally."[22] And second, he was sustained by hope for the future rather than disappointments of the present. "I hope I live a long time," he used to tell Melie. "I have so much I want to say."[23] His academic and theological work, the books he wanted to write before he died—and the books he *did* write: *Kultus und Evangelium, Gottesknecht und Davidsohn, The Lord's Prayer, Commentary on the Gospel of Matthew*—this upward call raised him above the gravitational pull of present problems.

Given the iniquitous legacy of the Wehrmacht and its attendant terror apparatus on the eastern front, it is hard to imagine—or believe—reports of German soldiers serving nobly in such an ignoble cause. But there were such soldiers. In January 1994, Israel honored Max Liedtke, an officer in the Wehrmacht on the eastern front who saved "numerous Jews in the Polish city of Przemysl,"[24] as a "Righteous Gentile" at Yad Vashem, the Holocaust memorial in Jerusalem. "Righteous Gentile" is the highest award given by the State of Israel to gentiles who aided Jews during the Holocaust.[25] The testimony of Fritz Kleemann Jr., Lohmeyer's bookkeeper and inseparable companion of three years, speaks similarly of Lohmeyer:

> I lived with Lohmeyer day in and day out from May 1940 until April 1943. Among the troops Lohmeyer had no enemies. His noble human qualities, his innate goodness, and the humanitarian way in which he conducted his command caused people to see him not as an officer but as a caregiver. Everyone—and this included the Russians with whom he was in constant contact—trusted that Lohmeyer would treat requests fairly and resolve them equably. He was never a National Socialist, and not infrequently he indulged in withering critique of the abuses of power among those who held power at the time. No one besides him could have done this with impunity. He was respected for his insistence on absolute truth as well as his uncommon sensitivity to human needs, and these qualities made even the thought of betraying him a cause for shame.

In every occupation zone his first resolve was to allow the Russian population, which often numbered in the thousands, to return to their homes. On one occasion he overtook 3,000 Russian prisoners of war. His own provisions did not suffice for their needs, so he commanded the Russians themselves to supply them with provisions. It was clear from the first day that the vast majority of prisoners of war were civilians, and Lohmeyer arranged for them to return to their homes unhindered. The next day, all but 300 Russian soldiers were released from confinement. He required everything left over in the kitchen to be divided among the Russian people. Lohmeyer did not tolerate mistreatment of Russians. He once punished a warrant officer to three-day detention for punching a Russian in a dispute over a pair of gloves. (That was the only punishment I remember him meting out.) A captured Russian officer once had to be watched for a day and night. Lohmeyer solved the problem by making the officer his guest in his own quarters, offering him a place at the same table, with the same food, drink, and tobacco, as the German officers. At night the Russian officer was put in a room with two beds: one for Lohmeyer and one for a German officer. Lohmeyer made a habit of turning necessity into virtue.[26]

Kleemann's testimony is both surprising and not surprising. It is surprising that anyone in Lohmeyer's situation would act so consistently admirably as Kleemann describes. Yet it is not surprising when one has followed Lohmeyer's life, for the wartime character Kleemann describes is the same character we have seen displayed throughout his life. He was caught up in the war, but he did not become like it. Lohmeyer traveled the same road that others traveled, but he succeeded throughout in taking a different journey.

The Return

In November 1942, three months after Lohmeyer had taken command of the Kuban, he and his troops were making what preparations they could to defend against the long and punishing winter ahead. Directly to the north and unknown to General Paulus's massive German troop encampment, the stalemate in the Battle for Stalingrad was but a brief reprieve before the total destruction of the German Sixth Army. In this calm before the storm, on November 6, to be exact, Dr. Kurt Deissner, professor of New Testament at the University of Greifswald, died. Three days after Deissner's death, the dean of the theology faculty at Greifswald wrote to the minister for science, art, and public education in Berlin requesting Lohmeyer's recall from the Russian front to succeed Deissner. Without Lohmeyer, wrote Dean Walther Glawe, the university would have to fill the position with interim appointments of foreigners from Sweden, Hungary, or Finland. Moreover, Glawe added, Lohmeyer was now fifty-two years old, and his only two sons were already war casualties. The older, Ernst-Helge, was missing and presumed dead, and the younger, Hermann-Hartmut, was convalescing with a serious head wound. Lohmeyer's academic qualifications, coupled with his age and adverse family circumstances, more than justified his release from military service.

On February 1, 1943—in the absolute vortex of the annihilation befalling the German Wehrmacht at Stalingrad—Lohmeyer responded to the university administrator's request for his return to assume the New Testament chair at Greifswald. "Your letters arrived at a very difficult and tense time," he wrote. "Everything is in commotion, and communications which until now had been stable are now torn apart."[27] The final decision in the matter lay in the hands of his commanding general, but Lohmeyer was optimistic the request would be granted. He nevertheless reminded the administrator of the immediate obstacles to the logistics of his return: winter weather was severe, ground communication was either severed or interrupted, and airmail sporadic. Delays in responses were inevitable. Lohmeyer begged forgiveness from the administrator for sending his reply via Melie, explaining that he needed to spare his final few airmail stamps.[28]

Following the defeat at Stalingrad, everywhere along the nearly fifteen-hundred-mile eastern front, from Leningrad in the north to the border of Turkey in the south, divisions of the Wehrmacht were in westward retreat in the spring of 1943. By then the Russian counteroffensive was full throttle, with Russians doing to German troops and civilians what German troops had done to them. Lohmeyer and his troops were no longer winning the war but losing it, and trying not to lose their lives in the process. German troops commenced the frightful withdrawal from Russia by truck or wagon, by cart or foot, by virtually any means possible to keep from falling into the hands of the enemy. Lohmeyer kept two diaries during the retreat. The first, written in a proper 5″ x 7″ diary with padded cover, extended from March 24 to April 6. He left a two-week gap of blank pages after the last date, evidently intending to fill in the missing interval later, but he never did. The first diary was followed by a second, smaller volume about the size of a pocket datebook. It contained only three entries—April 22, 23, and 24, immediately prior to his return to Greifswald. Both diaries were written in pencil, the first in cramped and brittle script that is barely legible, the second in his well-governed signature script.[29]

The two documents provide a broken narrative of the roughly six-hundred-mile return from the Kuban to Greifswald. The westward trek began very early each morning, between 3 and 4 a.m., with brief rests along the way. One day he covered twenty-five kilometers. Lohmeyer carefully governed the information in the diaries. Good accommodations are recorded, for example, but bad ones are omitted, as are virtually all references to other stresses and hardships endured. Lohmeyer encountered far worse circumstances in the flight from Russia than he recorded in the two diaries; he almost certainly wanted no pejorative references to Russia and Russians in his diaries if he were captured by the Red Army. Somewhat unexpected in the frantic flight westward was Lohmeyer's mindfulness of the church year, dating entries "Good Friday," "Easter Monday," or "Sunday." One Sunday he attended the only available church service, Roman Catholic. He noted the scarves covering women's heads and the piety of the worshipers, kneeling, fervent in prayer. The Eucharist sparked a half-page reflection on the doctrine of transubstantiation, that is, belief that the words of institution convert the bread and wine to the actual body and blood of Christ. On that Sunday, in those circumstances, the undoubted sincerity of the worshipers was more important for him than the theological complexities of the doctrine.

Lohmeyer began a number of diaries in his life but finished almost none of them. Nor are his diaries particularly transparent and revealing. If you want to feel Lohmeyer's pulse, you will not find it in his diaries. You must read his letters. There you have your hand on the strong and steady beat of his heart, and your mind is infused with the vitality of his mind and character and soul. His diaries were sporadic, but his letters flowed throughout his life, uninterruptedly, in all directions and to all destinations. There is an important insight into his personality in this observation. He was not interested in writing primarily as a way of processing his thoughts, or of speaking either about or to himself. For Lohmeyer, writing was not a mirror. It was a *conduit* for relationships with Melie and Hönigswald and Fridrichsen and the host of recipients, scholars and friends alike. The volume and quality of his correspondence reveal him to be a man who, by nature, belonged to the tribe of Buber—"I and Thou."

Two poignant vignettes from Lohmeyer's flight westward come from Melie's later account. German soldiers retreating before the Red Army passed through villages with starving and often critically ill inhabitants, "without absolutely any possibility of offering them shelter or help." In one instance, however, Lohmeyer reported to Melie, he succeeded in sheltering Russians infected with typhus and other illnesses in makeshift barracks, although there was not even fresh straw for them to lie on. And at transportation hubs along the westward path, Lohmeyer used his authority as a German commandant to arrange for Jews, who otherwise would have been shot by the SS, and also for Russian mayors and civic leaders, to be transported to the west either by train or plane.[30]

On April 24, 1943, there came a knock on the door of the Lohmeyer home on Arndtstrasse 3 in Greifswald. With all the men away at war, and with herself and Puppi alone in the house, Melie kept the door locked. She was not expecting anyone. Perhaps it was a beggar. Melie was not prepared for what she saw, nor was she until then aware of the toll that a son killed on the eastern front, another son critically wounded on the eastern front, and a husband commanding on the eastern front had had on her. She opened the door to see a man, aged and exhausted. Her heart stopped. There, standing before her, was Ernst.

Thirty years later she recalled her response to Ernst in that moment as the most regrettable of her life. "If only I had opened my arms to him and received him with a warm and loving heart our subsequent unhappiness would not have happened. But I was paralyzed, paralyzed in grief over Helge's gruesome death, paralyzed in the loneliness of my heart that had grown callous, because Ernst had for years left me inwardly alone. I was like a piece of wood, and he, who had awaited this moment with the deepest expectation and hope of his soul, was the same."[31]

CHAPTER 13

New Beginnings

We journey through the years and all our journeys are only
a standing still before God. We hold our life in trembling
hands and all our trembling is steadfast firmness. We lament
and we rejoice in our abilities. All affliction and joy are only
a faint reflection of a bright light. For wherever we go and
whatever we experience, in darkness and daylight, in weakness and strength, in evil and good, in everything God is
present. For God is light and in him there is no darkness;
the darkness passes away and the light remains shining.

Ernst Lohmeyer[1]

Return to Greifswald

Lohmeyer had not expected to survive the eastern front. Gudrun
later wrote, "My father thought he would never return home from
Russia. Now it had actually happened, but he brought the shadows
of the experience home with him."[2] He savored the joy of surviving the war alive, understandably. We need only recall his words to
Margarete Tschirley: "I escaped the sentence of death in the war.
You have no idea how dispensable life was."[3] But he also had to
learn how to live under its attending "shadows." His body was beset
with dysentery, his complexion yellow, and the visage staring back
at him from the mirror was gaunt and changed. The inevitable catastrophe awaiting Germany on account of "the hated Nazi regime
infuriated him and overshadowed his entire existence," said Melie.[4]

The catastrophe awaiting Germany had already befallen his own family. His oldest son, Helge, had disappeared in January of 1942 in "the hell of Damiansk," never to return. His second son, Hartmut, was alive but critically wounded. His life-giving vocation as a scholar had been interrupted for four profligate years. The four years, in fact, could potentially be extended. Lohmeyer's recall from the eastern front had not been an official discharge from military service—and would not be for another six months. Both joys and shadows were present in his return to Melie. He was at last back with his "Dear Heart," as he called her, but their nearness was not a warm and healing togetherness. "Despite the palpable happiness of being together again," he wrote Anton Fridrichsen two months after his return, "my wife and I find it strange to be living together again. If times were not so grave and ominous we might be able to learn more quickly what we need to learn."[5]

One of the immediate blessings of Lohmeyer's return was freedom from university classroom responsibilities until the fall. He had six months to convalesce, and he made the most of each day in the only way he knew to restore himself. He read. Especially literature of abiding cultural significance—Charles Dickens, Wilhelm Raabe, C. F. Meyer, Gottfried Keller, Hugo Hoffmannsthal, and always and above all Friedrich Hölderlin. And he wrote. In eight weeks he prepared a five-hundred-page edition of Martin Luther's commentary on Romans, which he never published.[6] Luther's 1515–1516 lectures on Romans were lost until they were discovered in 1908 by Johannes Ficker, professor of church history at Strasbourg, in the Secret Prussian Archive in Berlin-Dahlem—the same archive, incidentally, where I wrote the majority of this biography in 2016. It was presumably Ficker's lately discovered manuscript that Lohmeyer edited.[7]

In fall 1943 university duties resumed, ending Lohmeyer's six months' convalescence. The resumption of duties brought its own blessings. In November, he was officially discharged from the army, which meant he could not be redeployed in the war.[8] His reintegration into the teaching rotations of the theology faculty rejuvenated him. The university, not surprisingly, was not fully functional. Virtually everything needed for its operation was absent, in short supply, or rationed, including heating fuel, electricity, paper, medicines, food, and materials of all sorts. The vast majority of male students, including many faculty, were away at war. The university had to reduce its schedule and course offerings accordingly. Despite these exigencies, the Theology Department at Greifswald ironically *increased* in demand and size in 1943-1944. The universities of Cologne, Kiel, Rostock, Königsberg, Leipzig, Berlin, and Breslau had been bombed out, forcing theology students to go elsewhere to continue their studies. The universities of Tübingen and Greifswald, which had not been bombed, were still open, and many orphaned theology students divided themselves between the two to complete their studies. Lohmeyer plunged into a full teaching load. In winter semester 1943-1944 he taught on the Gospel of John and the apostle Paul. In summer 1944 he lectured on New Testament theology and the Sermon on the Mount, and in winter semester 1944-1945 he lectured on New Testament theology again and the Lord's Prayer. In addition, he taught the New Testament seminar in each of the foregoing semesters.[9] Seldom had his teaching responsibilities been heavier!

"Believing Theology"

In 1941 Rudolf Bultmann wrote an essay entitled "The New Testament and Mythology," in which he asserted that the New Testament worldview was essentially mythical in character. Bultmann believed this mythical worldview—its three-storied universe of heaven, earth, and hell, and its accompanying belief in miracles, angels, and demons—had been rendered obsolete by modern science, and as such was no longer credible to modern believers. He also believed, however, that imprisoned in this outmoded mythical worldview was a kernel of the gospel, which he referred to as the *kerygma*—the Greek word for the early Christian proclamation of the gospel. This captive kernel, Bultmann believed, was still valid. He proposed a program, which he called "demythologizing," of liberating the *kerygma* from its obsolete straitjacket. The task of theology was to strip the *kerygma* of its outmoded New Testament worldview, like corn is stripped of its husk, in order to render the gospel once again credible to modern scientific believers.[10] The end result of Bultmann's demythologizing project closely resembled in both terminology and concept the existential philosophy of human existence that Martin Heidegger set forth in *Being and Time*.

On January 9, 1944, Lohmeyer took the train from Greifswald to Breslau, presumably at the request of the Confessing Church there, to address the issue of demythologizing.[11] Lohmeyer did not regard demythologization as an unprecedented challenge to the church's understanding of Scripture. He saw it rather as a further attempt of the eighteenth-century Enlightenment project to emancipate "eternal ideas of reason from the cloak of tradition," thus purging eternal ideas "of every bit of mythological sense—or nonsense."[12] If "demythologizing" per se had not been specifically proposed before in the Enlightenment project, it was nevertheless part of the same project, a new railway car, so to speak, coupled to the long-established train of Enlightenment thinking. We should hardly be surprised that Lohmeyer's aesthetic sensitivities would resist Bultmann's disemboweling of the gospel imagery. Bultmann, of course, did not claim to alter the gospel but rather to liberate it from its imprisoned impotence. Lohmeyer argued, however, that he *had* altered it, indeed reduced it to a philosophy of life. He regarded Bultmann's demythologizing program as an "existentialist philosophy that is no more than a secularized form of Christian theology."[13] For Lohmeyer, existentialism was too narrow to deal with the range of theology, for existentialism was limited to human existence, thus making man the center of the universe, whereas theology—and myth—dealt with God and spiritual realities as well.

Shucking the husk from the kernels was a false analogy for Lohmeyer, for the simple reason that a husk was not essential to the kernel whereas the embodiment of the gospel was essential to its meaning. Demythologization did "violence to the inner and unbreakable unity in which permanent truth and historical form are combined."[14] To strip "flesh" from John's declaration that "the Word became flesh" destroys the incarnation; to object to "Father" and "heaven" in "Our Father who art in heaven" is to assert that God cannot be identified with anything creaturely; to discard "it was night" in John 13:30 eliminates the chief metaphor of evil from the Fourth Gospel.

The problem with demythologization, in Lohmeyer's mind, was its dualism, its division of reality into two spheres, essence and form, and discarding of the latter in order to "emancipate" and preserve the former. Bultmann was wholly committed to *kerygma*, proclamation of the gospel, but his program of proclamation required dismissing historical realities essential to "the Christ event." Lohmeyer rejected this bifurcation, which he believed to be overcome in the incarnation, to which Christian faith attests. "God requires faith—an almost tautological statement, but it includes the requirement of a believing theology. By this I mean a theology which starts with faith, raises it to a knowledge informed by faith, and produces a theological system. Every word of faith and every word of revelation which faith apprehends is not content until it has found its proper place in a believing theology."[15] Lohmeyer concluded his response to demythologization with a variation of Immanuel Kant's famous dictum from *Critique of Pure Reason* that "thoughts without contents are empty, [and] intuitions without concepts are blind." For Lohmeyer, the answer to demythologization—and to all biblical theology—was this: "Without believing theology all academic theology is empty, and without academic theology all believing theology is blind."[16]

The Lord's Prayer

The final complete work in Lohmeyer's theological legacy was his exposition of the Lord's Prayer in Matthew 6 and Luke 11.[17] *Das Vater-Unser—The Lord's Prayer*—could be considered his crowning achievement, for more than his other works, it united his incisive exegetical skills and his abilities as a theological synthesizer in producing a work on prayer that is rewarding to scholar and layperson alike. Only two of Lohmeyer's books have been translated into English. *The Lord's Prayer*, fortunately, is one of them, affording the English-speaking world an excellent and surprisingly complete example of Lohmeyer's work.[18] He began the book, as he had several earlier books, with a preparatory theological essay entitled "The Lord's Prayer as a Totality," which he published back in 1938 in *Theologische Blätter* (*Theological Papers*).[19] Lohmeyer worked intermittently on *The Lord's Prayer* in the following years, even in Russia, as several references in letters to Melie in 1942–1943 testify. He completed the study after his return to Greifswald in 1943. The work touched a deep chord within Lohmeyer's spiritual life. If it were marketed today, it might appear under the rubric "Spiritual Formation." Lohmeyer was aware that politically hermetic East Germany would scarcely be interested in a book on the Lord's Prayer, and he appealed to his son Hartmut, and after his arrest to Melie also, for assistance in getting the volume published by Günther Ruprecht in the West.

Lohmeyer launched the exposition with an insightful consideration of "Our Father." There are only two personal substantives in the Lord's Prayer—God and the first-person plural pronoun, "we/our." The first-person singular pronoun, "I," does not occur in the prayer. We come before God and stand before him only as "we." God makes human community possible in this world, and fellowship with God is not simply my personal destiny but *our* corporate final destiny. "Our" includes Christians and Jews, and indeed all people. The Lord's Prayer is not a particular individual's prayer nor the prayer of a particular group of people or nation or religion. It is devoid of all distinctive religious doctrines: there is no explicit reference to creation, exodus, covenant, law, prophecy, kingship, Israel, church, or even "the Lord" (= Jesus) himself. It is the simple prayer of "God's children as they stand before their Father."[20]

The second word of the prayer, "Father," identifies God. In Jesus's mother tongue of Aramaic, the word for "Father" would have been *Abba*. In Father-*Abba*, all that remained hidden and obscure and unapproachable in God's self-revelation to Moses as YHWH is made clear and near and intimate. The total mystery of YHWH is resolved and summed up in God as "Father," *Abba*. "God is there—there as Father—to all who ask." In this everyday word and relationship common to all humanity, in God as *Abba*, the mystery and secret of YHWH have been fulfilled and replaced.[21] We have spoken several times of Lohmeyer's theological insights that bore fruit in later New Testament scholarship. His insight with regard to

Abba in the Lord's Prayer is one of the most noteworthy, for Joachim Jeremias—who was Lohmeyer's predecessor at Greifswald—developed Lohmeyer's insight regarding *Abba* into a study that would distinguish Jeremias among New Testament scholars. Twenty years after Lohmeyer's *Lord's Prayer*, Jeremias proposed what has since become one of the assured consensuses of New Testament scholarship, that *Abba* is one of the truest and surest characteristics of Jesus's teaching not only about God but also by implication about *himself* as God's Son.[22] Jeremias, regrettably, did not credit Lohmeyer for his acute insight regarding *Abba*.

Lohmeyer understood all seven petitions of the Lord's Prayer in light of God as *Abba*. In the Lord's Prayer, Jesus instructed disciples how to approach and petition God, and in his own life and ministry he *demonstrated* how to do the same. An especially difficult petition is "on earth as it is in heaven," which was perhaps intended to follow each of the first three petitions—that God's name should be hallowed, his kingdom come, and his will be done. Lohmeyer warned against imagining that believers should expect the full realization of the kingdom of God in this world, and he further warned against concluding that the lack of its realization in this world rendered faith invalid. The incarnate Jesus lived within the same tension of pressing needs and unfulfilled hopes. Lohmeyer regarded Jesus's prayer in the Garden of Gethsemane, "*Abba*, Father, everything is possible to you. Take this cup from me, nevertheless, not my will, by Thy will be done" (Mark 14:36), as both a commentary on and model of the third petition of the prayer.

Lohmeyer followed the second-century church father Tertullian in his estimation of the Lord's Prayer as *breviarium totius evangelii*—a digest or compendium of the entire gospel! Lohmeyer interpreted the prayer not simply as a summary of the teaching of Jesus, or even of the four Gospels, but as a summary of the *gospel* itself. By *breviarium totius evangelii* Lohmeyer did not mean a compendium of the biblical witness, for as he noted, "there is not a single mention in the prayer of all the manifold gifts and commandments in which the Jews, as God's chosen people, prided themselves."[23] In the Lord's Prayer, rather, Jesus distilled faith to its absolute essence—that of a relationship of a child to his or her father. That essence depended solely on Jesus. "In the form of the Master the petitioner finds the surety of faith, for Jesus proclaims the coming Kingdom, he works through the Kingdom, and he gives this Kingdom prayer to his disciples."[24]

President Lohmeyer

In the spring of 1945, the westward Soviet advance crushed the failing defenses of the German Wehrmacht in the east. The Red Army had reached the Oder River, and Germany faced imminent and total defeat. Despite Hitler's scorched earth decree—that Germany, like Valhalla in Wagner's *Twilight of the Gods*, should face annihilation—the city fathers of Greifswald recognized the futility of attempting to defend the city and the inevitability of its destruction if a defense were attempted. A Russian military assault would result in senseless carnage in Greifswald, whose population of forty thousand was nearly doubled by the influx of refugees from the east. Lohmeyer counseled Dr. Carl Engel, president of the university, on the futility of a last stand. On the night of April 29, Engel, the commander of Greifswald's military resistance, two professors of the medical school, two drivers, and two interpreters drove twenty-five miles southeast to Anklam, which was burning in flames, to meet with Major General Borstschev of the Red Army to offer the capitulation of Greifswald. The offer was accepted. The artillery attack scheduled for Greifswald was withdrawn, and at noon on April 30, 1945, a dozen officials and leading citizens of Greifswald, Lohmeyer included, surrendered the city peacefully to the Soviet forces.

The Soviets required Greifswalders to cease all military resistance, surrender their weapons to the town hall, and refrain from plundering. For its part, the Red Army agreed not to station military forces within the city proper and guaranteed that administrative, business, and educational life of Greifswald, including the university, would proceed "without interruption under German auspices."[25] The peaceful surrender of Greifswald was a demonstration of courage and foresight in the face of Hitler's fanatical order of German self-extermination. It resulted not only in the preservation of Greifswald, one of the few cities in the Russian zone to escape destruction, but also in the preservation of the university, which was the sole university east of the Elbe to survive destruction.[26]

Three days after the surrender of the city, the university officially resumed limited operation. Within two weeks Greifswald University president Carl Engel was arrested by the Soviets. Engel was an unusual combination of vice and virtue. In terms of vice, Engel was an ardent and unrepentant member of the Nazi Party—and had been since 1933. But in terms of virtue, he was not a coward. Unlike the vast majority of Nazi Party members in the Russian sector who fled to West Germany before the advancing Soviet troops, Engel, who had a car and could have fled, remained in Greifswald at his post. In early May 1945 he was swept up in a wave of Soviet arrests and imprisoned in Fünfeichen, a former Nazi concentration camp that the Red Army had converted to a Soviet concentration camp. There Engel, along with some six thousand other Germans arrested and imprisoned by the Soviets between 1945 and 1948, died.

In the wake of Engel's arrest, Lohmeyer was named president of the university on May 15 by the Soviet Military Administration of Germany.[27] Contrary to German university protocol, Lohmeyer was not elected president de jure by the faculty but was *made* president de facto by the Soviet administration. This appointment surely constitutes one of the greater paradoxes in the postwar era—an officer who served in the German Wehrmacht on the Russian front being proposed and installed by the same Russians as president of a German university in Soviet-occupied East Germany.[28] Why the Soviets would have installed a man *like* Lohmeyer is perhaps the wrong question. The right question is why they installed *Lohmeyer.* Several reasons, not inconsiderable in the circumstances, commended him. His personal record of opposition to Nazism relieved him of suspicion of being a Nazi sympathizer, and his record as president of the University of Breslau and as commander of a large region of German-occupied Russia attested to his administrative abilities. Lohmeyer's record as a commandant on the eastern front, in fact, commended him as a man the Soviets could *trust.*

The choice of Lohmeyer as president was good for the university, but it did not improve his marital relationship with Melie. In fact, it almost certainly worsened it. He had told Melie nothing of the process leading to his appointment as president. This was perhaps due, in part, to his reticence regarding personal accomplishments, but it was more likely due to the breakdown in communication between the two. Melie wanted to spare Ernst from the toll that the presidency of Breslau had taken on him in the early '30s. "I was totally surprised," she later wrote, "when he mentioned in passing in the spring of '46 that he had been chosen as president of the university, and that he had accepted. I had no inkling of it. All plans had been made outside the house, and he simply came and went as a foreign and silent guest."[29] Melie made a mistake in the date of this entry (Lohmeyer was made president in spring 1945 rather than 1946), but there was unfortunately no mistake in her description of the state of their relationship.

In Melie's later memoir to her children, which I quoted at the end of the last chapter, she blamed their subsequent marital misfortunes on her coldness and unresponsiveness when Lohmeyer returned from Russia.[30] We have no way of calculating the effect on Ernst of her "paralysis," to use her word, but given his harrowing return from the East and his wasted condition, it must wounded him deeply. But in the same quotation Melie hinted that she responded as she did not only because of the loss of Helge at the Battle of Leningrad and Ernst's pitiful state but also because "for years Ernst had left her inwardly alone."[31] The effect of Lohmeyer's emotional abandonment of Melie would be equally difficult to calculate. His fervent academic camaraderie with colleagues like Hönigswald; his inexhaustible intellectual energy, as evinced by his academic publications in the 1920s and 1930s; his indefatigability in university politics—all were accomplished at a cost to his relationship with Melie. When we recall Lohmeyer's ode to productivity in his first sermon,[32] we can believe Melie's sense of inner loneliness. Lohmeyer's acceptance of the presidency of the University of Greifswald without consultation with his wife was a further instance of his inner migration away from Melie, and further cause for her isolation.

Nor was emotional distance the only bone of contention. Lohmeyer's collaboration with the Russian occupation in the process of reopening the university became a protracted point of disagreement between Ernst and Melie. His service on the eastern front had given him a sympathy for the Russian people, especially the peasants with whom he had had much contact. This sympathy seems to have inclined him to give the benefit of the doubt—sometimes even unquestioned endorsement—to the Russian occupation. Melie did not share this optimism or trust of the Russian occupation or of the persons associated with it. Her warnings to Ernst on this matter seemed, from her perspective, to fall on deaf ears, and what she judged as Ernst's uncritical collaboration with the Russian occupation became a standing point of contention between the two of them. The distance between them "remained the same," she said. "We were both cold and dead."[33]

The New Regime

Travel to distant places sometimes requires us to set our watches to new time zones. In the spring of 1945, something of the reverse happened to Lohmeyer: the Russian occupation brought a new "time zone" to Greifswald, and it was imperative that Lohmeyer—and all Germans in the Soviet sector—adjust his clock accordingly. The events that transpired rapidly and inexorably in Lohmeyer's life in 1945 cause one to ask whether he adjusted his clock—his understanding and modus operandi regarding the Russian occupation—sufficiently. The simple facts of the matter seem to require the question. The facts are these: Lohmeyer survived twelve years of the Third Reich, during which he comprehensively opposed Nazism in principle and on occasion opposed it in specific protests. He was never arrested or imprisoned, however. Yet within nine months of the communist takeover in Greifswald, without having opposed communist regulations to the same degree that he had opposed Nazi regulations, he was both arrested and imprisoned, and eight months later executed.

What happened? Why did it happen? Could Lohmeyer have acted otherwise to avoid it? There were surely few professors in Germany who opposed the Hitler era as clearly, steadfastly, and successfully (if you consider survival a success) as did Ernst Lohmeyer.

Did he lack the same perspicacity in his dealings with the Soviets in Greifswald? Did his sympathy for the Russian people as a commandant on the eastern front induce him to misjudge the Russian occupation of Greifswald? Melie would have answered these questions with at least a qualified yes. Events that unfolded in Lohmeyer's life seem to verify Melie's judgment. We should keep in mind, however, that Lohmeyer did not survive two years on the eastern front by misjudging similar matters, or by being naïve and foolish. Is it likely that Lohmeyer would be fox-smart regarding Nazis and ox-dumb regarding communists? We must reckon with the possibility that the Soviet occupation was simply more insidious and ruthless than Nazism had been in Germany. Josef Stalin's ruthless smashing of the landed peasantry in the early 1930s; his murder of some six million kulaks, as he ignominiously called them; his elimination of Russia's agricultural workers that resulted in a famine that took the lives of another two or three million Russians by starvation—all these were evidence of iron-fisted Soviet subjugation. The total number of Russians who perished at the hand of *Stalin* in the 1920s and 1930s approximated ten million people, a number that exceeded any single people-group murdered by the Nazis.[34] The Soviet Gulag equaled in size the Nazi concentration camp system. Descriptions of the Soviet prison system in Aleksandr Solzhenitsyn's *Gulag Archipelago* or in Victor Herman's *Coming Out of the Ice* are, sadly, no less terrifying than those of survivors of Nazi concentrations camps.

Nothing can be gained by arguing which of the two evils—Nazism or communism—was worse. But something may be gained by determining which was the more *invasive*. An understanding of this point may shed at least some light on Lohmeyer's situation in 1945-1946. Here I wish to share a personal experience that has made me stubbornly sympathetic with respect to his situation in Greifswald.

In the spring of 1971, I was in Berlin preparing to lead my first trip into East Germany with Berlin Fellowship. I had graduated from Princeton Seminary in 1970 and had just completed a year of New Testament study at the University of Zürich. The pastor who arranged the various teams and travels into East Germany from West Berlin was the Reverend Ted Schapp. Ted knew of my interest in theology and asked if I wanted to meet with a Marxist theologian in East Berlin. I welcomed this rare and intriguing opportunity. On a balmy spring evening, Ted parked his car at Kochstrasse in West Berlin. We both passed through Checkpoint Charlie and made our way to one of the modern and standardized high-rise apartments typical of communist East Berlin. After climbing several flights of stairs, we found the name Fink on a door.

There we were received by Dr. Heinrich Fink, professor of pastoral theology at Humboldt University in Berlin. The apartment was classic German Democratic Republic decor: soft linoleum flooring, pastel wall papering, living room that calved off into two bedrooms, all with a faint acrid smell of soft lignite coal, the main heating source in East Germany. The Finks had set the central coffee table with beer, wine, and pretzels for our visit. The only thing atypical in this apartment were the floor-to-ceiling bookcases that lined the living room walls. The Finks were avid readers, he as a theology professor at the university and his wife as a pastor.

Fink's Marxist convictions were well known. Among East Germany's intelligentsia, he was perhaps even a household name. He did not belong to the circle of pastors associated with Berlin Fellowship, and Ted and I had not visited him to talk about the Fellowship. We were interested in hearing how Fink's Marxist convictions accorded with his Christian beliefs. He had written his doctoral dissertation on Karl Barth, and he reminded us that although Barth was sharply antagonistic to Nazism, he had held a more accommodating position regarding communism. He was right on both points. The Finks' daughter suffered from a disability, the exact nature of which I can no longer recall, which both he and his wife assured us would have ill-fated her in Nazi Germany. This was also true. In socialist East Germany, by contrast, their daughter received special medical and educational benefits. In addition to socialized medicine, the Finks hailed prohibition of pornography and guns, lack of homelessness, low crime rates, and high social welfare as triumphs of communist East Germany.

Our conversation flowed like a stream, rapidly at some points and more leisurely at others. We talked mostly about modern theology, including liberation theology, the then-popular "theology of hope," the church in the States—especially with regard to the Vietnam War and civil rights—and the church in East Germany. The Finks' perspective on politics and theology, and their promise for the common good, was understandably much different from the perspectives of Ted and me. They were very able apologists for communism. Ted and I were skeptics—although we sought to be gracious skeptics. We all had assumed our differences from the outset, and the assumption freed us to hear the differences of the other without feeling coerced to agree. Cases were made on both sides with conviction and civility. I look back on the conversation as one of the more unusual and interesting of my life.

Shortly after midnight Ted and I excused ourselves, wound our way down the stairs, and walked back to the prefab East German checkpoint at Friedrichstrasse opposite Checkpoint Charlie. Ted preceded me in line at the checkpoint. After a brief moment at the counter, the border guard stamped Ted's passport, and he exited the building and walked the thirty or forty yards to Checkpoint Charlie in West Berlin. We had agreed to meet at Kochstrasse, where we had parked our car. The guard motioned me forward. I expected a repeat of the routine—a cursory inspection of my passport, the turning of a few pages, then a thump of the East German customs stamp that covered a whole passport page. Rather than a thump, however, the official motioned me to follow him down a hallway and into a barren room with a table and two chairs. Once we were seated, I was ordered to empty my pockets on the table. Among my possessions was a day calendar, which the officer went through methodically, expecting elaborations from me of various entries. A volley of questions commenced—Why was I in Berlin? Where had I come from? Where had I been in East Berlin, and what had I done there? With whom had I spoken? What had we talked about? These questions were repeated and rephrased, and others added to them, with Gatling gun relentlessness.

Answer questions without arousing suspicion, I reminded myself. The rule regarding interrogations at border crossings was to answer questions sufficiently to satisfy the interrogator but not so completely as to incriminate those in the East. This rule seemed eminently reasonable when I first heard it. But at the East German checkpoint the rule failed me, for it did not account for the element of fear. At the moment, the fear element was considerable. I reminded myself that I had done nothing wrong. I wasn't smuggling, wasn't exchanging money illegally, and my association with Berlin Fellowship, which would have been more problematic, was fortunately unknown and unmentioned. Such realities and rationalizations failed to quell the fear, however. The United States had no diplomatic relations with communist East Germany in 1971. The East German authorities could do whatever they wanted with me. Guilt or innocence was irrelevant. I would have no legal recourse.

There was a small window in the interrogation room, directly behind the officer questioning me. Through the window I could see the lighted guardhouse of Checkpoint Charlie in the middle of Friedrichstrasse. The silhouettes of men inside would be of US soldiers—Americans. The safety I had always taken for granted and now longed for was there at Checkpoint Charlie. But I wasn't there, and I wasn't safe. The thirty or forty yards in between separated the First World and the Second World. The two points seemed, quite literally, worlds apart.

After an hour or so, the interrogation ended as unceremoniously as it had begun. The official ushered me back down the hall, stamped my passport, and released me. As I walked toward Checkpoint Charlie, my legs began to ache and I felt short of breath—precisely the psychosomatic response the interrogation had been engineered to provoke.

In the following decades, I passed through East German checkpoints many times without anything remotely similar happening. As time passed I began to consider the above experience a rogue event, an anomaly that was bound to happen from time to time in East Germany. I ceased to think much about it. Nineteen years later, in June of 1990 to be exact, I was again in Europe. The Berlin Wall had been opened six months earlier, and I was traveling through East Germany and Czechoslovakia in order to witness firsthand the historic transition from communism to democracy. In East Berlin I tested the thaw in the political climate by walking into Humboldt University, something that had been strictly forbidden in the communist era. A directory in the atrium listed the names of professors. I scanned the list and saw "Dr. Heinrich Fink," who had been named president of Humboldt University two months earlier. It had been nineteen years since I had seen Fink, and I decided to pay him a visit. I introduced myself by recalling Ted's and my visit in his apartment in 1971. He invited me into his office, where we talked cordially for a half hour. He invited me to join him for a quick dinner and then attend a lecture on liberation theology at the university. I accepted both invitations and enjoyed our impromptu reunion. At the end of the evening we parted cordially.

Shortly after returning to the States in the summer of 1990, I leafed through a news magazine in which there was an article on high-level spies in East Germany. Heinrich Fink was one of the spies. He had been a Stasi agent for twenty-one years. When Ted Schapp and I visited him in 1971, he had already been in the service of the Stasi for three years. We, of course, had no idea that we were discussing theology with an upper-echelon Stasi agent. To be sure, there is nothing terribly surprising about that, for as Americans we had an untrained "sixth sense" for spies. The surprise was that East Germans, who had an acute "sixth sense" for such, were also unaware of Fink's long-standing Stasi affiliation. "German academe was shocked," wrote John Koehler, to learn that the man who had been promoted to president of Humboldt had been a master spy for the prior two decades.[35]

Lessons That Only a Spy Can Teach

I drew two conclusions from my reflections on the Heinrich Fink revelation. One was personal. My harrowing interrogation at Checkpoint Charlie in 1971 had evidently not been a rogue event. The border-guard bullying had likely been the result of a phone call from Fink. The Fink revelation also provided a probable explanation for my Stasi file, which I procured in 1993 from Joachim Gauck, who later became president of Germany (2012–2017). Although I had often been in East Germany in the 1970s and 1980s—some visits indeed more dodgy than my first visit in 1971—the only information preserved in my personal Stasi file pertained to the 1971 visit. The evidence again pointed to Fink.

The second and more important conclusion has to do with the invasiveness and pervasiveness of surveillance that accompanied the Russian occupation of East Germany in 1945, and it accounts for my stubborn sympathy with Lohmeyer in the trials he faced in reopening the University of Greifswald. In terms of pervasiveness, the East German Stasi differed from all other known spy organizations. For purposes of comparison, England's famous MI6 officially claims to employ 4,000 spies around the world. The earth's population is now about 7.5 billion people. That amounts to 1 MI6 agent for roughly every 2 million people. Not very invasive. More contemporary with Lohmeyer and thus more relevant for our purposes, the Nazis employed some 40,000 Gestapo agents in twelve nefarious years of existence. Germany had a population of some 80 million people during the war years, which amounted to approximately 1 Gestapo agent for every 2,000 German citizens. Much more invasive. Neither of these spy networks, however, was nearly as finely meshed as the Stasi. When the Berlin Wall fell in 1989, East Germany had a population of 17 million people and a full-time Stasi workforce in excess of 100,000 agents, with roughly another 175,000 "unofficial," part-time informants. The Stasi labyrinth totaled somewhere in the neighborhood of 275,000 pairs of seeing eyes, busy hands, and willing feet. That amounted to 1 Stasi agent for every 50 or 60 East Germans. Totally invasive. By the time East Germans had left their apartments in the morning and walked to the first cross street, they had been surveilled by a Stasi agent. Actually, they usually did not need to leave their apartments, for the most numerous informants were family members. If someone was informing on you in East Germany, it was most likely either your kids in the next bedroom or the spouse sleeping next to you.[36]

The Stasi per se did not exist in Lohmeyer's day—it would be officially formed with the founding of the German Democratic Republic in 1949. But the Soviet paranoia that lay behind the insidious Cheka in Russia and the later Stasi in East Germany was a virus that infected the Red Army, and the Red Army infected Greifswald in the spring of 1945. Lohmeyer doubtless knew of the Soviet intelligence network, but it would have been difficult for him to know at such an early date how intricate and pervasive and ultimately lethal it was. The degree of its surveillance, as noted above, vastly exceeded the possibilities that he and all Germans had associated with the Gestapo. Lohmeyer would experience its stinging reality as he labored to reopen the University of Greifswald in 1945. He was dependent on others for advice and assistance in the manifold duties required to reopen the university. Some of his aides and advisers, unfortunately, were viral agents who pretended to help but intended to destroy.

CHAPTER 14

One against Many

The way is not easy, and not without difficulty and struggle, but when our goals are clear and when we are armed with the strength that alone overcomes the darkness and power of destruction and oppression, then the semester will rise before us like the break of day: "The new day beckons us to sail to new shores!"

Ernst Lohmeyer[1]

Fervor to Reopen the University

The prospect of opening the University of Greifswald carried Lohmeyer forward on the crest of a wave of new possibilities. The Lohmeyer home at Arndtstrasse 3 became a hub of meetings—people coming and going, the telephone ringing constantly. Lohmeyer was on the go from morning till night with appointments at the university and throughout town. And further afield. Parleys with communist party authorities regarding reopening the university were regularly required in Schwerin, 100 miles to the west, and in Berlin, 150 miles to the south. Lohmeyer's shuttle diplomacy was greatly encumbered by the need for written permission from the major of Greifswald, who in turn needed to get permission from the Russian occupation, for each train trip out of Greifswald. Melie rued the demands on her husband and the disruption of their home, but Ernst was invigorated. The inevitable burdens of plans, responsibilities, and meetings were made tolerable by the vision of reestablishing in

Soviet-occupied Germany a true liberal arts university in the tradition of Wilhelm von Humboldt, free from the dogmas and policies that had warped universities in the Nazi era.

The new beginning in Greifswald was a *kairos* moment, as the Greeks would say, and Lohmeyer seized it with undiminished will. Even Melie's doubts were allayed by the initial promise of the hour. "Ernst's plans and measures were at first entirely approved in his negotiations with the Russian professors," she later wrote.[2] A subsequent assessment of Gudrun struck a similar note. In her father's labors to reopen the university in 1945, "he did not turn his back on responsibilities, especially when they seemed necessary."[3] Word on the street and at the university was no less enthusiastic about Lohmeyer. He was hailed as "a man of the future." A "new Weimar" seemed at hand. The university "had not seen the likes of such a president before."[4] This euphoria, if such it was, would be short-lived, however. "None of us perceived in these initial birth pangs of the new era that universities in the [Russian]-occupation zone were fated to be more or less purely political instruments," wrote Melie.[5]

An Anti-Nazi Damned as a Nazi Protector

Reopening the university tested and taxed Lohmeyer's energy and ideals to the maximum. The problems were legion. There were shortages of food and coal. The faculty and student body were depleted from the war, many having died in action, others now prisoners of war. A wave of arrests swept through Greifswald following the surrender of Germany, resulting in three of the delegates who negotiated the surrender of Greifswald to the Russians, including President Engel, being sent to the NKVD prison camp at Fünfeichen. The Russian occupation required students and faculty to swear an oath of allegiance to Soviet socialism. The medical program at the university faced obstacles on both material and moral fronts: there were shortages of medicines and supplies, and medical professors would now be required to perform abortions.

The Achilles' heel facing Lohmeyer, however, was the problem of "denazification." Ridding Germany of the Nazi cancer that had caused the loss of as many as 100 million people in the worst war in human history was at the top of the to-do list of the victorious Allied Powers, Soviets included. Like so many political realities, however, this goal was more easily set than accomplished. The extent to which individual Germans had been influenced by Nazism was difficult to know, and the point at which their succumbing to such influences was criminally culpable was difficult to determine. Most Germans were guilty of passive complicity with Nazism: in a totalitarian state without the right of free expression or civil opposition, it was difficult not to be passively complicit. Other Germans were guilty of active complicity, informing on neighbors, for example, or betraying Jews—or if not actually betraying them, then confiscating their possessions once they had been taken from their homes. Denazification was bewilderingly complex: if enforcement were too lax, the guilty were acquitted; if enforcement were too zealous, the innocent were punished. The golden mean between the two poles was as difficult to determine as it was to execute. And a pressing practical reality made it even more elusive, for this cancer operation could kill the patient. That is to say, a thoroughgoing implementation of denazification (if such were possible) would eliminate from the leadership of Germany the very echelon of persons essential to build a healthy new Germany. Denazification was punitive. It had to be held in tension with the values of reconciliation and cooperation if *democracy* were to succeed in Germany.

The Allied occupation responded to this sea of vagaries by adopting a principled and pragmatic policy of demonstrable guilt. The Berlin Three Power Conference, which included Russia, England, and America, sought to locate demonstrable guilt between the poles of "nominal" and "complicit." Persons who were Nazi Party members but had not acted criminally as such were to be judged "nominal" and free from punishment. Party members who were criminally complicit, on the other hand, must be punished according to the nature of their crimes. Lohmeyer endorsed this paradigm for the university. He had taught in German universities throughout the Nazi dictatorship. He knew the pressures that Nazi Party membership exerted on faculty, especially younger faculty trying to establish their careers. For many professors, party membership was tantamount to membership in labor unions, to use a modern analogy—a way of accommodation but not necessarily of culpability. Professors who had not misused their party affiliation to injure their profession, the university, or its students should be retained, in Lohmeyer's plan, whereas those who had failed in any of these criteria should be terminated.[6]

This policy, which seemed reasonable, practical, and just, and which the Three Power Conference endorsed, became a point of standing contention with the local communist blocs in Greifswald and Schwerin. It needs to be remembered that communism per se did not begin in Russia but rather was founded by *German* ideologues, Karl Marx (†1883) and Friedrich Engels (†1895), who coauthored *The Communist Manifesto* in 1848. Vladimir Lenin was of course the father of Russian communism, but the communism he introduced in Russia was learned by reading the works of Marx and discussing Marxist ideology in cafés during his exile in Zürich, Switzerland. Marxist socialism took deep root in Germany, becoming, as we noted in chapter 8, a major political opponent to Nazism in the 1920s and early 1930s. Nazi retaliation against German communists had been merciless, many of whom, not surprisingly, fled to Russia during the Nazi years. There they were schooled in Russian communism and groomed to serve back in Germany after the eventual victory of Stalinist communism over Hitlerian Nazism. These Moscow-schooled communists were now in their first posts in Schwerin and Greifswald, and they exhibited the noncompromising zeal of the newly and duly indoctrinated. On the issue of denazification, they judged Nazi Party membership per se culpable, irrespective of the member's behavior. Those who had been party members before 1937, that is to say, those who had *chosen* to join the party, were to be categorically dismissed, whereas those who had joined the party after that date, perhaps more by compulsion than choice, were to be deprived of all positions of leadership, although they might continue to teach.[7]

The consequences of this policy were especially dire at Greifswald. In its effort to consolidate all civil services under Nazism, the Third Reich attempted to assimilate all civil servants—and university professors were one class of civil servants—into party membership. The peaceful surrender of Greifswald had induced a large number of professors with Nazi affiliations—or who were suspected of such—to remain in the city rather than flee to the west. Half of the professors at the university were formal members of the Nazi Party when Greifswald capitulated to the Red Army in May 1945. The issue was not simply that a rigid enforcement of denazification would reduce the university faculty by 50 percent—although that catastrophe would have occurred. There were even more serious issues at stake. The university clinic was the only functioning medical clinic in Greifswald and the surrounding region of Pomerania. It was filled with victims of the ravages of the war—wounded soldiers and civilians, malnourished children, and sufferers of every illness and epidemic imaginable, especially typhus. All but four of the medical faculty were Nazi Party members. An enforcement of the denazification policy of the Greifswald and Schwerin hard-liners would overnight eliminate an entire health-care system.

This hard-line policy on denazification conflicted with the policy approved by Marshal Georgy Zhukov and the Russian Military Administration in Berlin-Karlshorst, which adopted the Three Power Conference agreement. The bully methods by which the Greifswald communist bloc advanced its doctrinaire policy may actually have been a compensation for its weakness. The Greifswald Communist Party numbered only 450 members at the time, with some 4,000 party members—at most—in all of north Germany. The Greifswald party was thus small, and its leadership weak and poorly organized. Its inflexibility on denazification may have been a ploy for credibility. Germany's defeat in 1945 had left Nazism discredited and people disillusioned, but twelve years of anticommunist propaganda during the Third Reich had not left Germans unaffected. The propaganda of communist functionaries following the Russian occupation in 1945, combined with the confiscation of properties, expropriation of farmlands, and ensuing arrests—often of innocent persons!—had reinforced rather than allayed Nazi-inculcated fears of communism. In the immediate postwar era, communist party communiqués were long on tirades against National Socialism but short on constructive solutions for the rebuilding of Germany. Had Big Brother in Moscow not backed the fledgling Communist Party of

Germany in the immediate postwar years, it is questionable whether it could have survived.[8] The University of Greifswald appeared to the communist blocs in Greifswald and Schwerin like an island of intellectuals nursing at the breast of the old order, unwilling to embrace the iron mistress of Russian-style socialism. Note the doctrinaire hubris of the Schwerin communist bloc in early February 1946: "We are in no way interested in providing operational cartels that are more or less fascist, which will simply be converted by fascists as vehicles for their own privileges."[9]

Lohmeyer's policy on denazification, reasonable as it may appear to us today, failed to gain the depth of root it needed to succeed, and its failure increasingly exposed him to opposition. Among communist bloc members in Schwerin and Greifswald, his moderation provoked resentment, and resentment hardened to mistrust. Of the thirteen members of the faculty senate in mid-May 1945, ten were dismissed because of alleged Nazi affiliations.[10] At the end of the month, the commander of the Soviet occupation in Stettin closed the university until the faculty had been "cleansed" of Nazi elements.[11] Attempts to resolve the issue throughout summer 1945 failed. Lohmeyer was like a field athlete competing with other athletes, some of whom—Marshal Zhukov being one—were playing the same game by the same rules that he was, whereas other athletes were playing by different rules, if not different games altogether. At the end of August Lohmeyer was summoned to a meeting with seven Russian generals who demanded that all Nazi Party members of the university, regardless of attenuating factors, be dismissed. Lohmeyer objected that implementation of the resolution, which had already reduced the faculty from 150 to 90 members, would render the university inoperable. Eighty percent of the law school had already been dismissed; the school of medicine would be left with but four faculty; and only the theology department would survive intact. Lohmeyer's objection failed, and the resolution carried.[12]

Throughout summer and fall 1945 Lohmeyer continued his shuttle diplomacy to Schwerin and Berlin in attempts to defuse the denazification bomb. His visits with Marshal Zhukov in Berlin-Karlshorst encouraged him, but dealings with Schwerin, in particular, left him drained and depleted. For her part, Melie was not consoled by Zhukov's supposed advocacy. She reminded her weary husband that nothing the general had said or done had materialized in effective aid for him or for the university. She further warned that if—and when—the local communist bloc checkmated Lohmeyer, Zhukov would not come to his aid.

Lohmeyer was left with little option but to hold his course. In September, Greifswald formally rejected the Three Power Conference policy of clemency for "nominal" Nazi Party members, "demanding categorical dismissal of every Nazi university professor, whether a formal Party member or a member of one of its affiliates, without regard either to the date of joining the Party or length of membership in it."[13] A codicil to the above communiqué declared that a university professor occupied a position in the state that was both educationally and *politically* significant and symbolic. Hence, a Nazi Party member, regardless of circumstances, had forfeited the right to teach in the new socialist Germany, and "politically unreliable elements needed to be replaced as quickly as possible."[14] This ruling effectively consigned the university to a witch hunt, for what evidence would be sufficient either to prove political reliability or defend against the charge of political unreliability? The mere *accusation* of being a Nazi was now fatal.

The memorandum mauling that had been so disastrous in Lohmeyer's life ten years earlier in Breslau began to replay itself in Greifswald. A wearisome correspondence ensued throughout the fall of 1945. Dossiers, files, and letters of reference were required of every member of the Greifswald faculty and staff, each requiring tiresome review, counsel, and meetings on Lohmeyer's part. In November, Schwerin demanded dismissal of forty-four university administrators because of Nazi Party membership.[15] The attempts of the university to moderate the effects of such demands by partial or alternative measures were viewed by the increasingly entrenched Schwerin bloc as acts of defiance.[16] Lohmeyer disliked power struggles. He believed that differences could be resolved through reason and dialogue. But the chasm between the politics of the communist blocs in Schwerin and Greifswald and his policies could not be bridged by reasonable discourse. Heaped with acrimony, he was reproached as a Nazi protector.[17]

Lohmeyer the Politician

The issue of denazification gave the university a cold in the spring of 1945, which by the fall of the year had developed into the flu. Even in illness, however, people find ways to carry on. Lohmeyer did too. Already in July 1945 his name, occupation, and address appear as the twenty-fifth member of the fledgling "Democratic Party," which in the fall of the year became the right-of-center Christian Democratic Union (CDU). The CDU is still today a major political party in Germany. Lohmeyer's ability to focus on other matters besides denazification exhibits his ability to hold a wide-angle leadership lens even in the midst of crises. His participation in the Democratic Party not only certified his opposition to Nazism, but more importantly at the time, it registered his commitment to a participatory democratic political spectrum in contrast to the Soviet-style totalitarianism that was taking root in eastern Germany. In late August he made an apology for this fragile and endangered freedom in a speech to the Culture Federation of Democratic Renewal[18] in Schwerin. One had to think twice about accepting an invitation to speak on freedom in East Germany in late 1945. That is perhaps why the initial invitee had declined the invitation. Lohmeyer was asked to be a substitute speaker, and he did not decline. He spoke on the necessity of freedom in a genuinely democratic culture. Citing the great apologists for such a culture—Bach, Goethe, Hölderlin, Herder, Dickens, Tolstoy, Plato—he ended with the greatest apologist of all, Jesus: "The ancient saying that 'the truth will make you free' is relevant in the immediate present, relevant from small daily matters to labor for great goals in the distant future. If you ask how such a culture can be founded, I answer in a single sentence: Culture is founded when we are free, for the deepest kernel of culture is the idea of freedom."[19] The message was not welcomed by communist party members present, one of whom wrote, "Professor Lohmeyer was unfortunately not as ideologically stalwart as we had hoped he would be. He showed himself to be a philosophical idealist and even something of a mystic, while his reserve regarding Soviet Russia and the Red Army was hardly concealed."[20]

Lohmeyer the Pastor

In addition to university and national politics, Lohmeyer's wide-angle lens also included the church. The German Evangelical Church had been reduced to a holding pattern during the Nazi years. Its last plenary gathering had been held in 1933, the year Hitler seized power in Germany. The power struggle between the German Christian Movement and the Confessing Church persisted throughout the duration of the Third Reich, the German Christian Movement, always the majority, roughly maintaining its size while the Confessing Church, virtually defenseless in the face of Nazi policies and persecution, suffering attrition to become a small but faithful remnant. Both sides, apart from a not-inconsiderable "moderate middle," remained polarized throughout the Third Reich. The dishonor that descended on Nazism with the defeat of Germany in 1945 resulted in equal dishonor for the German Christian Movement that was beholden to it. The Confessing Church, by contrast, emerged like a phoenix from the ashes, validated and respected as it had never been in the Third Reich. Its weakness and scorn were suddenly reversed by the necessity of reforming the vestiges of Protestantism in Germany. The Barmen Declaration and the Confessing Church, both of which had come into existence as an emergency response to Nazism, now, ironically, in a situation their founders could not have foreseen, faced their finest hour in reforming German Protestantism.

The task of officially reconstituting the German Lutheran Church fell to Dr. Otto Dibelius, bishop of Berlin-Brandenburg and president of the corresponding church districts throughout Germany. Dibelius was a warhorse. For the next decade and more, his leadership of the German church capitalized on strengths of the Confessing Church, of which he had been a member, as well as on lessons learned from its failures. There was much work to be done. The Stuttgart Confession of Guilt in October of 1945 publicly admitted the Confessing Church's failure to advocate more explicitly and effectively for Jews during the Third Reich. Early communiqués of the postwar church addressed pressing conditions of the hour as well, including the flood of refugees and displaced persons, the search for family members and lost relatives, and the repair of destroyed churches and property throughout Germany. A social catastrophe befell Germany after the capitulation in May 1945, and the Protestant churches were mobilized to respond to it as best they could.

And they required representatives from the various German states to attend a plenary church gathering in Berlin on October 2, 1945. Greifswald was in Pomerania, one of Germany's smaller states, whose representatives were Superintendent Karl von Scheven and "Professor Dr. Lohmeyer." Unfortunately, the ball and chain of denazification to which Lohmeyer was inseparably tethered in the fall of 1945 prevented him from participating either in the preparatory meeting planned for September 19 or in the plenary meeting in Berlin in October, at which the Stuttgart Confession of Guilt was received and the Evangelical Church of Germany was formally reconstituted.

In the fall of 1945, the director of the Church Consistory of Berlin-Charlottenburg, a Dr. Söhngen, wrote Bishop Dibelius about the need to do more than reform the church's bureaucracy and social outreach. The greater need, he maintained, was reformation of the church's *life*—its commitment to the gospel and its community of faith. He proposed the formation of a "Protestant academy" where believers might receive academic instruction and spiritual training. Dibelius directed Söhngen to Lohmeyer, whose theological expertise and ecclesiastical commitments he highly esteemed. Lohmeyer, Dibelius assured Söhngen, was the best resource he knew to form a Protestant academy. It was Söhngen's perception that the church had parted ways with its Christian past, resulting in the loss of its distinction from culture and in culture. The days were past, in Söhngen's judgment, for the church to be a chaplain to society or a purveyor of spiritual cultural values. The church needed reforming as badly as society did. In this three-page letter Söhngen articulated the critical divide between Christian faith and modern culture, a divide that we today characterize as "post-Christian."

Söhngen's concerns, and the understanding with which he addressed them, were prescient, even prophetic. Would that Lohmeyer had been able to form the Protestant academy Söhngen envisioned. But in late 1945, forces were converging on him that prohibited him from attending to the request, either then or in the future.[21]

Preparation for Inauguration

Despite the host of problems in 1945, Lohmeyer had accomplished much for the university. His energies had been tireless. He had initiated a number of new programs—one in preventative medicine, another in water purification, a third in research into the production of gas in the medical school, and a fourth in forestation in the School of Agriculture. Officials who had harassed his denazification effort were forced to commend his "splendid example"[22] in these initiatives. Equally praised was his expansion of satellite industries of the university that produced serum, medicines, pharmaceuticals, and even cosmetics.[23] Such products were manufactured in West Germany, but they were not available in the Russian sector. Lohmeyer's initiatives in such matters sought to ensure the viability of the medical school.

Most important, Marshal Zhukov, supreme commander of the Soviet Military Administration in the Russian sector, gave Lohmeyer a green light formally to reopen the university on February 15, 1946. The date was proposed by Zhukov, independent of and contrary to desires of the communist blocs in Schwerin and Greifswald. General Zhukov's authority in the Russian sector was the counterpart to General Dwight D. Eisenhower's or General George Marshall's authority in the American sector. Lohmeyer trusted—who wouldn't have?—that Zhukov's heft was more than sufficient to counteract any opposition on the matter that might arise from communist blocs in Schwerin or Greifswald.

Two anecdotes provide glimpses into the character that Lohmeyer continued to exhibit in the fraught lead-up to the inauguration. The first concerns Melie and him. At a lecture that Lohmeyer delivered on the Lord's Prayer in Greifswald, Melie noticed a soldier with only one arm standing next to a teenage girl about Gudrun's age. "You two need to get to know my daughter," Melie said, inviting them to dinner the following night. The soldier, Hans Pflugbeil, was suffering severe depression from the loss of his arm in the war. He was an accomplished organist, and the loss of his arm had forced him to give up playing the organ. Lohmeyer knew enough about music, and also about Pflugbeil's ability, to encourage him to resume the organ with his two feet and remaining arm and hand. He further requested Pflugbeil's assistance in reviving the Institute of Church Music and Musicology at Greifswald. Lohmeyer would not live to see the institute revived: his arrest, and the stagnating effect of communism in East Germany, would retard its establishment for several decades. But Lohmeyer's vision did not die. The institute was finally established at Greifswald after the collapse of communism in East Germany in 1989. By that time Pflugbeil himself had died, but his return to the organ in 1946, and his founding of the annual Bach Week Music Festival in Greifswald, which continues to this day, helped prepare the way for the establishment of the Institute of Church Music and Musicology at Greifswald.[24]

A second glimpse comes from a New Year's greeting to Lohmeyer from an unnamed student on January 1, 1946. A folded sheet of paper with a black-and-white photo of the university on the left contained the following message typed flawlessly on the right.

Dear Magnificence!

With admiring respect we wish you a happy New Year!

We all know how tirelessly you have contended for the preservation and life of the University of Greifswald.

You have already achieved and restored much, indeed very much.

Despite unflagging efforts, the university has suffered crippling blows. Surely very few know how personally you have suffered in all this.

The year 1946 now stands before us. May it bring you at last the final success. May the university live again with you at the helm!

A student.

Your alma mater—for all.[25]

This tender acknowledgment could not forestall the tides of opposition that were rising against Lohmeyer. But the testimony that "We all know . . ." assured him that he was not alone.

The "Gift" of Gottfried Grünberg

The English word "gift" and the German word *Gift* have very different meanings. The English word means a "present," but the German word means "poison." Both meanings of the word—one apparent and the other actual—apply to Gottfried Grünberg, a final pivotal character in the drama to reopen the university.

In December 1945 and January 1946, preparations for reopening the university accelerated to a "feverish pace," in Melie's words.[26] The single front of denazification with which Lohmeyer had until then primarily contended now split into several branches, all of which seemed to converge on him from different directions. In December the NKVD arrested several members of the Greifswald battalion who were suspected of complicity in Bromberg Bloody Sunday. Melie feared that Ernst too might be arrested, but he remained unshaken. His innocence and guilelessness, he maintained, were his best defense against political intrigue. "The Russians have too good an intelligence network not to know that I have nothing to do with that matter," he assured Melie.[27] She was not assured. She chided him that a clean conscience was no guarantee of impunity from the Russians in political matters.

Lohmeyer pursued his course of nonalignment with customary resolve. His adherence to that course in late summer 1945, although practically efficient, was strategically dangerous. In early December, Dr. Gottfried Grünberg, vice president and minister of public education of Mecklenburg-Pomerania, set a trap that Lohmeyer inadvertently stepped into. Grünberg, a former miner, had been schooled in Marxism-Leninism in Russia during the war. Melie distrusted him intensely, judging him an individual who had fortuitously received a position in life that he neither deserved nor possessed the characteristics to occupy justly. "*This* Grünberg," she would later write, "was a man who even in genuine communist circles was described as a very weak man whom people gladly looked to when they wanted something unpleasant done."[28] In the Lohmeyer home, in the presence of several professors, Grünberg suggested that Lohmeyer follow the Russian model of leadership. Specifically, he recommended abolishing the office of dean in order to consolidate the reins of power in Lohmeyer's hands during the emergency interim at the university. He assured Lohmeyer that this would allow him to re-open the university more swiftly. He then smiled, in Melie's later report, and added, "like a king in a little kingdom!"[29] Melie later warned Ernst, "That is a risky thing to do, for it leaves the whole matter hanging from your neck!"[30] Lohmeyer liked and admired Grünberg, however, and favored his plan. "Then I can act without interference," he told Melie.[31] Events would soon confirm Melie's judgment with regard to Grünberg. And also Gudrun's, who later declared that Grünberg intended to make Lohmeyer a scapegoat.

Lohmeyer followed Grünberg's advice. Why he chose to do so, especially given Melie's opposition, and perhaps Gudrun's as well, is not entirely clear. He was no stranger to intrigue, especially—if Melie's description of him is to be trusted—Grünberg's clumsy intrigue. Nevertheless, given the standing opposition he had faced from the communist blocs in Schwerin and Greifswald on the issue of denazification, along with their obstruction to reopening the university, it is perhaps not surprising that Lohmeyer would opt for a plan that promised to circumvent both obstacles. There are times in life when a bad plan seems preferable to no plan. As Grünberg predicted, the immediate advantage of the decision granted Lohmeyer emergency powers at a critical juncture in the university's existence. But it was a high-risk advantage, as Melie warned, for in case of failure Lohmeyer would be held solely responsible. The plan was effected in the fall of 1945. And it cleared the faculty senate. But the senate meeting in mid-January 1946 erupted in a sharp disagreement, in which Lohmeyer was forced to defend his abolishment of the dean's office. The minister director of public education of Mecklenburg-Pomerania, Dr. Manthey, was present, and he opposed Lohmeyer. The opposition to Lohmeyer from Schwerin was now formidable.

In January 1946 Lohmeyer was informed that "new directives from Berlin" reflected a hard line on denazification. This meant that Lohmeyer had lost the heavyweight in his corner—Marshal Georgy Zhukov, commander in chief of the Soviet Military Forces in the Russian sector of Germany. We do not know for certain why Berlin-Karlshorst changed positions on the issue, but we can guess. Zhukov was shortly thereafter transferred from command of the Soviet

Military Administration at Berlin-Karlshorst, in March 1946, and the "new directives" probably anticipated the policy of the successor administration. The guess is further supported by the fact that other policies of the communist bloc in Schwerin were also endorsed by the successor administration at Karlshorst.

Lohmeyer's ideal of an intellectually free Prussian university could not withstand the sustained pressure brought against it to conform to the politics introduced by the Soviet occupation. In mid-November, he was mandated by the German Central Administration for Public Education in the Soviet Occupation Zone[32] to form a Commission for Democratic Renewal for History Instruction[33] that would establish "the proper perspective for the new instruction in history,"[34] which would include instructors' manuals, student textbooks, pamphlets of approved sources, and examples of proper student outcomes. A quota system was instituted that limited enrollment at Greifswald to nine hundred students of approved socialist perspectives. In late November, Lohmeyer as president reminded the medical faculty that new directives to perform abortions in certain circumstances contravened earlier policies adopted by the university medical commission. He asked the six medical professors present "if it were not advisable to protest the new directives."[35] In mid-December of 1945, Lohmeyer wrote a direct and unambiguous letter to Schwerin asserting the right of the university to self-administration in the face of heightened attempts to administer and manage it from the outside.[36] Just two weeks earlier, he and Professor Johannes Stroux, president of Humboldt University in Berlin, had committed themselves "to preserve the heritage of the German university from the dangers threatening free inquiry" in the Soviet sector of Germany.[37] Grünberg's poison was now fatal in the bloodstream of the university. Melie's premonitions were quickly and irrevocably being fulfilled: the University of Greifswald was becoming "a more or less purely political instrument."[38]

Two weeks after the promulgation of the "new directives," Lohmeyer wrote to Schwerin, protesting the Ministry of Culture and Education's expropriation of the administrative services of the university, which had always been under the jurisdiction of the president.[39] When Grünberg spoke at the opening ceremonies on

February 15—the day Lohmeyer was arrested—he delivered a kill shot to Lohmeyer's hopes, dreams, and sacrifices for the university. "Never again will the university be self-contained, but it will work in the closest possible way with the life and work of the entire people. The university can only be strong and fruitful when it is the daughter of the working people."[40]

The Camelot that Lohmeyer envisioned and labored valiantly to effect had been scuttled. Perhaps he had tried to accomplish too much, or too much in too short a time. Perhaps, as in the case of Grünberg, he had failed to consider alternative consequences of actions. We who are removed from the hammering pressures of Lohmeyer's circumstances should be humble in our judgments of him. His opportunities were limited, his means to achieve them equally so, and the tides against him inversely aggressive.

Night of Stealth

The reopening ceremony was scheduled for Friday, February 15, 1946, at 11 a.m. in the baroque hall of the university. The ceremony would be a testimony to Lohmeyer's aspirations, his unflagging energy, and his vindication of human reason and character over the manifest forms of tyranny. The faculty would march in academic regalia, processing to Haydn and recessing to Beethoven. Speeches were scheduled for the lord mayor of Greifswald, Minister Solotuchin of the Russian occupation, and Dr. Gottfried Grünberg. The ceremony would be crowned by Lohmeyer's inaugural address, followed by his installation as Rektor Magnifizenz by Wilhelm Hoecker, president of Mecklenburg-Pomerania.

The inaugural address would never be delivered, however. Indeed, the greater part of it has been lost and never found. Only the following quotation, which appears to be Lohmeyer's conclusion, was preserved in the papers of one of his students and later quoted by his daughter Gudrun.

So this resumption of the university is more than a continuation of something that had been temporarily interrupted. It is, rather, a setting forth to new and yet old goals, in new and yet old ways, with new and yet old powers. Everything is new in the sense that in the wake of the catastrophe that has befallen us, nothing can be rebuilt where it formerly stood. Nevertheless, the old still remains, for even the most brutal force and worst despotism that have lasted so long have not been able to alter the face of true things and true problems. The way is not easy, and not without difficulty and struggle, but when our goals are clear and when we are armed with the strength that alone overcomes the darkness and power of destruction and oppression, then the semester will rise before us like the break of day: "The new day beckons us to sail to new shores!"[41]

But Lohmeyer's vision of a true liberal arts university in Soviet-dominated East Germany was not to be.

Melie gives the final account.

And so the fifteenth of February came, the day of the reopening. My husband was away from the house all day [on the fourteenth]. He did not come home for dinner, but simply phoned to say that he would come later. I waited in suspense. The doorbell rang about 11 p.m. and three men wearing the familiar uniforms of the NKVD came up the stairs and asked hurriedly for my husband. I said I was certain he was at the university. I immediately phoned, but was told that my husband had gone with a colleague to the local communist headquarters. In the meanwhile my husband returned home quite exhausted, but clearly of the opinion that none of this concerned him personally. It was not clear whether he took the whole thing seriously. He said that Dr. Müller had come to the university totally drunk and repeatedly slammed his fist on the table, shouting, "You're treading a dangerous path, you little monk!" Müller declared in the name of the government in Schwerin that my husband was removed from office, although the reopening would still take place in the morning. I told my husband that NKVD men had come to arrest him. "Oh nonsense," he said. "The Russians know everything about me, otherwise they would have come for me long ago. Maybe I'll have to boot out this person or that person before morning. The Russians like to run around at night."

About 12:30 a.m. the Russians came back and arrested my husband. They made a two-hour search of the house, during which they seized a bundle of valuable letters from scholars the world over, several photographs of my husband, and a radio. Other than that they were well-behaved. I had the feeling they recognized with whom they were dealing. For most of the time my husband stood by the stove, looking utterly miserable, dutifully and quietly answering their questions. What he was thinking I do not know. He said nothing personal. He seemed numb, or perhaps he thought the whole thing would blow over. In an almost childlike voice he said to the captain, "You want to arrest me? But I haven't done anything." When the time was up I woke our daughter, who ran crying to her father, but he did not speak to her either. He looked as though he were a wooden statue, motionless, with a dazed look on his face. When the search was over the captain told me to pack up some bed linens, toilet articles, and eating utensils. My husband put on his coat and the backpack, and then they left. My daughter went with him to the door, but he said nothing to her. He remained stiff and silent, and so he left us.[42]

When the soldiers left, Melie ran to the window. "From the balcony I called out as the three men walked away, my husband in the middle, 'Auf Wiedersehen.'" Melie did not report what he said in response. She only said, "I heard his voice for the last time."[43]

CHAPTER 15

Years of Silence

I have written this testimony not only for you who come from our father's flesh and blood. I think that it is important that a man of his intellectual significance, who contributed to the scholarly pursuit of the Christian religion, should not be consigned to the bureaucratic files of Russian prisoners. It must be made known how this valuable and innocent life was exterminated. The day will certainly come when you will be asked about these things. That is why I have written you.

Melie Lohmeyer[1]

Turmoil in the Faculty

A whirlwind of confusion swept through the faculty on the morning of February 15, 1946. Vice President Grünberg, on hand for the ceremonies, hastily convened a meeting of the faculty senate with Dr. Franz Wohlgemuth. Wohlgemuth, who at one time had studied Roman Catholic theology, was Communist Party secretary for the university. He was a German hard-liner who had been schooled in Russian communism during the war, and since returning to Germany, he, along with Grünberg, had often been in the Lohmeyer home working to reopen the university.[2] Like Grünberg, Wohlgemuth was no ally in Lohmeyer's project. The true agenda of both surfaced six weeks after Lohmeyer's arrest, when Grünberg appointed Wohlgemuth administrator of the university. This was the same Grünberg who, it will be remembered, had prevailed on Lohmeyer to abolish the office six months earlier! Some twenty faculty were present for the emergency meeting Saturday morning, none of whom would accept the office of president in Lohmeyer's stead. The faculty in attendance were adamant: "For us Professor Lohmeyer is the president," they insisted. "He is not dead, and he should be freed by those who are trying to hinder him from the exercise of his office."[3] The meeting was deadlocked, and Grünberg adjourned it for the opening ceremonies.

The inaugural ceremony was tense and awkward. President Wilhelm Hoecker was prevailed on by Grünberg and General Skocyrew, head of Russian administration in Schwerin, to make some impromptu remarks. Next to Hoecker on the podium was the vacant presidential chair, draped with the necklace and medallion designated for Lohmeyer's inauguration. Grünberg ordered Dr. Müller, who in a drunken rage hours earlier had denounced Lohmeyer as a wretched little monk, to remove the presidential insignia. Speeches were given as scheduled, but all references to Lohmeyer in the morning speeches were scratched out. The expunging of his person had begun. It fell to Wohlgemuth, not the least untarnished figure on the platform, to announce that "due to extenuating circumstances his Magnificence was unable to participate in the opening ceremonies."[4]

The faculty's Saturday morning valor on behalf of Lohmeyer was commendable. Had it been sustained, it may have played a favorable role in Lohmeyer's release, although we shall never know. Rudolf Hermann, a fellow New Testament professor who had taught with Lohmeyer at both Breslau and Greifswald, maintained contact with Melie in the years following Lohmeyer's arrest, and he wrote twice in his behalf in 1948.[5] But on the whole, efforts from both church and university were too little, too late. Particularly in the university, where each faculty dossier was being scrutinized for political correctness, fears of offending the ever-hardening political autocracy in the Russian sector inhibited efforts on behalf of Lohmeyer. Four years later, Otto Dibelius, bishop of Berlin-Brandenburg, would speak of the "reserve"[6] with which the church responded to the tens of thousands of people who disappeared in Germany during the Russian occupation. Ernst Lohmeyer was among this number.

Six years of war, Dibelius noted, robbed the church of "its inner freedom to raise an outside voice of protest."[7] The only letter of formal protest of Lohmeyer's arrest from the Greifswald faculty preserved in the Secret State Archive of the Prussian Cultural Heritage Foundation in Berlin is Professor Seeliger's, who against his wishes was appointed acting president following Lohmeyer's arrest.[8] In a plenary meeting of the faculty senate three days after the arrest, only two professors—a pharmacologist and a chemist—spoke in Lohmeyer's behalf.

As for the subsequent inaugural festivities on February 15, apart from some procedural awkwardness on the morning platform, out-of-town visitors may have participated in the event unaware of what had transpired with the university president. This was especially true of the Epicurean zest of the afternoon banquet. Melie, of course, was not included in celebratory events. It went without saying that the wife of a victim of communist repression was guilty by association. The apprehensions that inhibited Greifswalders from advocating for Ernst Lohmeyer inhibited them from advocating for Melie as well. Melie later wrote to Hartmut and Gudrun, "Throughout the university people were stifled with fear and depression. Even rumors about dear father were quasi-comforts, for people talked and whispered about 'a dark military affair,' about which one could not learn more."[9] Fearing similar vulnerability for their political leanings, eight Greifswald professors and several of their assistants fled to the West the week following Lohmeyer's arrest.

Letter from Cell 19

Following his arrest, Lohmeyer was imprisoned in the Criminal Justice Building, two doors down from the university, at Domstrasse 6/7. Conditions in the prison, a former Gestapo prison that had been converted to an NKVD prison in May of 1945, were grim. Cells were overcrowded and unhygienic, and prisoners were incarcerated indiscriminately—young with old, criminals with political victims.[10] "The battle for your father's fate now fell to me," Melie later wrote to her children.[11] She quickly learned that Lohmeyer was held in an exterior cell facing the city wall. From this cell Lohmeyer waved his hand so that Melie and Gudrun could recognize him, and they waved in return. Mother and daughter walked along the city wall daily at 1 p.m. and 5 p.m., hoping, as Melie later wrote, "to give him the feeling of belonging to us."[12]

The only letter Lohmeyer succeeded in smuggling to Melie in his seven-month imprisonment began "Cell 19, begun on 3/31/46." He thanked her for a package she had sent, which included a jar of marmalade, but begged her not to deprive herself on his account. She needed food more than he did, he insisted. His self-description seems to echo Psalm 31:12, "I am an old piece of scrap metal."[13] He had been in prison for six weeks and was still in the dark about the reasons for his arrest. He had been interrogated by "little"[14] Captain Ivanoff, the same officer who had arrested him on the night of February 14. A "Professor Ivanoff" first appears in Greifswald records a week before, when he arrived from Berlin to hold "immediate conversations" with concerned parties.[15] It was Lohmeyer's impression that Ivanoff was only a conduit for questions of his NKVD superior, Colonel Lurykow. Lohmeyer had been interrogated about his military activities in Poland, Belgium, and Russia, but, as he wrote to Melie, he "had the impression that they were looking for things on which they could hook and hold me, as if these questions veiled their real motives, which lay on political grounds, of which the local NKVD itself is unaware."[16] Lohmeyer bluntly summarized the case against him to that point: "I still think the whole thing is a plot hatched in Schwerin, in which the Communist Party is not entirely free from guilt."[17] The Communist Party in Schwerin, in other words, and not the Soviets or NKVD, were setting the rules of play in his case. "I'm groping in the darkness," he concluded, "and hoping that my imprisonment will end as suddenly as it began, even if it is certain to last a long time."[18] Years later Melie reported that Ernst did not seem to take his arrest entirely seriously. "I think he was convinced that Berlin-Karlshorst would be able to get him out of prison."[19] "Berlin-Karlshorst," of course, referred to Marshal Zhukov, in whose advocacy Lohmeyer trusted. Melie was further concerned about her husband's trust in his innocence. "It was not clear to him that in totalitarian politics innocence or guilt plays absolutely no role."[20]

The brutalities of the German Wehrmacht in Russian territories during the war made the accusation of German atrocities an easy charge to bring against Germans who had served on the eastern front. Lohmeyer was an easy prey of such accusations. As late as November 1949, a month after the founding of the German Democratic Republic, its Ministry of Foreign Affairs propagated this accusation. Lohmeyer's arrest, it maintained, "was made not on political but on military grounds."[21] In the next chapter we shall discover the probable source of this allegation in a denunciation of Franz Wohlgemuth. Suffice it to say that, had Lohmeyer's military activities been suspect, the Russians would never have approved his appointment as university president in May 1945. The predominant and virtually only reason for Lohmeyer's arrest attested in the records immediately surrounding it is political, not military. The faculty meeting on February 16, following Lohmeyer's arrest, presided over by Ministry Director Manthey,[22] Chief Administrative Counselor Dr. Müller,[23] and General Skocyrew of the Russian Military Administration in Berlin, brought a barrage of charges against Lohmeyer, none of which was military. He had not followed "guiding principles"[24] from Berlin, his presidency resulted in a "breach of trust,"[25] and the faculty—above all the medical faculty, which "during the Nazi era was deplorable"[26]—had been insufficiently purged. Ministry Director Manthey declared "the personal political views of the president patently false,"[27] and he had "allowed certain forces to be harbored in the university that had no place in a democratic state."[28] All these, the report maintained, were Lohmeyer's responsibility, and his failure to fulfill his responsibility according to Communist Party directives "had sabotaged the opening of the university."[29] As Lohmeyer reported to Melie in his letter from cell 19, the reasons for his arrest were *political*, often with reference to denazification. Manthey's political accusation against Lohmeyer went so far as to contravene the authority of the Russian occupation in Germany, asserting that Lohmeyer's "direct agreements with the Central Administration in Berlin had no validity."[30] Melie had long warned Ernst that if local communist functionaries opposed him, Marshal Zhukov would not come to his aid. Manthey's assertion fulfilled her prediction.

Lohmeyer was sparing in parsing out the case against him. He soon turned to prison conditions themselves. Prison fare was "bearable,"[31] he noted laconically. He was doing no physical labor, so the morning and evening regimen of carrot and potato soup sufficed well enough. At the end of March his rations were augmented by a pound of bread, and of late, even a teaspoon of sugar and a little butter. Prisoners were roused at 5:30 a.m. to carry out their waste buckets, given five minutes at the water faucet to wash, and then expected to clean their cells with rags. The tedium of prison life contained some small but happy surprises, unexpected laughter and lightheartedness among the prisoners, for example. But the overall routine of prison life was oppressive: doing nothing, lying on one's bunk, staring at the ceiling.

Lohmeyer's description of the Greifswald prison was less forbidding than descriptions of the same conditions reported by other prisoners. This was likely the result of his desire to mitigate, if possible, Melie's anxieties. But he does not disguise his own anxieties. Would the four thousand marks left in her bank account be enough to live on? he asked. His only personal request was for Melie to oversee the publication of his book *The Lord's Prayer*. She should contact Vandenhoeck & Ruprecht, his default publisher of many years and many subjects. Perhaps Joachim Jeremias at Göttingen or Rudolf Bultmann at Marburg could be prevailed upon to undertake its final edits. He briefly imagined teaching somewhere far removed from Greifswald, in Tübingen, perhaps. His deepest remorse was the hardships Melie had to undergo in the wake of his arrest, and no less, the burden of knowing that Gudrun would be deprived of her place at the University of Greifswald because of his arrest. "If ever a human abuse could make bitter, it is this!" he confessed.[32]

Rumors Bred by Silence

The letter from cell 19 was Melie's last personal communication from Ernst. In the spring of 1946, sometime after writing the letter, Lohmeyer was transferred from single cell 19 to communal cell 27 on the top floor, facing the university courtyard. Cell 27 was not visible from the city wall, thus ending the communication by hand movements that Lohmeyer had shared with Melie and Gudrun. Silence ensued. When a pheasant hunter pauses momentarily in a field and remains absolutely still, it often causes the birds to flush. Silence at the Criminal Justice Building had a similar effect on Greifswald: it gave flight to rumors. Melie knew that Ernst was scheduled to be tried by the Russians sometime in May or June. Trial by Russians may actually have caused Lohmeyer faint hope. He knew he was innocent of war crimes, and he knew—or thought he knew—that the Russians knew the same. This, combined with his fairly sanguine view of Russian leadership in immediate post-war Germany, may have accounted for his hint to Melie in the letter from cell 19 that he hoped for release, even if not soon. We can be fairly certain that he also counted on the advocacy of Marshal Zhukov in Karlshorst in his defense. Melie, as we have seen, entertained no such optimism about Russian intentions in Germany. Russia's exercise of "justice," she repeatedly reminded Ernst, had nothing to do with actual guilt or innocence. As for Zhukov himself, Lohmeyer could not have known that as of March 1946—the same month Lohmeyer penned his letter from cell 19—Zhukov had been relieved of his command of the Soviet Military Administration in Germany. This eliminated the supposed ace—the only card, in fact—in Lohmeyer's hand in the high-stakes political poker game with the Russians. Lohmeyer's guarded optimism, nevertheless, was evidently shared by others, for in early summer 1946 Melie was informed by three different parties, among them a former mayor and prison translator, that her husband was about to be released. The translator was a prison insider, whose report presumed to be the most credible of the three. Melie, wisely, did not spread her wings in a flight of fancy. June came and went, then July, but without release or word of Ernst. Melie later wrote to her children, "One has to conclude that his release was undesired."[33]

The Stalinist web of suspicion and guilt that typified the arrest of Lohmeyer in February included not only Ernst but also Melie and the children. Lohmeyer's salary was severed the day of his arrest, leaving the family without income. The same day the water heater was turned off; the next day the telephone was disconnected. The following weeks and months witnessed a parade of Russians coming at will into the Lohmeyer house to look over their things and take what they wanted. Their furniture was confiscated. Gudrun's seat at the university was revoked, and with it her hopes to study medicine. She had, fortunately, already completed her qualifying examination to become a church musician. In hopes of allowing the children to pursue their remaining unbroken vocational options, Melie moved the family from Greifswald to Berlin in the fall of 1947.

Intercessory Efforts

Already on March 1, Rudolf Bultmann wrote to Melie expressing his distress at the news of Lohmeyer's arrest two weeks earlier. He wrote again on April 20, warmly agreeing to Melie's request to edit *The Lord's Prayer* for publication. Sporadic letters of commiseration and support arrived throughout spring and summer of 1946, and even more in the fall when silence appeared to dash Lohmeyer's hoped-for release. Communications arrived from various quarters—personal acquaintances, scholars, church leaders, and former students from around Europe. Later, in 1951, some even arrived from America. The personal letters expressed sorrow at Melie's misfortune, offering support and prayer on her behalf. Scholars and church officials, on the other hand, usually adopted a professional format, attempting to roll back the grim accusations against Lohmeyer by attesting to his moral character, scholarly preeminence and promise, and personal innocence. The chief element in common with all letters on his behalf, whether personal or professional, was Lohmeyer's uncompromised opposition to National Socialism.[34]

A striking number of letters were written by Jewish scholars—Martin Buber, Israel Heinemann, Richard Koebner, Ernst Joseph Cohn, Richard Hönigswald, Eugen Rosenstock-Huessy. No one apart from Melie knew Lohmeyer better or corresponded with him longer than had Richard Hönigswald, his closest colleague at Breslau. The Secret State Archives in Dahlem preserve over two hundred letters from Hönigswald to Lohmeyer, many of which have appeared in a volume of correspondence between the two.[35] Hönigswald spoke for virtually all character references in attesting that Lohmeyer was a man of the "highest human conviction . . . absolutely incapable of dishonorable behavior or of the least inhumanity. I know Professor Lohmeyer as an unconditional opponent of National Socialism and an implacable enemy of any anti-Semitic tendency. At all times there were always Jews among his closest circle of acquaintances, and never, not even at the peak of Nazi domination, did he shrink from openly and unreservedly embracing his Jewish friends."[36]

Ernst Joseph Cohn, the Jewish professor at Breslau who subsequently fled to England, wrote in slightly misleading English in 1956 on Lohmeyer's behalf. "When Professor Lohmeyer believed me to be personally threatened," testified Cohn, "he tried to shield me against students who wanted to attacke [*sic*] me with his own person."[37] Martin Buber, Israel Heinemann, and Richard Koebner wrote from Hebrew University in Jerusalem attesting to Lohmeyer's "passionate opposition to National Socialism, one of the very few Germans who openly expressed their mind."[38] The importance of three prominent Jewish intellectuals attesting to the character of an officer serving in an army that routinely murdered Jews cannot be overemphasized. The three Hebrew University professors attested not only to Lohmeyer's innocence but also to the bridge that his life and scholarship had built with the Jewish community. Cohn's letter, again written in English, attested to the same bridge—and to its utter uniqueness: "Lohmeyer belongs to those convinced and upright Christians of whom I as a tractising [*sic*] Jew can only think in terms of profound admiration and gratitude for all they have done for me and my coreligioniste [*sic*] and for everybody else who suffered from Nazi-persecution."

Other letters came from Confessing Church leaders, including Martin Niemöller, Gottfried Fitzer, Hanna Sommer, Katharina Staritz, and, later, Hans Lilje, Otto Dibelius, and Heinz Zahrnt. In October 1946 Niemöller wrote in words that virtually paralleled those of Fitzer, that Lohmeyer had paid a high personal price for his public opposition to Nazism, being dismissed and demoted to Greifswald. Lohmeyer, testified Niemöller, "stood loyally on the side of the Confessing Church in its battle against the claims and despotism of National Socialism."[39]

The majority of references came from Protestant professors and former students, including Rudolf Bultmann, Hans von Campenhausen, Martin Dibelius, Julius Schniewind, Rudolf Seeliger, Fritz Lieb, and Anton Fridrichsen. From Switzerland Fritz Lieb wrote to Wilhelm Pieck, the president of the Communist Party in Schwerin, appealing for Lohmeyer's release.[40] Bultmann wrote from Marburg that Lohmeyer's character was best attested by Lohmeyer himself, in a letter he had written to Bultmann during the war: "The best we can hope for in the occupied territory of Poland," Lohmeyer wrote to Bultmann, "is to try to protect the local population from the atrocities of the Browns (= SA) and Blacks (= SS troops)."[41]

Bultmann concluded his testimony by writing that "people like Prof. Lohmeyer are urgently needed to rebuild the Germany in a new mind."[42] Others reacted in barely suppressed outrage at the charges against Lohmeyer. "The charge that Lohmeyer is a war criminal is utterly laughable," wrote Campenhausen. Equally emphatic in her testimony on behalf of Lohmeyer was Katharina Strauss, wife of Otto Strauss. The latter was professor of Sanskrit and Indo-European languages at Breslau and a member of "the Lohmeyer Circle," who died in exile in Holland in 1940. "[Lohmeyer's] fanatical rejection of National Socialism exposed him to extreme danger. He was the only professor known to me who bravely resisted the commandos who came to confiscate 'Jewish Marxist' books from the library, which by their definition also included the Bible."[43]

The only official letter on behalf of Lohmeyer from the communist sector of Germany came from Professor Rudolf Seeliger, who was appointed acting president of Greifswald after Lohmeyer's arrest. At the time and in the circumstances, Seeliger's letter of advocacy for an "enemy of the state" was unquestionably courageous—and dangerous. All other letters came from "the West." Months turned to years, and the steady stream of letters diminished to a trickle. The hearts that pounded loud and fast for Lohmeyer's release in spring and summer 1946 began to beat more slowly and quietly by the fall of the year. The occasional letters that arrived in

Melie's mailbox expressed steadfast solidarity, but they inevitably, if unintentionally, accentuated her loneliness and isolation as well. The lapse of time and the silence about Lohmeyer were like a slow but powerful countercurrent separating Melie further and further from the possibility of rescue.

In other parts of Germany and among Lohmeyer's friends and colleagues, life was slowly but happily returning to prewar conditions. Bultmann reported that his house in Marburg had fortunately been spared damage during the war. The American occupation had not laid claim to it, and he was busy rebuilding his academic career. How bitter Lohmeyer's fate—and Melie's with it—by comparison. No letter could have driven home her ill fate and isolation more poignantly than a letter of April 15 from Hönigswald. After recounting his misfortunes after leaving Breslau, which we related in an earlier chapter, Hönigswald wrote to Melie from New York, where now, gratefully, he had resumed a successful academic career and his wife, an equally successful commercial career.

The above correspondence consisted of one letter, or in rare cases of two or three letters, to Melie personally or to the authorities on behalf of Lohmeyer's release. One correspondent among the advocates, however, moved beyond condolences to a decade-long consolation. The consoler was Günther Ruprecht, editor of many of Lohmeyer's theological commentaries and books published by Vandenhoeck & Ruprecht in Göttingen. Melie had contacted Ruprecht regarding the publication of *The Lord's Prayer*, in hopes that its publication might stimulate Lohmeyer's release from prison. Ruprecht rendered yeoman's service in bringing out *The Lord's Prayer* in a record three months, in November 1946. Lohmeyer was dead by then, but neither Ruprecht nor Melie nor anyone else who sought his release knew that at the time.

Ruprecht's success in expediting the publication of *The Lord's Prayer* was matched by his personal consideration for Melie herself. He perceived the fuller dimensions of her loss and abandonment beyond the veneer of the academic venture with which she had approached him. "It was with great consternation that we heard a few days ago that your husband was arrested in mid-February," Ruprecht wrote on March 20.[44] Further missives followed, assuring Melie of his deep concern in the past weeks and months. Melie opened up to his vicarious identification with her. Rumors of Lohmeyer's imprisonment here, his transport there, his impending release then, flared up and died out like little grass fires, exacerbating Melie's anxiety. She oscillated between trust in God's guidance and near despair. As weeks lengthened to months and years, she processed her understanding of events with Ruprecht. He listened wisely, without offering palliatives of false hope or fulminating in righteous indignation. Nor did he abandon Melie to the increasing possibility that Lohmeyer's disappearance might never be resolved. In late 1950 he wrote yet again, perhaps his most sympathetic pastoral missive:

> God has now drawn an unerasable line under all the "ifs" and "buts." To accept this and not to fight it is not easy. I now understand how particularly distressful the past quarter of a year has been for you. And yet, we want to be grateful that in the midst of this dire distress which sometimes can bring us to despair, we are permitted firmly to trust that God leads us in grace and love, indeed very personally, even when we often do not understand. The gift of holding the Father's hand firmly in the midst of the surrounding darkness is more than "an experience of God" and mystical immersion. It is the simple and comforting truth that makes us true human beings, for which we again and again, even through tears, must be grateful.[45]

A False Lead Eliminated

I mentioned earlier the German Academic Exchange Program grant that I received in 1993 to investigate Lohmeyer's mysterious disappearance and death. In 1993 it was commonly believed that at some point Lohmeyer had been transferred from the Criminal Justice Building in Greifswald to a Soviet concentration camp in East Germany at Fünfeichen, where Carl Engel, his predecessor as president, had been incarcerated, along with many other Germans who in one way or another were deemed "enemies of the state." The "Fünfeichen hypothesis" was rooted in reasonably good evidence, or so it seemed to those who were trying to solve the puzzle of Lohmeyer's fate. The evidence was a personal remembrance of a woman named Erika Harmel, whose father, Karl Hagemann, was a judge who had been incarcerated in Fünfeichen and later released. Frau Harmel reported to Günter Haufe, professor of New Testament at the University of Greifswald and longtime researcher into Lohmeyer's fate, that her father "had played chess with Prof. Lohmeyer in Fünfeichen."[46]

When I went to Germany in 1993, I searched East German archives, by then opened after the collapse of communism, to verify Frau Harmel's report. In the forty years of communist control of East Germany, no installations and industries had been more carefully guarded, or trespass of their grounds more severely punished, than those of the military, the Stasi, and the communist party. The headquarters of the communist party in Schwerin, formally known as the Socialist Unity Party, was a handsome multistory building in the city center. In the communist era, not only the party headquarters but also a full city block perimeter around it was carefully guarded. In my several visits to Schwerin in the 1970s and 1980s, I gave the headquarters a wide berth, as did everyone, when walking through the city. By 1993, however, the two Germanys were reunited, and barely three years afterward, ordinary citizens were permitted access to buildings like the former headquarters of the Socialist Unity Party. Like the Nazis, communists were meticulous record keepers. All files concerning Fünfeichen were kept in Schwerin's former Socialist Unity Party headquarters. This was the place that likely could prove or disprove the report of Lohmeyer's incarceration in Fünfeichen.

The apprehension I felt upon approaching the former Socialist Unity Party headquarters in Schwerin was similar to what I felt the first time I drove a car in England over the crest of a hill on a two-lane road. Having driven all my life in the States, I had to summon up a strong combination of mind and will not to swerve the car into the right-hand lane. I had to employ similar self-discipline as I approached the former communist party headquarters. My nasty experience at Checkpoint Charlie in 1971 replayed itself in my memory.

My appointment at the former headquarters was scheduled for 9 a.m. I anticipated a frosty reception, vetting procedures, being shunted to various offices, and hopefully eventual, if reluctant, access to the proper files. Needless forebodings in this instance! I introduced myself at the front desk and was immediately greeted as though I were a dignitary. Two members of the staff, Herr Schlombs and Herr Funk, came cascading down the stairs to greet me. I cannot recall what either man looked like, but I cannot forget how eager both were to accommodate me. They escorted me to a conference room on the second floor, where comfortable chairs, coffee service, and cakes awaited us. A companion table was stacked with several files, especially procured for my investigation.

Their superior, a Dr. Radow, was present in the room, and he was no less solicitous than Funk and Schlombs. I was secretly hoping for a brief tour to see what a former communist party headquarters was like. No time for that. Schlombs and Funk wanted to know about my research, rehearsing their own data related to the matter, which was surprisingly complete. They began slamming files down on the table beside me, pointing to this and that, showing me my reserved work area, where I could copy any materials of interest (free of charge). They would be available all morning, they assured me, but a clerk on duty could answer my questions. They introduced me to him.

A celebrity, or perhaps a politician, might expect the reception I was receiving from these solicitous civil servants, but for an academic—especially one who had approached the former communist party headquarters with foreboding—this was a complete surprise. The Lohmeyer agenda was momentarily arrested, at least in my mind. I had anticipated an unpleasant experience at the former headquarters, resistance at best, perhaps even animosity. But from my first footstep inside the building I had been genuinely welcomed. The remarkableness of what was happening momentarily overcame my inhibitions. I paused and made eye contact with all three men. Not quite sure what to expect, they settled down. "Three years ago this meeting would have been impossible," I said. "Our countries were mortal enemies. Yet today I am sitting in a building I could not even approach then, and you are treating me with undreamt-of hospitality. Can you explain that?"

People in former East Germany had learned not to express personal opinions in public, and given the time and place, my question surely transgressed the boundaries of social etiquette. But this particular meeting seemed too historic for mere social conventions. At this moment, in this room, we were experiencing the fall of the Wall and end of the Cold War. The First World and Second World were no longer locked in conflicting political ideologies and military strategies. We were free to meet and talk and experience one another not as the embodiment of our respective governmental stereotypes but as the unique individuals we were. What was happening to us was the exact opposite of what Lohmeyer had experienced nearly fifty years earlier. In 1945 a political climate turned quickly, mysteriously, from friendly to antagonistic. In 1993 we were experiencing a happy reversal, a political thaw, longtime antagonists now friends.

I savored the momentary polite agreement that prevailed after my question. But soon my eager hosts returned to the business of pleasing their guest. I spent the next three hours combing through the names of several thousand prisoners in the Fünfeichen records. The name of Lohmeyer was not among them. Lohmeyer had almost certainly not been incarcerated there. As I searched the names, a possible cause of the error became evident. Although Lohmeyer's name was not in the Fünfeichen records, the name of his predecessor as president, Professor Engel, was. When I returned to Greifswald, I reported my findings to Professor Haufe. We called Frau Harmel on the telephone and asked if she possibly confused the names of Lohmeyer and Engel? A moment of silence ensued on the line, after which Frau Harmel responded. "I suppose that is possible. I was a young girl at the time. What stuck in my memory is that father played chess with a university professor. I can't remember the professor's name. It must have been Engel rather than Lohmeyer."

Lohmeyer had not been transferred to Fünfeichen. He ended his incarceration where it began—in the Criminal Justice Building in Greifswald.

Two Soldiers and the Roar of an Engine

The exchange of information among prisoners was as important as the exchange of cigarettes or foodstuffs. As the postwar years lengthened, the information was no longer limited to World War II, although it continued to include it. In Soviet-occupied postwar Europe, disappearances and deaths of people like Lohmeyer had become commonplace. They disappeared mysteriously on the way to work or on the way home from work, while out walking or while sitting in their homes. Some were taken from their beds at night. Many were simply never heard from again, their deaths by execution or starvation or forced labor in remote work camps shrouded by the same cloud of mystery that occluded their disappearance. Some were taken to concentration camps in eastern Germany— the same camps built by the Nazis. Some 120,000 Germans were incarcerated between 1945 and 1949 in eleven "special camps" of the NKVD in the Soviet sector of postwar Germany.[47] Many of the camps had been Nazi concentration camps, including Buchenwald, Sachsenhausen, Ravensbrück, and Fünfeichen. Some of the camps, including Buchenwald and Ravensbrück, would be used until 1955, which meant they were used *longer* by the Soviets than they had been by the Nazis. Given the vortex of silence into which imprisoned and dead prisoners were swept, exchange of prisoner information was a critical part of camp life.

In 1950, the clouds of silence and darkness that had shrouded Ernst Lohmeyer's disappearance for the previous four years were momentarily broken by a clearing of blue sky. The Russians closed Sachsenhausen, the infamous concentration camp on the northern edge of Berlin, in that year. A number of prisoners who had earlier been incarcerated in Neubrandenburg were now in Sachsenhausen, and they exchanged information about Lohmeyer. Upon their release, they wrote to Melie on June 17, 1950. "It is our grievous duty to inform you today that the Ernst Lohmeyer that you are looking for is reported by a former prisoner to have died in prison in Greifswald in fall 46."[48] The letter had been sent from Berlin, and Melie made her way to the return address on the letter, only to be informed that its source, a Karl Heinz Schröder, had left for Sweden three weeks earlier. She wrote to Schröder in Sweden, requesting further information about her husband. On June 29 she received a letter from Schröder, who reported being in the Greifswald prison with Lohmeyer through August of 1946. According to Schröder's testimony, Lohmeyer had first been tried in relation to the Bromberg Massacre in Poland in September of 1939, but the "accusations against him were unsubstantiated."[49] Schröder said he was then charged for crimes that German troops had committed in Russia under his authority as a captain in the Wehrmacht. On the basis of these charges, a Russian military tribunal condemned Lohmeyer to death in late August 1946. At that point Lohmeyer was removed from the cell he had shared with Karl Heinz Schröder and transferred to a corner cell on the ground floor with prisoners condemned to death. One of the prisoners in the death cell was a namesake, a Manfred Schröder, whose sentence was later commuted to ten years of hard labor. The two Schröders, Karl Heinz and Manfred, were both sent to Sachsenhausen, where in 1949 they met in the infirmary and exchanged information. Karl Heinz Schröder testified to Melie that the following report came from the mouth of Manfred Schröder, who had sworn him to communicate it truthfully to Lohmeyer's wife.

> On the same day—I believe it was September 1946, when your husband saw you with your daughter for the last time by the city wall—the following events transpired: a Russian officer entered the cell and called his (= Lohmeyer's) name. Your husband was lying on the bunk dressed in shirt, pants, and stockings. He got up and began to gather his things together and finish dressing, whereupon the officer said that would not be necessary. Two Russian soldiers then entered the cell and tied Lohmeyer's hands behind his back. They led him out of the cell, and a short while later the noise of engines starting in the waiting vehicles could be heard.[50]

Karl Heinz Schröder concluded his letter to Melie: "[Manfred] Schröder was convinced that your husband went the way that many before him had gone. When your husband was led out of the cell he instructed Manfred to greet you."[51] "I confirm this description of events," concluded Karl Heinz. "The verdict was executed, and it was my duty to communicate the prisoner's testimony to you." He signed the letter, "With deepest respect, Karl Heinz Schröder."[52]

Melie wrote a return letter of gratitude to Karl Heinz Schröder, informing him that his information corresponded with that of a certain Hans Tobis, whom she had recently visited. The independent reports of Schröder and Tobis verified one another. "The dreadful expression on Tobis's face," reported Melie, "left no doubt that he knew dear father had been shot."[53] Tobis added that in the three months of his incarceration in Greifswald, he knew of twenty-three men who were taken away and shot to death.

In Karl Heinz Schröder's final letter to Melie, he passed a single piece of information that, however insignificant it may have seemed to him, was a small joy amid a sea of sorrow to Melie. She had asked Schröder if her husband had done any academic work in prison. Schröder doubted that he had, because "only the New Testament had been left to him."[54] Lohmeyer's Greek New Testament, which had not parted from his pocket in war and peace, had been with him to the end.

Melie's indefatigable quest to discover Ernst's fate had come to an end. In September 1946, he had been shot by the NKVD. Rumors, of course, continued to spin, although with the increase of years their frequency decreased. A church newspaper reported that Lohmeyer was allegedly imprisoned in Poland, other sources that he was imprisoned in Russia, a few that he was even in West Germany. Melie had visions of him somehow, sometime, against all odds, showing up at the front door. Throughout the early 1950s, as Russia sporadically released its German prisoners of war, husbands supposedly dead occasionally returned. But the long pursuit of Lohmeyer's fate had by then chastened Melie of fantasies. It was not a surprise—perhaps it was even one of those severe mercies whose sole virtue is that bad news finally puts to rest all cheating fantasies to the contrary—that on December 6, 1957, nearly twelve years after Ernst's arrest, the Russian Red Cross delivered a cruelly brief message to the family: "Lohmeyer, Ernst, born 1890 Dorsten. Died on September 19, 1946, in camp."[55]

Confirmation of Lohmeyer's death in 1957 did not end Melie's labors on his behalf, although it shifted them from information about his death to preservation of his memory, and above all to *honoring* his memory. Melie died in 1971, but her two surviving children, Hartmut and Gudrun, continued nursing the flame of that memory. Her labors were also carried on by Professor Günter Haufe, who in 1972 occupied the chair of New Testament at the University of Greifswald formerly occupied by Lohmeyer. Despite the blackout on Lohmeyer's name in communist East Germany, Haufe labored to determine the details of Lohmeyer's disappearance and death. In 1974 I first encountered the name of Ernst Lohmeyer in the mysterious reference in his commentary on the Gospel of Mark, and I too joined the small company of people dedicated to remembering, recovering, and recording the life of Ernst Lohmeyer.

CHAPTER 16

Return to the Posthumous Inauguration

We all must die. There is no tragedy in dying. The tragedy is dying without honor.

Gudrun Lohmeyer Otto, 1996

Prophet in a Smoke-Filled Office

Professor Haufe finished his eulogy at the posthumous inauguration of Ernst Lohmeyer. The piano quartet played Bach's *Prelude f-Moll* from *The Well-Tempered Clavier*. My mind turned from the years that had brought me to this day to the events of the day itself, Thursday, September 19, 1996.

It had begun with a visit to Manfred Herling at the Greifswald University Archive. Herling and his assistant Barbara Peters had aided me in many helpful ways in my research into Lohmeyer's mysterious disappearance and death. Peters was not in the archive when I arrived, but Herling was sitting in his smoke-filled office with papers, files, books, and documents stacked on every flat surface. The scholarly clutter excited my imagination like a smorgasbord would a hungry person. The portraits on the walls, their dark colors further darkened by decades of smoke and soot, and the heavy nineteenth-century furnishings probably looked much the same in 1896 as they did in 1996. Herling received me exuberantly. He was a cauldron of ideas and passions. The more passionate he became, the more eloquently he spoke. Three presidents of Greifswald University had been murdered, he reported with affect. "Its founder Heinrich

Rubenow, Carl Engel, and Lohmeyer himself. Surely that's some sort of record in German universities," he proffered. "Take Engel," he said, dropping his arm emphatically on the desk. "He was an unrepentant Nazi . . . and public about it! When the Russians rolled into Greifswald, he had a car and could have escaped to the West as many others did. But he didn't! He stayed in Greifswald and resisted the communist intruders." Herling proceeded to Engel's grim and inevitable fate. "Engel was arrested, of course—within a week of the arrival of the Red Army. It was his arrest that caused Lohmeyer to be named president of the university." Engel had been taken to Fünfeichen—a former Nazi concentration camp turned into a communist concentration camp after the war. "There he died—starved to death." Herling leaned forward and held me in the crosshairs of his eyes: "Character can come from people you don't expect," he declared solemnly.

A new thought occurred to him about which he was even more passionate. The current residents of Arndtstrasse 3—the Lohmeyer home—refused to allow a plaque to Lohmeyer to be affixed to the wall of their building. "They're afraid the Russians will come back and they'll be sent to the Gulag as imperialist collaborators," he fulminated. His ire was accompanied by brilliant and borderline vulgarisms. Herling and his wife had both lost their fathers in World War II. He had an indomitable aversion to totalitarianism and utopianism alike, both of which, he declared in a dogmatic crescendo, led to the worst inhumanities and barbarisms. And he hated cowardice! "What hope is there for Christianity and civilization if people are afraid to confess their faith out of fear of trifles?" he thundered.

A Professor Detective

I took reluctant leave of this prophet in a smoke-filled archive and climbed two flights of stairs to the office of Martin Onnasch, professor of church history. As soon as I entered the office, Onnasch placed two documents in my hands. One was a German translation of Lohmeyer's complete Russian trial record. The other was an official exoneration of Lohmeyer by the Russian government. These two documents, so long sought and impatiently awaited, were now present in my hands.

I had combed German archives in vain looking for Lohmeyer's trial record during my German Academic Exchange Program sabbatical in 1993 and 1994. I concluded that it did not exist in Germany, and if it still existed, it must be in Russia. I was right on both matters, but it was not I who located it. It was Gudrun, fittingly, who succeeded in locating it . . . or having it located. An acquaintance of Gudrun's put her in touch with a Dr. Hans Coppi, whom she did not personally know, to undertake the mission. Hans Coppi was the son of Hans and Hilde Coppi, both of whom were executed by the Nazis in Berlin's gruesome Plötzensee Prison for their participation in *Rote Kapelle*—"The Red Chorus"—a communist resistance movement. *Rote Kapelle* sent secret telegraph messages to Stalin warning of Operation Barbarossa, the impending German invasion of Russia in June 1941. Its information could not have been more accurate . . . nor Stalin's rejection of it more total! Hans Sr. was executed by the Nazis in Plötzensee in 1942. Hilde was pregnant with Hans Jr. when she was in Plötzensee. Three months after he was born in 1943, Hilde was also executed. Young Hans grew up in communist East Germany, where he rose to various positions of prominence in its political apparatus. As a child of parents martyred by the Nazis, he was assured, indeed almost destined, for a leadership role in communist East Germany.

The collapse of East Germany in 1989 was a *kairos* moment in the search for Lohmeyer's fate. Gudrun and Hans Coppi had something in common: both had something that the other needed. Gudrun needed Coppi's expert knowledge of Russian archives. If Lohmeyer's trial record existed in Russia, Coppi likely knew where it was and how to get it. But Coppi also needed Gudrun. After the fall of East Germany in 1989, Coppi, like all members of its leadership apparatus, found himself discredited, indeed a virtual pariah, in newly united Germany. The aid he could render to Gudrun by helping to resolve the fate of her father was a unique and invaluable service—both to Gudrun and to the rehabilitation of his own reputation. The alliance between Gudrun and Hans Coppi worked a wonder. Within ten days of her request, Coppi had produced Lohmeyer's trial record—still written in Russian—from a former communist archive known only to him, to which he alone had access.

It was this document—Ernst Lohmeyer's Russian trial record—that Professor Onnasch placed in my hands. Along with the trial record, Onnasch included a copy of Lohmeyer's plea for clemency to Josef Stalin. The original trial record was in Russian, and Lohmeyer's original plea in German. Neither had been translated into the other language until summer 1996. The Slavic Department of Greifswald University had translated the Russian trial record into German and transcribed Lohmeyer's handwritten plea of clemency into German typescript only days before Onnasch placed the document in my hands.

The second document Onnasch placed in my hands was the official Russian rehabilitation of Lohmeyer in August 1996, fifty years after his execution. Onnasch made it available to me on condition that I not publish from or about it for six months. He closed the door of his office, told me to sit down, and explained why. The process of exoneration typically takes months and sometimes years to complete, but Lohmeyer's case had been expedited more quickly. He explained the reason. Before coming to the University of Greifswald, Onnasch had directed the Hannah Arendt Institute in Dresden. While there, he and the Arendt Institute had supplied the Russian office tasked with processing cases of political exoneration with both money and supplies, including paper, ink, photocopiers, copy fluids, spare parts, and so forth. Such technology and supplies, indispensable for the administrative process of exoneration, were either unavailable or difficult to procure after the Soviet Union collapsed in the early 1990s. The head of the Russian exoneration unit was Leonid P. Kopalin, chief justice and director of the Division of Rehabilitation of the Central Military Administration of the Federation of Russia.[1] Kopalin was a personal friend of Onnasch. The Russian exoneration process of Lohmeyer under Kopalin had occurred in record time—it was rendered in Moscow on August 15, 1996, and hand-delivered by Kopalin's wife in Greifswald on August 18. Onnasch hoped that a six-month time lapse would spare Kopalin from possible charges of corruption and bribery in rendering Lohmeyer's rehabilitation.

Onnasch closed with two parting words of advice. First, there was more to the story about how Greifswald had procured Lohmeyer's exoneration so rapidly, but that was for a physician, a man named Dr. Horst Hennig, to relate. Hennig, Onnasch informed me, would contact me at the dinner after the posthumous inauguration. And second, Onnasch told me that the trial record did not recount the way the trial was actually conducted, but the way the Soviets wanted the trial to appear to have been conducted. Its purpose was not to record the impartial presentation of evidence but to produce evidence in support of a prior judgment of Lohmeyer's guilt.

Physician Sleuth

Visits with Herling and Onnasch had been the two main events leading up to the evening service. My thoughts returned to the inauguration ceremony. The Bach *Prelude* was followed by a prayer, and the posthumous inauguration concluded with Bach's *Fuge f-Moll*, also from *The Well-Tempered Clavier*. Following the service, photos were taken at the front of the festival hall, after which the family, dignitaries, and invited guests retired to Hotel am Dom on Langestrasse for dinner. Unfortunately, Gudrun could not be present at the posthumous inauguration. She was undergoing cancer treatments at the time that, although they extended her life until 2004, prevented her from attending the service of her father's rehabilitation for which she had labored so indefatigably. Her husband, Klaus, was there, however, as was their thirty-six-year-old daughter Julia, who was practicing veterinary medicine near Frankfurt, Germany. I sat next to Julia at dinner and talked with her and several professors from the University of Rostock.

As I was leaving the dining room after dinner, a man stopped me, introduced himself hurriedly as Dr. Horst Hennig, and asked to meet me in the restaurant at 10 p.m. I showed up at the agreed time and place, and Hennig ushered me to a quiet table and presented me with a sheaf of materials. We talked till nearly midnight. In 1950, Hennig, a twenty-four-year-old studying medicine at the

University of Halle in East Germany, was alarmed by the tyranny growing in the Russian sector of Germany. He allied himself with various democratic reform movements. Along with other students, he was arrested and imprisoned. For three months he was held in solitary confinement, without light, and subjected to beatings and hunger. He was then sentenced to twenty-five years of hard labor in Workuta, one of the countless camps in Russia's infamous Gulag Archipelago. Workuta lay north of the Arctic Circle, where winter temperatures plummeted to minus 40–50 degrees Celsius. A twenty-five-year sentence in such a camp was a death sentence. In 1953, two years after his arrival in Workuta, prisoners demonstrated for more humane treatment. The Soviets responded to the demonstration with gunfire, killing 53 and critically wounding 123 others. In 1955 Hennig succeeded in gaining release from the Gulag and returning to Germany.

He chose not to put the experience "behind him," however. With the collapse of Soviet communism in 1990, Hennig employed his facility in Russian and his knowledge of the Soviet penal system to advocate for the posthumous rehabilitation of German prisoners who, unlike himself, had not been fortunate enough to return alive from the Gulag. He had spent the greater part of his adult life being hunted, defamed, and persecuted by Soviet communism. The innuendos and coded generalities in which he couched the narrative he recounted in the Hotel am Dom indicated that his past was still present . . . and probably always would be.[2]

It was with Horst Hennig that the process leading to Lohmeyer's rehabilitation finally gained traction. Hennig specialized in rare diseases. Leonid Kopalin's daughter suffered from a disease that Hennig had successfully treated. Hennig knew from personal experience how the Soviet legal system worked. He knew that Lohmeyer had been an innocent victim of it, and that the fiftieth anniversary of his murder was approaching. He appealed to Leonid Kopalin on behalf of Ernst Lohmeyer. Kopalin responded by expediting the review of Lohmeyer's case.

The documents in my hands now allowed me to assemble remaining pieces of the puzzle to achieve as complete a picture as may ever be possible of Lohmeyer's trial and conviction.[3]

Arrest

Immediately following Lohmeyer's arrest on the night of February 14/15, 1946, he was taken to the Criminal Justice Building at Domstrasse 6/7, which the NKVD utilized as a prison. In the succeeding months he was placed on various floors and in various cells of the building, but he was held exclusively in this location until his execution by shooting on September 19, 1946. The primary reason for his arrest was his strong and independent character and his commitment, indeed his *vocation*, to reopen the University of Greifswald according to the ideals of a historic German university, free from doctrinaire interference of the Russian occupation. The presenting reason for his arrest was his failure to satisfy the requirement of the communist party blocs in Schwerin and Greifswald to dismiss all university professors who were members of the Nazi Party. Lohmeyer refused to comply with this requirement on the grounds that dismissal of all party members would have closed the university, including the medical faculty, which was providing critical relief to the war-wounded at the time. Lohmeyer's decision was fully in accord with the Three Power Agreement, signed by Russia, America, and Britain, that culpable and nefarious party members should be terminated whereas nominal party members who were not guilty of criminal offenses should be retained. The report of Dr. Naas, representative of the German Central Administration of Public Education in Berlin, on the morning of Lohmeyer's arrest, that his "activity had not been good for the University," corroborates this point.[4]

A second reason for Lohmeyer's arrest was his endeavor to reopen the university on February 15, 1946. In this too Lohmeyer acted in accord with the highest authority, for the Russian Military Administration in Berlin, which supported reopening the university on the above date, supervened the authority of the communist party blocs in Schwerin and Greifswald that opposed it. Two further reasons may have played roles in his arrest, although whether they did, and to what extent they did, is not entirely clear. First, the arrest of a strong and independent leader like Lohmeyer was strategically utilitarian, for it sent a forewarning to other universities and university presidents in the Russian sector that they were not immune from Soviet authority. The arrest of Lohmeyer made undeniably clear that the ideal of an educational organ independent of Soviet political authority would not be tolerated. Second, the communist authorities may have interpreted Lohmeyer's membership in the Democratic Party, which he joined in June of 1945 (and which in the fall of the year became the Christian Democratic Union [CDU]), to signal his commitment to "bourgeois" rather than "proletariat" politics, both as a community leader and as president of the University of Greifswald.

In the final analysis, however, the exact reasons for Lohmeyer's arrest are not fully resolved, and probably cannot be fully resolved, for already on the morning of February 15, 1946, information about his arrest consisted of a snarl of opposing reasons and evidence. To take but one of the above-mentioned reasons as an example, Lohmeyer's Russian trial record mentions his membership in the CDU eight times disapprovingly. This would appear to be evidence for its role in his arrest. On the other hand, a report, ostensibly produced by the Communist Party of Germany and dated February 16, 1946—*one day* after his arrest—lists Lohmeyer as the first of five theology faculty members who were *unbelastet*—communist jargon for "politically clean." This critically dated memo expressly denies that Lohmeyer was arrested for political reasons.[5]

The fact that Lohmeyer was arrested by the NKVD, the Soviet secret military police, indicates that *military* grounds played a role in his arrest. Such grounds would require a military reason, a denunciation related to military matters, for example. Precisely such a denunciation was supplied by a memorandum of Dr. Franz Wohlgemuth, leader of the Communist Party of Germany in Schwerin-Greifswald, who accused Lohmeyer of having participated in the Bromberg Massacre in Poland in 1939. Wohlgemuth further stated that Lohmeyer had served in the German Wehrmacht in the Ukraine, which insinuated further criminal culpability on his part. The date of the memo is critical—February 14, 1946! The memo bears the imprimatur of "Franz Wohlgemuth, leadership of the Community Party of Germany."[6] One day before Lohmeyer's arrest, Wohlgemuth provided the NKVD with a military denunciation that required Soviet military justice to hear Lohmeyer's case.[7] We are thus faced with a curious and contradictory circumstance: one and the same communist party both exonerated and condemned Lohmeyer in separate memos within twenty-four hours of each other. That the Bromberg Massacre was a false pretext for Lohmeyer's arrest is proven by the fact that it was *unmentioned* in the Russian trial record, for the Russians by then knew that Lohmeyer was not in Poland at the time of the massacre. Wohlgemuth, it will be remembered, was himself appointed *Kurator*—university administrator—by Gottfried Grünberg six weeks after Lohmeyer's arrest. Wohlgemuth was an occupational predator. He was not above destroying another man's career—or, as in Lohmeyer's case, another man's *life*—if it resulted in the advancement of his own. That he used Lohmeyer's removal as president to seize his position—and wrote his denunciation to achieve both purposes—seems virtually beyond doubt.

Trial

Throughout the spring of 1946, Lohmeyer communicated from his prison cell by hand movements with Melie and Gudrun, who stood on the promenade beside the old city wall. On several occasions Melie managed to send him food packages. Lohmeyer was interrogated on and off by Captain Ivanoff, the same officer who was present at his arrest. No grounds for arrest were communicated to Lohmeyer. Ivanoff himself, in fact, appeared no clearer on the grounds for the arrest than Lohmeyer was. In March, Lohmeyer wrote a last letter to Melie attributing his arrest to "a Schwerin intrigue,"[8] a ploy of the communist party blocs. He reckoned with a lengthy incarceration, but nursed hopes of eventual release. He fantasized about moving to Tübingen, or someplace where he and Melie could start anew.

The woolly ambiguity surrounding his arrest and detention lasted three and a half months. On May 30 his trial by the Russians began, and on June 6 charges were presented. The nearly fifty-page trial record preserves a volley of accusations. As a commandant in German-occupied regions of the Soviet Union, Lohmeyer was accused of serving the interests of the fascist state. Included in the interests, the record continues, was that German "fascist invaders"[9] arrested and killed 550 innocent Russian citizens. Lohmeyer was further accused of arresting as many as 70 Soviet citizens, of whom some 20 were submitted to trials. Other accusations followed, even more general in nature: Lohmeyer had unleashed a "witch hunt against Soviet citizens";[10] he had committed "crimes"[11] in Soviet-occupied territories; he had subjected Soviet citizens to forced labor without pay, and had arrested, imprisoned, and shot others. These acts of arbitrary violence, submitted the trial record, could not have happened without Lohmeyer's knowledge and participation as commandant. Lohmeyer's membership in the CDU, as noted above, was mentioned eight times as an act deserving punishment. In the near book-length trial record, only one accusation was accompanied by a specific name, date, and place: that Lohmeyer was responsible for the execution of a partisan named Ivan Nozka.

These accusations need to be understood in light of the following. The trial was conducted in Russian, a language Lohmeyer did not know. He was dependent on a translator throughout. He was not permitted to speak unless asked; and when asked, he was not permitted to remain silent. Lohmeyer was not permitted a lawyer or legal counsel of any kind. Above all, he was not permitted to bring evidence or witnesses relative to his guilt or innocence. That fifty of Germany's intellectual and cultural leaders testified to Lohmeyer's impeccable character; that Jewish voices such as Ernst Cohn, Martin Buber, Jochen Klepper, and Jewish colleagues at Breslau avowed that Lohmeyer would never shoot innocent civilians; and that a man who opposed Nazism as bravely, persistently, and sacrificially as Lohmeyer was scarcely likely to participate in its most heinous crimes—none of this was admissible evidence.

The trial was not about credible evidence but about accusations, all but one of which lacked specifics. The 70-some Soviet citizens that Lohmeyer allegedly arrested and tried, and the 550 persons he was accused of slaughtering, all lacked names, witnesses, dates, and places of alleged crimes. No reputable court of justice would entertain such accusations without such corroborating information. How might one refute killing 550 unnamed people at an unidentified place on an unspecified date? The logical mind may counter that an accusation for which there is no refuting evidence is equally one for which there can be no convicting evidence. This, of course, was the crux of the matter, for a conviction of Lohmeyer was based not on evidence but solely on accusations.

The atrocities perpetrated in Russia by the German Wehrmacht between 1941 and 1944 resulted in an insatiable demand for retribution. A quota of guilty perpetrators needed to be found as a token of atonement for each of the violated regions of the nation. Accusations alone were sufficient to satisfy the demand for retribution. Indeed, to demand *evidence* could be interpreted as an attempt to exonerate the accused, to "privilege the enemy" and "betray the class struggle." Lohmeyer was a sacrificial lamb on which the plenary sins of the German army could be heaped.[12]

When allowed, Lohmeyer spoke to the various charges brought against him. More than once he rejected the charge that the populace had been reduced to forced labor.[13] To another charge he replied, "I do not regard that as a crime."[14] More often, "I confess that I am not guilty of this accusation."[15] And in conclusion, "I am a person of faith and consequently cannot do acts of cruelty."[16] He emphatically denied committing acts of rapacity, forced labor, arbitrary arrests, and above all, shooting civilians. He admitted that the Wehrmacht had committed atrocities in the Kuban before his command of the region, and especially by retreating German troops after his command there. But atrocities and injustices had not been committed or permitted under his command. "The police forces under my command carried out no shootings of Soviet citizens."[17] Conditions on the Russian front were unspeakably brutal, but Lohmeyer repeatedly testified that he used what little power and opportunity he had to do the little good he could.

Lohmeyer affirmed only one accusation in the long trial record—the sole incident that was accompanied by corroborating details, a name and a date. A partisan named Ivan Nozka had been arrested in November 1942 for cutting telephone lines. Without telephone communications the lives of German soldiers under Lohmeyer's command were at risk. Lohmeyer confessed to allowing Nozka to be hanged for this act. Although Lohmeyer was not present at the hanging, he maintained that the sentence of hanging for such an act was not a crime.[18]

The Defendant

The legal advocate that Lohmeyer was denied in summer 1946 was granted to him fifty years later in Leonid Kopalin. According to Kopalin, in the 1990s Soviet archives contained more than 200,000 dossiers on German citizens who were either imprisoned or executed by the Soviets in the postwar era. Of this number, 30,000 dossiers were of German prisoners of war in the Soviet Union, another 40,000 dossiers of Germans convicted by Soviet military tribunals in East Germany, and nearly 130,000 dossiers of Germans imprisoned and sentenced to hard labor in East German internment camps. When Kopalin filed his report in 1996, he and his office had been reviewing German files since 1993, for three years. Of 6,000 dossiers reviewed in that time period, only 6 percent of the accused—360 persons—were found to be guilty of their alleged crimes. That is to say, in Kopalin's first three years as chief justice and director of the Division of Rehabilitation of the Central Military Administration of the Federation of Russia, 94 percent of Germans arrested, tried, and punished by the NKVD following World War II were innocent. Such dossiers, like Lohmeyer's, are replete with forced confessions, unsupported denunciations and accusations, and falsifications of both accusations and evidence.[19]

These staggering statistics may cause us to lose sight of something in Kopalin's report that is easily overlooked. It is rare for nations to confess their crimes against other nations and peoples. Kopalin's statistics of exoneration demonstrate, however, that in the 1990s Russia made a clear and public admission of its guilt in the postwar era. The exoneration of Ernst Lohmeyer and the thousands of innocent victims like him, which had been rendered impossible in the previous seventy-five years, was finally achieved following the collapse of Soviet communism in Russia. And, with the slide of Russia back into autocracy under Vladimir Putin in the early years of the new century, it would again be rendered impossible. Only in the window of opportunity opened by Boris Yeltsin in the final decade of the twentieth century was the exoneration of Lohmeyer by Leonid Kopalin possible.

In his exoneration, Kopalin presented the counterevidence and arguments that had not been allowed in Lohmeyer's case. Lohmeyer, said Kopalin, did not expropriate Russian agriculture and industry for the Third Reich but used the same to aid the Russian population. He protected civilians from arrests, deportations, and punishments. He neither ordered nor took part in shootings of civilians; on the contrary, his administration was mild and humane. He permitted three hundred noncombatant communist and Jewish prisoners, and a communist leader named Lasutkin, to return to their homes. Kopalin found no evidence of criminal activity in the Kuban under Lohmeyer's jurisdiction, and he insisted that Lohmeyer could not be held culpable for war crimes committed there both before and after his command of the region. Lohmeyer's imprisonment and trial, averred Kopalin, had been a protracted violation of legal due process. Kopalin concluded:

> Lohmeyer took no personal part in shootings of Soviet civilians or in other punitive actions, and he never gave orders or directives regarding the same. As commandant of the region of Slaviansk from 27 August 1942–18 March 1943 (approximately a half-year) he sought to reduce the consequences of the war for the entire civilian population. . . . When the facts are considered one must conclude that Ernst Lohmeyer was arrested and convicted without sufficient cause and on the basis of political motives alone. Therefore, in accordance with Paragraph 3 of the Law of the Russian Federation, "Concerning Rehabilitation of Victims of Political Repression," of 18 October 1991, Ernst Lohmeyer stands fully rehabilitated and all his rights pertaining thereto restored (posthumously).[20]

The exoneration is signed "L. P. Kopalin" and dated August 15, 1996.

Verdict

Kopalin based his verdict on evidence, not on accusation, which unquestionably required a verdict of innocence in Lohmeyer's case. The actual trial in the summer of 1946 was simply window dressing for a predetermined conclusion, however. On June 18, 1946, the court found Lohmeyer guilty of all accusations presented against him in the trial. The name authorizing the verdict of guilty was "N. Ivanoff"—the same Ivanoff who arrested Lohmeyer in his home six months earlier, who interrogated him throughout the spring, and who now, ostensibly, determined his final guilt. Recall that throughout the summer of 1946 reports from persons supposedly in the know found their way to Melie of Lohmeyer's imminent release from jail. The trial record shows that such reports were mere rumors, and gravely mistaken.

Ivanoff's verdict of guilt in June was not accompanied by a sentence of punishment. For the latter, Lohmeyer was required to wait another two months in his prison cell. At 6 p.m. on August 28 an all-Russian military triumvirate, consisting of a major, sergeant, and staff sergeant, reconvened to announce the sentence. No witnesses were allowed at the hearing. Lohmeyer was given two hours to plead his case. He closed with talking points that summed up his life:

> I am a man of Faith and therefore cannot commit atrocities.
>
> I am a professor known world wide. I have lectured not only in Germany but in many other countries like America, Belgium, and Sweden.
>
> I am an honorary member of an American theological society [Society of Biblical Literature].
>
> I have many friends who opposed Nazism throughout the world.
>
> I could never commit the crimes of which I am accused.
>
> I was not free not to serve in the Wehrmacht.
>
> I have always said that war is a crime.[21]

At 8 p.m. the tribunal adjourned for two hours. It reconvened at 10 p.m., and Major Jakovcenko delivered the sentence. Lohmeyer was to remain, as before, in prison. He was guilty of all charges brought against him. He had imposed a "fascistic administration"[22] in Russia, he had "gathered a circle of traitors to the Fatherland around himself,"[23] and he was guilty of the "crime of German-Fascist aggression."[24] He was ordered to be shot and his property confiscated. The decision could not be appealed. At 10:30 p.m. the major dropped his gavel and the trial ended.

The next day Lohmeyer picked up his pen for the last time to write an appeal for clemency to Josef Stalin. His hand was steady and the words flowed flawlessly. In two and a half pages he made only two minor changes. "I am a professor of Protestant theology and a faithful member of the Christian church," he began.[25] He reviewed his commitment to theology and scholarship and his contribution to the same in books, lectures, and personal renown, as well as his relationships with professors in Sweden, Holland, France, America, England, and Switzerland. He repeated his opposition to Nazism, and its cost to his career. He fought in the war not because he wanted to—he believed it to be a criminal act from the outset—but because he was forced to.

At this point in the letter Lohmeyer made an abrupt key change, so to speak. He turned from his accomplishments and worthiness to something more essential—the issue of being *a moral human being* in a world of violence and chaos. "Wherever I served in occupied territories I sought to honor the fundamentals of what it means to be human. I assure you again that I never ever took part in the shooting of Soviet citizens or ordered such. On the contrary, I sought in all regions to alleviate the ravages of war where I could, and I made no distinction between my comrades in the German Wehrmacht or communist Soviet citizens."[26] He closed by saying that his punishments as commandant—even for minor infractions—were milder than required. Moreover, he had not fled to the West at war's end, but he stayed in the Russian sector and fulfilled the highest humanistic ideals in the administration of the University of Greifswald. And finally, there was his family. One son was killed in the war, another critically wounded; his wife, sixty years of age, was ill; and his young daughter longed for an education. "Therefore, I appeal to you once again for mercy."[27]

No groveling, no self-pity, no hollow self-justifications, no fabrications, no heroics. It is a simple testimony, but in its simple truth a masterpiece of what it means to be a moral human being in a world in which both morality and humanity had almost ceased to exist. Lohmeyer stood tall, an upright human being, hoping for the same from Josef Stalin. The German word for an appeal for clemency is *Gnadengesuch*, literally, "appeal for grace." We have no knowledge of Stalin ever being motivated by grace. Whether he would have been in this instance we shall never know, for the letter that Hans Coppi brought back from Russia had never been translated into Russian. Stalin never saw Lohmeyer's *Gnadengesuch*.

Execution

At the end of August Lohmeyer was moved into a cell for prisoners awaiting execution. He was imprisoned with Manfred Schröder, who remained with him until he was taken away, and to whom we are indebted for the last report on his life. On Thursday, September 19, 1946, NKVD operatives entered the prison cell, bound Lohmeyer's hands, and took him away. Silence ensued thereafter for nearly fifty years.

In my research into Lohmeyer's death, the most commonly suggested place of his execution has been in nearby Hanshagen. Melie believed her husband had been killed outside Greifswald, perhaps in Hanshagen or elsewhere. The NKVD, she stated, did not kill its victims at the place of incarceration but at remote sites outside it. This has remained the majority opinion on the matter, and it may be correct. We know from the report of Hans Tobis, the young man who survived his incarceration in the NKVD prison at the time of Lohmeyer's imprisonment, that some twenty-three prisoners at the Criminal Justice Building in Greifswald were executed in the spring of 1946.[28] That would suggest a killing site outside the prison. But if such a site existed, one would expect there to be some knowledge of it. Executions, especially mass executions over several years, were hard to conceal from villagers, farmers, hunters, herders, and locals living and working in the region where they took place. No bones have been uncovered from a mass grave. No killing site has been identified in the environs of Greifswald. Lack of corroborating evidence makes it difficult to know if the Hanshagen hypothesis is reliable oral tradition or baseless rumor. All this does not refute the hypothesis, but it cautions acceptance of it as fact.

I am inclined to think that Lohmeyer was shot in the parking lot of the Criminal Justice Building at Domstrasse 6/7. Suchdienst München, the division of the German Red Cross that investigates Germans who disappeared or were incarcerated/executed during the Russian occupation of eastern Germany, reports that "the USSR never identified either the place or cause of death"[29] of prisoners other than occasionally reporting "in the territory of the USSR"[30]—which would include East Germany. The Russian Red Cross's earliest version of Lohmeyer's death announcement, however, actually identifies a place of death: "Lohmeyer, Ernst, born 1890 in Dorsten. Died on 19th September 1946 *im Lager*."[31] "*Im Lager*"—literally "in the camp"—means the place of detention. The Russian trial record also refers to Lohmeyer's incarceration "*im Lager*," which appears to signify the Criminal Justice Building at Domstrasse 6/7. The German Red Cross concluded that "on the basis of several authorities [Ernst Lohmeyer] was shot in the fall of 1946 in the MWD [Russian abbreviation for 'Ministry of Internal Affairs'] prison in Greifswald."[32] The judgment of the German Red Cross on this matter is based on "well over 90,000 pages"[33] of NKVD files related to the fate of Germans who were incarcerated in Russian camps in East Germany.[34] Such a knowledge base warrants serious consideration. The most important evidence, however, comes from the Russians themselves. The forty-eighth and final page of the Russian trial record reports that Lohmeyer's death sentence "was executed on September 19, 1946, *in Greifswald*."[35] According to Kopalin's explanation in his rehabilitation of Lohmeyer, this acknowledges that the Russians killed Lohmeyer "in Greifswald"—although it does not identify where they disposed of his body.

The premises of Domstrasse 6/7 were a convenient and relatively secure place for execution. A surrounding wall obscured the interior driveway and parking place from the sight of those outside the premises. The roar of truck engines—which Manfred Schröder reported hearing shortly after Lohmeyer was taken from the prison cell—would muffle the sound of a single pistol shot to the head. Lohmeyer's body would have been thrown into the back of the truck, taken out of town, and disposed of. No sound, no sight, no trace. Like so many other murder victims of the NKVD, it would be *als ob er nie extierte*, "as though he never existed."

And so it was—almost.

Honor

Before I departed Greifswald following the September 1996 posthumous inauguration, I returned to the university for a final visit. The baroque festival hall was empty and still. Its vermilion walls and white pillars were luminous in the pale afternoon sunlight. At the front of the hall were the plaque and photograph of Lohmeyer from the celebration of the night before. His bust, not yet returned to its place in the president's office, remained on top of the polished black August Foerster grand piano. To the right of the piano was the empty president's chair. I sat in stillness. My chance encounter with this man twenty years before had reached its conclusion. The half-century blackout on his fate, the puzzle of his "mysterious disappearance and death," as Gerhard Sass referred to it, had at last been resolved—at least as far as human resources can resolve such things. Lohmeyer seemed to be looking back at me from his picture. It was an ineffable moment.

A liturgical staple in Lohmeyer's spiritual life had been the daily Bible readings of the Herrnhuter Brethren in Germany. The reading for September 19, 1946, his death day, was Mark 7:37, "[Jesus] has done all things well." Lohmeyer found this verse particularly rich and meaningful. In his Mark commentary he wrote about verse 37 as follows: "In Jesus . . . the eschatological fulfillment of what from the very beginning had been a long and dark history of God's people is at hand. Here is the fulfillment of Old Testament eschatological prophecy."[36] "[Jesus] has done all things well." Lohmeyer's death was the fulfillment of the same hope.

On the flight back to the States I reread the fifty-page Russian trial record. Even when one understands that this was theater, a show trial without an audience, a volley of accusations that was a *folly* of accusations, sufficient in themselves to assure a death sentence, it is a brutal read. What it was like for Lohmeyer to endure it alone we can only imagine. Or perhaps we *cannot* imagine.

Two weeks after I returned home I received a telephone call from Germany. Gudrun was calling. Her preferred method of communication was, like her father's, with paper and pen—although Gudrun mercifully typed her letters. I had not received a phone call from her before. She thanked me for my role in rehabilitating her father's reputation. I was moved once again by this woman's gentleness, her thoughtfulness and integrity, her affirmation of me, an outsider, in a matter that drew me inevitably into the life of her family, which had been so dismembered by outsiders. I thanked her for her kindness. "I only wish it had brought him back to life," I said. "Ah," she gently chided, "that was never the issue. My father would no longer be alive now anyway. We all must die. There is no tragedy in dying. The tragedy is dying without honor. You have helped restore his honor."

CHAPTER 17

The Last Letter

The school of life has some difficult classes, but it is in such classes that one learns the most. Most difficult for me were the four walls of a prison cell that was six steps long and two steps wide, and a door that could only be opened from the outside. Beyond was a fence with four strands of electrified barbed wire, and a gate guarded by men with machine guns.

Corrie ten Boom[1]

The Secret Prussian Archive

In 2016 I received an invitation from the University of Greifswald to present a lecture on Ernst Lohmeyer at a symposium commemorating the seventieth anniversary of his death. The symposium was entitled "Hopeful Beginning, Violent End." A half-dozen other scholars, from Germany, Italy, and England, also presented. The symposium, hosted by the theological faculty of the University of Greifswald, kept the candle of Lohmeyer's memory burning and explored his enduring significance as a theologian. I lectured on Lohmeyer's understanding of martyrdom, a theme that played a prominent role in three different works he published while a professor at Breslau in the late 1920s. I concluded by quoting Philippians 3:10, a verse that Lohmeyer considered essential to understanding the Christian life. "I want to know him, and the power of his resurrection and the fellowship of his sufferings, and in so doing to be conformed to his death."

Following the lecture my wife and I went to Berlin, where I continued research on Lohmeyer in the writing of this book. We rented an inviting third floor loft for three months in Dahlem, a beautiful section of Berlin. Each morning I walked twenty-five minutes along tree-lined streets and past impressive villas to the archive where I did my research. On the way I passed the house where Albert Einstein lived until he emigrated from Germany to America in 1933. Three blocks farther I passed the former Kaiser Wilhelm Institute with its distinctive rounded turret and black-slate roof crowned with a prominent spike, resembling a Teutonic helmet, where Einstein conducted physics experiments, and where in 1938 Otto Hahn, Fritz Strassmann, Lise Meitner, and Max Delbrück first split the atom. Farther still I passed the Jesus Christ Church, from which Pastor Martin Niemöller founded the Pastors' Emergency League in 1933, which morphed into the Confessing Church the following year. Nearer the archive I walked through the sprawling Free University of Berlin, which was founded in the 1950s, with major financial support from the Ford Foundation and the Marshall Plan in America. The Free University had been established to provide Berlin with a university free—hence the name—from communist control, since Humboldt University lay in then-communist East Berlin. My walk brought me to the Secret State Archive of the Prussian Cultural Heritage Foundation, a stately two-story neo-baroque building with two symmetrical wings that reach out to the visitor in a dignified welcome.

In the year 2000 Gudrun and Klaus Otto willed the remaining corpus of Lohmeyer's letters and papers, which they had inherited from Melie, to the Secret Prussian Archive. The archive already possessed some fifteen cartons of Lohmeyer materials, each carton roughly the size of a small suitcase. The bequest from Gudrun and Klaus swelled the Lohmeyer materials to thirty-five cartons, the most complete repository of Lohmeyer materials.

I had contacted the associate director of the archive, Frau Dr. Schnelling-Reinicke, in preparation for my research. Dr. Schnelling-Reinicke had all thirty-five cartons of materials numbered and stacked in sequence on two rolling carts in the acquisition room for my use. In addition, she had personally prepared a forty-seven-page inventory of the materials contained therein. Her catalogue, which aided my research invaluably, rivaled one of the feats of Hercules. The spacious reading room on the second floor was appointed for optimum scholarly productivity. It contained the essentials of comfortable study chairs, nice writing surfaces, and good lighting in a classic reading room with large windows facing the courtyard and bookcases crowned with Latin sayings and marble busts. All distractions were eliminated—no talking among scholars or on cell phones, no cell-phone photography, no WiFi for email, no backpacks, no private materials, and minimal photocopying services. Laptop computers were of course allowed. In organization and policies the archive offered scholars optimum access to original source materials, while protecting those irreplaceable materials from theft, misuse, and deterioration. In my three months there, I succeeded in accomplishing more research and writing on this book than I had accomplished on any project of similar nature in my life.

File 146

My first day in the archive was October 28, 2016, my birthday. The reading room was filled with scholars poring over discolored old handwritten documents that exuded the faint and alluring stench of antiquity. I examined Dr. Schnelling-Reinicke's critical catalogue. At the end of the catalogue my eye fell on file 146, a letter written from Ernst to Melie dated March 31–April 4, 1946. It had been six weeks since his arrest in mid-February 1946, and Lohmeyer wrote to Melie on tissue packing paper that she had somehow managed to get to him in prison and that had not been confiscated. I had seen a portion of this letter before but not its entirety.

The file contained a 5″ x 6″ envelope, the edges of which were framed in a seventy-year-old shaded patina. Melie had written on the envelope, "The last letter of Ernst! That it will not be lost."[2] At the top of the envelope was the figure of a cross, not made with single vertical and horizontal strokes but etched with repeated vertical and horizontal strokes, pen pressed hard against the envelope, leaving a darkly engraved cross. Inside the envelope was a second envelope marked simply "Last letter."[3] This second envelope contained two folded letters. The larger of the two was written in Melie's rounded upright script. Folded inside her letter was a second letter written in pencil in Lohmeyer's tight script on the thin packing paper that Melie had managed to get to him in prison. This letter was eight pages long, the script of which was so minuscule and written within a hairsbreadth of the edges of the paper, that Melie herself had had to transcribe it to render it more legible. Lohmeyer had folded this original letter into a two-inch square and compressed it until it was no thicker than a book of matches, small enough to be smuggled out of the prison under the insole of a boot, or in a folded shirt cuff, or in a hat brim. A vague hint in the letter suggested that he had enlisted a custodial worker to smuggle it out of the prison and deliver it to Melie. The two handwritten letters were thus the same letter, Ernst's original prison letter accompanied by Melie's larger and more legible copy. At some point Melie had converted the contents of this letter to double-spaced typescript, thirteen pages in length, which was also contained in file 146. In his seven months' imprisonment in Greifswald, Lohmeyer had succeeded in smuggling only one written communication to Melie. This was it.

The Happening

The letter was entitled "Cell 19," with a date, "begun on 31.3.46,"[4] and a postscript dated "4 April."[5] Writing the letter had been a five-day investment on Lohmeyer's part. The first part of the letter, which I had seen before, reported on prison conditions.[6] But Lohmeyer had not written to Melie primarily to report on such conditions and his fate, important as they were, for in the typescript version these were concluded in the first four pages. Nine pages still remained. On page 5 he turned to what was paramount on his mind. "Thanks be to God," he forcefully inserted, for what he wanted to say was no longer conditioned by "when I am released."[7]

> O my love, something important has happened to me and in me, a jolt has set me free from so much, a gust of wind has landed

me on new ground. I am still working through what happened to me. On the night that I was arrested, you came to me with light and lively steps—I was in my room with the interpreter—and you kissed me warmly and firmly on the mouth. There was a sudden knowledge of things that I had not seen until then, which my eyes had almost overlooked. And as Puppi then came into the room, driven by a dark feeling—or what was it?!—a lightness of heart came almost wholly upon me: the oneness of our hearts was there, the oneness found again, and everything was open and there was nothing more to hide. In this way, in this way it was bound to come, in this way it had to happen, in everything God's finger was clear to see.[8]

Lohmeyer did not describe the experience more precisely. He did not refer to it as a dream or vision or visitation, only as a *Geschehen*. It was not something he thought or felt, not something he envisioned or imagined, but something that *happened*. He reported only that it happened on the night of his arrest and that his interpreter was with him in the cell. Lohmeyer may not have been clear himself about exactly what had happened, and when and how, for he omits further details. But *that* something profound had happened he left no doubt. His 160-word German account has a stream-of-consciousness quality to it—phrases spliced loosely together with dashes, colons, and question marks, with only three full stops. This was wholly atypical of Ernst Lohmeyer, but similar to sections of Augustine's *Confessions*, more so to Paul's Damascus road experience, most of all to Pascal's dramatic encounter with God in terms of fire! It has the hallmarks of a divine inbreaking in which a Reality altered the coordinates of time, space, and language.

Lohmeyer continued—but now in his distinctive diction. In his first days and weeks in prison, he reviewed his life, and he trembled at what he saw. His work had ensnared him with its roots and tendrils, and he had not been able to free himself from them. This was the same work he had celebrated as a divine calling in his ordination sermon of 1912, but the work had somehow usurped the calling and become the sum of his life. But in the disconcerting self-inventory he also discovered comfort and peace. The pendulum of his life had swung between the specter of death and the hope of life. The pendulum stopped at neither pole, neither at what had happened to him nor even at his failings, but at a different and more permanent place, at *who he was*. In the remainder of the letter, Lohmeyer shared his self-realization honestly and vulnerably, but above all hopefully.

Self

"It is now clear to me that for more than twenty years I have followed the wrong course," he began.[9] The wrong course had not evolved over a long period of time, as it does perhaps for many people, camouflaged by the responsibilities and pressures of careers and advancement and families. It began with a decision in the summer of 1925 that was clear in his mind. Melie had wanted to bear another child—the child would be Gudrun—his close and adoring daughter. Ernst reluctantly consented, but "in conceding to your wish for another child," he confessed, "I decided to devote myself entirely to my work."[10] There seemed to be good reasons for him to make a decision that he later came to regret. He was a gifted intellectual, and he believed his work was a calling from God. His academic career had taken strong root and was growing year by year. But other factors, including Hönigswald's influential friendship, came into play as well. "Perhaps I had also been enticed by the alluring and impressive example of Hönigswald,"[11] he conceded. The decision to pursue his work with such resolve was neither new nor in itself wrong, of course, as Lohmeyer himself noted. The "fundamental error," rather, had been in pursuing his work "so exclusively, and in so doing push[ing] everything related to our love into second place."[12]

Their common love, which until then had made Lohmeyer's academic work fruitful, became simply one factor among others in his life. The pressure to succeed fueled and blew out of proportion Lohmeyer's egoism. He admitted to Melie, "I really wanted to extinguish my ego and allow my accomplishments to speak for themselves."[13] But the more success he experienced—especially *theological* success in the things of God—the more he came to believe he had chosen the right course. When he was toppled from the pinnacle of success at Breslau, both as president and professor, his fall to the less prestigious University of Greifswald should have been the wake-up call he needed to see his error. But something other and worse happened: his self-obsession exerted itself more strongly. We certainly have no trouble understanding why this might have happened: the forces that had conspired against him so ruthlessly at Breslau had taught him to rely on no one but himself. Henceforth he had pursued his own work "with stony bitterness."[14] His work became not merely the first thing in his life but virtually the only thing, separating him from other things, including Melie.

The war, for all its trials and horrors, had strangely reinforced Lohmeyer's self-occupation, for the recognition and authority he enjoyed as an officer in the Wehrmacht helped restore the honor of which he had been so unjustly deprived at Breslau. Lohmeyer employed his military authority in an attempt to lessen the burdens of the war on others, but even this benevolence, he confessed, was "a quest to fulfill *my* life, to satisfy *my* needs."[15] "I continued to believe that I was able to achieve all things through my own powers, and I failed to see that what is ultimate and best in life should and must be given to us. What I did, I did without heart and without love; you sensed it all along, and I myself knew but failed to see it honestly."[16]

The miracle of Melie's warm and loving kiss in cell 19 reminded Lohmeyer that what God had granted him in life had been granted with and through her. "The gift of the fulfillment of *my* life was bound to the same fulfillment of *your* life, [for] both fulfillments were no longer divided but, like two roots, had grown—or were meant to grow—into the single tree of *our* life."[17] But, continued Lohmeyer, again strongly reminiscent of Augustine's *Confessions*, "my life did not permeate my love, and my love permeated my life too little, so my heart remained unfulfilled, and as such open for many dreams and realities."[18] That Melie's life was also and perhaps equally leached he did not see—or his immersion in work did not permit him to see.

The war came, and their isolated lives, which until then had shared a common space and circumstances, were thrust into radically different spaces and circumstances. What transpired in the violent world into which Lohmeyer was thrust is most fittingly related in Melie's later words. Melie wrote for the benefit of Hartmut and Gudrun, and she referred to Ernst as "your father."

> In the midst of the hell [of the eastern front] your father found a woman friend, his interpreter, an older woman with a fourteen-year-old son and an older husband. Your father took care of them all as far as possible. The woman gave her whole heart to your father, allowing both her husband and son to make their way to the West in order to remain with your father, with whom, as father later said, she vowed to die. That is how grim the situation was. He made his way back with X and they parted in Lodz [Poland], where X hoped to be taken in by friends. It was probably a difficult parting. Fellowship in hell is binding.[19]

That Ernst had told Melie of his "wrong way"[20] before the last letter is clear from the way he referred to it. This is also clear from Melie's above description, which is more complete than was Ernst's in the last letter. Melie's description is also more understanding, I might add, than is Ernst's self-confession. In his own words, "That such happenings and experiences were possible shows clearly enough how distant they were from our life together. How they contradicted our relationship; how they confirmed my sorry and impoverished self! I will say once more, my Dearest: forgive me this violation of your heart that I saw but did not see, sensed but did not admit. Forgive me all I have done for the sake of the love that you have for me and that, despite all I have done, I have for you."[21]

Lohmeyer's relationship with his interpreter unmasked his emptiness before God, and it triggered, in his words, "an inner collapse."[22] Serious as the collapse had been, it had motivated him to return to Melie and, as a form of atonement, to attempt to remain sexually chaste until he did. But the Happening in prison had caused, or better, *forced* Lohmeyer to see that his "final and deepest transgression"[23] was not against human love but against divine love. In Lohmeyer's case, however, it was particularly true that the transgression against divine love was so closely intertwined with the transgression of human love with Melie that the two scarcely could be separated. "In these long years I have often sought for God, but my search was only one search among others, not the one and only search. I have even thought myself sometimes to be near God, but I did not feel or find him. How could I have? I have looked in many places and thought to find him where he was not; and at the one place where he was present for me and should be present for me, and where I could have found him, which was in our love, there I no longer found him."[24]

The Finger of God

At the point of ultimate and apparently final separation, with no chance of touching one another and little hopes of ever seeing each other again, the redemptive Happening came to Lohmeyer. The Happening dominated the end of the letter.

> Were it not for this imprisonment and this warm kiss—and both belong together, for I cannot separate them—you and I would have remained separated. God signaled gently with his finger, and the walls crumbled and the springs of water that had been choked burst forth. I went away from you and Puppi relieved and freed; imprisonment could no longer rob me of the gift of our united hearts. Here, in these long days and nights, it has become clear to me how gracious and wise God's judgment has been—as right and precise as the measure of a single hair. His sentence has been one of both judgment and grace, and both in equal measure. He wrenched me from all the constraints and dealings and work that until then had spelled danger and damage for me and set me entirely alone, where I could do nothing except face myself. He cut to shreds the artificial web in which I had bound my wrong choices and failures so that he could bind me at the same time in the mantle of your love and his love. He took from me the freedom, which until then I had used to try to do everything by my own powers, and compelled me to kneel before his command that seemed senseless and foolish. He made me as one fettered, in order to fetter me to himself and to you, and in so doing he gave me the gift of inner freedom from all the mortal burdens of my

life. He did all this to me, an innocent victim in the world's eyes, the martyr of a good cause—and only he and you know that in so doing he was truly just and truly consoling. I am now a prisoner, and yet I have everything I have longed for. . . . In everything I am free and inwardly certain, no longer because of myself but because of the bond of unity that binds me to God and to you.[25]

Here Lohmeyer assured Melie of the obvious: he had not been apotheosized or achieved a state of transcendental immunity. He found himself, as ever, torn between doubt and confidence, complaint and comfort, anxiety and peace. He recalled a Bach "Lamento" that Melie used to sing, "Oh, that I had waters sufficient to regret my sin, that my eyes were streams of tears!" Lohmeyer now understood and treasured the "Lamento" as never before.[26] He cautioned Melie, however, against being overly hopeful that her efforts could win his release: "Humans are sand," he reminded her, "on which one cannot build."[27] Finally, and above all, he dared hope that the vision of Melie and Gudrun gaily coming to him would be a harbinger of their reunion. He asked a question that I find so poignant that it seems more like a prayer: "Would God have given me all this simply to allow it to perish behind these prison walls?"[28] Was not the Happening—whatever it was—a harbinger of the reuniting of their family? Had God not sent Melie to him, so that God could send him to Melie? These questions . . . these questions were all that mattered in life. And along with these questions, the precious word of Scripture, "In quietness and trust shall be your strength."[29] His final sentence recalled his near-miraculous but painful return to Melie from the eastern front, when he and Melie were at last reunited but she had not embraced him: "If only you will still love me, if only I can be certain of your love? Then it is again possible that you will embrace me in your arms!"[30] In Lohmeyer's handwritten original, it is impossible to tell whether the final punctuation of that sentence was a question mark or an exclamation mark. The punctuation in the typed copy is the result of Melie's hand. It is an *exclamation* mark, Melie's clear affirmation of his hope!

Lest This Perish behind These Prison Walls

We read and write biographies because of some historical magnetism that attracts us to a person. Not all aspects of the person attract us to the same degree. Some aspects may even repel us, like when the same poles of two magnets are held closely together. This is inevitable. Biographies are about *life*, and life is always and only a combination in varying degrees of the noble, the ordinary, and the shameful. Even in an autobiography—indeed, *especially* in an autobiography—we would have to face—if we were as honest as Lohmeyer was—the glaring polarities in ourselves that Lohmeyer revealed about himself.

Of greater importance to me than the faults Lohmeyer confessed in the last letter was the way he dealt with them. Most of us, I suspect, would be prepared to extend certain allowances to a man who faced the opposition Lohmeyer had faced at Breslau under Nazism and at Greifswald under communism, and especially given the circumstances he had endured on the eastern front. In the last letter Lohmeyer made no plea for such allowances. No lies, denials, excuses, pleas for pity, dismissiveness, or attempts at "damage control" were made in an effort to mitigate his responsibility. The way had not been easy, but he never appealed to its difficulties as an excuse for his misdeeds. He grieved them, he grieved their consequences, and he sought to deal with them in the only way possible for a man of moral character and Christian faith—by confession, asking forgiveness, making amends as possible. That is called *character*. It was the character I had always seen in Lohmeyer, but now at the end of my quest I saw in the last letter its truest expression. Lohmeyer never strove or expected or presumed to be a hero, and whether or not he was a hero, readers will have to decide for themselves. What he strove to be was *a man of faith and character*. The way of confession allowed him to remain a man of faith and character, indeed to become a man greater in both.

For me personally, Lohmeyer's letter from cell 19 was not simply his last letter, it was his ultimate letter. In writing this biography I had been like an electrician installing cable and splicing wires in a building without current. I had succeeded in wiring "the Lohmeyer house," so to speak—the scholar, theologian, pastor, humanist, aesthetic, man of letters, independent thinker, example of moral courage. All these were in place, and the wires seemingly connected. But in the last letter, the cables and wires that I had until then innocuously manipulated suddenly hummed and surged with current. I was no longer speaking about Lohmeyer. He was now speaking to me, even *for* me. Not his weaknesses but his strengths had posed the greater temptations and potential downfalls in his life. This exceptional and versatile theologian names perhaps the chief danger that all who devote their lives to the study of theology inevitably face, which is to shift God from the subject of one's life to the object of one's inquiry, and thence to a mere idea. Not the incidentals of his life but the divine call to productive work—the very thing in which Ernst Lohmeyer had preeminently succeeded—was given such prominence that it threatened to usurp the One who bestowed the gift. The "inordinate preoccupation with self"[31] that chafes at the lack of recognition and honor that we think ourselves due seems to justify our seeking it in other ways. Our most sacred commitments—how easy to take them for granted and allow them to grow cold. And suffering. In the last fifteen years of life, Lohmeyer's cup was filled with suffering. How terribly difficult to surrender trials and sufferings to the "finger of God," to God's redemptive purposes that we cannot now see and understand. The last letter is like a litany of confession. It names the sins we would rather forget or deny about ourselves. But in naming and confessing, we, like Lohmeyer, are brought to a true self-understanding and to the possibility of a deep and enduring renewal of life.

What happened in the visit of Melie and Gudrun "jolted"[32] Lohmeyer from the rut of his accomplished but exhausted existence to a place of freedom and newness of life. He no longer wanted to protract the same life but to live new life. As a free and innocent man, he had been made a guilty prisoner, but as a prisoner he had become a free man, and in confessing his guilt—not the false guilt heaped on him by a rogue regime but the true guilt revealed by his Judge—he became both forgiven and innocent. His freedom hoped and pleaded for the love that he had lost, and his freedom rejoiced in the Love that had found him.

The arrest and imprisonment of Lohmeyer in 1946 became the severe mercy of God that reignited the flame of a beautiful and powerful marriage that neither Ernst nor Melie alone could reignite. The letter from cell 19 was Lohmeyer's most valiant effort to save that marriage. Recapturing Melie's love was more important than news of his prison conditions or prospects of survival, for with her love he could face whatever he had to face. His composure in the trial, his letter to Stalin, the testimony of Manfred Schröder to his prison demeanor—all these testify to a groundedness, faith, perhaps even peace as he faced the end. Melie's prison visits, and her networking with people of influence, unceasing letters, and advocacy for his life, testify to the same on her part. When the years extended to decades, when all hope of his return home had been lost, she learned to embrace him in a new way by laboring indefatigably for his memory.

In cell 19 Lohmeyer "came to himself," as Jesus said of the younger son who abandoned his home and father for a distant land. In "coming to himself," the son returned to the father to receive what the father ever longed to give. Lohmeyer hoped that God would use the personal renewal he experienced in cell 19 so that he could return to his family as a new and better husband and father, to his scholarship as a new and better scholar, to his faith as a more faithful disciple. God used the renewal of cell 19 to prepare him for other ends that Lohmeyer did not will, but ends, if God willed them, he would accept. On September 19, 1946, he fulfilled a vow he made back in 1926: "I want to know him, and the power of his resurrection and the fellowship of his sufferings, and in so doing to be conformed to his death" (Phil. 3:10).

Abbreviations

Notes

CHAPTER 1

1. "Niemand weiss, wo Lohmeyer seine letzte Ruhe gefunden hat. Wir alle aber wissen, wer er war und für uns noch immer ist: ein hervorragender Theologe, ein grosser Mensch, voller Lauterkeit und Arglosigkeit, ein Märtyrer für die Freiheit der Universität, in der Sprache Israels: ein 'Gerechter under den Völkern'" (Günter Haufe, "Ein Gerechter unter den Völkern. Gedenken an Ernst Lohmeyer" [address at the University of Greifswald on the occasion of the fiftieth year of Lohmeyer's execution, September 19, 1996]). All translations from German to English in this book are my own unless otherwise noted.

2.

In memoriam
ERNST LOHMEYER
geboren am 8.7.1890
Professor für Neues Testament
Greifswald 1935–1946
Rektor der Universität ab 15.5.1945
verhaftet vom NKWD am 15.2.1946
zu Unrecht hingerichtet am 19.9.1946
rehabilitiert am 15.8.1996

CHAPTER 2

1. "Bis ihn höhere Gewalt einem bis heute ungeklärten Schicksal entgegenführte" (Gerhard Sass, "Ergänzungsheft," 4, published with Ernst Lohmeyer, *Das Evangelium des Markus*, KEK I/2, 8th ed. [Göttingen: Vandenhoeck & Ruprecht, 1967]).

2. "So erfreulich die Tatsache ist, dass der Markuskommentar Prof. Lohmeyers nunmehr in 2. Auflage erscheint, so schmerzlich ist es zugleich für Wissenschaft und Kirche, dass der Verfasser nicht mehr selbst die Herausgabe der Neuauflage übernehmen kann. Sein mir vorliegendes Handexemplar zeigt wie er ständig an der Verbesserung und Ergänzung gearbeitet hat, bis ihn höhere Gewalt einem bis heute ungeklärten Schicksal entgegenführte" (Sass, "Ergänzungsheft," 4).

CHAPTER 3

1. Oberkonsistorialrat in Münster.
2. *Evangelisches Choralbuch für Kirche und Haus.*
3. Heinrich Lohmeyer to Maria Niemann, June 23, 1884 (GStA PK, VI. HA, NI, Lohmeyer, E., No. 2).
4. "Lasst mich ein Beispiel gebrauchen! In der Zeit, da wir noch Kinder waren, lag all unser Leben, unser Glück und unsere Freude in den Händen unseres Vaters und unserer Mutter. Von ihnen empfingen wir alles. Denn wir waren nichts und waren alles nur in ihrer Liebe. Das war unser Leben und unsere Freude" (Andreas Köhn, ed., *Ernst Lohmeyers Zeugnis im Kirchenkampf: Breslauer Universitätspredigten* [Göttingen: Vandenhoeck & Ruprecht, 2006], 28).
5. "Wie in so vielen Pfarrhäusern lebte man auch bei den Lohmeyers in Vlotho a.d. Weser der Musik. Grossmutter Marie spielte gewandt Klavier, der Vater sass gern improvisierend in seinem Studierzimmer am Harmonium, jedem Kind wurde ein Instrument zugedacht, und sonntägliches Musizieren gehörte zum Wochenendprogramm" (Gudrun [Lohmeyer] Otto, "Erinnerung an den Vater," in *Freiheit in der Gebundenheit*, ed. Wolfgang Otto [Göttingen: Vandenhoeck & Ruprecht, 1990], 45).
6. "Dann war es das vierhändige Klavierspielen, . . . das wir später so perfektionierten, dass wir uns ohne Skrupel an alles heranwagten, sicher nicht zum Vergnügen der Mithörenden" (Otto, "Erinnerung an den Vater," 39).
7. "Das Griechentum hat mich immer aufs Höchste entzückt, denn dieses stellt ja eine überschwenglich reiche Blüte des Menschengeistes dar, und die Ursache davon ist, dass seine ganze Kultur auf künstlerischer Grundlage ruht, das freischöpferische Werk menschlicher Phantasie ist bei den Hellenen der Ausgangspunkt ihres so unendlich reichen Lebens. Darum ist uns von hellenischem Boden jeder Zoll heilig. . . . In Hellas ist jeder Stein belebt, individualisiert, die Naturstimme zum Bewusstsein ihrer selbst erwacht. Und die Männer, die dieses Wunder vollbracht, stehen vor us, von

den halb fabelhaften Zeiten des trojanischen Krieges an bis zur Herrschaft Roms: Helden, Herrscher, Krieger, Denker, Dichter, Bildner. Hier ward der Mensch geboren, fähig ein Christ zu sein" (Otto, "Erinnerung an den Vater," 41–42). Much of the information on Lohmeyer's youth in the previous section is taken from Gudrun Otto ("Erinnerung and den Vater," 36–52) and Andreas Köhn, *Der Neutestamentler Ernst Lohmeyer*, WUNT 2.180 (Tübingen: Mohr Siebeck, 2004), 5–7.

8. "Die Beherrschung sprachlicher Mittel—auch im Griechischen—ist schon so gross, dass der Blick für geistige Zusammenhänge frei werden kann und ihm eine emotionale Identifizierung möglich macht" (Otto, "Erinnerung an den Vater," 41–42).

CHAPTER 4

1. "Mich freut, dass Du besonders für Deine musikalischen Neigung ein Feld der Tätigkeit gefunden hast.... Du kannst auch einige Meisterstunden nehmen, um den feinen Schliff im Bogenstriche zu bekommen" (Gudrun [Lohmeyer] Otto, "Erinnerung an den Vater," in *Freiheit in der Gebundenheit*, ed. Wolfgang Otto [Göttingen: Vandenhoeck & Ruprecht, 1990], 45).

2. Lohmeyer's correspondence with Haering and Zimmern is preserved in GStA PK, VI. HA, NI, Lohmeyer, E., No. 4a.

3. Lohmeyer to Stroux, November 30, 1945: "Angesichts der damit drohenden Gefahren fühlen wir uns verpflichtet, den ererbten Charakter einer deutschen Universität dadurch fester zu bewahren, dass wir das Moment der Forschung deutlicher in den Vordergrund schieben" (UAG R. 458/VII, p. 51).

4. Lionel R. M. Strachan, "Translator's Preface," in *Light from the Ancient East* (Grand Rapids: Baker, 1978), xix.

5. GStA PK, VI. HA, NI, Lohmeyer, E., No. 17.

6. "Mir erschien er als das Reinste und Klarste und Echteste, was mein Leben je berührt hatte. Sein fast kindliches Aussehen kontrastierte seltsam mit diesen ausdrucksvollen grünen Augen, die er vom Vater geerbt hatte, und mit der hohen denkerischen Stirn, die so viele Gedanken verriet. Ein geheimer Wille und eine geheime Leidenschaft stand hinter diesen Zügen. Doch war mir das damals nicht klar, der sanfte Zauber seines Wesens, seine vermeintliche Ausgeglichenheit, seine Zartheit der Gesinnung, seine Ritterlichkeit waren weit grösser, überwogen und liessen keine Rätzel zu" (Otto, "Erinnerung an den Vater," 42).

7. "Soll ich ihn Dir beschreiben? Er ist ein kleiner lieber, fast hübscher Junge mit langen bis zur Schulter herabhängenden schwarzen Haaren und

grossen leuchtenden braunen Augen; in seinen Bewegungen bisweilen noch ganz kindlich ungebärdig und doch wiederum jungenhaft bestimmt. Er steht auf der Schwelle von früher Kindheit zu wirklicher Jugend, und so ist's oft ein seltsames, reizendes Gemisch von beidem. Sein ganzes Wesen ist mir so innig lieb und verwandt. Mit seinen grossen Augen schaut er mich immer an, wenn ich etwas erzähle, und hängt an meinen Lippen; und dann kommen wundervoll kindliche, besinnliche Fragen aus seinem Munde. Ich hatte ihm einmal eine Geschichte aus dem alten Testament erzählt, ganz in naiver Weise: Der liebe Gott sprach . . . usw. Da fragte er denn: Ach, sagen Sie doch, spricht der liebe Gott auch jetzt noch? Ich: Oja, wenn man einmal ganz still ist und ihn um etwas bittet, dann antwortet er auch. Er: Spricht er dann so, wie ich zu ihnen spreche, hören Sie's? Ich: Nein, so nicht; aber wenn man etwas gebeten hat, dann wird man plötzlich ganz froh und weiss, was man tun soll, und dann weiss man auch, dass der liebe Gott einem etwas gesagt hat. Und dann nach einer kleinen stillen Pause: Aber wenn ich in den Himmel komm, dann spricht er doch ganz richtig mir mir? Ich: Ja, das tut er ganz gewiss. Er: Ich möchte so gern jetzt gleich zu ihm gehen. . . . Und dann weiter: Ist der liebe Gott immer allein? Ich: Nein, er hat eine ganze Menge lieber kleiner Engel, mit denen is er immer zusammen und ist ganz fröhlich mit ihnen. Er: Sagen Sie, wann ist der liebe Gott eigentlich geboren? Ich: O nein, der ist nicht geboren; er war schon, als gar keine Menschen auf der Erde waren. Er: Aber hat er denn keinen Vater und keine Mutter? Ich: Nein, die hat er nicht. Er: Ach dann ist der liebe Gott eine Waise. . . . Aber dann will ich ganz bald zu ihm gehen und mit ihm sprechen; dann freut er sich doch gewiss, nicht wahr? Da nahm ich den lieben Jungen, der die ganze Zeit still an mich gelehnt gestanden hatte, in meinen Arm und gab ihm einen Kuss. Ja, geh Du nur ganz bald zum lieben Gott, dann freut er sich gewiss. Und danach sprang er fort, und lief fröhlich wie ein Kind im Park herum und wollte ein Eichhörnchen fangen" (a letter preserved by Klaus Otto, made available to Andreas Köhn on December 16, 2001. See Köhn, *Der Neutestamentler Ernst Lohmeyer*, WUNT 2.180 [Tübingen: Mohr Siebeck, 2004], 8).

8. GStA PK, VI. HA, NI, Lohmeyer, E., No. 17.

9. Lohmeyer's dissertation was published as *Diatheke: Ein Beitrag zur Erklärung des neutestamentlichen Begriffs* (Leipzig: Hinrichs, 1913).

10. "Von ungemeiner Wichtigkeit" (Lohmeyer, *Diatheke*, 121).

11. For the Damascus Document, see Lohmeyer, *Diatheke*, 115–16.

12. "Labyrinth literarkritischer Hypothesen" (Lohmeyer, *Diatheke*, 53).

13. "Die Quelle aller Wissenschaft und aller Wahrheit und aller Gewissheit und aller Realität ist die Liebe."

14. "Dafür halte uns jedermann," Predigt E. Lohmeyers über 2 Kor 4,1–6 (Berlin, 1911), in Andreas Köhn, ed., *Ernst Lohmeyers Zeugnis im Kirchenkampf. Breslauer Universitätspredigten* (Göttingen: Vandenhoeck & Ruprecht, 2006), 26–35.

15. "Und so irren wir wie Flüchtlinge umher, ungewiss, wo wir uns sicher gründen sollen, bis uns das Bewusstsein geschenkt ist, dass unser Leben in Gott ruht, dass wir in ihm, in seiner Liebe leben dürfen, bis uns Barmherzigkeit widerfahren ist" (Köhn, *Ernst Lohmeyers Zeugnis im Kirchenkampf*, 29).

16. Augustine, *Confessions* 1.1.

17. "Ihre Gestalten treten dann zu uns und reden mit uns wie vertraute Freunde, die sich einst ebenso sehnten, wie wir es tun und Ruhe gefunden haben" (Köhn, *Ernst Lohmeyers Zeugnis im Kirchenkampf*, 29).

18. "Und wenn wir so leben, in einem überweltlichen Leben in der Welt, dann haben wir das Recht und die tiefe Gewissheit, dass wir arbeiten dürfen, und nimmermüde Freudigkeit dazu. Alles Leben drängt nach Tat, weil es unversiegliche Kraft in sich birgt; es will Arbeit, um in freier Fülle sich zu entfalten" (Köhn, *Ernst Lohmeyers Zeugnis im Kirchenkampf*, 33).

CHAPTER 5

1. "So ist denn auch Freiheit vorhanden, solange Vernunft in uns ist, die Gerechtigkeit zu erkennen, und Wille, sie zu bewahren" (Ernst Lohmeyer, *Die Lehre vom Willen bei Anselm von Canterbury* [Leipzig: Deichert, 1914], 47–48).

2. Ernst Lohmeyer, "Die Lehre vom Willen bei Anselm von Canterbury" (Inaugural Dissertation zur Erlangung der Doktorwürde der hohen Philosophischen Fakultät der Friedrich-Alexanders-Universität Erlangen, Lucka S.-A, Reinhold Bergen, 1914).

3. See Wade Davis, *Into the Silence: The Great War, Mallory, and the Conquest of Everest* (New York: Knopf, 2011), 15–16.

4. Über Stock und über Stein
Schrittst das brave Deutsche Bein.
Lange Strümpf von Wolle rein
Strickst man noch viel Liebe ein
Für das brave Deutsche Bein
Wird der Marsch noch besser sein.
(GStA PK, VI. HA, NI, Lohmeyer, E., No. 177)

5. GStA PK, VI. HA, NI, Lohmeyer, E., No. 159.

6. GStA PK, VI. HA, NI, Lohmeyer, E., No. 73, letter sent to Melie, January 30, 1916.

7. Ernst's correspondence with Melie appears in GStA PK, VI. HA, NI, Lohmeyer, E., No. 60.

8. GStA PK, VI. HA, NI, Lohmeyer, E., No. 74.

9. GStA PK, VI. HA, NI, Lohmeyer, E., No. 95.

10. "Ob Ferien oder Semester, Wochen- oder Feiertag, Stadt oder Land, es verging kein Tag ohne wissenschaftliche Arbeit. Es lässt sich schwer vorstellen, besonders für die jungen Menschen unter uns, was es für ihn bedeutet haben muss, fast neun Jahre in seinem Leben Soldat gewesen zu sein" (Gudrun [Lohmeyer] Otto, "Erinnerung an den Vater," in *Freiheit in der Gebundenheit*, ed. Wolfgang Otto [Göttingen: Vandenhoeck & Ruprecht, 1990], 44).

11. "Wenn ich schreibe, so kann ich in allen Höhen und Tiefen jauchzen und traurig sein!" (quoted from Günter Haufe, "Ein Gerechter unter den Völkern. Gedenken an Ernst Lohmeyer" [address at the University of Greifswald on the occasion of the fiftieth year of Lohmeyer's execution, September 19, 1996]).

12. Ernst Lohmeyer, *Vom göttlichen Wohlgeruch*, SHAW.Philosophisch-historische Klasse, Jahrgang 1919, 9. Abhandlung (Heidelberg: Carl Winters Universitätsbuchhandlung, 1919).

13. "Die vernichtende Kraft des Protestantismus hat den [Weihrauchs] glauben in die Sphäre des Volksaberglaubens hinabgedrückt" (Lohmeyer, *Vom göttlichen Wohlgeruch*, 50–51).

14. Gerhard Delling's article on "aroma" in *TWNT* 5:492–95 relies heavily on Lohmeyer's *Habilitation*.

15. For *Angriff*, see GStA PK, VI. HA, NI, Lohmeyer, E., No. 17, pp. 101–4.

16. "Nein, das ist nicht wahr."

17. "Das scheint mir über behaupt."

18. "Ja—Ja mein Geliebster. Ich freue mich."

19. *The Treaty of Peace between the Allied and Associated Powers and Germany* (London, 1919).

CHAPTER 6

1. Blaise Pascal, *Pensées* 6.347.

2. "Die Härten des Krieges, das lange Soldatenleben hatten ihn männlicher werden lassen und seine von Natur aus vorhandenen praktischen Fähigkeiten und seinen Sinn für reale Gegebenheiten ausgebildet, was ihm später bei der verwaltenden Universitätsarbeit zustatten kam" (Gudrun [Lohmeyer] Otto, "Erinnerung an den Vater," in *Freiheit in der Gebundenheit*, ed. Wolfgang Otto [Göttingen: Vandenhoeck & Ruprecht, 1990], 46).

3. Ernst Lohmeyer, *Christuskult und Kaiserkult* (Tübingen: Mohr Siebeck, 1919).

4. A complete list of Lohmeyer's lectures at Heidelberg, Breslau, and Greifswald is offered by Ulrich Hutter, "Theologie als Wissenschaft. Zu Leben und Werk Ernst Lohmeyers (1890–1946)," *Jahrbuch für schlesische Kirchengeschichte* 69 (1990): 123–69.

5. "Vom preussischen Kultusministerium erhielt ich heute den Ruf, als Ihr Nachfolger nach Breslau zu kommen. Es ist mir eine Ehre und Freude zugleich, gerade den Lehrstuhl inne haben zu können, den Sie bisher bekleidet haben" (Hutter, "Theologie als Wissenschaft," 154).

6. "Reichlich fremd und reichlich östlich"; "sehr freundlich" (Hutter, "Theologie als Wissenschaft," 131).

7. Lohmeyer's letter to Bultmann appears in Hutter, "Theologie als Wissenschaft," 154.

8. GStA PK, VI. HA, NI, Lohmeyer, E., No. 174.

9. "Am 17. Feb., mittags 1 Uhr, starb uns unser einziges Kind, unsere kleine Beate-Dorothee nach 5-wöchentlichen mit holdseliger Geduld getragenen Qualen im zarten Alter von 1 Jahr. Prof. E. Lohmeyer und Frau Melie Lohmeyer" (*Heidelberger Tageblatt*, February 19, 1921).

10. Ernst Lohmeyer, *Soziale Fragen im Urchristentum* (Leipzig: Quelle und Meyer, 1921; Darmstadt: Wissenschaftliche Buchgesellschaft, 1973).

11. Georg Liebster, "K. Kautskys *Ursprung des Christentums*," *Christliche Welt* 8 (1910): 170–75, quoted from Andreas Köhn, *Der Neutestamentler Ernst Lohmeyer*, WUNT 2.180 (Tübingen: Mohr Siebeck, 2004), 17–18.

12. Erik Esking, *Glaube und Geschichte in der theologischen Exegese Ernst Lohmeyers: Zugleich ein Beitrag zur Geschichte der neutestamentlichen Interpretation*, ASNU 18 (Lund: Gleerup, 1951), 152.

13. Pascal, *Pensées* 6.347.

14. For an insight into Eduard Schweizer's personal thoughts about theology and life, see "*En Route* with My Teachers," in *Jesus Christ: The Man from Nazareth and the Exalted Lord* (Macon, GA: Mercer University Press, 1987), 57–91. The above quotation is found on p. 90.

15. *The White Rose: The Student Resistance against Hitler, Munich 1942/43* (Weisse Rose Stiftung e.V., Ludwig-Maximilians-Universität, Munich), 35.

16. On George's influence on the Stauffenberg plot, see Tobias Kniebe, *Operation Walküre. Das Drama des 20. Juli* (Berlin: Rowohlt, 2009), 86–89, 106, 153–64.

17. Bruce McCormack, *Karl Barth's Critically Realistic Dialectical Theology* (Oxford: Clarendon, 1995), 43–44, speaks of the relationship between the *noumena* and *phenomena* as "the thing-in-itself (*noumena*)

which, by forcing itself upon us from without, gives rise to our knowing (*phenomena*)."

18. For a helpful assessment of both Richard Hönigswald and neo-Kantianism in Lohmeyer's life and theology, see Ulrich Hutter-Wolandt, "Ernst Lohmeyer und Richard Hönigswald. Um die Wissenschaftlichkeit neutestamentlicher Exegese," in *Studien zur Philosophie Richard Hönigswalds*, ed. E. W. Orth and D. Aleksandrowicz (Würzburg: Königshausen & Neumann, 1996), 205–30.

19. Aristotle, *Rhetoric* 2.4.

20. Wolfgang Otto, ed., *Aus der Einsamkeit—Briefe einer Freundschaft. Richard Hönigswald an Ernst Lohmeyer* (Würzburg: Königshausen & Neumann, 1999).

21. "vielleicht auch verlockt von dem verführerischen und imponierenden Beispiel Hönigswalds," in "Brief aus dem Gefängnis der GPU in Greifswald" (GStA PK, VI. HA, NI, Lohmeyer, E., No. 146, p. 6.

22. "Die Frage ist, natürlich, wieweit er hiermit die Intentionen des Apostels richtig erfasst" (quoted from Köhn, *Der Neutestamentler Ernst Lohmeyer*, 173).

23. See Köhn, *Der Neutestamentler Ernst Lohmeyer*, 133.

24. William Baird, *History of New Testament Research* (Minneapolis: Fortress, 2003), 2:469.

CHAPTER 7

1. "Die Wahrheit immer zuerst, und nachher die feineren Gefühle und das übrige" (quoted from R. Hönigswald, "Alois Riehl," *Unterhaltungsbeilage der Schlesischen Zeitung* [Breslau], February 22, 1925).

2. Deutscher Akademischer Austausch Dienst.

3. "Schweres Gespräch" (GStA PK, VI. HA, NI, Lohmeyer, E., No. 146, p. 5).

4. "Erlaube ich mir mitzuteilen, dass mir heute früh eine Tochter geboren wurde, die den Namen Gudrun Richarda tragen soll. Ich bitte ergebenst Anweisung zu geben, dass mir auch für dieses Kind die festgelegte Zulage ausgezahlt werde" (UAG, PA, 347, Band 1, 117).

5. "Ich war die Jüngste, das einzige Mädchen und mit den Sonderrechten bedacht, die das Kleinste in der Familie wohl immer erfährt. Mein Vater tadelte mich nie, strafte schon gar nicht, half mir bei allem, wenn ich ihn darum bat, und meine Erinnerungen konzentrieren sich auf diese Augenblicke entspannten Zusammenseins, von denen ich schon sprach, in denen nicht der Ansatz eines Missklanges zu spüren war. Unzählige Stunden

verbrachte ich auf seinem Schoss, was er langmütig nie verweigerte, sei es am Ende der mittäglichen Runde oder auch im häuslichen Studentenkreis. Wir spielten alle üblichen Kinderspiele allein oder mit den Brüdern zusammen. Das tat er nicht nur uns zuliebe, sondern es machte ihm selbst Spass, so, wie er mit unseren schlesischen Bauern oft skatspielend zusammensass. Und dann war es das vierhändige Klavierspielen, das wir langsam begannen und das wir später so perfektionierten, dass wir uns ohne Skrupel an alles heranwagten, sicher nicht zum Vergnügen der Mithörenden. Schularbeiten erledigte er sachlich und altersgemäss mit einem gewissen Vergnügen für mich, wenn die Zeit drängte, und er unterbrach dabei stets seinen eigne Arbeit" (Gudrun [Lohmeyer] Otto, "Erinnerung an den Vater," in *Freiheit in der Gebundenheit*, ed. Wolfgang Otto [Göttingen: Vandenhoeck & Ruprecht, 1990], 38–39).

6. "Es kommt mir fast verwunderlich vor, dass ich einen Vater hatte, wie ich ihn mir nicht besser oder anders hätte vorstellen wollen" (Otto, "Erinnerung an den Vater," 38).

7. "Er hatte die naturhafte Gabe, sich auf schlichte Menschen einstellen zu können, ob es unsere schlesischen Bergbauern waren, . . . oder seine ihm unterstellten Soldaten während des Krieges" (Otto, "Erinnerung an den Vater," 39).

8. "Die Verklärung Jesu nach dem Markusevangelium," *ZNW* 21 (1922): 185–215.

9. The incident involving Lohemeyer's "kleines Mädelchen" is described in Andreas Köhn, *Der Neutestamentler Ernst Lohmeyer*, WUNT 2.180 (Tübingen: Mohr Siebeck, 2004), 49n65.

10. For a full discussion of Lohmeyer's correspondence with Vandenhoeck & Ruprecht, see Köhn, *Der Neutestamentler Ernst Lohmeyer*, 30–51.

11. Ernst Lohmeyer, *Kyrios Jesus: Eine Untersuchung zu Phil. 2,5–11*, SHAW 18 (Heidelberg: C. Winters, 1928).

12. Lohmeyer, *Kyrios Jesus*, 7.

13. In addition to *Kyrios Jesus* and *Die Briefe an die Kolosser und an Philemon*, already cited, and *Die Briefe an die Philipper*, KEK IX/1 (Göttingen: Vandenhoeck & Ruprecht, 1928), helpful discussions of Lohmeyer's treatment of Phil. 2:5–11 are found in Erik Esking, *Glaube und Geschichte in der theologischen Exegese Ernst Lohmeyers: Zugleich ein Beitrag zur Geschichte der neutestamentlichen Interpretation*, ASNU 18 (Lund: Gleerup, 1951), 160–67; William Baird, *History of New Testament Research* (Minneapolis: Fortress, 2003), 2:462–70; and Ralph Martin, *Carmen Christi: Philippians 2:5–11 in Recent Interpretation and in the Setting of Early Christian Worship* (Grand Rapids: Eerdmans, 1983), 25–30.

14. "[Die Offenbarung] ist das Buch eines Märtyrers für Märtyrer, und

durch sie für alle Gläubigen" (Ernst Lohmeyer, *Die Offenbarung des Johannes*, 2nd ed., HNT 16 [Tübingen: Mohr Siebeck, 1953], 202).

15. Ernst Lohmeyer, "Die Idee des Martyriums im Judentum und Urchristentum," *ZST* 5, no. 2 (1927): 232–49.

16. Ernst Lohmeyer, *Die Briefe an die Philipper*.

17. "The Road Not Taken."

18. Nationalsozialistische Deutsche Studentenbund.

19. "Wir sind heute ein durch und durch politisches Geschlecht. Auch unsere Frage nach dem 'Heil' wird in der Dimension des Politischen wach. Nicht um den Frieden mit Gott geht es den Menschen unserer Tage, sondern um Überwindung der politischen Not im weitesten Sinne" (cited from Köhn, *Der Neutestamentler Ernst Lohmeyer*, 55).

20. On the rising tide of Nazism at the time of Lohmeyer's accession to the presidency of Breslau, see Köhn, *Der Neutestamentler Ernst Lohmeyer*, 54–55.

21. "... die Wurzeln unseres Daseins zu greifen als dort, wo alles Erkennen zur Tat treibt und alles Tun in Erkenntnis sich gründet, in der Geschichte. Denn das im Wandelbaren ein Unwandelbares Gestalt und Begriff werde, das ist Geschichte" (Ernst Lohmeyer, "Glaube und Geschichte in vorderorientalischen Religionen" [speech given at the introduction to the Rekotrat on November 3, 1930, Breslauer Universitätsreden, Heft 6, Ferdinand Hirt, Breslau, Königsplatz 1, 1931], 4).

22. "Glaube behauptet einen ewigen Sinn und eine ewige Wirklichkeit in untrüglicher Wahrheit und eindeutiger Gewissheit zu besitzen" (Lohmeyer, "Glaube und Geschichte in vorderorientalischen Religionen," 5).

23. "Unverrückbarkeit ewiger Gesetze" (Lohmeyer, "Glaube und Geschichte in vorderorientalischen Religionen," 6).

24. "Geschichte ist nicht gegebenes Schicksal, das man empfängt, sondern aufgegebenes Ziel, um das man sich strebend müht ... nicht im Triumph der Macht, sondern im Sieg des Guten des weisen Gottes ewiges Gesetz" (Lohmeyer, "Glaube und Geschichte in vorderorientalischen Religionen," 11).

25. "Wenn also im Judentum der Gedanke des Messias und seiner Gemeinde den Lauf der Geschichte krönt, so kommt darin nur ein grundsätzlicher Gedanke aller Geschichte zum Ausdruck. Darum ist dieser Messias ein bestimmtes Ich, aus der Geschichte lebend und in der Geschichte wirkend; und der Gehalt dieses Lebens und Wirkens ist nichts anderes als der Gehalt der Gemeinschaft, die er schafft und regiert" (Lohmeyer, "Glaube und Geschichte in vorderorientalischen Religionen," 24).

26. "Wen Gott setzt, den bestimmt er zu dem einzigen Ort seiner

Wahrheit und Wirklichkeit und vollendet durch ihn alle Gemeinschaft und Geschichte . . . sein 'Wort Fleisch wird'" (Lohmeyer, "Glaube und Geschichte in vorderorientalischen Religionen," 25).

27. "Darum ist er Gewissheit des ewig Gegenwärtigen und Sehnsucht nach dem 'Kommenden', Erfüllung und Verheissung in Einem. In solcher eschatologischen Vollendung des Unvollendbaren wird auch die Geschichte zu eigenem und ursprünglichem Gange frei. Sie bleibt in ewigem Wandel des Geschenens und ewiger Unwandelbarkeit ihres Sinnes, unerschöpflich und mannigfaltig in ihrem Werden und Vegehen, durchsichtig und einheitlich in ihrem Sinn, immer gerichtet und immer gerettet. So im Ganzen ihres Sinnes webend, so im Tatsächlichen ihres unendlichen Laufes sich regend, wird sie immer was sie ist und ist sie immer was sie wird. . . . Das Verhältnis von Glaube und Geschichte erschliesst—, wenn das Johannesevangelium von Jesus die Sätze pragt: 'Und das Wort ward Fleisch und wohnte unter uns. Und wir sahen seine Herrlichkeit'" (Lohmeyer, "Glaube und Geschichte in vorderorientalischen Religionen," 27).

CHAPTER 8

1. Sebastian Haffner, *Anmerkungen zu Hitler* (Munich: Fischer Taschenbücher, 1978).

2. Ernst Lohmeyer, *Grundlagen paulinischer Theologie*, BHT 1 (Tübingen: Mohr Siebeck, 1929).

3. "Ich bringe grundsätzlich keine Aufsätze, die ich selbst nicht verstehen kann." "Esoterische Sondersprache" was Lietzmann's expression for academic jargon. His letter is preserved in Dieter Lührmann, "Ernst Lohmeyers exegetisches Erbe," in *Freiheit in der Gebundenheit*, ed. Wolfgang Otto (Göttingen: Vandenhoeck & Ruprecht, 1990), 63.

4. "Alle beteiligten müssen sich über die letzten Grundsätze historischer Methode einig sein" (quoted from Andreas Köhn, *Der Neutestamentler Ernst Lohmeyer*, WUNT 2.180 [Tübingen: Mohr Siebeck, 2004], 227).

5. "Die beigefügte Abschrift des Lietzmannschen Briefes hat mich empört. . . . Zunächst einmal würde auch ich zur Sache absolut *nicht* schweigen." Letter of Hönigswald to Lohmeyer, dated December 18, 1931, appears in *Aus der Einsamkeit—Briefe einer Freundschaft. Richard Hönigswald an Ernst Lohmeyer*, ed. Wofgang Otto (Würzburg: Königshausen & Neumann, 1999), 48–49.

6. "Wie aber soll man anders in wissenschaftlicher Weise von diesen Prinzipien sprechen als dadurch, dass man sich in die wissenschaftliche Tradi-

tion dieser Prinzipienlehre einordnet? Sie reicht von Plato bis Leibniz und Kant; ihre Sprache ist es, die ich nachsprechen, ihr Denken, das ich nachzudenken versuche" (quoted from Lührmann, "Ernst Lohmeyers exegetisches Erbe," 60-61).

7. "So müsste ich eigentlich fragen ... welchem Umstande Sie Ihr Wächteramt verdanken. Wollen Sie wie in einer Schule als praeceptor theologiae germanicae Forschern vorschreiben, was an ihren Arbeiten 'legitim' ist?" (quoted from Köhn, *Der Neutestamentler Ernst Lohmeyer*, 229).

8. See Ernst Lohmeyer, "Zur evangelischen Überlieferung von Johannes dem Täufer," *JBL* 51 (1932): 302.

9. "Ich bin nicht durch einen Evangelisten erweckt, nicht durch eine Predigt erschüttert, nicht aus einem unordentlichen, sündigen Leben herausgerufen worden. Ich habe nicht Vergebung der Sünden verlangt, sondern ich suchte den Sinn meines Lebens. Ich fand ihn am Schluss meines ersten Semesters in der Begegnung mit der Gestalt Jesu Christi" (quoted from F. W. Bautz, ed., *Biographisch-Bibliographisches Kirchenlexikon* [Hamm, Germany: Verlag Traugott Bautz, 1975], 1:1242).

10. Bautz, *Biographisch-Bibliographisches Kirchenlexikon*, 1:1242-48.

11. An interview of Ron Eyrie with Elie Wiesel in "Judaism," *The Long Search* video series.

12. "Gesinnungsmässigen Zusammensetzung der Breslauer Studentenschaft."

13. "Die Rasse, die am 9. November 1918 schuld ist, an dem Tage, an dem unser deutsches Volk verraten wurde."

14. "Hörsaal V total überfüllt, Scharren, Pfiffe, 'vaterländische Lieder,' 'Juden raus!,' 'Cohn raus!'"

15. "Juden raus!," "Wir wollen deutsche Professoren!," "Synagoge!," "Juda verrecke!," "Fort mit den Juden!"

16. "Rektor, Polizei, Räumung, Flucht ins Dozentenzimmer und unter Polizeischutz durch die Universität, aus der Universität und durch das Universitätsviertel."

17. The quotations and above description of the Cohn affair are indebted to Köhn, *Der Neutestamentler Ernst Lohmeyer*, 61-62.

18. Cohn's testimony (including the misplaced prepositional phrase at the end), written in English a decade later from his exile to England, is found in GStA PK, VI. HA, NI, Lohmeyer, E., No. 18.

19. "Professor Lohmeyer hat ... gegen die Einflüsse nationalsozialistischer Politik auf das Leben und die Arbeit der Universität scharfe Stellung genommen. ... Er hat als [Cohns] Verteidiger schwersten Angriffe ausgesetzt, dies aber nicht gefürchtet, sondern auch seine Stellung einige Male Massen tobender Studenten gegenüber verteidigt. Er wurde deswegen und weil seine

Person sowie sein Haus als Zuflucht für die bedrängten jüdischen Kollegen und Studenten galten (in seinem Sommerhäuschen in Glasegrund . . . hat er mehreren dieser bedrängten Menschen Aufenthalt und Ruhe gewährt!)" (in Köhn, *Der Neutestamentler Ernst Lohmeyer*, 64).

20. Data related to the conclusion of the Cohn affair is found in Köhn, *Der Neutestamentler Ernst Lohmeyer*, 65–68.

21. "Gefährlicher Scharfsinn."

22. "[Hönigswald] verficht eine leerlaufended Dialektik."

23. "Ich muss auch heute noch die Berufung dieses Mannes an die Universität München als einen Skandal bezeichnen, der nur darin seine Erklärung findet, dass das katholische System solche Leute, die scheinbar weltanschaulich indifferent sind, mit Vorliebe bevorzugt, weil sie gegenüber den eigenen Bestrebungen ungefährlich und in der bekannten Weise 'objektive-liberal' sind." The above quotations were taken from Martin Heidegger's letter of denunciation in Otto, *Aus der Einsamkeit*, 20

24. "[Hönigswald] wurde unter dem direkten Einfluss des Philosophen Martin Heideggers aus der Universität herausgedrängt" (Otto, *Aus der Einsamkeit*, 20).

25. For a brief printed reminiscence of Henry Hönigswald, see Otto, *Aus der Einsamkeit*, 23–24.

26. William Shirer, *The Rise and Fall of the Third Reich: A History of Nazi Germany* (New York: Simon & Schuster, 1960), 211.

CHAPTER 9

1. "Der christliche Glaube ist nur so lange christlich, als er den jüdischen in seinem Herzen trägt; auch ist der jüdische Glaube nur so lange jüdisch, als er den christlichen in sich zu hegen vermag" (Ernst Lohmeyer to Martin Buber, August 19, 1933).

2. Gerhard Kittel, *Die Judenfrage* (Stuttgart and Berlin: Kohlhammer, 1934), 92.

3. To Ruprecht's credit, he repeatedly refused Lohmeyer's encouragement.

4. Kittel, *Die Judenfrage*, 77: "echter National Sozialismus."

5. "Ein Recht und eine Pflicht, wenn [die Nation] sich nicht selbst aufgeben wolle" (Kittel, *Die Judenfrage*, 57).

6. "Der Jude wird christlicher Bruder, aber nicht deutscher Bruder" (Kittel, *Die Judenfrage*, 80).

7. See Sebastian Haffner, *Anmerkungen zu Hitler* (Munich: Fischer Taschenbücher, 1978).

8. For a thorough and judicious discussion of Gerhard Kittel, see Robert P. Ericksen, *Theologians under Hitler: Gerhard Kittel/Paul Althaus/Emanuel Hirsch* (New Haven: Yale University Press, 1985), 28–78. Further, see Leonore Siegele-Wenschkewitz, *Neutestamentliche Wissenschaft vor der Judenfrage: Gerhard Kittels theologische Arbeit im Wandel deutscher Geschichte* (Munich: Christian Kaiser Verlag, 1980).

9. "Wie ernst ich gerade Ihre Lebensarbeit nehme und wie ich Sie und Ihresgleichen mir im tiefsten verbündet zu wissen glaube."

10. "Feindselig."

11. "Es lag mir daran, der 'völkischen' Bewegung einen Weg zu zeigen, der dem Berechtigten an ihr Rechnung trägt, der aber *zugleich* dem Judentum wirklich als solchem gerecht würde." Kittel's letter to Buber is found in *Martin Buber: Briefwechsel aus sieben Jahrzehnten. Band II: 1918-1938* (Heidelberg: Verlag Lambert Schneider, 1973), 486–87.

12. "Mit der besonderen Aufmerksamkeit gelesen" (*Martin Buber*, 487).

13. "Worüber in der Tat ein Einvernehmen bestehen oder entstehen kann" (*Martin Buber*, 487).

14. "Ich kann es . . . nicht gerecht finden" (*Martin Buber*, 487).

15. See *Martin Buber*, 487–88.

16. "Glasegrund bei Habelschwerdt, 19.8.1933. Sehr verehrter Herr Kollege, Ich las soeben Ihren offenen Brief an Gerhard Kittel, und es drängt mich Ihnen zu sagen, dass mir jedes Ihrer Worte wie aus meinem Herzen gesprochen ist. Aber was mich drängt, ist nicht nur dieses Gefühl geistiger Verbundenheit, wenngleich das in diesen Tagen um seiner Seltenheit willen mich begleitet, sondern es ist, um es offen zu sagen, etwas wie Scham, dass theologische Kollegen so denken und schreiben können, wie sie es tun, dass die evangelische Kirche so schweigen kann, wie sie es tut, und wie ein Führerloses Schiff von dem politischen Sturmwind einer doch flüchtigen Gegenwart sich aus ihrem Kurse treiben lässt; und dieser Brief soll Ihnen nur ein Zeichen sein, dass nicht alle in den theologischen Fakultäten, auch nicht alle Neutestamentler, Kittels Meinungen teilen.

"Ich möchte freilich nicht den Eindruck erwecken, als nähme ich die Frage, von der Sie schreiben, nicht bitter ernst. Aber es wäre schon vieles gewonnen, wenn man nur klar erkennen wollte, wo und wie sie zu stellen ist. Nicht von Mensch zu Mensch, auch nicht unter Gesichtspunkten des Staates, des Volkes, der Rasse oder welche fürchterlichen Schlagworte jetzt immer ihr Wesen treiben oder besser ihr Unwesen—es gibt da keine Möglichkeit, zu fragen oder auch zu antworten, weil jede gesicherte Vorausssetzung fehlt und jede Diskussion in These und Antithese, in Pathos und Sentiment abgleiten muss. Und allem, was auf diesen Gebieten an Bedrückendem sich ereignet, ist nicht durch Worte, sondern nur durch Hilfe zu begegnen. Es bleibt die Frage des Glaubens—die ebenso enge Verbundenheit und Gebundenheit an das eine Buch und die ebenso deutliche Geschiedenheit. Und es scheint, als sei es dem deutschen Christentum besonders schwer, diese Doppelheit der Beziehungen zu tragen und zu begreifen. Es bedürfte einer weitreichenden Klärung all der geschichtlichen und sachlichen Voraussetzungen, auf denen dieses zweifache Verhältnis ruht; ich kann sie jetzt nicht geben und brauche sie Ihnen nicht sagen. Ich hoffe, dass Sie mit mir darin übereinstimmen werden, dass der christliche Glaube nur so lange christlich ist, als er den jüdischen in seinem Herzen trägt; ich weiss nicht, ob Sie auch der Umkehrung beistimmen werden, dass auch der jüdische Glaube nur so lange jüdisch ist, als er den christlichen in sich zu hegen vermag. Das soll zunächst nichts weiter sagen, als dass diese Frage von Judentum und Christentum nicht wie zwischen Part und Wierpart hin- und hergeworfen werden kann, sondern dass es eine innere, den eigenen Ernst und die eigene Wahrheit erschütternde Frage des Glaubens ist. Ich wüsste für einen christlichen Theologen fast nichts wo das 'Tua res agitur' ihn so gefangennehmen sollte, wie diese Frage des Judentums. Und es ist für mich eine bittere Erfahrung, dass in unserer christlichen wie theologischen Öffentlichkeit man so leichthin politischen oder sonstwie gefärbten Schlagworten zuneigt, wie es etwa in Kittels Begriff vom 'Gehorsam gegen die Fremdlingschaft' geschieht, der einer politischen Massnahme ein religiöses Mäntelchen, fadenscheinig und voller Löcher, umhängt. Un noch bitterer ist es, dass, wenn die 'Diffamierung' politisch und sozial durchgeführt wird, dass dann kein Theologe und keine Kirche nach dem Beispiel ihres Meisters zu den Verfemten spricht: Mein Bruder bist Du, sondern von ihnen fordert, statt ihnen zu helfen. Aber alles Geschehene ist ja nur zu begreifen, wenn man sich immer wieder sagt, dass wir kaum jemals so weit vom christlichen Glauben entfernt waren wie eben jetzt, und es bleibt uns nur die leise Hoffnung auf eine Erneuerung des Christentums, wie Sie sie für die Erneuerung des Judentums hegen. Dann erst scheint mir auch der Boden recht bereitet zu sein, um die jedem im anderen entstehende Frage fruchtbar zu lösen. Ich danke Ihnen herzlich für Ihren offenen Brief und bin mit aufrichtigem kollegialem Gruss, und wenn ich Ihnen auch nicht persönlich bekannt bin, dennoch in alter und nun wieder neuer Verbundenheit" (Ernst Lohmeyer, in *Martin Buber*, 499–501).

17. Ernst Lohmeyer, *Grundlagen paulinischer Theologie*, BHT 1 (Tübingen: Mohr Siebeck, 1929).

18. Ernst Lohmeyer, *Das Evangelium des Markus*, KEK I/2, 8th ed. (Göttingen: Vandenhoeck & Ruprecht, 1967), 6.

19. Martin Buber, *I and Thou*, trans. W. Kaufmann (New York: Scribner's Sons, 1970), 158.

20. "Später, als die Situation sich schon recht verschärft hatte, besuchte er (= Lohmeyer) mich in meinem Wohnort Heppenheim, . . . und sagte im Hotel, in dem er abstieg: Ich bin hergekommen, um Herrn Professor Buber zu besuchen" (Gudrun [Lohmeyer] Otto, "Erinnerung an Ernst Lohmeyer," *DP* 81 [1981]: 359.

CHAPTER 10

1. "Herrn Lohmeyers antinationalsozialistisches Verhalten und seine antinationalsozialistische Gesinnung ist eine offenkundige Tatsache" (Dr. Gustav Walz, president of the University of Breslau, letter to the German minister of education, 1934, cited in Ulrich Hutter, "Theologie als Wissenschaft. Zu Leben und Werk Ernst Lohmeyers [1890–1946]," *Jahrbuch für schlesische Kirchengeschichte* 69 [1990]: 164).

2. "Alles Leben drängt nach Tat. . . . Nur auf persönlichen Wege können wir den Menschen das Leben bringen, wie es uns einst selbst nur auf persönlichen Wege nahte. . . . Ein Leben in Gott and in seiner Liebe, und ein Leben unter den Menschen und in der Arbeit an ihnen, beides unlöslich ineinander verschlungen, das ist die täglich neue Gabe und Aufgabe unseres 'Berufes.'" Lohmeyer's sermon appears in Andreas Köhn, ed., *Ernst Lohmeyers Zeugnis im Kirchenkampf. Breslauer Universitätspredigten* (Göttingen: Vandenhoeck & Ruprecht, 2006), 26–35 (quotations from 33 and 35).

3. "Jesus lehrt beten: Führe uns nicht in Versuchung, und hat von diesem 'uns' niemanden—nicht einmal sich selbst—ausgenommen. Versuchungen sind da and bleiben, solange Menschen wissen und wählen, was sie tun; keiner bleibt verschont, und keiner darf je verschont bleiben: Er hätte sonst aufgehört, lebendig zu raten und zu taten" (Köhn, *Ernst Lohmeyers Zeugnis im Kirchenkampf*, 113).

4. "Liebe Freunde, scheuen wir uns nicht vor der Frage: Würden nicht Not und Grauen aufhören, würden nicht Friede und Eintract unter der Menschheit wohnen, die nie so zersplittert und zerrissen war, wie sie es heute ist?" (Köhn, *Ernst Lohmeyers Zeugnis im Kirchenkampf*, 116).

5. "Alles Grenzenlose Sehnen ist im tiefen Sinne wider Gott gerichtet" (Köhn, *Ernst Lohmeyers Zeugnis im Kirchenkampf*, 117).

6. "Gott ist nicht das Traumbild des Phantasten, und nichts Phantastisches ist in ihm; von Gott reden heisst von der strengen Gebundenheit unseres Lebens auch an alle seine Notdurft reden" (Köhn, *Ernst Lohmeyers Zeugnis im Kirchenkampf*, 116).

7. "On Temptation," a sermon of Lohmeyer on Matt. 4:1–11, February 22, 1931, in Köhn, *Ernst Lohmeyers Zeugnis im Kirchenkampf*, 112–17.

8. "Wir hören jetzt so viel von Pflicht des Einzelnen, Gemeinschaft zu halten mit allen, die ihm durch Blut oder Abstammung, durch Lebensfügung oder -führung nahe sind. Und diese Pflicht ist unumstösslich; aber alle diese Formen der Gemeinschaft reichen nicht in den Grund, auf dem der Glaube seine Gemeinschaft gründet. Denn in ihm hat und hält der Einzelne nicht Gemeinschaft, sondern er *ist* die Gemeinschaft. Er ist sie eben so sehr, wie er Gemeinschaft mit Gott ist; und das ist der Sinn jenes Doppelgebotes Jesu: Du sollst Gott lieben und Deinen Nächsten wie Dich selbst" (Köhn, *Ernst Lohmeyers Zeugnis im Kirchenkampf*, 76).

9. "Und weiten wir etwas den Blick auf unsere Gegenwart: Was gibt uns die Sicherheit des Standes und Weges? In ihr sind alle Gegensätze aufs fürchterlichste gewirrt: Jauchzen und Weinen, Not und Heil, Tod und Leben. . . . Hier hören wir: Ein neuer Frühling geht durch unser Land, und dort sehen wir, wie Kummer und Sorge sich immer tiefer in die Herzen und Gesichter gräbt" (Köhn, *Ernst Lohmeyers Zeugnis im Kirchenkampf*, 138).

10. "Es ist gut für euch, dass ich hingehe" (Köhn, *Ernst Lohmeyers Zeugnis im Kirchenkampf*, 139).

11. "Alles ist gut" (Köhn, *Ernst Lohmeyers Zeugnis im Kirchenkampf*, 139).

12. "'Alles ist gut'—auch und gerade der Tod dieses Herrn. Dies ist die letzte Sicherheit, und dieses die einzige Wahrheit. Da geht es nicht mehr um dich und mich, nicht um Wollen und Wünschen, nicht um Klagen und Verzweiflung; über allem Leben und Tod, über allem Wechseln und Wandeln steht dieses eine: Es ist gut" (Köhn, *Ernst Lohmeyers Zeugnis im Kirchenkampf*, 139–40).

13. "Sie reden schlicht von Gottes Wirklichkeit in diesem einen Tode und versenken in ihn alle Wahrheit und allen Trost. Sie sprechen von Leitung und nicht von Forderung, von Verkündung und nicht von Anspruch, sie sprechen von einem einmaligen Geschehen, das alle Not und allen Tod zu dem einen Pfade wandelt, auf dem wir sicher and behütet wandeln" (Köhn, *Ernst Lohmeyers Zeugnis im Kirchenkampf*, 142).

14. "Das Ende seiner Breslauer Zeit kam, und meinen Vater traf es hart. Es war ein Kaltstellen von einem Tag zum anderen, ein demütiger Abbruch einer 15 jährigen produktiven Zeit" (Gudrun [Lohmeyer] Otto, "Erinnerung an Ernst Lohmeyer," *DP* 81 [1981]: 359).

15. "Es ist merkwürdig, dass wir als Kinder von den Spannungszuständen, in denen er oft lebte, nichts merkten oder gar in the der Reaktion uns gegenüber spürten. Erklärbar scheint es mir nur so zu sein, dass sich sein eigentliches Leben im rein Geistigen vollzog und das reale, zu dem wir gehörten, bei aller Liebe nicht den gleich Stellenwert hatte" (Gudrun [Lohmeyer] Otto, "Erinnerung an den Vater," in *Freiheit in der Gebundenheit*, ed. Wolfgang Otto [Göttingen: Vandenhoeck & Ruprecht, 1990], 39).

16. "Er war immer offen für andere Meinungen, konnte zuhören und war immer ausgeglichen und deshalb ausgleichend. Nie wurde er scharf, sondern blieb auch in der Auseinandersetzung sachlich und vornehm. Er glaubte sich nicht im Besitz der Wahrheit, sondern sah sich hineingestellt in einen Prozess des Lernens und Forschens, der seinem Wesen nach ein unendlicher Prozess ist" (Gerhard Sass, "Die Bedeutung Ernst Lohmeyers für die neutestamentliche Forschung," *DP* 8 [1987]: 357).

17. "Wirkungslose Scheinwissenschaft" (Andreas Köhn, *Der Neutestamentler Ernst Lohmeyer*, WUNT 2.180 [Tübingen: Mohr Siebeck, 2004], 80).

18. "[Die] selbstverständliche Pflicht und Aufgabe, dass wir Theologen deutsch denken und fühlen" (Köhn, *Der Neutestamentler Ernst Lohmeyer*, 80).

19. "[Der] sklavisch an den Text der Bibel" . . . "unchristlich und undeutsch" (Köhn, *Ernst Lohmeyers Zeugnis im Kirchenkampf*, 81).

20. "Nicht ohne Grund haben wir im Mai 1933 auf dem Schlossplatz deutschfeindliche Bücher verbrannt" (Köhn, *Ernst Lohmeyers Zeugnis im Kirchenkampf*, 80).

21. Köhn, *Ernst Lohmeyers Zeugnis im Kirchenkampf*, 74.

22. "Von jeher einen schweren Kampf gegen die Gegner des Nationalsozialismus" (Köhn, *Ernst Lohmeyers Zeugnis im Kirchenkampf*, 81).

23. "Von der bürgerlich-demokratisch-nationalen Seite her die Bewegung aufs schärfste bekämpften" (Köhn, *Ernst Lohmeyers Zeugnis im Kirchenkampf*, 81).

24. "Judenfreundlichkeit" (Köhn, *Ernst Lohmeyers Zeugnis im Kirchenkampf*, 81).

25. See Köhn, *Der Neutestamentler Ernst Lohmeyer*, 72–73.

26. See Hutter, "Theologie als Wissenschaft," 138. The article against Adam was entitled "Kleine Geister in grosser Zeit," and the one about the Emergency League, "Unerhörte Herausforderung des Nationalsozialismus."

27. "Teufelsbewegung" and "Gekränkte Pastoren" (Köhn, *Der Neutestamentler Ernst Lohmeyer*, 78).

28. "Reaktionärer Kreise, die . . . die *Aufbauarbeit der nationalsozialistischen Regierung sabotieren* . . . müssen unschädlich gemacht werden, auch wenn sie im Gewande eines Dieners Gottes ihr verwerfliches Handwerk ausüben" (Köhn, *Der Neutestamentler Ernst Lohmeyer*, 78).

29. "Völlig untragbar" (Hutter, "Theologie als Wissenschaft," 163).

30. "Ein sehr bedenkliches, rechtswidriges Verhalten" (Hutter, "Theologie als Wissenschaft," 164).

31. "Eine ganze Reihe Gründe" (Hutter, "Theologie als Wissenschaft," 164).

32. "Herr Lohmeyers antinationalsozialistisches Verhalten und seine

antinationalsozialistische Gesinnung ist eine offenkundige Tatsache, für die ich weitere Belege zu bringen nicht für erforderlich halte" (Hutter, "Theologie als Wissenschaft," 164).

33. "Missbilligung" (Hutter, "Theologie als Wissenschaft," 165).

34. "Die Folgen Ihres Verhaltens werden Sie in vollem Umfange zu tragen haben" (Hutter, "Theologie als Wissenschaft," 165).

35. "Provozierend" (Hutter, "Theologie als Wissenschaft," 167).

36. See the letter in Hutter, "Theologie als Wissenschaft," 167.

37. "Das Verhalten von Prof. Lohmeyer is völlig unmöglich und seine weitere Lehrtätigkeit für eine Universität im nationalsozialistischen Staate untragbar. Die Studentenschaft fordert deshalb sofortige Abberufung von Prof. Lohmeyer. Der alleinige Rücktritt von Prof. Lohmeyer als Seminardirektor genügt der Studentenschaft nicht" (Hutter, "Theologie als Wissenschaft," 138).

38. "Nach der Einführung des deutschen Grusse kann es möglich sein, dass ich aus alter Gewohnheit meinen Hut gezogen habe, wenn ein Student mich durch Erheben des rechten Armes grüsste" (GStA PK, VI. HA, NI, Lohmeyer, E., No. 12).

39. For Lohmeyer's letter to University Administrator Hahnke, dated January 30, 1934, see GStA PK, VI. HA, NI, Lohmeyer, E., No. 12.

40. Letter preserved in Hutter, "Theologie als Wissenschaft," 165–66.

41. "Ich möchte Ihnen die dringende Bitte zum Ausdruck bringen, dass Sie das Schreiben am Beginn der nächsten Vorlesung verlesen. Ich habe den Führer der Studentenschaft in diesem Sinne informiert, der mir gegenüber die Garantie übernommen hat, dass jegliche Unruheäusserung unterbleibt. Ich bin vollkommen Herr der Studentenschaft. Ich muss Sie nun aber wirklich im eigensten Interesse bitten, im besprochenen Sinn die Sache zu beschliessen." Walz's letter to Lohmeyer is dated January 30, 1934 (GStA PK, VI. HA, NI, Lohmeyer, E., No. 12).

42. Lohmeyer's letter of February 1, 1934, to President Walz is preserved in the GStA PK, VI. HA, NI, Lohmeyer, E., No. 12.

43. "Von dem was ich in diesen Gesprächen gesagt habe, habe ich nichts zurückzunehmen und werde ich nichts zurücknehmen" (letter of Lohmeyer to students, GStA PK, VI. HA, NI, Lohmeyer, E., No. 12).

CHAPTER 11

1. "Wenn etwas uns fortgenommen wird, womit wir tief und wunderbar zusammenhängen, so ist viel von uns selber mit fortgenommen. Gott aber

will, dass wir uns wiederfinden, reicher um alles Verlorene und vermehrt um jeden unendlichen Schmerz" (Rainer Maria Rilke, letter to Princess Cathia von Schönaich-Carolath, 1908).

2. "Eine sofortige Abberufung von Herrn Lohmeyer" (letter of Walz to the Minister für Wissenschaft, Kunst, und Volksbildung, January 26, 1934, in Ulrich Hutter, "Theologie als Wissenschaft. Zu Leben und Werk Ernst Lohmeyers [1890–1946]," *Jahrbuch für schlesische Kirchengeschichte* 69 [1990]: 163–64).

3. The student signatories of *Confession and Constitution* were reported by Lohmeyer in his personal account of the events surrounding his dismissal as chair of the theological faculty. See GStA PK, VI. HA, NI, Lohmeyer, E., No. 12.

4. For Huber's final testimony before People's Court Judge Roland Freisler, see *Dying We Live*, ed. Helmut Gollwitzer, Käthe Kuhn, and Reinhold Schneider, trans. Reinhard Kuhn (London: Collins, 1956), 146–48.

5. "Wissenschaftliche Gründlichkeit . . . ohne die kein ehrlicher und dauerhafter Frieden möglich ist," in Andreas Köhn, *Der Neutestamentler Ernst Lohmeyer*, WUNT 2.180 (Tübingen: Mohr Siebeck, 2004), 87.

6. GStA PK, VI. HA, NI, Lohmeyer, E., No. 12, p. 50. The letter of Dean Lothar is dated January 8, 1936.

7. "Der schärfste Vorkämpfer der Benenntniskirche in Königsberg" (UAG PA, 347, Band 1, p. 57).

8. "Ausserordentlich starken Einfluss" (UAG PA, 347, Band 1, p. 57).

9. "Bei D. Lohmeyer wurde wenigstens dieser starke persönliche Einfluss nicht ganz so zur Auswirkung kommen" (UAG PA, 347, Band 1, p. 57).

10. Documentation related to Lohmeyer's *Strafversetzung* to Greifswald comes from UAG PA, 347, Band 1.

11. "Übrigens ist die Nachricht von meiner Berufung eines der bekannten Täuschungsmanöver. Es ist in Wirklichkeit eine Versetzung, und zwar wie mir mündlich zugegeben worden ist, eine Strafmassnahme wegen kirchlicher Haltung und Betätigung im Sinne der bekennenden Kirche" (quoted in Köhn, *Der Neutestamentler Ernst Lohmeyer*, 93).

12. "Gottes Wort entbindet uns von keinem Ringen, es nimmt uns nicht die tägliche Mühsal des Lebens, ja wir müssen sagen, erst dort wo wir sein Heil sehen, wird uns das Unheil unseres Lebens voll bewusst. Wir sind gerade dann die Angefochtenen, wenn Er uns aus allem Streit reisst; und die Anfechtung ist unendlich tiefer und grösser als alle Anfechtungen, die wir von Menschen und Verhältnissen erdulden mögen. Aber liebe Freunde, auch in der tiefsten Anfechtung wird noch der Klang Seiner Stimme vernehmbar und weht sie hinweg wie einen leichten Rauch. Ihr wisst es wohl, dass es hier keine

Beweise gibt; ... Wir können uns auch ihr versagen, und Generationen von Menschen haben sich ihr versagt. Wir können uns auch der Stimme Gottes versagen—und wie viele sind es die es tun—und wie oft tun wir es selbst. Aber auch noch dem Versagenden schenkt Er seine Stimme; wie das Meer braust und niemals stumm wird, wie die Wasserströme frohlocken und ihren Lauf nicht hemmen können, so klingt auch durch unser Leben, wir mögen uns ihr entziehen oder uns ihr aufschliessen, das Wunder Seiner Stimme, unfassbar und dennoch immer vernehmlich. Und wem er diese Seine Stimme schenkt, und wem schenkt er sie nicht, der kann nicht anders als mit dem Psalmisten sprechen: Singet dem Herrn ein neues Lied" (GStA PK, VI. HA, NI, Lohmeyer, E., No. 8).

13. In addition to Schönherr's testimony, I am indebted here to Dirk Alvermann and Karl-Heinz Spiess, eds., *Universität und Gesellschaft. Festschrift zur 550-Jahrfeier der Universität Greifswald, 1456–2006, Band 1, Die Geschichte der Fakultäten im 19. und 20. Jahrhundert* (Hinstorff: Rostock, 2006), 90–91.

14. Die Herren Theologieprofessoren sollten "doch gefälligst auch einmal ihren Studenten sagen!" (Köhn, *Der Neutestamentler Ernst Lohmeyer*, 99).

15. "Unter dem Niveau eines Sekundaners befunden" (Köhn, *Der Neutestamentler Ernst Lohmeyer*, 99).

16. On the Gauleiter episode, see Köhn, *Der Neutestamentler Ernst Lohmeyer*, 98–100. Andreas Köhn, "Von der 'Notwendigkeit des Bekennens': Theologie als Martyrium am Beispiel Ernst Lohmeyers (1890–1946)," in *Martyrium im 20. Jahrhundert*, ed. Hans Maier and Carsten Nicolaisen (Annweiler, 2004), 109–21.

17. "Das geschah sicher nicht deshalb, weil er das Katheder für wichtiger hielt, sondern weil ihm die Verantwortung für das auf der Kanzel, also im Auftrag und Namen Gottes zu Sagende so unendlich gross und schwer erschien. ... Wie kann flüchtiges Wort Bleibendes aussagen und im Unvollkommenen Vollkommenes aufleuchten? Wie kann ein Mensch den Weg zeigen zur Quelle des Lebens selbst? Solche Gedanken erklären Lohmeyers Zurückhaltung gegenüber eigenem Predigtdienst in den letzten Wirkungsjahren" (Gerhard Sass, "Die Bedeutung Ernst Lohmeyers für die neutestamentliche Forschung," *DP* 8 [1987]: 357).

18. "In der gegenwärtigen Lage von Theologie und Kirche und für die Zukunft des Meyerschen Kommentars scheint mir nichts nötiger zu sein als eine gründlich von 'neuen Ideen' geleitete Forschung am Neuen Testament. ... Wenn Sie in den letzten Jahren Ihre Ansicht geändert haben sollten, so tut mir das aufrichtig leid, aber ich kann deswegen nicht von den Prinzipien meiner Arbeit lassen" (letter to Günther Ruprecht, dated November 13, 1936, cited in Köhn, *Der Neutestamentler Ernst Lohmeyer*, 94).

19. Ernst Lohmeyer, "The Right Interpretation of the Mythological," in *Kerygma and Myth: A Theological Debate*, ed. H. W. Bartsch, trans. R. H. Fuller (New York: Harper & Row, 1961), 134.

20. "Ich sehe keinen Pfad aus diesem Dunkel" (Köhn, *Der Neutestamentler Ernst Lohmeyer*, 83).

21. "Gott hat für sein eschatologisches Werk und Evangelium das verachtete Galiläa erkoren" (Ernst Lohmeyer, *Galiläa und Jerusalem*, FRLANT 34 [Göttingen: Vandenhoeck & Ruprecht, 1936], 34).

22. "Der Weg des eschatologischen Vollendung ist von Gott so bestimmt, dass er in dem von Jerusalem verfemten, jetzt aber erwählten Galiläa begann. Aus dem Lande des eschatologischen Anbruchs führt er Jesus in die Stadt der Feinde und Sünder, aus der von Gott erkorenen Heimat—der doppelten Heimat des Evangeliums and des Menschensohns—in den Ort der Fremde und des Todes" (Lohmeyer, *Galiläa und Jerusalem*, 34).

23. Ernst Lohmeyer, *Das Urchristentum, 1. Buch: Johannes der Täufer* (Göttingen: Vandenhoeck & Ruprecht, 1932).

24. See Köhn, *Der Neutestamentler Ernst Lohmeyer*, 200-201.

25. "An diesem kleinen Abschnitt des Markusevangeliums zeigte sich, dass jeder Satz und jedes Wort von einer bestimmten theologischen Anschauung getragen ist. Hier ist nichts naive Geschichtserzählung, sondern alles bewusster Glaubensbeweis; und das Gleiche ist in anderer Weise bei Matthäus und Lukas, wie selbstverständlich bei Johannes, der Fall" (Ernst Lohmeyer, "Zur evangelischen Überlieferung von Johannes dem Täufer," *JBL* 51 [1932]: 318).

26. "Voraussetzung ist freilich, dass die Frage der Quellentheorien nicht mehr, wie es eine Zeit lang üblich war, in erster, sondern in dritter und vierter Linie steht" (letter of May 1, 1928, quote from Köhn, *Der Neutestamentler Ernst Lohmeyer*, 43).

CHAPTER 12

1. "Schwerer ist noch, dass man in dies fürchterliche Chaos von Grauen und Schuld mit verflochten ist, gewiss als ein Unschuldiger, mancher wohl auch als einer, der mit allen Kräften draussen und drinnen versucht hat, einen geringen Teil solcher Schuld wieder gut zu machen—aber die Verflechtung bleibt" (Lohmeyer to Anton Fridrichsen, October 1943, cited in Gudrun [Lohmeyer] Otto, "Erinnerung an den Vater," in *Freiheit in der Gebundenheit*, ed. Wolfgang Otto [Göttingen: Vandenhoeck & Ruprecht, 1990], 49).

2. The exact number of deaths on both sides of the Bromberg Massacre,

like the exact number of deaths in the Allied bombing of Dresden on February 14, 1945, for example, differs in reputable sources and makes definite pronouncements on the matter difficult. My figures regarding the massacre follow *Deutschland im Zweiten Weltkrieg*, Band 1, *Vorberetiung, Entfesselung und Verlauf des Krieges bis zum 22. Juni 1941* (Leitung: Gerhart Hass, Berlin, 1974), 178ff.; Heinz Neumeyer, *Westpreussen: Geschichte und Wandel* (Universitas, 1993), 439nn202ff.

3. On the entire atrocity, see James Edwards, "Ernst Lohmeyer—ein Schlusskapitel," *EvT* 56 (1996): 323n8.

4. "Es ist so viel Unmögliches und Unsagbares in den besetzten Gebieten geschehen, dass es tausend Mal besser gewesen wäre, nicht anzufangen.... Nein, moralisch haben wir alles verloren in diesen Gebieten" (Günter Haufe, "Ein Gerechter unter den Völkern. Gedenken an Ernst Lohmeyer" [address at the University of Greifswald on the occasion of the fiftieth year of Lohmeyer's execution, September 19, 1996], 3).

5. Lohmeyer's movements and meetings in early 1940 are taken from his field diary (GStA PK, VI. HA, NI, Lohmeyer, E., No. 171).

6. Ernst Lohmeyer, *Kultus und Evangelium* (Göttingen: Vandenhoeck & Ruprecht, 1952), was translated into English and published under the title *Lord of the Temple: A Study of the Relation between Cult and Gospel*, trans. Stewart Todd (Richmond, VA: John Knox, 1962).

7. On Lohmeyer's Sweden visit, see Andreas Köhn, *Der Neutestamentler Ernst Lohmeyer*, WUNT 2.180 (Tübingen: Mohr Siebeck, 2004), 106–7.

8. For Melie's correspondence, see GStA PK, VI. HA, NI, Lohmeyer, E., No. 132.

9. "Wir sind in schwerer Sorge um unseren ältesten Jungen, von dem wir seit dem 23. Jan. aus dem Osten nichts mehr gehört haben, und leben von Tag zu Tag in Erwartung einer frohen oder schlimmen Nachricht. Darüber vergeht die Möglichkeit zu schreiben, und mir kommt es fast vermessen vor, in solchen Tagen noch ein Buch herauszugeben. Ich tue es nur mit schwerem Herzen" (cited in Köhn, *Der Neutestamentler Ernst Lohmeyer*, 109–10).

10. On Ernst's and Melie's correspondence, see GStA PK, VI. HA, NI, Lohmeyer, E., Nos. 140, 141, 142.

11. Postcard of June 23, 1942 (GStA PK, VI. HA, NI, Lohmeyer, E., No. 143).

12. Letter dated June 27, 1942 (GStA PK, VI. HA, NI, Lohmeyer, E., No. 143).

13. The information and statistics are taken largely verbatim from the Topography of Terror Museum in Berlin, November 2016.

14. Letter of June 28, 1942 (GStA PK, VI. HA, NI, Lohmeyer, E., No. 143).

15. Letter of July 1, 1942 (GStA PK, VI. HA, NI, Lohmeyer, E., No. 143).

16. Letter of Ernst to Melie, July 26, 1942 (GStA PK, VI. HA, NI, Lohmeyer, E., No. 143).

17. "Denn ich bin seit Anfang September draussen, wie vor 25 Jahren, und bin aus aller Arbeit herausgerissen" (cited from Köhn, *Der Neutestamentler Ernst Lohmeyer*, 104).

18. "Die Meinen sind daheim und in verhältnismässiger Sicherheit—auf mich kommt es ja nicht so sehr an. Der Dienst ist hier in allem unendlich schwerer und aufreibender. Ich bin mager und hager geworden, nur noch Haut und Knochen und sehr grau—was Menschen für ein Inferno bereiten können, habe ich erfahren" (cited from Köhn, *Der Neutestamentler Ernst Lohmeyer*, 110).

19. See John Keegan, *The Second World War* (New York: Penguin Books, 1989), 227–37.

20. "Fast hätte ich ihn nicht wiedererkannt. Das war nicht mehr der jugendliche, schon durch sein ansprechendes Äusseres seine Hörer gewinnende Dozent, als den ich ihn gekannt hatte. Er hatte die Zähne verloren, das Gesicht war eingefallen, u. er wirkte sehr gealtert. Nur wenn er sprach, wirkete er wie früher: überlegt und überlegen. 'Du erschrickst über mein Aussehen. Verlust der Zähne. Skorbut. Ernährungsmangel. Kleine Vitamine.' In Verbindung damit erzählte er, dass in seinem Verwaltungsgebiet eine Quadratkilometer grosse Apfelplantage gelegen hätte. Die dazu gehörenden Konservenfabriken waren zerstört. Sein Vorgänger hätte bei strengster Strafe verboten, dass jemand von der Bevölkerung Äpfel pflückte. Er habe in einem Anschlag bekanntgegeben, dass, wer Äpfel pflückte und eine bestimmte Menge abliefere, mit nach Hause nehmen dürfe, soviel er tragen könne. 'Es ist kein Apfel am Baum geblieben, die Soldaten hatten Äpfel und die Bevölkerung auch.' In diesem Zusammenhang fiel der Satz, der sich mir unvergesslich eingeprägt hat: 'Ich bin auf nichts stolz in meinem Leben' (im Zusammenhang war deutlich, dass er eine Universitätslaufbahn u. seine Bücher meinte) 'aber auf eins bin ich stolz: dass ich an dieser Stelle ohne Todesurteil ausgekommen bin. Du ahnst nicht, wie leichtfertig damit umgegangen wird" (cited in Köhn, *Der Neutestamentler Ernst Lohmeyer*, 152n82).

21. "Es mag heute schwer begreifbar sein, dass ein Mann, der in führender Position schon die Bedrängnis der Nazi-Zeit an sich selbst erfahren, der Einsicht durch seine Funktion as Bestazungsoffizier in Verfahrensweisen der Bolschewisten gewonnen hatte, dass ein Mann von so hoher Intelligenz und tief verwurzelter Menschlichkeit sich für dieses Amt zur Verfügung stellte" (Gudrun [Lohmeyer] Otto, "Erinnerung an Ernst Lohmeyer," *DP* 81 [1981]: 360).

22. "Ich glaube, zwei Gründe sind da zunächst zu nennen: Mein Vater entzog sich nie einer Verantwortung, wenn sie ihm notwendig erschien. Er hatte die merkwürdige Gabe, sich für Menschen und Dinge einsetzen zu können, ohne die Gefahr für die eigene Person in Erwägung zu ziehen (Otto, "Erinnerung an Ernst Lohmeyer," 360).

23. "Hoffentlich bleibt mir noch etwas Zeit. Ich habe noch so viel zu sagen" (Otto, "Erinnerung an Ernst Lohmeyer," 360).

24. "Liedtke wurde für die Rettung zahlreicher Juden in der polnischen Stadt Przemysl gewürdigt [mit dem Titel 'Gerechter unter den Völkern']."

25. "Ehemaliger Wehrmachtsoffizier in Israel geehrt," *Der Tagesspiegel*, January 6, 1994, 4.

26. "Ende Mai 1940 wurde er [Lohmeyer] zu unserer Einheit versetzt und damit lebte ich mit ihm bis zum April 1943 tagtäglich zusammen. Lohmeyer hatte innerhalb der Truppe wohl keinen Feind. Seine hohen menschlichen Qualitäten, sein vornehme Güte, seine humanitäre Art, alle Dinge zu regeln, liessen in ihm nie den Offizier, aber stets den Seelsorger sehen. Jedermann (selbst der Russe der mit ihm zu tun hatte), hatte Vertrauen, dass sein Anliegen gerecht behandelt und gelöst wird. Er war nie Nationalsozialist und übte häufig genug rücksichtslose Kritik an den Machenschaften der damaligen deutschen Machthaber. Niemand anders als er konnte das ungestraft tun, weil die Achtung von seinem Streben nach absoluter Wahrheit und von seinem seltenen Menschlichkeitssinn jeden Verrat vor Scham unmöglich gemacht hat. Das rein Menschliche überwog bei allen seinen Entscheidungen. Er war Humanist in idealster Form.

"In jedem Einsatzorte sorgte er zu allererst dafür, dass die russische Bevölkerung die oft zu Tausenden versprengt war, wieder in ihre Heimat kam. Als er einmal 3000 Gefangene zu übernehmen hatte, rief er die russische Bevölkerung auf, diesen mit Verpflegung zu helfen, weil seine Vorräte hiezu nicht ausreichend gewesen sind. Noch am ersten Tage wurde festgestellt, dass es sich zum weitaus grössten Teil der Gefangenen um Zivilisten handelt, und kurzentschlossen hat Lohmeyer für diese Pässe ausgestellt, damit sie ungehindert in die Heimat reisen konnten. Am anderen Morgen waren alle bis auf 300 Mann wirkliche russische Soldaten aus der Gefangenschaft entlassen. Alles, was in der Küche übrig blieb, musste an die russische Bevölkerung verteilt werden. Unerbittlich war Lohmeyer bei Misshandlung von Russen. So bestrafte er einen Stabsfeldwebel zu 3 Tagen Mittelar[rest], weil dieser im Streit um in Paar Handschuhe einem Russen eine Ohrfeige gegeben hatte. (Übrigens die einzige Strafe, die ich mir ersinnen kann, die Lohmeyer gegeben hat.) Einmal musste ein gefangener russischer Oberst einen Tag und eine Nacht bewacht werden. Diese Aufgabe löste Lohmeyer in der Form, dass der Herr Oberst bei bester Unterhaltung im Casino sein Gast war, am gleichen Tisch wie wir übrigen Off. Platz zu nehmen hatte, dasselbe Essen, dasselbe Trinken und dasselbe Rauchen vorgesetzt bekam. Dem Herrn Oberst wurde ein Zimmer mit zwei Betten (eines davon für einen deutschen Off.) zur Verfügung gestellt. Lohmeyer versuchte stets aus jeder Not eine Tugend zu machen" (Fritz Kleemann's testimony to Lohmeyer is found in GStA PK, VI. HA, NI, Lohmeyer, E., No. 18).

27. "Denn die Briefe trafen in eine sehr schwierige und angespannte Zeit. Alles ist in Bewegung, Verbindungen, die bisher bestanden, sind zerrissen" (UAG PA 347, Bd. 2, 126).

28. UAG PA 347, Bd. 2, 120, 126.

29. For both diaries, see GStA PK, VI. HA, NI, Lohmeyer, E., No. 171.

30. For the quotation "es waren absolut keine Möglichkeiten, diese Menschen unterzubringen oder ihnen zu helfen," and report of the westward flight, see Melie Lohmeyer, "Väterchens Ende," GStA PK, VI. HA, NI, Lohmeyer, E., No. 147, p. 2.

31. "Und nun kommt das Traurigste, was ich zu sagen habe. Hätte ich ihn damals mit beiden Armen geöffnet mit warmem lebendigen Herzen empfangen können, das ganze Unglück später wäre nicht geschehen. Aber ich war erstarrt, erstarrt durch Helges grauenhaftes Ende, erstarrt in der Einsamkeit eines gänzlich überzogenen Herzens, denn er hatte mich schon seit Jahren innerlich alleine gelassen. Ich war wie aus Holz und er wahrscheinlich in tiefster Seele erwart[g]ungs- und hoffnungsvoll, war es auch." Lohmeyer's return home in April 1943 is related by Melie in "Väterchens Ende," 3.

CHAPTER 13

1. "So wandern wir durch die Jahre und alles Wandern ist nur ein Stille-Stehen vor Gott. So tragen wir unser Leben in zitternden Händen und alles Erzittern ist unverbrüchliche Festigkeit. So mühen wir uns und freuen uns an unseren Kräften. Und alle Mühsal und Freude ist nur ein schwacher Abglanz eines hellen Scheines. Denn wohin wir fahren und was wir erfahren, in Finsternis und Helle, in Ohnmacht und Macht, in Bösem und Gutem, in allem widerfährt uns Gott. Denn Gott is das Light und Finsternis ist nicht in ihm; die Finsternis vergehet und das Licht scheinet jetzt" (Ernst Lohmeyer, from a sermon at Breslau, July 19, 1931, cited in Ulrich Hutter, "Theologie als Wissenschaft. Zu Leben und Werk Ernst Lohmeyers [1890–1946]," *Jahrbuch für schlesische Kirchengeschichte 69* [1990]: 147).

2. "Mein Vater hatte geglaubt, aus Russland nicht mehr heimzukehren.

Nun war es doch geschehen, aber die Schatten umgaben ihn auch zu Haus"
(Gudrun [Lohmeyer] Otto, "Erinnerung an Ernst Lohmeyer," *DP* 81 [1981]:
360).

3. See above, p. 182.

4. "Der zunehmende Druck des ihm von jeher verhassten Naziregimes
empörte und beschattete sein ganzes Dasein" (Melie Lohmeyer, "Der Fall
Lohmeyer," GStA PK, VI. HA, NI, Lohmeyer, E., No. 186, p. 1).

5. "Meiner Frau und mir ist es ein fremdes, wenn auch täglich emfun-
denes Glück, dass wir wieder zusammen leben können. Vielleicht würden wir
es schneller lernen, wäre nicht die Zeit so ernst und drohend" (Otto, "Erinnerung an Ernst Lohmeyer," 360).

6. See Andreas Köhn, *Der Neutestamentler Ernst Lohmeyer*, WUNT
2.180 (Tübingen: Mohr Siebeck, 2004), 112, and Otto, "Erinnerung an Ernst
Lohmeyer," 360.

7. On the discovery of Luther's *Lectures on Romans* by Johannes Ficker,
see *Luther: Lectures on Romans*, trans. and ed. Wilhelm Pauck, Library of Christian Classics (Philadelphia: Westminster, 1961), xii; Martin Luther, *Commentary on the Epistle to the Romans*, trans. and ed. J. Theodore Mueller (Grand
Rapids: Zondervan, 1954), 5.

8. UAG, PA 347/III, 1.

9. For a complete list of Lohmeyer's lectures and courses, see Hutter,
"Theologie als Wissenschaft," 148–53.

10. See Rudolf Bultmann, *Kerygma and Myth*, ed. H. W. Bartsch, trans.
R. H. Fuller (New York: Harper & Row, 1961), 1–44.

11. Köhn, *Der Neutestamentler Ernst Lohmeyer*, 112.

12. Ernst Lohmeyer, "The Right Interpretation of the Mythological," in
Bultmann, *Kerygma and Myth: A Theological Debate*, 124.

13. Ernst Lohmeyer, "Right Interpretation of the Mythological," 134.

14. Ernst Lohmeyer, "Right Interpretation of the Mythological," 125,
127.

15. Ernst Lohmeyer, "Right Interpretation of the Mythological," 134.

16. Ernst Lohmeyer, "Right Interpretation of the Mythological," 135.

17. Ernst Lohmeyer, *Das Vater-Unser* (Göttingen: Vandenhoeck &
Ruprecht, 1946).

18. Ernst Lohmeyer, *The Lord's Prayer*, trans. John Bowden (London:
SPCK, 1965).

19. Ernst Lohmeyer, "Das Vater-Unser als Ganzheit," *TBl* 17 (1938):
217–27.

20. Ernst Lohmeyer, *Das Vater-Unser*, 202–7.

21. Ernst Lohmeyer, *Das Vater-Unser*, 27.

22. Joachim Jeremias, *The Prayers of Jesus*, trans. John Bowden (Philadelphia: Fortress, 1967), 11–57. On Jeremias's indebtedness to Lohmeyer on *Abba*, see also Henning Theissen, "Die Bibel als Begründungsanfang der evangelischen Theologie. Eine systematisch-theologische Erinnerung an den Breslauer und Greifswalder Neutestamentler Ernst Lohmeyer," *Gdanski Rocznik Ewangelicki* 8 (2014): 271–74.

23. "Von all den vielfältigen Gaben und Aufgaben, deren das jüdische Volk als das erwählte sich rühmt, ist hier nicht eine genannt" (Ernst Lohmeyer, *Das Vater-unser*, 205).

24. "An der Gestalt des Meisters hängt diese Bürgschaft, welcher das Kommen des Gottesreiches verkündet, aus diesem Gottesreich heraus wirkt und seinen Jüngern dies Gebet schenkt" (Ernst Lohmeyer, *Das Vater-unser*, 206).

25. GStA PK, VI. HA, NI, Lohmeyer, E., No. 17, p. 115.

26. On the peaceful surrender of Greifswald, see Köhn, *Der Neutestamentler Ernst Lohmeyer*, 114–15; Jasper von Altenbockum, "Die Greifswalder kennen die Geschichten, die Geschichte kannten sie lange Zeit nicht," *Frankfurter Allgemeine Zeitung*, April 29, 1995, 6; Greifswalder Physikalische Hefte, 8, Ernst-Moritz-Arndt Universität Greifswald (Greifswald, 1986), 12.

27. Sowjetische Militäradministration Deutschlands (SMAD).

28. So too Günter Haufe, "Ein Gerechter unter den Völkern. Gedenken an Ernst Lohmeyer" (address at the University of Greifswald on the occasion of the fiftieth year of Lohmeyer's execution, September 19, 1996).

29. "So war ich völlig ahnungslos, als er mir im Frühjahr 46 auf einmal erzählte, er sei zum kommenden Rektor der Universität gewählt worden und er habe auch angenommen. Ich hatte keine Ahnung gehabt. Alle Besprechungen waren ausserhalb des Hauses gewesen und er selbst ging ein und aus wie ein fremder stummer Gast" (Melie Lohmeyer, "Väterchens Ende," GStA PK, VI. HA, NI, Lohmeyer, E., No. 147, p. 4).

30. See above, p. 188.

31. ". . . den er hatte mich schon seit Jahren innerlich alleine gelassen" (Melie Lohmeyer, "Väterchens Ende," 3).

32. See above, pp. 38–39.

33. "Zwischen uns beiden blieb es das gleiche, wir waren beide kalt und tot" (Melie Lohmeyer, "Väterchens Ende," 4).

34. See Aleksandr I. Solzhenitsyn, *The Gulag Archipelago, 1918–1956: An Experiment in Literary Investigation I–II*, trans. W. Whitney (New York: Harper & Row, 1973), chap. 2. Solzhenitsyn writes that "there was nothing to be compared with [the elimination of the kulaks] in all Russian history" (54). It was the first experiment in genocide, "subsequently repeated by Hitler with the

Jews, and again by Stalin with nationalities which were disloyal to him or suspected by him" (55).

35. "German academe was shocked to learn that Heinrich Fink, professor of theology and vice chancellor at East Berlin's Humboldt University, had been a Stasi informer since 1968. After Fink's Stasi connections came to light, he was summarily fired." See John O. Koehler, *Stasi: The Untold Story of the East German Secret Police* (Boulder, CO: Westview, 1999), 9.

36. Joachim Gauck, *Die Stasi Akten: Das unheimliche Erbe der DDR* (Hamburg: Rowohlt, 1991), remains a primary source for information related to Stasi files.

CHAPTER 14

1. "Der Weg ist nicht leicht, nicht ohne Not und Anstrengung, aber wenn die Ziele klar sind und die Kräfte gerüstet, die Nacht und Macht der Zerstorung und Bedrückung zu überwinden, dann wird es mit dem anhebenden neuen Semester gehen wie mit dem anbrechenden Morgen: 'Zu neuen Ufern lockt ein neuer Tag!'" (Ernst Lohmeyer, address prepared for the reopening of the University of Greifswald, February 15, 1946, cited in Gudrun [Lohmeyer] Otto, "Erinnerung an Ernst Lohmeyer," *DP* 81 [1981]: 361).

2. "Seine Pläne und Massnahmen wurden damals in den Verhandlungen mit den russischen Professoren durchaus gebilligt" (Melie Lohmeyer, "Der Fall Lohmeyer," GStA PK, VI. HA, NI, Lohmeyer, E., No. 186, pp. 2–3).

3. "Mein Vater entzog sich nie einer Verantwortung, wenn sie ihm notwenig erschien" (Otto, "Erinnerung an Ernst Lohmeyer," 360).

4. "In Greifswald selbst . . . hatte sich eine richtige Welle von Bewunderung, Anerkennung und Bejahung gebildet. Wir haben 'Klein Weimar,' 'so etwas von Rektor haben wir seit langen Zeiten nicht gehabt,' 'ein Mann der Zukunft' und so weiter" (Melie Lohmeyer, "Väterchens Ende," GStA PK, VI. HA, NI, Lohmeyer, E., No. 147, p. 5).

5. "Niemand von uns durchschaute in diesen ersten Geburtswehen der neuen Aera, dass die kommenden Universitäten in der Besatzungszone mehr oder weniger als rein politische Instrumente gedacht sind" (Melie Lohmeyer, "Der Fall Lohmeyer," 2–3).

6. On the Three Power resolution, see Bezirksleitung Schwerin der SED, Bezirksparteiarchiv, Landesleitung der KPD Mecklenburg, Kreisleitung der KPD Greifswald 1945–1946, 1. Mappe, I/11, p. 216. See also Helge Matthiesen, "Eine tödliche Intrige," *Frankfurter Allgemeine Zeitung*, March 15, 1996, 10.

7. On the exact conditions of denazification, see Dirk Alvermann and

Karl-Heinz Spiess, eds., *Universität und Gesellschaft. Festschrift zur 550-Jahrfeier der Universität Greifswald, 1456–2006*, Band 1, *Die Geschichte der Fakultäten im 19. und 20. Jahrhundert* (Hinstorff: Rostock, 2006), 1:101.

8. On the early role of the Communist Party of Greifswald, see Bezirksleitung Schwerin der SED, 1. Mappe, I/11, pp. 46–47, 98–99.

9. "Im übrigen sind wir in keiner Weise daran interessiert, dem mehr oder weniger faschistischen Unternehmertum Kartelle zu schaffen, die sie in die Lage versetzen ihren faschistischen Kundenkreis noch mehr zu bevorzugen" (Bezirksleitung Schwerin der SED, Bezirksparteiarchiv, Landesleitung der KPD Mecklenburg, Kreisleitung der KPD Greifswald 2. Mappe, 1945–1946, I/11a, p. 121).

10. Greifswalder Physikalische Hefte, 8, 12–13.

11. UAG R 580/7, 6–7.

12. Bezirksleitung Schwerin der SED, 2. Mappe, 1945–1946, I/11a, pp. 112–13.

13. "Der Block der antifaschistischen Parteien zu Greifswald fordert grundsätzlich die Entlassung jedes Hochschullehrers, der der NSDAP als Pg. oder ihren Kampfverbänden sowie dem NS Dozentenbund als Mitglied angehört hat, ohne Rücksicht auf den Zeitpunkt des Eintritts oder die Dauer der Mitgliedschaft" (Bezirksleitung Schwerin der SED, 1. Mappe, I/11, p. 216).

14. "Politisch unzuverlässige Kräfte so schnell wie möglich zu ersetzen" (Bezirksleitung Schwerin der SED, 1. Mappe, I/11, pp. 216–17).

15. UAG R 580/1, 47.

16. UAG R 580/1, 67.

17. "In Schwerin als auch bei den kommunistischen Krisen Greifswalds wurde er sehr falsch ausgelegt, und man hiess ihn einen 'Naziprotektor'" (Melie Lohmeyer, "Der Fall Lohmeyer," 3).

18. Kulturbundes zur demokratischen Erneuerung.

19. "Das alte Wort, die Wahrheit wird euch freimachen, (...) gilt auch in der unmittelbaren Gegenwart, gilt von der kleinen Arbeit des Tages wie von der Arbeit auf grosse Ziele und auf ferne Zeiten. Sie werden auch aber fragen, wieso wird auf diese Weise Kultur begründet: Und ich antworte mit dem Satz, von dem ich ausging: Kultur is damit begründet, dass wir frei geworden sind. Denn allerinnerster Kern der Kultur ist der Gedanke der Freiheit" (Andreas Köhn, *Der Neutestamentler Ernst Lohmeyer*, WUNT 2.180 [Tübingen: Mohr Siebeck, 2004], 121).

20. "Leider hat Prof. Lohmeyer nicht restlos in der Ideologie gesprochen, die wir gewünscht hätten. Er hat sich als ein philosophischer Idealist und sogar etwas als Mystiker gezeigt, mit einer sogar mehr als angedeuteten Re-

serve gegenüber Sowjetrussland und der Roten Armee" (Köhn, *Der Neutesta-mentler Ernst Lohmeyer*, 121).

21. Correspondence relating to Lohmeyer's involvement in the newly formed Evangelical Church is found in GStA PK, VI. HA, NI, Lohmeyer, E., No. 16. The reconstitution of the Church of Pomerania, and the name of Lohmeyer as one of its representatives, is in letter 9; Söhngen's letter is 25.

22. "Schönes Beispiel" (Bezirksleitung Schwerin der SED, 1. Mappe, I/11, p. 227).

23. This three-page positive report was written in Schwerin on February 10, 1946, four days before Lohmeyer's arrest (Bezirksleitung Schwerin der SED, 1. Mappe, I/11, pp. 227–29).

24. See " 'Lass dir nicht grauen und entsetze dich nicht. . . .' Kriegsende und Wiederaufbau Kirchenmusik," ein Interview mit Annelise Pflugbeil von Irmfried Garbe, *Zeitgeschichte regional*, July 2005, 108. I owe this anecdote to a conversation with the Reverend Wolfgang Nixdorf in Schwerin, Germany, December 10, 2016.

25. "Euer Magnifizenz! Mit bewundernder Nachachtung grüssen wir Sie am Neujahrsmorgen./ Wir alle wissen, wie Sie in unermüdlichem Streben um die Erhaltung und das Leben der Universität Greifswald kämpfen./ Viel, sehr viel haben Sie bisher schon erreicht und gerettet./ Aber auch schwere Schläge hat die Universität erleiden müssen trotz Ihres nie erlahmenden Bemühens./ Vielleicht nur wenige wissen, wie Sie persönlich darunter leiden./ Das Jahr 1946 steht vor uns. Möchte es Ihnen schliesslich doch den endgultigen Erfolg bringen! Möchte die Universität mit Ihnen an der Spitze wieder aufleben!/ Ein Student/ Ihrer alma mater für alle" (GStA PK, VI. HA, NI, Lohmeyer, E., No. 17, p. 118).

26. "Die Vorbereitungen für die Wiedereröffnung wurden fieberhaft betrieben" (Melie Lohmeyer, "Der Fall Lohmeyer," 3–4).

27. "Die Russen haben einen viel zu guten Nachrichtendienst, als dass sie nicht wüssten, dass das mich nichts angeht" (Melie Lohmeyer, "Der Fall Lohmeyer," 2).

28. "Dieser Grünberg wurde, wie ich später hörte, auch in echt kommu-nistischen Kreisen als ein sehr schwacher Mensch geschildert, den man gerne verschob, wenn etwas Unangenehmes zu machen war" (Melie Lohmeyer, "Väterchens Ende," 7).

29. "Er lächelete dabei und sagte, 'also einen König in einem kleinen Königreich'" (Melie Lohmeyer, "Väterchens Ende," 7).

30. "Ich sagte nachher zu Väterchen: 'Das ist aber eine riskante Sache, da hast Du ja die ganze Sache alleine auf dem Hals" (Melie Lohmeyer, "Vä-terchens Ende," 7–8).

31. According to Melie, Lohmeyer's exact words with respect to Grünberg were "Ich liebe und verehre diesen Mann." And with regard to his plan, "[Er] ist mir ja auch viel lieber, da kann mir keiner reinfunken" (Melie Lohmeyer, "Väterchens Ende," 7–8).

32. Deutsche Zentralverwaltung für Volksbildung in der sowjetischen Besatzungszone (UAG R 458/VII, 35).

33. Kommission für die demokratische Erneuerung des Geschichtsunterrichtes (UAG R 458/VII, 35).

34. "Richtlinien für den neuen Geschichtsunterricht" (UAG R 458/VII, 35).

35. "Ob es angezeigt sei, gegen diese Verfügung vorstellig zu werden" (UAG R 458/VII, 56).

36. "Die in den gegenwärtigen Verhältnissen gesteigerten Aufgaben der äusseren Verwaltung und Bewirtschaftung haben die Universität genötigt, den Gedanken der Selbstverwaltung stärker auszuprägen" (UAG R 458/VII, 37).

37. In a letter of November 30, 1945, Lohmeyer wrote to President Stroux at Humboldt: "Angesichts der damit drohenden Gefahren fühlen wir uns verpflichtet, den ererbten Charakter einer deutschen Universität dadurch fester zu bewahren, dass wir das Moment der Forschung deutlicher in den Vordergrund schieben" (UAG R 458/VII, 51).

38. "Mehr oder weniger rein politisches Instrument" (Melie Lohmeyer, "Der Fall Lohmeyer," 2–3).

39. UAG R 458/VII, 37.

40. "Nie wieder Abgeschlossenheit der Universität, sondern engstes Zusammenleben und Zusammenarbeiten mit dem ganzen Volk. Die Universität kann nur stark und fruchtbar sein als Tochter des werktätigen Volkes" (UAG R 580/2, 25).

41. "So ist dieser Wiederbeginn mehr als ein Fortsetzen dessen, was eine Zeitlang unterbrochen war, es ist ein Aufbrechen zu neuen und doch alten Zielen auf neuen und doch alten Wegen mit neuen und doch alten Kräften. Neu ist dies alles, weil nach dem erlittenen Zusammenbruch nichts mehr dort begonnen werden kann, wo es bisher stand, und dennoch ist dies alles auch alt, weil auch die brutalste Gewalt und die schlimmste Willkür auf die Dauer nicht das Antlitz der wahren Dinge und Probleme enstellen können. Der Weg is nicht leicht, nicht ohne Not und Anstrengung, aber wenn die Ziele klar sind und die Kräfte gerüstet, die Nacht und Macht der Zerstörung und Bedrückung zu überwinden, dann wird es mit dem anhebenden neuen Semester gehen wie mit dem anbrechenden Morgen: 'Zu neuen Ufern lockt ein neuer Tag!'" For the preservation of the excerpt by Werner Schmauch, Lohmeyer's student, see

Christfried Boettrich, "Ernst Lohmeyer zum 19. September 2006," in *Ernst Lohmeyers Zeugnis im Kirchenkampf. Breslauer Universitätspredigten*, ed. Andreas Köhn (Göttingen: Vandenhoeck & Ruprecht, 2006), 9n1. The quotation itself is from Otto, "Erinnerung an Ernst Lohmeyer," 361.

42. "Es kam nun der 15. Februar 1946, der Tag der Wiedereröffnung, heran. Mein Mann war den ganzen Abend ausser Haus—kam auch nicht zum Abendessen, telefonierte bloss, er käme später. Ich wartete bedrückt. Da schellte es gegen 11 Uhr, und es kamen 3 mir der Uniform nach wohlbekannte Männer der NKWD die Treppe herauf und fragten hastig nach meinem Mann. Ich sagte, er sei in der Universität und wusste Bescheid. Es war so weit.—Ich telefonierte sofort, erfuhr aber nur, mein Mann sei mit einem Kollegen zur Kreiskommandantur gegangen. Mittlerweile kam dann mein Mann nach Hause, sehr erschöpft und eigentlich in einer Verfassung, als ginge es ihn selber nicht wesentlich an, oder als nähme er es nicht ganz für ernst. Er erzählte, Dr. Müller sei inzwischen in der Universitä gewesen in schwer angegrunkenem Zustand, habe dauernd auf den Tisch geschlagen und geschrien: 'Mönchlein, Du gehst einen schweren Gang' und habe ihn im Namen der Schweriner Regierung abgesetzt. Die Eröffnung fände aber morgen trotzdem statt. Ich sagte meinem Mann, es seien inzwischen die Männer der NKWD dagewesen, ihn zu verhaften. 'Ach Unsinn,' sagte er, 'die Russen wissen schon über mich Bescheid, sonst hätten sie mich längst geholt. Vielleicht soll ich noch die und die vor morgen rausschmeissen. Die Russen laufen ja gern nachts herum.' Gegen ½ 1 Uhr etwa kamen die Russen jedoch wieder und verhafteten ihn. Sie machten 2 Stunden Haussuchung, bei der sie einen Stoss wer[t]voller Gelehrtenbriefe aus aller Welt, einige Photographien meines Mannes und unser Radio mitnahmen. Sie benahmen sich übrigens durchaus anständ[ig]. Ich hatte so das Gefühl, dass sie selber merkten, bei wem sie war[en]. Mein Mann stand während dieser Zeit meist am Ofen, sah entsetzlich elend aus und gab ruhig auf alle Fragen Antwort. Was in ihm vor[ging] weiss ich nicht. Er sagte nichts Persönliches. Er was wohl ganz erstarrt, oder aber er hielt es nur für eine vorübergehende Massnahme. Er sagte dem Kapitän nur in fast kindlichem Tonfall: 'Sie wollen mich verhaften? Aber ich habe doch nichts gemacht.' Ich wec[kte] als die Zeit vorgeschritten war, unsere Tochter, die sich weinen[d] an den Vater drängte, aber auch mit ihr sprach er nicht. Er sah aus wie aus Holz geschnitzt—unbeweglich und auch mit einem erstarrten Gesichtsausdruck. Gegen Ende der Haussuchung forderte mich der Capitän auf, Wäsche, Toilettesachen, Essgeschirr und Besteck zusa[mmen]zupacken. Mein Mann zog sich an, nahm den Rucksack um, und dann gingen sie. Meine Tochter brachte ihn bis zur Haustüre. Auch ihr hat er nichts mehr gesagt—er blieb erstarrt und stumm, und so g[ing] er" (Melie Lohmeyer, "Der Fall Lohmeyer," 4).

43. "Vom Balkon aus rief ich, als die drei Männer davongingen, meinen Mann in der Mitte: 'Auf Wiedersehen,' und ich hörte zum letzten Male seine Stimme" (Melie Lohmeyer, "Väterchens Ende," 10).

CHAPTER 15

1. "Ich habe diese Niederschrift nicht nur für Euch als Väterchens Fleisch und Blut verfasst. Ich denke, es ist gut, dass ein Mann von seiner geistigen Bedeutung, von seiner Arbeit für die Wissenschaft der christlichen Religion nicht nur in den amtlichen Annalen als tot in russischen Gewahrsam gebucht wird. Es muss gewusst werden, auf welche Weise dieses wertvolle Leben schuldlos zu Grunde gerichtet wurde. Es kommt sicher der Tag, an dem Ihr danach gefragt werdet. Auch aus diesem Grund habe ich geschrieben" (Melie Lohmeyer, writing to her two children, May 2, 1965, in Melie Lohmeyer, "Väterchens Ende," GStA PK, VI. HA, NI, Lohmeyer, E., No. 147, p. 27).

2. Melie Lohmeyer, "Väterchens Ende," 5–6.

3. "Für uns ist Professor Lohmeyer Rektor, er ist nicht gestorben, also soll er von denen, die ihn an der Ausübung seines Amtes, hindern, freigegeben werden" (Gottfried Grünberg, *Kumpel, Kämpfer, Kommunist* [Berlin: Militärverlag der Deutschen Demokratischen Republik, 1977], 294).

4. "Dass seine Magnifizenz besonderer Umstände halber nicht an der Eröffnung teilnehmen könne." The account of the senate meeting and opening ceremony comes from Grünberg, *Kumpel, Kämpfer, Kommunist*, 293–95. Grünberg is not an unbiased witness, and errors in his report extend to the misspellings of the names of both Lohmeyer and Skocyrew. In the above description I have followed Grünberg only when his report is corroborated by other sources.

5. Arnold Weibel, "'Der Fall L.' in Greifswald, Schwerin, und Berlin—Was wurde zur Rettung Ernst Lohmeyers unternommen?" *Zeitgeschichte Regional—Mitteilungen aus Mecklenburg-Vorpommern* 1 (1997): 29–34.

6. "Zurückhaltung."

7. "Was andere Völker in 6 Kriegsjahren erlitten haben, hatte die Kirche nicht die innere Freiheit, Anklage nach aussen zu erheben" (Dibelius's quotation is from Mathias Rautenberg, "Der Tod und die SED. Zum 65. Todestag Ernst Lohmeyers," *Zeitgeschichte Regional. Mitteilungen aus Mecklenburg-Vorpommern* 15, no. 2 [2011]: 26–27).

8. GStA PK, VI. HA, NI, Lohmeyer, E., No. 18.

9. "In der ganzen Universität, die damals in dumpfer Angst und Bedrückung lebte, war ein Gerücht über Väterchen so quasi eine Beruhigung,

denn man sprach und flüsterte von einer 'dunklen militärischen Sache,' und da konnte man ja weiter gar nichts machen" (Melie Lohmeyer, "Väterchens Ende," 13).

10. Wretched prison conditions are recorded in Bezirksleitung Schwerin der SED, Bezirksparteiarchiv, Landesleitung der KPD Mecklenburg, Kreisleitung der KPD Greifswald 2. Mappe, 1945–1946, I/11a, p. 37.

11. "Es begann nun für mich der Kampf um Väterchens Schicksal" (Melie Lohmeyer, "Väterchens Ende," 13).

12. "Um ihm ein Gefühl der Zugehörigkeit zu uns zu geben" (Melie Lohmeyer, "Väterchens Ende," 12).

13. "Ich bin ein Stück weggeworfenes altes Eisen" (Ernst Lohmeyer, "Brief aus dem Gefängnis der GPU in Greifswald," GStA PK, VI. HA, NI, Lohmeyer, E., No. 146, p. 1).

14. "Kleinen" (Ernst Lohmeyer, "Brief aus dem Gefängnis," 1).

15. "Herr Professor Ivanoff wäre aus Berlin gekommen, der sie sofort sprechen möchte" (UAG, R 580/1, 68).

16. "Ich habe den Eindruck, als suchten sie erst nach Dingen, bei denen sie einhaken und mich fassen könnten, und als ob diese Fragen nur die wahren Motive verschleiern sollen, die auf politischem Gebiet liegen und der hiesigen NKWD selbst nicht bekannt sind" (Ernst Lohmeyer, "Brief aus dem Gefängnis," 2).

17. "Ich halte das ganze immer noch für eine Schweriner Intrige, bei der die KPD nicht ganz unschuldig ist" (Ernst Lohmeyer, "Brief aus dem Gefängnis," 2).

18. "So tappe auch ich eigentlich im Dunkeln und hoffe nur, dass ebenso plötzlich wie meine Haft begann, sie auch enden wird, wenn es sicher lange dauern wird" (Ernst Lohmeyer, "Brief aus dem Gefängnis," 2).

19. "Ich glaube, er war der Überzeugung, dass man ihn durch Berlin-Karlshorst schon wieder herausholen könnte" (Melie Lohmeyer, "Vaterchens Ende," 11).

20. "Es war ihm nicht klar, dass bei totalitärer Politik Recht oder Unrecht gar keine Rolle spielen" (Melie Lohmeyer, "Vaterchens Ende," 11).

21. "Seitens der Regierung wurde am 16.2.46 mitgeteilt, dass diese Verhaftung nicht politische, sondern militärische Gründe habe" (Ministerium für Auswärtige Angelegenheiten der Deutschen Demokratischen Republik, in UAG PA 347, Band 4, no page).

22. "Ministerialdirektor."

23. "Obereregierungsrat."

24. "Richtlinien."

25. "Vertrauensbruch."

26. "Während des Nationalsozialismus erbärmlich gewesen."

27. "Die Personalpolitik des Rektors als offenbar falsch."

28. "Dass in diesem Unternehmen gewisse Kräfte untergebracht werden sollten, für die im demokratischen Staat eigentlich kein Platz sei."

29. "Die Eröffnung der Universität sei sabotiert worden." These accusations are documented in the minutes of the Saturday, February 16, 1946, faculty meeting (Meckl. Landeshauptarchiv Schwerin, Landesregierung Mecklenburg, Ministerium für Volksbildung, Signatur 2464, 179–84).

30. "Min. Dir. Manthey erklärt weiter, dass direkte Vereinbarungen mit der Zentralverwaltung in Berlin keine Gültigkeit haben." These accusations are also documented in minutes of the Saturday, February 16, 1946, faculty meeting.

31. "Erträglich" (Ernst Lohmeyer, "Brief aus dem Gefängnis," 2).

32. "Wenn mich eine menschliche Schmählichkeit noch erbittern könnte, so ist es dieses!" (Ernst Lohmeyer, "Brief aus dem Gefängnis," 4).

33. "Man muss den Schluss ziehen, als sei seine Freilassung unerwünscht gewesen" (Melie Lohmeyer, "Der Fall Lohmeyer," GStA PK, VI. HA, NI, Lohmeyer, E., No. 186, p. 5).

34. Letters of reference for Lohmeyer are preserved in GStA PK, VI. HA, NI, Lohmeyer, E., No. 18.

35. Wolfgang Otto, ed., *Aus der Einsamkeit—Briefe einer Freundschaft. Richard Hönigswald an Ernst Lohmeyer* (Würzburg: Königshausen & Neumann, 1999).

36. "Lohmeyer war ein Mann von humanster Gesinnung, . . . Ich halte ihn einer unehrenhaften Handlung oder auch nur der kleinsten Inhumanität für absolut unfähig. Ich kenne Professor Lohmeyer als bedingungslosen Gegner der nationalsozialistischen Herrschaft in Deutschland und als unversöhnlichen Feind jeder antisemitischen Tendenz, wie sich denn zu allen Zeiten in seinem engsten Freundeskreis Juden befanden, und er sich niemals, auch nicht auf der Höhe der nationalsozialistischen Herrschaft, gescheut hat, sich offen und rückhaltlos zu seinen jüdischen Freunden zu bekennen" (Otto, *Aus der Einsamkeit*, 119). Unless otherwise noted, all letters of reference in the section "Intercessory Efforts" come from GStA PK, VI. HA, NI, Lohmeyer, E., No. 18.

37. E. J. Cohn, "Declaration."

38. "Herr Professor Lohmeyer ist von jeher ein leidenschaftlicher Gegner des Nationalsozialismus; er ist einer der sehr wenigen Deutschen, die ihre Gesinnung offen bekannt haben."

39. "Professor D. Ernst Lohmeyer . . . hat sich im Kampf der Bekennenden Kirche gegen Anmassung und Gewaltherrschaft des Nationalsozialismus

treu auf die Seite der Bekennenden Kirche gestellt" (Martin Niemöller, "Bescheinigung").

40. The Lieb letter is taken from Andreas Köhn, *Der Neutestamentler Ernst Lohmeyer*, WUNT 2.180 (Tübingen: Mohr Siebeck, 2004), 139.

41. "Das Beste, was er in dem besetzten Gebiete tun könne (er stand damals in Polen), sei, dass er die Einwohner vor den Grausamkeiten der 'Braunen und Schwarzen' (der SA und SS) schützte" (Rudolf Bultmann, "Gutachten über Herrn Professor D. Ernst Lohmeyer [Greifswald], Marburg, Oktober 18, 1946").

42. "Menschen wie Prof. Lohmeyer sind für den Aufbau Deutschlands in einem neuen Geiste dringend notwendig."

43. "Seine fanatische Ablehnung des Nationalsozialismus brachten ihn häufig in allergrösste Gefahr. Er ist der einzig mir bekannt gewordene Dozent, der sich mannhaft der Beschlagnahme 'jüdisch-marxistischer' Bücher aus seiner Bibliothek widersetzte, indem er dem Abholungskommando entgegenhielt, dass sie dann auch die Bibel als ein von Juden verfasstes Buch mitnehmen müssten."

44. "Zu unserer grossen Bestürzung hörten wir vor wenigen Tagen, dass Ihr Mann Mitte Februar verhaftet worden sei" (quoted in Köhn, *Der Neutestamentler Ernst Lohmeyer*, 138).

45. "Gegenüber all diesem Wenn und Aber hat Gott nun einen unwiderruflichen Schlussstrich gesetzt. Damit fertig zu werden und nicht zu hadern ist nicht leicht. Und ich verstehe jetzt, welche Note Ihnen besonders das letzte Vierteljahr gebracht hat. Und doch wollen wir dankbar sein, dass wir selbst in solcher äussersten Not, die bisweilen zur Verzweiflung werden kann, fest daran glauben dürfen, dass Gott uns in Gnade und Liebe führt, und zwar uns ganz persönlich, auch wenn wir es manchmal nicht verstehen. Dies im Dunkel sich an der Vaterhand festhalten dürfen ist mehr als alles 'Gotterleben' und alles mystische Versenken. Es ist die schlichte und tröstende Wahrheit, die uns erst wahrhaft zu Menschen macht und für die wir immer wieder, wenn auch unter Tränen, danken müssen" (quoted from Köhn, *Der Neutestamentler Ernst Lohmeyer*, 147. For the entire correspondence between Melie and Ruprecht, see Köhn, 137–56).

46. "Dass ihr Vater, Landesgerichtsrat Karl Hagemann, 1946 im Lager von Neubrandenburg/Fünfeichen als Mithäftling mit Ernst Lohmeyer Schach gespielt hat" (Günter Haufe, "Gedenkvortrag zum 100. Geburtstag Ernst Lohmeyers," in *In Memoriam Ernst Lohmeyer*, Greifswalder Universitätsreden, n.s., 59 [Greifswald: Ernst-Moritz-Arndt-Universität Greifswald, 1991], 16n2).

47. Markus Wehner, "Propaganda der Tat. Neue Quellen zur Sowjetischen Militaradministration in Deutschland," *Frankfurter Allgemeine Zeitung*, November 1, 1995.

48. "Wir haben die traurige Pflicht, Ihnen heute mitteilen zu müssen, dass der von Ihnen gesuchte Ernst Lohmeyer nach Aussagen eines ehemaligen Häftlings im Herbst 46 im Gefängnis Greifswald verstorben ist" (Melie Lohmeyer, "Väterchens Ende," 19).

49. "Diese Anklage erwiess sich aber als haltlos" (Karl-Heinz Schröder, letter to Melie written from Skogsby, Sweden, June 29, 1950, made personally available to me by Gudrun Otto; also Melie Lohmeyer, "Väterchens Ende," 21).

50. "Am selben Tage im, ich glaube es war im September 1946, wo Ihr Gatte Sie mit Ihrem Frl. Tochter zum letzten Mal auf dem Wall sah, spielte sich folgendes ab: Ein russischer Offizier betrat die Zelle und rief seinen Namen. Ihr Gatte lag auf seiner Pritsche mit Hemd, Hose, und Strümpfen bekleidet, er erhob sich und wollte seine Sachen zusammenpacken und sich ankleiden, worauf der Offizier sagte, es sei nicht nötig. Im selben Moment betraten zwei russische Soldaten die Zelle, rissen seine Hände auf dem Rücken und banden ihn. Sie führten ihn aus der Zelle, worauf kurze Zeit später das Motorengeräusch der bereitstehenden Wagen ertönte" (Melie Lohmeyer, "Väterchens Ende," 21–22).

51. "Für Schröder stand fest, dass er denselben Weg gegangen ist wie viele andere vor ihm. Beim Herausführen aus der Zelle hat er dem Schröder noch Grüsse an Sie aufgegeben" (Melie Lohmeyer, "Väterchens Ende," 22).

52. "Auch für mich stand nach dieser Schilderung fest, dass das Urteil vollstreckt wurde und ich hielt es für meine Pflicht es der Kampfgruppe zu melden. . . . Hochachtungsvoll, Karl-Heinz Schröder" (Melie Lohmeyer, "Väterchens Ende," 22).

53. "Vorher hatte ich diesen Tobis besucht und sah in dem hellen Entsetzen seines Gesichts, dass er genau Bescheid wusste und mir bestätigte, dass Väterchen erschossen worden wäre" (Melie Lohmeyer, "Väterchens Ende," 22).

54. "Als einzige hat man ihm das Neue Testament gelassen" (Melie Lohmeyer, "Väterchens Ende," 24).

55. "Lohmeyer, Ernst, geb. 1890 Dorsten. Gestorben am 19. September 1946 im Lager."

CHAPTER 16

1. Oberst der Justiz und Leiter der Abteilung Rehabilitierung bei der Haupt-Militärstaatsanwaltschaft der Russischen Föderation.

2. In addition to articles photocopied from various newspapers and jour-

nals about his experiences, Horst Hennig gave me a volume devoted to Workuta that he had edited three months earlier. See Horst Hennig, *Erfahrung aus den Diktaturen—Folgerungen für Gegenwart und Zukunft*, Vorträge auf dem Halle-Forum III, 18.-20.05.1996 (LagGern Workuta/GULag in der Union der Opferverbände kommunistischer Gewaltherrschaft—UOKG).

3. All material in the foregoing section related to the posthumous inauguration, and meetings with Manfred Herling, Martin Onnasch, and Horst Hennig, comes from personal notes written within hours of the events described.

4. "In diesem Punkte sei die Tätigkeit Prof. Lohmeyers für die Universität nicht gut gewesen" (Naas's declaration is from Meckl. Landeshauptarchiv Schwerin, Landesregierung Mecklenburg, Ministerium für Volksbildung, Signatur 2464, p. 183).

5. The five *unbelastet* theology faculty members were Lohmeyer, Koepp, Hermann, Haendler, and Prost (note that Lohmeyer's name heads the list).

6. This denunciation was uncovered by Helge Matthiesen, "Eine tödliche Intrige," *Frankfurter Allgemeine Zeitung*, March 15, 1996, 10. The original is in the Vorpommersches Landesarchiv in Greifswald, Akte IV/4/02/46/16/Blatt 64 des Bestandes "Kreisleitung Greifswald."

7. On charges of war crimes placing the accused under Soviet military authorities, see Mathias Rautenberg, "Der Tod und die SED. Zum 65. Todestag Ernst Lohmeyers," *Zeitgeschichte Regional. Mitteilungen aus Mecklenburg-Vorpommern* 15, no. 2 (2011): 23.

8. "Eine Schweriner Intrige" (Lohmeyer, "Brief aus dem Gefängnis der GPU in Greifswald," GStA PK, VI. HA, NI, Lohmeyer, E., No. 146, p. 2).

9. "Die deutschen faschistischen Eroberer" (Untersuchungsakte No. 2313, GStA PK, VI. HA, NI, Lohmeyer, E., No. 25, p. 20).

10. "Eine Hetzjagd auf sowjetische Bürger" (GStA PK, VI. HA, NI, Lohmeyer, E., No. 25, pp. 3-4).

11. "Verbrechen" (GStA PK, VI. HA, NI, Lohmeyer, E., No. 25, p. 15).

12. On the historical context of Russian trials of the time, see Rautenberg, "Der Tod und die SED. Zum 65. Todestag Ernst Lohmeyers," 20, 28.

13. "Die Bevölkerung wurde nicht gezwungen."

14. "Das erachte ich nicht als Verbrechen."

15. "Ich bekenne mich der Anklage nicht schuldig."

16. "Ich bin ein gläubiger Mensch und kann daher keine Greueltaten vollbringen."

17. "Die Gendarmerie, die mir unterstand, hat keine Erschiessungen von sowjetischen Bürgern durchgeführt."

18. The complete trial record, in the original Russian and also in German translation, is located in GStA PK, VI. HA, NI, Lohmeyer, E., No. 25.

19. See Leonid P. Kopalin's speech to the Halle Forum, May 18–20, 1996, printed in Hennig, *Erfahrung aus den Diktaturen*, 39–60.

20. "An Erschiessungen sowjetischer Bürger sowie an anderen Strafaktionen nahm er persönlich nie teil und erteilte niemals derartige Befehle oder Weisungen. Als Kommandant des Kreises Slawjansk im Zeitraum 27. August 1942–18. März 1943 (etwa ein halbes Jahr) bemühte er sich, die Folgen des Krieges für die gesamte Zivilbevölkerung zu mildern. . . . Unter diesen Umständen muss man zu der Schlussfolgerung gelangen, dass Ernst Lohmeyer ohne ausreichende Gründe und nur aus politischen Motiven heraus verhaftet und verurteilt wurde. Deshalb gilt Ernst Lohmeyer gemäss Paragraph 3 des Gesetzes der Russischen Föderation 'Über die Rehabilitierung der Opfer politischer Repressionen' vom 18. Oktober 1991 vollständig rehabilitiert und alle seine Rechte wiederhergestellt (posthum)" (GStA PK, VI. HA, NI, Lohmeyer, E., No. 19).

21. "Ich bin ein gläubiger Mensch und kann daher keine Greueltaten vollbringen. Als Professor bin ich in der ganzen Welt bekannt. Ich habe nicht nur in Deutschland, sondern in vielen anderen Ländern wie Amerika, Belgien oder Schweden Vorträge gehalten. Ich bin Ehrenmitglied der theologischen Gesellschaft Amerikas. Ich habe viele Freunde unter Antifaschisten in der ganzen Welt. Ich konnte eine derartige Anzahl an Verbrechen nicht begehen. Ich bin unter dem Druck der Faschisten in die Armee eingetreten. Ich habe immer gesagt, dass Krieg ein Verbrechen ist" (GStA PK, VI. HA, NI, Lohmeyer, E., No. 25).

22. "Errichtung der faschistischen Ordnung."

23. "Ausserdem hat Lomeyer [*sic*] um sich herum einen Kreis von Vaterlandsverrätern versammelt."

24. "Verbrechen der deutschen-faschistischen Eroberer" (the above quotations come from "Protokoll der Gerichtsverhandlung," 28 August 1946, GStA PK, VI. HA NI, Lohmeyer, E., No. 25, p. 42).

25. "Ich bin Professor der evangelischen Theologie und ein treues Mitglied der christlichen Kirche."

26. "Ich habe deshalb wo ich nur konnte, versucht, gerade in den besetzten Ländern die Grundsätze der Menschlichkeit hochzuhalten. . . . Ich versichere nochmals, dass ich an keiner Erschiessung von Sowjetbürgern je teilgenommen oder gar sie veranlasst habe, ich habe in Gegenteil auch hier für die Sowjetbevölkerung die Leiden des Krieges zu mildern gesucht, und habe dabei keinen Unterschied zwischen Mitarbeitern der deutschen Wehrmacht und kommunistischen Sowjetbürgern gemacht" (GStA PK, VI. HA NI, Lohmeyer, E., No. 25).

27. "Daher bitte ich nochmals um Begnadigung" (GStA PK, VI. HA NI, Lohmeyer, E., No. 25).

28. See above, p. 242.

29. "Nie ein Sterbeort und nie die Todesursache mitgeteilt" (personal letter to me from Deutsches Rotes Kreuz-Suchdienst, Infanteriestrasse 7a, Munich, dated January 19, 1994).

30. "Auf dem Territorium der UdSSR verstorben" (personal letter from Deutsches Rotes Kreuz-Suchdienst, January 19, 1994).

31. The death announcement is dated December 6, 1957, and the accuracy of the translation of the Russian original (made by Lea Beinroth) is attested by the USSR Executive Committee of the Alliance of the Societies of the Red Cross and the Red Halfmoon.

32. "Nach Aussagen mehrerer Gewährspersonen wurde er [Ernst Lohmeyer] im Herbst 1946 im MWD-Gefängnis Greifswald erschossen" (personal letter to me by Deutsches Rotes Kreuz-Suchdienst, Infanteriestrasse 7a, Munich, January 10, 1994).

33. "Weit über 90 000 Blatt Papier mit Listen der Verstorbenen, Entlassenen etc" (personal letter from Deutsches Rotes Kreuz-Suchdienst, Munich, January 10, 1994).

34. Personal letter from Deutsches Rotes Kreuz-Suchdienst, Munich, January 10, 1994.

35. "Das Urteil ... zum Tode durch Erschiessen verurteilten Ernst Lohmeyer, geb. 1890 in Dorsten, wurde am 19. September 1946 in Greifswald vollstreckt."

36. "In ihm [Jesus] ... eschatologischer Vollendung kommt, was in einer langen dunklen Geschichte der Gottesgemeinde vom ersten Anfang an angelegt war. Hier ist Erfüllung at.licher eschatologischer Prophetie geschehen" (Ernst Lohmeyer, *Das Evangelium des Markus*, KEK I/2, 8th ed. [Göttingen: Vandenhoeck & Ruprecht, 1967], 151).

CHAPTER 17

1. "Die Schule des Lebens hat einige schwierige Klassen. Aber man lernt in diesen Klassen am meisten. Am schwersten war es für mich, als mich die vier Wände meiner Zelle umgaben, einer Zelle sechs Schritte lang, zwei Schritte breit, mit einer Tür, die nur von aussen zu öffnen war. Nachher waren es vier elektrisch geladene Stacheldrahtzäune und ein Tor, das Männer mit Maschinenpistolen bewachten" (Corrie ten Boom, *In Ihm Geborgen. Meine Lebensgeschichte* [Wuppertal: R. Brockhaus Verlag, 1969], 5).

2. "Letzter Brief von Ernst! Dass er nicht verlorgengeht."

3. "Letzter Brief."

4. "Zelle 19, begonnen am 31.3.46."

5. "4. April."

6. See above, p. 230.

7. "Gott sei Dank . . . wenn ich frei komme."

8. "Ja, mein Liebes, es ist wohl etwas mit mir und in mir geschehen, ein Ruck, der mich von vielem frei gemacht, ein Windstoss, der mich auf einen anderen Boden versetzt hat, und an diesem Geschehen habe ich noch immer zu arbeiten. In der Nacht, das ich verhaftet wurde, kamst Du einmal mit leichtem, schwingendem Schritt auf mich zu—es war in meinem Zimmer in Gegenwart des Dolmetschers—und küsstest mich warm und fest auf den Mund—da war es wie ein plötzliches Erkennen von Dingen, die ich bisher nicht gesehen hatte, und mir waren fast die Augen übergegangen. Und als dann Puppi hinzukam, von einem dunklen Fühlen getrieben—oder was war es?!—da wurde mir vollends fast leicht ums Herz: die Einheit der Herzen war da, sie war wieder gefunden, und es war alles offen und nichts mehr zu verschliessen. So, so sollte es kommen, so musste es geschehen und in dem allen war Gottes Finger deutlich zu merken" (Ernst Lohmeyer, "Brief aus dem Gefängnis der GPU in Greifswald," GStA PK, VI. HA, N1, Lohmeyer, E., No. 146, p. 5).

9. "Nun will mir scheinen, dass ich seit mehr als 20 Jahren einen falschen Weg eingeschlagen habe" (Ernst Lohmeyer, "Brief aus dem Gefängnis," 5).

10. "Damals, als ich Deinem Wunsche nach noch einem Kinde nachgab, beschloss ich, mich ganz meiner Arbeit hinzugeben" (Ernst Lohmeyer, "Brief aus dem Gefängnis," 6).

11. ". . . vielleicht auch verlockt von dem verführerischen und imponierenden Beispeil Hönigswalds" (Ernst Lohmeyer, "Brief aus dem Gefängnis," 6).

12. ". . . aber dass es so ausschliesslich geschah und damit alle Dinge unserer Liebe in die zweite Linie rückte, das war das Grundverkehrte" (Ernst Lohmeyer, "Brief aus dem Gefängnis," 6).

13. "Ich wollte wohl auch dann 'mein Ich auslöschen und die Dinge reden lassen'" (Ernst Lohmeyer, "Brief aus dem Gefängnis," 6).

14. "Es hat mich auf meine eigentliche Arbeit zurückgeworfen und die habe ich mit einer steinernen Erbitterung getrieben" (Ernst Lohmeyer, "Brief aus dem Gefängnis," 7).

15. "Die Sucht nach Erfüllung meines Lebens, meiner Befürfnisse" (Ernst Lohmeyer, "Brief aus dem Gefängnis," 7).

16. "[Ich] glaubte auch immer, aus eigenen Kräften alles leisten zu können, und achtete das nicht, dass uns das Letzte und das Beste geschenkt werden soll und muss—es war herz- und lieblos, und Du hast das immer gespürt, und ich selbst wusste und sah es nicht mit dem ehrlichsten Willen" (Ernst Lohmeyer, "Brief aus dem Gefängnis," 7–8).

17. "Ich sah ... wie sehr diese geschenkte Erfüllung meines Lebens an der gleichen Erfüllung Deines Lebens hing, wie beides nicht mehr geschieden, sondern wie aus doppelter Wurzel zu dem einen Baume unseres Lebens verwachsen war oder doch verwachsen sollte" (Ernst Lohmeyer, "Brief aus dem Gefängnis," 8).

18. "Das Leben drang nicht in die Liebe und die Liebe zu wenig in das Leben; so blieb auch das Herz nicht erfüllt und war für viele Träume und manche Realitäten offen" (Ernst Lohmeyer, "Brief aus dem Gefängnis," 8).

19. "Väterchen hatte damals in dieser Hölle eine Freundin gewonnen, seine Dolmetscherin. Eine ältere Frau mit 14-jährigem Sohn und einem alten Mann, für die Väterchen so weit sorgte, als es ihm möglich war. Die Frau hing ihr ganzes Herz an Väterchen, liess Mann und Sohn alleine in den Westen fahren und blieb bei ihm, um, wie Väterchen später sagte, mit ihm unterzugehen. So war damals die Situation. Er fuhr dann mit X zusammen zurück und setzte sie vor Lodz ab, wo X hoffte, bei früheren Bekannten unterzukommen. Es war wahrscheinlich ein schwerer Abschied. Gemeinschaft in einer Hölle verbindet" (Melie Lohmeyer, "Väterchens Ende," GStA PK, VI. HA, NI, Lohmeyer, E., No. 147, pp. 2–3). I have omitted the woman's name and referred to her as X in Melie's quotation and in my English translation.

20. "Irrweg."

21. "Aber dass solche Geschehnisse und Erlebnisse möglich waren, das zeigt genug, wie fern das alles von der Gemeinsamkeit unseres Lebens stand, wie es ihm widersprach und nur noch—und wie dürftig!—mein armes Ich bestätigte. Ich will es noch einmal sagen, mein Liebstes: verzeih mir diesen Frevel an Deinem Herzen, den ich gesehen und doch nicht gesehen, gespürt und doch nicht erkannt habe, verzeih mir dies alles, um der Liebe willen, die Du zu mir hast und die ich trotz allem zu Dir habe" (Ernst Lohmeyer, "Brief aus dem Gefängnis," 9).

22. "Innere Zusammenbruch" (Ernst Lohmeyer, "Brief aus dem Gefängnis," 10).

23. "Ein letzter und tiefster Mangel meines Lebens" (Ernst Lohmeyer, "Brief aus dem Gefängnis," 9).

24. "Ich habe in diesen langen Jahren oft nach Gott gefragt, aber es war eine Frage neben anderen, nicht die eine und einzige; ich habe auch bisweilen geglaubt, ihm nahe zu sein, aber ich habe ihn nicht gefühlt und gefunden. Wie sollte ich's auch? Ich habe ihn an vielen Orten gesucht und zu finden geglaubt, wo er nicht war, und an dem einzigen Ort, wo er für mich vorhanden war und vorhanden sein sollte, dass ich ihn hätte greifen können, da habe ich ihn nicht mehr gefunden, in unserer Liebe" (Ernst Lohmeyer, "Brief aus dem Gefängnis," 9–10).

25. "Und so wären wir wohl geschieden geblieben, wäre nicht diese Haft und dieser warme Kuss—und beides gehört zusammen, und ich kann es nicht trennen—geschehen. Gott hat leise mit dem Finger gewinkt, und schon barsten die Mauern und sprudelten die verschütteten Quellen. Ich ging von Dir und Puppi ganz leicht und wie befreit fort; diese Haft konnte die wiedergeschenkte Gemeinschaft der Herzen nicht mehr rauben. Und hier, in diesen langen Tagen und Nächten ist mir dann aufgegangen, wie haargenau und richtig, wie gnädig und weise dieses Gottesurteil ist—ein Urteil, das ebenso Gericht wie Geschenk ist. Er riss mich aus allen Bindungen, die mir bisher Gefahr and Schaden gewesen waren, aus allen Geschäften und aller Arbeit und stellte mich ganz allein dem Nichtstun, das heisst: mir selbst gegenüber. Er zerschnitt all das künstliche Geflecht, in das ich mein Irren und Fehlen gehüllt hatte, und hüllte mich doch zugleich in den Mantel Deiner und seiner Liebe. Er nahm mir, der ich bisher alles aus eigenen Kräften hatte leisten wollen, die Freiheit und nötigte mich, mich dem Gebot, auch dem unsinnigen und unverstandenen, zu beugen. Er machte mich zu einem Gebundenen, um mich an sich und Dich zu binden, und schenkte mir darin die inner Freiheit, von aller toten Last meines Lebens. Und er tat das alles, so dass ich nach aussen der unschuldig Leidende, der Märtyrer einer guten Sache bin, und nur er und Du wissen, dass er mich darin wahrhaft gerichtet, wahrhaft getröstet hat. Nun bin ich ein Häftling und habe darin alles, was ich suchte. . . . Ich bin doch in alledem frei und innerlich gewiss, nicht mehr durch mich, sondern durch das Band der Einheit, das mich mit Gott und Dir verbindet" (Ernst Lohmeyer, "Brief aus dem Gefängnis," 9–10).

26. "Ach, dass ich Wassers genug hätte, zu beweinen meine Sünden, dass meine Augen Tränenbäche wären" (Ernst Lohmeyer, "Brief aus dem Gefängnis," 12). The "Lamento" was not written by Johann Sebastian Bach but by his great uncle Johann Christoph Bach, composed from Jer. 9:1, Ps. 38:5, and passages from Lamentations. I am grateful to the grandchildren of Ernst and Melie Lohmeyer, Frau Dr. Julia Otto and Herr Stefan Rettner, for a letter dated October 19, 2017, identifying this "Lamento" of Johann Christoph Bach (1652–1703).

27. "Die Menschen sind Sand, auf die man nicht bauen kann" (Ernst Lohmeyer, "Brief aus dem Gefängnis," 12).

28. "Hätte mir Gott dies alles nur geschenkt, um es hinter Gefängnismauren zu vergraben?" (Ernst Lohmeyer, "Brief aus dem Gefängnis," 12).

29. Isa. 30:15.

30. "Ach, mein Herz, wenn Du mich nur lieb behalten willst, wenn ich Deiner Liebe gewiss sein kann? Ist es denn noch möglich, dass Du mich in die Arme schliessen willst!" (Ernst Lohmeyer, "Brief aus dem Gefängnis," 13).

31. "Ich-Besessenheit."

32. "Rücken."

Bibliography

Books by Ernst Lohmeyer (arranged by date of publication)

Diatheke: Ein Beitrag zur Erklärung des neutestamentlichen Begriffs.
Leipzig: Hinrichs, 1913.

Die Lehre vom Willen bei Anselm von Canterbury. Leipzig: Deichert,
1914.

Christuskult und Kaiserkult. Tübingen: Mohr Siebeck, 1919.

Vom göttlichen Wohlgeruch. SHAW.Philosophisch-historische Klasse,
Jahrgang 1919, 9. Abhandlung. Heidelberg: Carl Winters Universitätsbuchhandlung, 1919.

Soziale Fragen im Urchristentum. Leipzig: Quelle und Meyer, 1921;
Darmstadt: Wissenschaftliche Buchgesellschaft, 1973.

Vom Begriff der religiösen Gemeinschaft. Wissenschaftliche Grund-
fragen 3. Leipzig: Teubner, 1925.

Die Offenbarung des Johannes. HNT 16. Tübingen: Mohr Siebeck, 1926,
2nd ed. 1953, 3rd ed. 1970.

Kyrios Jesus: Eine Untersuchung zu Phil. 2,5-11. SHAW 18. Heidelberg:
C. Winters, 1928.

Der Brief an die Philipper. KEK IX/1. Göttingen: Vandenhoeck &
Ruprecht, 1928, 2nd ed. 1953, 3rd ed. 1954, 4th ed. 1956, 5th ed.
1961, 6th ed. 1964, 7th ed. 1974.

Grundlagen paulinischer Theologie. BHT 1. Tübingen: Mohr Siebeck,
1929.

Die Briefe an die Kolosser und an Philemon. KEK IX/2. Göttingen: Vandenhoeck & Ruprecht, 1930, 2nd ed. 1953, 3rd ed. 1954, 4th ed.
1956, 5th ed. 1961, 6th ed. 1964, 7th ed. 1974.

Das Urchristentum, 1. Buch: Johannes der Täufer. Göttingen: Vanden-hoeck & Ruprecht, 1932.

Galiläa und Jerusalem. FRLANT 34. Göttingen: Vandenhoeck & Ruprecht, 1936.

Das Evangelium des Markus. KEK I/2. Göttingen: Vandenhoeck & Ruprecht, 1937, 2nd ed. 1951, 3rd ed. 1953, 4th ed. 1954, 5th ed. 1957, 6th ed. 1959, 7th ed. 1963, 8th ed. 1967.

Kultus und Evangelium. Göttingen: Vandenhoeck & Ruprecht, 1952. English: *Lord of the Temple: A Study of the Relation between Cult and Gospel.* Translated by Stewart Todd. Richmond, VA: John Knox, 1962.

Gottesknecht und Davidsohn. Symbolae biblicae upsalienses 5. Uppsala, 1945; FRLANT 61. Göttingen: Vandenhoeck & Ruprecht, 1953.

Das Vater-unser. Göttingen: Vandenhoeck & Ruprecht, 1946, 2nd ed. 1948, 3rd ed. 1952, 4th ed. 1960, 5th ed. 1962. English: *The Lord's Prayer.* Translated by John Bowden. London: SPCK, 1965 = *"Our Father": An Introduction to the Lord's Prayer.* New York: Harper & Row, 1966.

Das Evangelium des Matthäus. KEK. Göttingen: Vandenhoeck & Ruprecht, 1956, 2nd ed. 1958, 3rd ed. 1962, 4th ed. 1967.

Articles by Ernst Lohmeyer (arranged by date of publication)

"Die Verklärung Jesu nach dem Markusevangelium." *ZNW* 21 (1922): 185–215.

"Urchristliche Mystik." *ZST* 2 (1925): 3–18.

"Von urchristlicher Gemeinschaft." *TBl* 4 (1925): 135–41.

"Das zwölfte Kapitel der Offenbarung Johannis." *TBl* 4 (1925): 285–91.

"Das Proömium des Epheserbriefes." *TBl* 5 (1926): 120–25.

"Vom Neutestamentler- und Kirchenhistorikertag 1926 in Breslau." *TBl* 5 (1926): 282ff.

"SUN CRISTWI." In *Festgabe für Adolf Deissmann*, 218–57. Tübingen: Mohr Siebeck, 1927.

"Die Idee des Martyriums im Judentum und Urchristentum." *ZST* 5, no. 2 (1927): 232–49.

"Apokalyptik." In *RGG*, 1:402-6. 2nd ed. Tübingen: Mohr Siebeck, 1927.

"Probleme paulinischer Theologie, I. Briefliche Grussüberschriften." *ZNW* 26 (1927): 158-73.

"Über Aufbau und Gliederung des vierten Evangeliums." *ZNW* 27 (1928): 11-36.

"Über Aufbau und Gliederung des ersten Johannesbriefes." *ZNW* 27 (1928): 225-63.

"August Tholuck." In *Schlesische Lebensbilder*, 3:230-39. Breslau, 1928.

"Probleme paulinischer Theologie, II. Gesetzeswerke." *ZNW* 28 (1929): 177-207.

"Kritische und gestaltende Prinzipien im Neuen Testament." In *Protestantismus als Kritik und Gestaltung*, edited by Paul Tillich, 41-69. Darmstadt, 1929.

"Der Begriff der Erlösung im Urchristentum." In *Deutsche Theologie*, 2:22-45. Göttingen: Vandenhoeck & Ruprecht, 1929.

"Probleme paulinischer Theologie, III. Sünde, Fleisch und Tod." *ZNW* 29 (1930): 1-59.

"Caspar Schwenckfeld von Ossig." In *Schlesische Lebensbilder*, 4:40-49. Breslau, 1931.

"Hegel und seine theologische Bedeutung, zum Gedenken an seinen 100. Todestag." *TBl* 10 (1931): 337-42.

"Vom Baum und Frucht. Eine exegetische Studie zu Matth. 3,10." *ZST* 9 (1932): 377-97.

"Zur evangelischen Überlieferung von Johannes dem Täufer." *JBL* 51 (1932): 300-319.

"'Und Jesus ging vorüber.'" *NTT* 23 (1934): 206-24.

"Die Offenbarung Johannes 1920-1934." *TRu*, n.s., 6 (1934): 269-314; n.s., 7 (1935): 28-62.

"Die Versuchung Jesu." *ZST* 14 (1937): 619-50.

"Das Abendmahl in der Urgemeinde." *JBL* 56 (1937): 217-52.

"Vom urchristlichen Abendmahl." *TRu*, n.s., 9 (1937): 168-227, 273-312; n.s., 10 (1938): 81-99.

"Vom Abendmahl im Neuen Testament." *DP* 42 (1938): 97ff., 173ff.

"Om nattvarden i Nya testamentet." *STK* 14 (1938): 333-45.

"Vom Sinn der Gleichnisse Jesu." *ZST* 15 (1938): 319-46.

"Das Vater-Unser als Ganzheit." *TBl* 17 (1938): 217-27.

"Der Stern der Weisen." *TBl* 17 (1938): 289-99.

"Die Fusswaschung." *ZNW* 38 (1939): 74-94.

"Vom urchristlichen Sakrament." *DT* 6 (1939): 112-26, 146-56.

"Die Reinigung des Tempels." *TBl* 20 (1941): 257-64.

"Das Gleichnis von den bösen Weingärtnern." *ZST* 18 (1941): 243-59.

"Das Gleichnis von der Saat." *DT* 10 (1943): 20-39.

"Die rechte Interpretation des Mythologischen." In *Kerygma und Mythos*, 154-65. Hamburg, 1948. English: "The Right Interpretation of the Mythological." In *Kerygma and Myth: A Theological Debate*, edited by H. W. Bartsch, translated by R. H. Fuller, 124-37. New York: Harper & Row, 1961.

"A und O." In *RAC*, 1:1-4.

"Antichrist." In *RAC*, 1:450-57.

"Mir ist gegeben alle Gewalt. Eine Exegese von Mt. 28,16-20." In *In Memoriam Ernst Lohmeyer*, edited by W. Schmauch, 22-49. Stuttgart: Evangelisches Verlagswerk, 1951.

Selected Works about Ernst Lohmeyer

Altenbockum, Jasper von. "Die Greifswalder kennen die Geschichten, die Geschichte kannten sie lange Zeit nicht." *Frankfurter Allgemeine Zeitung*, April 29, 1995, 6.

Alvermann, Dirk, and Karl-Heinz Spiess, eds. *Universität und Gesellschaft. Festschrift zur 550-Jahrfeier der Universität Greifswald, 1456-2006*. Band 1, *Die Geschichte der Fakultäten im 19. und 20. Jahrhundert*. Hinstorff: Rostock, 2006.

Baird, William. *History of New Testament Research*. 3 vols. Minneapolis: Fortress, 1992-2013.

Beintker, Horst J. E. "Ernst Lohmeyers Stellung zum Judentum." In *Freiheit in der Gebundenheit*, edited by Wolfgang Otto, 98-134. Göttingen: Vandenhoeck & Ruprecht, 1990.

Böttrich, Christfried, ed. *Ernst Lohmeyer. Beiträge zu Leben und Werk*. Greifswalder theologische Forschungen 28. Leipzig, 2018.

Edwards, James R. "Ernst Lohmeyer." In *Dictionary of Major Biblical*

Interpreters, edited by D. McKim, 671–75. Downers Grove, IL: InterVarsity Press, 2007.

———. "Ernst Lohmeyer—ein Schlusskapitel." *EvT* 56 (1996): 320–42.

———. "Martyrium: gesetztes Ziel in Lohmeyers Theologie, erreichtes Ziel in seiner Biographie." In *Ernst Lohmeyer. Beiträge zu Leben und Werk,* edited by Christfried Böttrich. Greifswalder theologische Forschungen 28. Leipzig, 2018.

Esking, Erik. *Glaube und Geschichte in der theologischen Exegese Ernst Lohmeyers: Zugleich ein Beitrag zur Geschichte der neutestamentlichen Interpretation.* ASNU 18. Lund: Gleerup, 1951.

Haufe, Günter. "Ein Gerechter unter den Völkern. Gedenken an Ernst Lohmeyer." Address at the University of Greifswald on the occasion of the fiftieth year of Lohmeyer's execution, September 19, 1996.

———. "Ernst Lohmeyer—Theologische Exegese aus dem Geist des philosophischen Idealismus." In *Freiheit in der Gebundenheit,* edited by Wolfgang Otto, 88–97. Göttingen: Vandenhoeck & Ruprecht, 1990.

———. "Gedenkvortrag zum 100. Geburtstag Ernst Lohmeyers." In *In Memoriam Ernst Lohmeyer.* Greifswalder Universitätsreden, n.s., 59. Greifswald: Ernst-Moritz-Arndt-Universität Greifswald, 1991.

———. "Lohmeyer, Ernst." In *Theologische Realenzyklopädie,* 21:444–47. Berlin: de Gruyter, 1991.

Hutter, Ulrich. "Theologie als Wissenschaft. Zu Leben und Werk Ernst Lohmeyers (1890–1946)." *Jahrbuch für schlesische Kirchengeschichte* 69 (1990): 123–69.

Hutter-Wolandt, Ulrich. "Lohmeyer, Ernst." In *RGG,* 5:503. Tübingen: Mohr Siebeck, 2002.

Köhn, Andreas. *Der Neutestamentler Ernst Lohmeyer.* WUNT 2.180. Tübingen: Mohr Siebeck, 2004.

———. "Ernst Lohmeyer und die Apokalyptik." In *Eschatologie und Ethik im frühen Christentum,* edited by Christfried Böttrich, 149–67. Greifswalder theologische Forschungen 11. Frankfurt: Lang, 2006.

————, ed. *Ernst Lohmeyers Zeugnis im Kirchenkampf. Breslauer Universitätspredigten.* Göttingen: Vandenhoeck & Ruprecht, 2006.

————. "Von der 'Notwendigkeit des Bekennens': Theologie als Martyrium am Beispiel Ernst Lohmeyers (1890–1946)." In *Martyrium im 20. Jahrhundert*, edited by Hans Maier and Carsten Nicolaisen, 109–21. Annweiler, 2004.

Kollmann, B. "Lohmeyer, Ernst." In *Dictionary of Biblical Interpretation*, edited by John H. Hayes, 2:86–87. Nashville: Abingdon, 1999.

Kuhn, Dieter. *Metaphysik und Geschichte. Zur Theologie Ernst Lohmeyers.* Berlin: de Gruyter, 2005.

Lührmann, Dieter. "Ernst Lohmeyers exegetisches Erbe." In *Freiheit in der Gebundenheit*, edited by Wolfgang Otto, 53–87. Göttingen: Vandenhoeck & Ruprecht, 1990.

————. "Lohmeyer, E." In *A Dictionary of Biblical Interpretation*, edited by R. J. Coggins and J. L. Houlden, 1:408–9. London: SCM, 1990.

Otto, Gudrun (Lohmeyer). "Erinnerung an den Vater." In *Freiheit in der Gebundenheit*, edited by Wolfgang Otto, 36–52. Göttingen: Vandenhoeck & Ruprecht, 1990.

————. "Erinnerung an Ernst Lohmeyer." *DP* 81 (1981): 359–62.

Otto, Wolfgang, ed. *Aus der Einsamkeit—Briefe einer Freundschaft. Richard Hönigswald an Ernst Lohmeyer.* Würzburg: Königshausen & Neumann, 1999.

————. "Ernst Lohmeyer—Gelehrter—Bekenner—Demokrat." Unpublished paper.

————. "Ernst Lohmeyer und Jochen Klepper." In *Freiheit in der Gebundenheit. Zur Erinnerung an den Theologen Ernst Lohmeyer anlässlich seines 100. Geburtstages*, edited by Wolfgang Otto, 135–80. Göttingen: Vandenhoeck & Ruprecht, 1990.

————, ed. *Freiheit in der Gebundenheit. Zur Erinnerung an den Theologen Ernst Lohmeyer anlässlich seines 100. Geburtstages.* Göttingen: Vandenhoeck & Ruprecht, 1990.

Rautenberg, Mathias. "Der Tod und die SED. Zum 65. Todestag Ernst Lohmeyers." *Zeitgeschichte Regional. Mitteilungen aus Mecklenburg-Vorpommern* 15, no. 2 (2011): 20–33.

Reinmuth, Eckart. "Vom Zeugnis des Neuen Testaments zum Zeugnis für das Neue Testament: Ernst Lohmeyer." In *Greifswalder theologische Profile. Bausteine zur Geschichte der Theologie an der Universität Greifswald*, edited by I. Garbe, T. Beyrich, and Th. Willi, 259–73. Greifswalder theologische Forschungen 12. Frankfurt: Lang, 2006.

Rogerson, John. *The Case for Ernst Lohmeyer*. Sheffield: Sheffield University Press, 2016.

Sass, Gerhard. "Die Bedeutung Ernst Lohmeyers für die neutestamentliche Forschung." *DP* 8 (1987): 356–58.

Schmauch, W., ed. *In Memoriam Ernst Lohmeyer*. Stuttgart: Evangelischer Verlagswerk, 1951.

Theissen, Henning. "Die Bibel als Begründungsanfang der evangelischen Theologie. Eine systematisch-theologische Erinnerung an den Breslauer und Greifswalder Neutestamentler Ernst Lohmeyer." *Gdanski Rocznik Ewangelicki* 8 (2014): 265–79.

Weibel, Arnold, "'Der Fall L.' in Greifswald, Schwerin, und Berlin—Was wurde zur Rettung Ernst Lohmeyers unternommen?" *Zeitgeschichte Regional. Mitteilungen aus Mecklenburg-Vorpommern* 1 (1997): 29–34.

Index

Note: In this index EL stands for Ernst Lohmeyer.

331

Earth Changes

Earth Changes

Student Objectives
I will be able to:

- **Read and analyze firsthand accounts and informational texts about Earth changes.**

- **Share ideas with my peers.**

- **Build my vocabulary knowledge.**

- **Conduct research to write a firsthand fictional account.**

Credits
Editor: Joanne Tangorra
Contributing Editors: Jeffrey B. Fuerst, Brett Kelly
Creative Director: Laurie Berger
Art Directors: Melody DeJesus, Kathryn DelVecchio-Kempa, Doug McGredy, Chris Moroch
Production: Kosta Triantafillis
Director of Photography: Doug Schneider
Photo Assistant: Jackie Friedman

Photo credits: Table of Contents C: duchy/shutterstock.com; Page 2: © Manpreet Romana/Getty Images; Page 3A: © MARK COSTANTINI/San Francisco Chronicle/Corbis; Page 15: Courtesy of Ximonic; Page 17: © Allo/Corbis; Page 19C: ©warrengoldswain/shutterstock.com; Page 22: ©Bettmann/Corbis

Tips for Text Annotation

As you read closely for different purposes, remember to annotate the text. Use the symbols below. Add new symbols in the spaces provided.

Symbol	Purpose
<u>underline</u>	Identify a key detail.
☆	Star an important idea in the margin.
① ② ③	Mark a sequence of events.
⟨magma⟩	Circle a key word or phrase.
?	Mark a question you have about information in the text. Write your question in the margin.
!	Indicate an idea in the text you find interesting. Comment on this idea in the margin.

Your annotations might look like this.

The Gold Rush

Notes

16   The migration on the Oregon Trail became an annual event. Thousands of emigrants began ① to join the wagon trains heading West. Then in ② ☆ 1848, gold was discovered in California. The ⟨lure⟩ of rich farmlands now changed to fields of gold. ③ By 1850, more than fifty thousand people traveled ! the Oregon Trail West. <u>Instead of turning toward Oregon near the end of the trail, many turned to California.</u> They hoped to find their fortune mining or panning for gold instead of farming. ?

That's a lot of people!

Who was the first person to discover gold?

LEXILE® is a trademark of MetaMetrics, Inc., and is registered in the United States and abroad.

E-book and digital teacher's guide available at benchmarkuniverse.com.

BENCHMARK EDUCATION COMPANY
145 Huguenot Street • New Rochelle, NY • 10801

Toll-Free 1-877-236-2465
www.benchmarkeducation.com
www.benchmarkuniverse.com

Table of Contents

Essential Question

How do Earth's natural processes impact our lives?